Luminos is the Open Access monograph publishing program from UC Press. Luminos provides a framework for preserving and reinvigorating monograph publishing for the future and increases the reach and visibility of important scholarly work. Titles published in the UC Press Luminos model are published with the same high standards for selection, peer review, production, and marketing as those in our traditional program. www.luminosoa.org

God's Property

ISLAMIC HUMANITIES

Shahzad Bashir, Series Editor

Publication of this Luminos Open Access Series is made possible by the Islam and the Humanities Project of the Program in Middle East Studies at Brown University.

1. *Forging the Ideal Educated Girl: The Production of Desirable Subjects in Muslim South Asia*, by Shenila Khoja-Moolji
2. *Witness to Marvels: Sufism and Literary Imagination*, by Tony K. Stewart
3. *God's Property: Islam, Charity, and the Modern State*, by Nada Moumtaz

God's Property

Islam, Charity, and the Modern State

Nada Moumtaz

UNIVERSITY OF CALIFORNIA PRESS

University of California Press
Oakland, California

Suggested citation: Moumtaz, N. *God's Property: Islam, Charity, and the Modern State*. Oakland: University of California Press, 2021.
DOI: https://doi.org/10.1525/luminos.100

Library of Congress Cataloging-in-Publication Data

Name: Moumtaz, Nada, author.
Title: God's property : Islam, charity, and the modern state / Nada Moumtaz.
Other titles: Islamic Humanities ; 3.
Description: Oakland, California : University of California Press, [2020] | Series: Islamic Humanities ; 3 | Includes bibliographical references and index.
Identifiers: LCCN 2020027438 (print) | LCCN 2020027439 (ebook) | ISBN 9780520345874 (paperback) | ISBN 9780520975781 (ebook)
Subjects: LCSH: Waqf—Lebanon. | Endowments—Lebanon. | Islam—Charities. | Charitable uses, trusts, and foundations (Islamic law) —Lebanon. | Charity laws and legislation—Lebanon.
Classification: LCC BP170.25 .M68 2020 (print) | LCC BP170.25 (ebook) | DDC 297.5/4—odc23
LC record available at https://lccn.loc.gov/2020027438
LC ebook record available at https://lccn.loc.gov/2020027439

Manufactured in the United States of America

24 23 22 21 20
10 9 8 7 6 5 4 3 2 1

CONTENTS

ACKNOWLEDGMENTS

This book has been long in the making. Encounters with many wonderful mentors, interlocutors, friends, and family developed my roots and interests into this beast. Its shortcomings are the result of my own limits, my well-known stubbornness, and my very slow thinking.

The book emerged from the intellectual milieu that was CUNY's Graduate Center between 2003 and 2012 as it intersected with personal experiences and the intellectual and political commitments I developed in my training at the Department of Architecture and Design (ArD) of the American University of Beirut (AUB). The ArD and AUB pushed me out of my Beiruti middle-class bubble and expanded my horizons, developing my interest in socio-spatial dialectics and bent to social justice. I am still traveling the roads Marwan Ghandour has opened for me in ways of thinking and approaching the world. I blame Mona Fawaz's wisdom for landing me in anthropology. Along with Mona Harb, Howayda al-Harithy, and Jala Makhzoumi, she has shown excitement for and support of my work that has always brought forth its relevance to the place I always come back to: Beirut.

At the Graduate Center, Talal Asad provided unwavering support, close engagement, and an immediate understanding of the intellectual and personal project that this work is. His writings, questions, and insights resonated deeply and changed profoundly the way I think. He has continued to extend generous support and encouragement in the years since I graduated. David Harvey's intellectual curiosity, interest, patience, generosity, humor, and friendship allowed me to follow my own interests and pushed me to find my voice while keeping in mind the larger picture. Vincent Crapanzano always read with insight and charity, able to uncannily understand my thought process and to see where I was heading. Katherine Verdery, who in her first semester at CUNY offered extensive comments on the first draft of my proposal before she even knew me or was on my committee, helped me place this project within anthropological debates and generously supported me. Louise Lennihan's enthusiasm for an early draft of a proposal for this project provided me the encouragement and confidence to undertake it. Mandana Limbert kindly agreed to be on my exam committee and provided many helpful suggestions. Don Robotham's humor, knowledge, support, and third-worldism made me feel at home in an otherwise very American program. Life at the GC would have been miserable without the guidance of Ellen de Riso. Supportively led by Julie Skurski, the anthropology dissertation group initiated my writing. While the composition varied across the years, Alessandro Angelini, Vivian Berghan, Sam Byrd, Christine Folch, Amy Jones, Andy Newman, Jeremy Rayner, and Ted Sammons pushed me to articulate the stakes of the project. The short-lived but so very inspiring Middle East dissertation group provided intellectual affinities and trust. I am particularly thankful to Aleksandra Majstorac-Kobiljski and Sara Pursley, who pulled us together, and to Shea McManus, Raja Abillama, Jeff Culang, Yunus Doğan Telliel, and Seçil Yılmaz, for their engagement and comments. Others read my various attempts to pull the various strands of this project into a coherent proposal: Diana Allen, Giancarlo Casale, Sam Haselby, Trenholme Junghans, and Paul Spohr.

New York, its consortium, and its bustling intellectual-academic life allowed me to meet scholars whose work and engagement left deep marks on this book. Brinkley Messick's *Calligraphic State* and its discussion of waqf was foundational for this project and so I was thrilled when he accepted to be my external reader. I am particularly grateful for his taking the time for a long discussion following my defense. His capacity to highlight the particularities of my work, which I take for granted, helped me see what I was doing. I am grateful that he continues to be a generous interlocutor. Michael Gilsenan engaged and supported this work in precarious times: its early and still confused phases. Wael Hallaq, without knowing me, responded to my emails and queries as an entitled graduate student. He gave me some of his precious time on many occasions and shared material, thoughts, and insights. His *Sharīʿa* was crucial to my making sense of my materials in the first iteration of this book as a dissertation. Etem and Sibel Erol's contagious passion for the Turkish language and Turkish literature could not have been a better introduction. Etem's shared interest in Ottoman waqf opened the door for me to the Turkish literature on the matter, as he slowly walked me through reading some of the material. He left us way too early.

I have been extremely fortunate to have had generous financial and institutional support to produce this work. The Graduate Center's Writing-Across-the-Curriculum Fellowship and Dissertation Writing Fellowship, the Wenner-Gren Foundation, the National Science Foundation, the Charlotte W. Newcombe Foundation, Europe in the Middle East—The Middle East in Europe (EUME) program, and the MIT Agha Khan Program in Islamic Architecture provided generous financial support and most importantly time to read and think. I would like to thank George Khalil and Gudrun Krämer for hosting me in Berlin, and Nasser Rabbat and Jim Wescoat for hosting me at MIT. I have been blessed with tremendously supportive departmental chairs. At Ohio State University, Kevin van Bladel strongly endorsed and arranged for a leave so I could spend a year in Germany at EUME. Both John Kloppenborg, chair of the Department for the Study of Religion (DSR), and Tim Harrison, chair of Near and Middle Eastern Civilizations (NMC), arranged for me to go through my third-year review early and take a year-long leave, without which I don't know how I would have finished my revisions. A book workshop was generously supported by the DSR, NMC, and the Centre for Diaspora and Transnational Studies, chaired by Kevin O'Neill. Anver Emon, and the Institute of Islamic Studies provided consistently enthusiastic support and research assistantship at the exact moment I needed it.

Many people helped me develop this book from its dissertation form, commented on the proposal, and generously introduced me to editors, providing endorsement and support at times of unknowns. I am forever grateful to Hussein Ali Agrama, Lalaie Ameeriar, the late Saba Mahmood, Amira Mittermaier, Kevin O'Neill, and Joel Wainwright. I still don't know what I have done to deserve Hussein's insight, intellectual companionship, and mentorship. Amira has answered an inordinate number of miscellaneous requests from me and supported and encouraged me in numerous ways. Kevin gave trust and support without ever asking for anything. Philip Sayers provided a sharp external eye on a few chapters and helped me see how to trim them. I am indebted to Shahzad Bashir's trust and his kindness. I thank Eric Schmidt for his advice and patience as events in Lebanon and life delayed my submissions and for his support around various stressors. Austin Lim was a kind nudger. Cindy Fulton let me be and was very matter-of-fact. Marwan Kaabour stepped in to help me with a cover crisis, which was averted. I especially thank Barbara Armentrout for her light editorial hand and her consistent human compassion, even when I tested her patience. Joud al-Korani lent her insight and eloquent style. Eagle-eyed Basit Iqbal accommodated a moving schedule for the index and kindly thought with me about multiple miscellaneous questions in the final stretch. Sadaf Ahmed meticulously read the last version.

My deepest gratitude goes to the many generous and brilliant colleagues and friends who read the manuscript in its entirety and participated in the book workshop: Guy Burak, Mohammad Fadel, Jairan Gahan, Jens Hanssen, Pamela Klassen, Katherine Lemons, Astrid Meier, Amira Mittermaier, and Kevin O'Neill. For the fine-toothed comments, for thinking with me about the conceptual framework and the substantive arguments, and for the stylistic suggestions, I am thankful. These were the comments I kept going back to while revising. Katherine Lemons lent me her brilliant mind and precious time as I was revising. Astrid Meier could not join us in Toronto and generously and gracefully hosted me at her place in Halle, where I was lucky to be the recipient of her deeply informed comments and extensive knowledge on waqf. Guy Burak could not make it to the workshop either, but his creative reading helped me bring out some of the arguments I did not realize I was making. I am lucky that Mohammad Fadel is at the University of Toronto. His sharpness, knowledge of the Islamic legal tradition, and generosity have made this manuscript far better even if we might still disagree.

Even before I had thought about a book workshop, Mariana Valverde showed interest in the project, sending me novels and articles, and then reading the entire manuscript and providing me very constructive comments. Her continuous encouragement, wisdom, and support while revising kept the process in perspective even if I could not let go. Raja Abillama, Ziad Aburrish, Saleh Agha, Rosie Bsheer, Fadi Bardawil, Yazan Doughan, Chris Gratien, Katherine Lemons, Khaled Malas, Lama Mourad, Arzoo Osanloo, Sara Pursley, Nisrine Salti, Noah Salomon, and Ana Vinea read various parts of the book, engaging me generously and supportively. Raja Abillama's incisive comments helped me string together all the feedback and attempts at answering the eternal cursed question, What is this book about? I thank the external readers for their support and suggestions.

In Beirut, waqf makers, lawyers, judges, and various individuals dealing with waqf were incredibly generous with their time. I will not name them for the purpose of anonymity. The archival research would not have been possible without the help of Shaykh Muhammad ʿAssaf, who allowed me to draw on his expertise on waqf and bother him with questions. Abu Ali welcomed me and chatted with me in his archive. Research on the contemporary period would not have kick-started without the help of brother Omar Hajjar, who trusted me and introduced me to contacts without any hesitations. It was a happy coincidence to rekindle with Ali Chalak and discover our intellectual affinities. He was also very kind to help me set up some interviews.

I would not have had the ease and extent of access I had in Beirut without my family. My mother's family talked to me at length about their family waqf and shared documents with me. Tante Alia, Tante Asma, Teta, and Tante Inʿam always answered with much detail any question I had—and I always had some under my belt at any meeting or occasion. Tante Alia's passing has made it so that I cannot but look back at these moments with a sense of both happiness to have captured them and sadness at not being able to live more of them with her. I miss bumping into her walking the streets of Beirut on her daily rounds of visits to friends and family. Without ʿAmmo ʿAbida, I simply could not have had access to archives in Beirut. He put me in touch with innumerable acquaintances, always coming up with new people I should talk to. My cousin Omar always looked to introduce me to anyone who could help me. The work of ʿAbd al-Latif Fakhoury, his enthusiasm and deep knowledge of the law, the shariʿa court, its records, and Ottoman Beirut facilitated my inquiries and provided for exciting discussions and debates. He also generously shared sources and documents.

In Istanbul, the staff of the Başbakanlık—to name a few whom I pestered a lot: Fuat bey, Ayten hanım, Elif, Ertuğrul, the photographers, and the staff of the tea pantry and the cafeteria—made it a pleasure to work there. Huricihan İslamoğlu not only arranged for my affiliation at Boğaziçi University but also talked Ottoman property regimes and political economy with me and opened her home when I was feeling estranged. In Ankara, staff and researchers at NIHA, in particular Aslı D. Kaymak-van Loo and Funda Demir, welcomed me and made my two-week research trip in a completely new city an unexpectedly pleasant stay. The staff at the Vakıflar Genel Müdürluğü (VGM) were very helpful despite the lack of facilities for researchers, letting me use their own computers. Ismail bey patiently humored my obsessive-compulsive quests. In Istanbul and in Ankara, a number of scholars chatted with me about my project and shared insights and their own research findings. I learned from Kürşat Çelik, Özer Ergenç, Zouhair Ghazzal, Eda Güçlü, Alp Yücel Kaya, Oktay Özel, Amr Shalakany, Yücel Terzibaşoğlu, and Merve Tezcanlı.

Many friends and colleagues have read papers, given comments, listened to me in mock job talks and conferences, encouraged me, and thought with me about the puzzles that my material presented to me. Some of them can probably recognize their insights in the pages of this book. I thank them for their support and their generosity: Asad A. Ahmed, Başak Çandar, Melissa Curley, Ahmad Dallal, Julia Elyachar, Michael Gasper, Ahmad Gharbieh, Humeira Iqtidar, Cricket Keating, Saba Mahmood, Becky Mansfield, Dody McDow, Ethan Menchinger, Aria Nakissa, Arzoo Osanloo, Junaid Quadri, Aziz Rana, Kirsten Scheid, Yunus Doğan Telliel, Mary Thomas, Fabio Vicini, Isaac Weiner, and Max Woodworth.

Al-daktorat Hiba Bou Akar and Ghenwa Hayek deserve their own paragraph. Their camaraderie, support, encouragement, faith, immediate and last-minute critical reading and comments, and brutal honesty allowed me to survive writing this book and life more generally.

Many wonderful people and friends made me feel at home and helped me grow in the different cities where I lived in the course of the many years that this book was in the making. In New York, it was Raja Abillama, Fadi Bardawil, Akissi Britton, Diana Coryat, Yunus Doğan Telliel, Abu Farman, Saygun Gökariksel, Amy Jones, Banu Karaca, Laura Kaehler, Mustafa Jundi, Mounira Khayyat, Yasmine al-Machnouk, Philippe Marius, Nada Matta, Shea McManus, Ceren Özgül, Christine Pinnock, Jeremy Rayner, Jana Saleh, Douaa Sheet, and Ana Vinea. In Istanbul, it was Sena Arçak and Dilek Ayaş, Saygun Gökariksel, Kristina Hamza, Ebru Karaca and Erol Tınmaz, Milia Maroun, and Ali Wick, Dahlia Gubara, and their lovely daughter, Amalia. In Ankara, it was Zeynep Oğuz and Yunus Doğan Telliel. In Berlin, it was Refqa Abu-Remaileh, Saima Akhtar, Başak Çandar, Yazan Doughan and Sultan Doughan, Karim Sadek, and Nahed Sammour. In Columbus, it was Ziad Aburrish, Justin Acome, Amna Akbar, Lisa Bhungalia, Morgan Liu, Smoki Musaraj, Ila Nagar, Juno Parreñas, Johanna Sellman, Noah Tamarkin, Inés Valdez, Aurélie Vialette, Michèle Vincent, Liz Vivas and Paul Anderson, and Joel Wainwright. In Boston, it was Hayal Akarsu and Hakan Karpuzcu, Rosie Bsheer, Yazan Doughan, and Sultan Doughan, Rania Ghosn, El Hadi Jazairy and Taha, Gökçe Günel, Chris Gratien, Nisrine Salti, Dilan Yıldırım, and the members of PAWG/PEWG (Political Anthropology Working Group/Political Ecology Working

Group). In Toronto, it is Judy Han and Jenny Chun, Jens Hanssen, Muhammad Ali Khalidi and Diane Riskedahl, Jeannie Miller and Mario Carrieri, Ruth Marshall, Amira Mittermaier, Alejandra Jimenez, and Felix, Yigal Nizri, Natalie Rothman and Alejandro Paz, Rania Salem, and Barton Scott.

I am blessed with a crew of friends who constantly remind me that these relations are what make this world worthwhile. For endless conversation, sharing meals, tea and coffee, and laughter and tears, for keeping me on the straight and narrow, and for humoring me and thinking with me about this book, I am thankful to Toufoul Abou-Hodeib, Saleh Agha, Amna Akbar, Vartan Avakian, Fadi Bardawil, Sultan Doughan, Yazan Doughan, Raffy Doulian, Michael Gasper, Rania Ghosn, Dahlia Gubara and Ali Wick (and Amma and Shammousa), Mohamad Hafeda, Lana Halabi, Laura Kaehler, Banu Karaca, Zeina Maasri, Khaled Malas, Yasmine al-Machnouk, Nada Matta, Basma Moumtaz, Ceren Özgül, Karim Sadeq, Khaled Saghieh, Nisrine Salti, Johanna Sellman, Kawkab Shibaru, Ali Shreif, Jana Traboulsi, Nurfadzilah Yahaya, Inés Valdez, Aurélie Vialette and Jesús Velasco, and Ana Vinea.

It was my family (mama, baba, Ghina, and Youmna) who, knowingly or unknowingly, drove me to this research, and I would not have been able to complete it without their love and support. Despite my unorthodox choices, they never hesitated to extend their help in many different ways and always made the labor they invested in my life and happiness look effortless. I was lucky that Mustafa Fakhoury and Mazen Saghir joined our family. Mazen's going through the same experience helped in the translation of the academic experience and provided camaraderie and support. I did not let Mustafa take off his lawyer's hat even during lunch break. During our family lunches, he graciously answered all the miscellaneous questions I had about the court and various legal processes and projects. He provided me with innumerable laws and references while I was writing and revising all over the world. My partner, love, and no.1 cheerleader, Ted Sammons, has put up with many hours I decided to spend on this book instead of together. With his brilliance and breadth of knowledge, he pushed my thinking, provided a pair of eyes and ears at any time of the day or night, read numerous drafts, trusting me and collecting me when I was falling apart. Most importantly, his love and humor have kept me sane and showed me other ways of being in this world.

NOTE ON TRANSLITERATION, TRANSLATION, AND DATATION

For transliteration from Arabic, Ottoman, and Turkish, I have used the *International Journal of Middle East Studies*' transcription system. All non-English words are italicized, except the words that exist in common English use, those that exist in the *IJMES* list of such words (ex: *fatwa*), and those that are often repeated, like *waqf*. For proper names, named places and structures, institutions, and the like, I have avoided diacritics. For Ottoman, I have used a hybrid that keeps the long vowels but follows modern Turkish voweling.

Translations are my own, unless otherwise noted. When translating legal manuals, I use the masculine to be faithful to the text. However, outside literal translations, I use *he or she* or just *she* when both women and men could be the subjects of certain actions, and *he* when only men could be subjects.

As is common in ethnographic writing, I have anonymized many interlocutors, while keeping the names of those who requested it and the names of officials when speaking as officials. I have used the Gregorian calendar, but when referring to a document dated in *hijri* years, I have included that date in brackets.

The Muslim months are abbreviated as shown below:

Muḥarram	M
Ṣafar	S
Rabīʿ al-Awwal	Ra
Rabīʿ al-Thānī	R
Jumādā al-Awwal	Ca
Jumādā al-Thānī	C

Rajab	B
Shaʿbān	Sh
Ramaḍān	N
Shawwāl	L
Dhū al-Qaʿda	Za
Dhū al-Ḥijja	Z

Introduction

Between 2007 and 2013, I found myself arguing a lot with my interlocutors about what *waqf* (/wɒkf/) was. Waqf, lawyers would say, is a member of the family of trusts or endowments or perhaps even the ancestor of the trust.[1] When founding waqfs, founders surrender the ownership of possessions to God, dedicating their revenues to charity in perpetuity.[2] Land and buildings or parts thereof are the most common kinds of waqfs. Besides their many worldly advantages, waqfs bring Muslims closer to God in the hereafter and continue to do so as long as waqf revenues serve charitable purposes.[3] In the archive of the Muslim Sunni

1. Some scholars (e.g., Gaudiosi 1988) have argued that English trusts were an adaptation of the Islamic waqfs because they arose after a period of intense contact between England and the Islamic world through the Crusades. Although it may be unfamiliar to scholars who do not work on the Muslim world, waqf was a pervasive institution there before the twentieth century, garnering a 47,506-word entry in the second edition of the *Encyclopedia of Islam*.

2. Waqf was defined in Islamic law, although arguments about its origins abound (see Oberauer 2013 for a recent take that addresses early studies). Waqf foundations, as partly property transactions, could be established by non-Muslims to support purposes that were considered pious "for us and for them," as Muslim jurists in the dominant school of law in the Ottoman Empire put it (e.g. Ibn ʿAbidin, *Ḥāshiya*, 3:360). Such purposes include the non-Muslim poor but not their places of worship (since that is not a pious purpose for Muslims) or a mosque (since that is not a pious purpose for non-Muslims). For Christian waqfs in Lebanon, see van Leeuwen (1994), Slim (2007), and Mohasseb Saliba (2008).

3. Scholars have shown the ways waqfs were used to plan property devolution and family relations and avoid estate fragmentation through inheritance (Doumani 2017), divert state revenues to private pockets (Petry 1998), colonize newly conquered land (Yıldırım 2011), provide public services and establish political and religious legitimacy (Debasa 2017), in addition to gaining prestige and religious capital. For a recent article that synthesizes the various worldly advantages of waqf, see Igarashi (2019).

court in Beirut, I had noticed a surge in waqf foundations starting in the 1990s, after a fifty-year lull. I was discussing these new waqfs with founders, administrators, officials, and scholars, but we continually debated: Could these waqfs be sold, or were they inalienable? Did they need to involve a rent-yielding asset, or could they just create a legal entity? Were waqfs simply nonprofits? The debates were endless.

It is true that I had my own preconceptions. Vaguely familiar with the waqf from growing up in Beirut, I was returning home in September 2007, after four years of coursework in anthropology; and since anthropological studies of contemporary waqfs were few, I had mostly read historical and legal studies of waqf and learned about the many forms that waqfs had taken in Islamic history.[4] In the Ottoman Empire, which included Beirut from the sixteenth into the early twentieth century,[5] when the French Mandate was imposed (1920–1943), the most visible waqfs included institutions and infrastructure: mosques, shrines, madrasas, soup kitchens, fountains, wells, cisterns, bridges, and even railways.[6] But waqfs also included vast arable lands, whole villages, and shops whose revenues funded the upkeep of these institutions and the salaries of their imams, teachers, students, caretakers, administrators and various employees. These were large foundations established by the rich and powerful—sultans, their mothers, wives, viziers, and dignitaries. But there were also myriad smaller waqfs, which account for the majority of waqfs founded in Beirut in the nineteenth century.[7] In Beirut, men and women of much lesser means surrendered the ownership of rooms, shops, houses, small pieces of land, and even trees to support the mosques and the Sufi lodges of the city and beyond, distribute bread to the poor, pay reciters to read parts of the Qur'an, provide shade to passersby, and especially support the families of founders.[8]

These were the waqfs I encountered in the nineteenth-century archive of the Sunni court in Beirut, and they differed very much from the new waqfs of the 1980s, 1990s, and 2000s. Today, although most waqfs were dedicated to the building and foundation of new mosques and Islamic centers, others did not

4. Some studies of contemporary waqf are Reiter (2007) and Hovden (2019). Erie's article (2016) is one of the very few anthropological studies of contemporary waqf. There is a robust literature particularly from the Muslim world about reviving and reforming the waqf today. See Moumtaz (2018b).

5. Between 1831 and 1840, Beirut fell to the Egyptian rule of Muhammad Ali and his son Ibrahim Pasha. Despite the short period of Egyptian rule and its characterization as extortive and highly taxing, nationalist historians place tremendous weight on that period in the "modernization" and "development" of Lebanon.

6. For monographs on Ottoman waqfs, see, for example, Hallaq (1985), Yediyıldız (1985), Deguilhem-Schoem (1986), Akgündüz (1988), Behrens-Abouseif (1994), Hoexter (1998a), van Leeuwen (1999), 'Afifi (1991), Singer (2002), Güran (2006), Adada (2009), Doumani (2017).

7. For studies of these smaller waqfs, see Yediyıldız (1985) and Doumani (2017).

8. Waqfs in Beirut and in other cities and villages far from the Ottoman imperial capital Istanbul supported the sanctuaries and poor of Mecca and Medina, as well other significant places in an expansive Muslim geography.

resemble anything I had seen in the archive. For instance, in one of the foundation documents noted in the registers of the Sunni shariʿa court archive for 2005, two Muslim men earmarked $200 to create a waqf supporting "human rights regardless of race, religion, and belief."[9] I was truly puzzled because supporting human rights did not look like the forms of Islamic charity I had previously encountered and $200 seemed like very little to sustain an eternal waqf.[10]

As I was to realize, my discussions and arguments with various interlocutors about these new forms of waqf were inevitable given my familiarity with nineteenth-century waqf practices. They reflect the vast changes in conceptions of religion, property, and charity that have made waqf practices and understandings very different today from those I had seen in Islamic legal manuals and historical records. If waqf was the "material foundation" of Islamic society, as Marshall Hodgson famously described it (1974, 2:124), then the changes to the economic foundations of the Islamic world with the rise of world capitalism were bound to change waqf. Indeed, with capitalism, land became a financial asset and real estate wealth that needed to be grown to benefit the nation's economy.[11] This new understanding of land competed with existing approaches to land as a (taxable) source of livelihood through agricultural production and rent and as a place of dwelling, among others. Waqfs that were tied in eternity to the particular purposes willed by founders had to be "liberated" for the benefit of the nation's economic progress.[12] And since waqf created particular relations between founders, their inner

9. MBSS.H 2005/1250.

10. Cash itself was not an oddity as an object of endowment because some Ottoman jurists allowed the practice, which others considered problematic on many levels: waqfs are supposed to have a use and usufruct that does not "extinguish" the object, which is not the case for cash. Furthermore, some scholars considered that cash waqfs constituted lending with interest, contradicting what some traditions cast as a prohibition on interest, *ribā* (see, e.g., Fadel 2007). See Mandaville (1979), Özcan (2003, 2008), Karataş (2011) for a discussion of the legal debate on cash waqfs. In Ottoman cash waqfs, however, the endowed sum was a large principal (not $200) that was lent, and the profits incurred were dedicated to charitable purposes.

11. My positing a change in the approach to land with capitalism does not mean that land was not used to speculate and make profit in the early modern and medieval eras. For a discussion of the main changes that happen to land with capitalism—namely, its transformation into a form of fictitious capital or a pure financial asset—see Harvey (2006, ch.11) and Polanyi (2001). The transformation of property into wealth (and their equivalence) has been noted by Hannah Arendt (1998, 22–78), who shows that for the Greeks and Romans, property was what gave one a position in this world and was in some ways inalienable, whereas the pursuit of wealth was considered a lowly occupation that distracted one from accomplishing true humanity through participating in politics.

12. My emphasis on grounding these transformations in the new property regime and modern ideas about economy and progress builds on arguments put forward by Powers (1989) and expanded on by Hallaq (2009, 433–36, 471–72). Another important explanation of the attack on waqf is that it was necessary to undermine those religious authorities that competed with the new states, as waqfs provided religious scholars with independent sources of income. However, the historical sources I use below show that the bigger concern was the "liberation" of alienated waqf properties and thus control over the resources they provided.

self, God, their family, their neighbors, their city, and the Muslim world as they imagined it, these relations were also remade.

God's Property argues that the financialization of land and its transformation into real estate wealth involved a process of secularization of land and of waqf, subjecting waqf to the question, Is the waqf a (private) religious or an economic thing? Secularization, when analyzed through an institution as complex as the waqf, appears under different guises, from the absence of an orientation towards an elsewhere or an afterlife to the emptying of God from certain spheres.[13] However, in these different guises, secularization most importantly involves *the continuous quest of separating religion from economy* and privatizing it. The latter form of secularization follows the argument that secularization implies a differentiation of "secular" spheres such as law, economics, and politics and the development of a separate sphere of religion, along with their overlap on the public and the private, but it differs in considering these processes a project essential for modern forms of governing, rather than as a normative indicator of modernity.[14] Furthermore, my use of the phrase "the continuous quest" gestures to Hussein Ali Agrama's argument that secularism is a "set of processes and structures of power wherein the question of where to draw a line between religion and politics arises and acquires a *distinctive salience*" (2012, 27; Agrama's italics). The expression "distinctive salience" indicates that the differentiation of various spheres is not in and of itself an indication of secularization; it is not simply the fact that polities recognize and differentiate between religion and politics that marks secular power. It is the rise of the *question* about the separation of spheres and the need to restrict (privatized) religion from encroaching on various other (public) spheres that is particular to

13. The orientation towards an elsewhere is my reformulation of Charles Taylor's "transformative perspective," the "perspective of a transformation of human beings which takes them beyond or outside of whatever is normally understood as human flourishing . . . [, which] sees our highest goal in terms of a certain kind of human flourishing, in a context of mutuality, pursuing each his/her own happiness on the basis of assured life and liberty, in a society of mutual benefit" (2007, 430). Taylor argues that with secularization, the transformative perspective becomes one option among many.

14. This argument regarding structural differentiation appears as early as Weber but has lately been elaborated by José Casanova (1994). The argument proposes that modernity brought about the creation of various spheres (economy, politics, culture, science), each with its rationality that is "emancipated" from religious norms and institutions. Casanova argues that such differentiation is enough for secularization and does not require the privatization of religion. Contra Casanova, I agree with Asad, who argues that whenever "religion" gets out of the private sphere, there is no reason for "religious reasons" not to interfere in other spheres, which are then hybridized (Asad 2003, 182). Thus, the fact that late Ottoman Islamic law distinguished between religious law derived from the sacred sources and state law based on public benefit (Fadel 2017) does not mean the Ottoman state was secular, as there is no privatization of religion and the constant questions and anxiety over the separation of religion from politics or economy does not arise. Moreover, as Agrama (2012) observes, even within a state riddled with the question of secularism, such as Egypt today, certain spaces like the Fatwa Council of Al-Azhar are "asecular" in the sense that concern over the relation between religion and politics does not arise there.

secularism as a mode of modern power. In Agrama's case, the constant attempt to separate religion from politics and to privatize it, especially through law, always creates more reasons for the state to interfere (because of the indeterminacy of law), to legislate, and thus to entrench state sovereignty. The analysis of the waqf, however, shows something different—namely, the rise of the question of where to draw a line between religion and the economy (rather than politics), a question in which sovereignty does not first appear prominent. Yet, the separation of religion from economy, along with its privatization, requires certain flows of capital from religious groups to the state, implicating state sovereignty beyond its entanglements in the delimitation of religion. Furthermore, examining the secularization of waqf shows that this constant questioning is also the result of the impossible demand to consolidate an institution as complex as the waqf in these spheres and the constant overflow that an institution embodying a different logic produces.

Secularization was accompanied by a private property regime, in the form of the "ownership model," which assumes an individual owner, a delimited object of property, and the absolute rights of the owner to exclude (Singer 2000).[15] This model of property, as anthropologists have noted, is far from universal, in its separation of people and things, its possessive impulse, and its disenchantment. Its implementation in the Ottoman Empire required a remaking of the Ottoman property regime, including its secularization, in the senses both of the expulsion of God from property relations and the distancing of property law from religion. Furthermore, in the course of the nineteenth century, individual and absolute ownership replaced the much more layered understanding of property, where each parcel's rights of use, revenues, and alienation (e.g., the right to cultivate, right to a portion of the harvest, right to taxes, right to sell) were spread among different people (and many times the state) (İslamoğlu 2000; Mundy and Smith 2007). In one of the nineteenth-century waqfs I discuss, a house with a garden, the state had rights to taxes; the daughter of the founder had the right to rent of the land; her husband and his family had the right to inhabit or rent the house; and the right to sell was confined to God. In the mid-twentieth century, the rights to the rent of the land and the house and the right to sell all became limited to the founder's daughter's heirs.

Waqf, God's property, provides a privileged site to analyze the secularization of property and its effects on relations to self, family, and community. As this book shows, under the new property regime, God was no longer the owner of the waqfs' property; instead, according to the letter of the law, each waqf had a legal personality and could itself own property, giving waqfs a new life as legal entities that could

15. On the intersection of secularism and the private property regime, see Klassen (2014, 176). Scholars have demonstrated how European theorists and jurists justified this regime based on Christian theology and defined it in contrast to the ways indigenous people of the Americas related to the land (e.g., Waldron 2002). Locke (2005, 286), for example, proposed that God gave the Earth to humankind in common and that private property stemmed from God's injunction to fructify the land.

navigate state control. Collectively, waqfs were defined in French Mandate law as the *religious* patrimony of the still undifferentiated Muslim community, itself a legal person, and thus became an important site to create Muslims as one sect (or *ṭāʾifa*; pl. *ṭawāʾif*, as religious communities are called in Lebanon) among others in the Lebanese state. This "sectarianization" of waqf transformed waqf from an individual endeavor with various worldly and otherworldly advantages to an institution tied to and reproducing a national legal-political-religious community. Concurrently, in this new property regime, which included new debt regimes that forwent forgiveness and prioritized foreclosure, founders became suspicious when making inalienable waqf as they were putting real estate property outside the reach of creditors. Their intent in waqf founding became open to scrutiny, bolstering a new sense of interiority to the self along with a new form of skepticism about motives. These new conceptions of self, along with new ideas about its *real* motivations, became the foundation of shifting criteria for distinguishing between truly charitable (for collective benefit) as opposed to self-interested (for private benefit) behavior, making waqfs dedicated to families appear to be not *really* charitable. Based on these distinctions between public and private, a notion of public utility was articulated, defined by the state and centered around its preservation and economic progress, that separated "religious" and "economic" waqfs and emphasized the perpetuation of "religious" waqfs (mosques, Sufi lodges, madrasas), while making other waqfs partake in the capitalist market and its perpetual improvement and accumulation.

A MODERN REVIVAL AND THE GRAMMAR OF CONCEPTS

The new waqfs I was seeing in the twenty-first century were not only new in their conceptualization. They were also new in the trend they represented: a revival of the waqf after a long absence of new foundations in the period between Lebanon's independence in 1943 and the late 1980s. Indeed, early in the twentieth century, when Beirut was still part of the Ottoman Empire, thousands of people depended on such largesse, and entire neighborhoods were made into endowments to support a charitable institution like a mosque or a soup kitchen. But with the fall of the Ottoman Empire and the imposition of the French Mandate on Lebanon at the end of World War I, things changed. For one, the French were not interested in reproducing an "Islamic society." Instead, they sought to create a civil state that remained equidistant from the "personal status law" or "family law" (governing marriage, divorce, waqf, and for some inheritance and custody) of eighteen Muslim, Christian, and Jewish sects given official recognition and legal sovereignty.[16] This legal secular arrangement transformed religious

16. The jurisdiction of Christian courts was limited to marriage and divorce; see Méouchy (2006) for the reasons behind these differences.

communities into (legal) sects, but it is distinct from what is often termed political sectarianism, or consociationalism, namely the distribution of public office and civil service based on the religious balance in Lebanon.[17] But also, for the French, waqfs stood against the freedom of circulation of land and property because they tied up a lot of the real estate wealth. Thus, regulations sought to eliminate many forms of the waqf and facilitate their conversion to private property. Between 1943 and the late 1980s, almost no new waqf foundation appears in court registers because of the entrenchment of these new understandings of religion as a separate sphere and of property as real estate wealth, a redefinition of the role of the state in provisioning its citizens, and laws that aimed at eradicating waqf as a practice.[18] It was only in the 1990s that new waqfs started appearing again in the registers. Between 1990 and 2009, some seventy new waqfs were founded and recorded in the court adjudicating the personal-status issues of the Sunni community in Beirut.

The revival of waqf in Beirut coincides with a larger waqf revival initiated by Kuwait in the early 1990s, while the trajectory of waqf decline and eradication in colonial and postcolonial states was common in the Middle East—with the exception of Jordan and Palestine, where waqf has stood in the way of land appropriation by Jewish settlers, and Saudi Arabia, where the main legal system remains shariʿa-based.[19] This is a notable change in the trend of waqf foundation and the

17. Thus, seats in Parliament are divided between the various sects, and the president is a Maronite, the prime minister a Sunni, and the speaker of the house a Shiʿi. Political sectarianism is a prime research area in Lebanon and often considered a major cause of Lebanon's underdevelopment and problems, including the 1975–1990 civil war and limited sense of national belonging (the people, it is said, have more affiliation to their religious community than to their national one). Sharara (1975) and Makdisi (2000) show that the phenomenon is a modern one rather than the expression of deep-seated pre-modern identities. For an example of historical studies about the making of sectarian identities, see Weiss (2010). For recent anthropological studies of sectarianism, see, for example, Nucho (2016), Mikdashi (2017), and Bou Akar (2018). The legal arrangement I describe here, while connected to political sectarianism, is different from it, because political sectarianism could be abolished while upholding this legal arrangement that allows different religious laws for different religious sects. Recent changes allowing the Lebanese to "cross out" their sect from their state records and IDs pose the question as to which personal status laws should be followed. As Abillama (2018) compellingly argues, the possible creation of a civil marriage and personal status law would not change the current legal arrangement; both religious and civil marriage "belong to the same secular configuration" (149). However, this change that somehow creates a new "civil sect" affects political sectarianism because it poses the question of the political representation of these citizens who legally belong to the "civil sect."

18. For an excellent study documenting the rise of the idea and practice of the state providing for the poor in Egypt, see Ener (2003).

19. In the introduction of the edited volume on waqf by Deguilhem and Hénia (2004, 7), a note from the publisher, the Public Secretariat of Waqfs (al-Amana al-ʿAmma li'l-Awqaf) in Kuwait, founded in 1993, describes the book as part of a "strategy to promote waqfs" adopted by the Executive Committee of the Conference of the Ministry of Waqfs and Islamic Affairs in Muslim Countries in 1997. It designated Kuwait as the coordinating state for this project to "revive waqf and develop its socio-economic possibilities for the benefit of Muslim societies" (2004, 7). Scientific research on waqf and its law and historical manifestations was encouraged through an international competition, a scientific journal, and even fellowships for doctoral students. Both Joseph (2014) and Abdallah (2018,

perception of waqf, even if in Beirut the number of new foundations remains far less than the average of new foundations in the nineteenth century in relation to the number of inhabitants. While the increase is modest in number and has not caught the attention of outside observers in the way the increase of veiling among women did, it is significant because waqf stands at the intersection of the social, economic, political, religious, moral, and aesthetic. As I show throughout this book, it is a window onto the modern world and the transition to modernity, and the making of much of what we moderns take for granted in these domains.

The revival of the waqf, like the surge of charity worldwide, also coincides with the rise of neoliberalism, the retreat of the welfare state, and the delegation of the provision of social services to nonprofits and individual benefactors, the so-called third sector. It is in this context that the United Nations Economic and Social Commission for Western Asia has jumped on the waqf bandwagon and advanced the waqf as a deeply rooted practice that can be mobilized in the new welfare mix where the state is not the main provider of social services (ESCWA 2013). Many contemporary writings in the Muslim world, which aim to revive the waqf, embrace the neoliberal rhetoric of the need to decrease state expenditures and see the waqfs as a third sector that can help with this aim and concurrently redistribute wealth (for an academic version, see, e.g., Çizakça 2000; for a popular version, see the many papers by Monzer Kahf, e.g., 2004). Quite a bit of Islamic charity has espoused neoliberal logic, promoting entrepreneurialism as an Islamic virtue and investing in human capital to "teach a man how to fish" to uproot the source of poverty (Atia 2013). Yet, tying Islamic charity to neoliberalism, both in terms of its causes and its form, would be to miss an important part of the story, as Amira Mittermaier (2019) has shown in Egypt, where giving practices like feeding the poor continue traditions that long predate neoliberalism and that exceed neoliberal logics.[20]

This revival of the waqf is also a part of what has been termed the Islamic Revival, the rise of political Islam and Islamic sensibility and practice in Muslim-majority countries since the 1970s.[21] With the Iranian Revolution often serving as the Revival's watershed moment, this religiosity is described in academic scholarship

70) mention this waqf revival but do not provide any more detail than I do here. The revival definitely warrants further research. For a description of the decline trajectory in the modern Middle East and North Africa, see Aharon Layish's section in the Waḳf entry in *Encyclopedia of Islam*, 2nd ed. For the particular cases of Palestine, see, for example, Ashtiyya (2001), Dumper (1994), Khayat (1962), Reiter (1996, 2007), Yazbak (2010) for Muslim waqfs, and Shaham (1991) for Christian and Jewish waqfs. For a study of Saudi Arabia's legal system, which unfortunately does not discuss waqf, see Vogel (2000).

20. Mittermaier (2019) describes a practice of giving that is done out of duty, for God, rather than out of compassion for the poor, and is not aimed at social justice and eradicating poverty.

21. Osanloo (2019) shows how, in a place like Iran, where Islamic foundations are part of this Islamic Revival and attempt to Islamicize society, foundations have come, through activists' efforts, to also serve populations like sex workers and drug users, which the Islamic state does not want to see.

and by its own participants as a revival after a period of decreasing religiosity. Indeed, some of the large Muslim-majority modern nation-states like Turkey and Iran had actively pursued policies of secularization and privatization of religion following World War I and into the 1970s. In Beirut, the Revival had to wait for the Lebanese Civil War (1975–1990) to end before it could bloom.[22] Study circles burgeoned and Islamic satellite channels from across the Arab world appeared on Beiruti television screens, while formal organizations and informal study groups sought to instruct Muslims about their religious duties and to instill in them the desire to live a good Muslim life. Charitable giving, a pillar of the Islamic tradition, was given pride of place in both teaching and practice as one of the best ways to be close to God. Waqf, as a perpetually giving kind of charity, was one of the charitable Islamic institutions that organizations themselves started using and enjoined Muslims to use.

Yet the revival of a centuries-old practice, taking place under a very different architecture of state, law, and religion and accompanied by a new property regime, came to refigure what waqf was in nineteenth-century Beirut. Indeed, today's waqf, anchored in Islamic law, reflects larger transformations in the Islamic tradition.[23] The modern state, capitalism, modern pedagogy and technology, and new forms of authority have deeply reordered and created ruptures in the tradition.[24] In particular, shariʿa was deeply refigured under the modern state. Before that, shariʿa laid claim to governing society and was a "legally productive mechanism" that asserted ultimate legal sovereignty (Hallaq 2005, 169; 2009, 361; 2013). Indeed, shariʿa described how to live one's life and assessed all actions on a scale of obligatory, recommended, indifferent, reprehensible, and prohibited; thus it included many legal ordinances justiciable in the here-and-now, and it provided the limit of the legally possible for Islamic polities that governed in its name. The modern state challenged both these monopolies (law production and sovereignty) and replaced the shariʿa as the organizing principle of society, the "machine of

22. The efforts of the Revival in Lebanon on the Sunni side have not been the object of sustained anthropological research (for political scientific approaches see Rougier 2007 and Pall 2013, 2018). Groups as varied as Jamaʿa Islamiyya, Jamʿiyyat al-Mashariʿ al-Islamiyya (known as al-Ahbash), the Sahariyya (the Lebanese branch of the Syrian Qubaysiyyat), along with unaffiliated individuals trained by particular teachers, have directed their effort at *daʿwa*, the invitation to an Islamic way of life, through teaching, study circles, and schools, even though some of them are also involved in the state and party politics. For an interesting discussion of the term *daʿwa*, see Mahmood (2005, 157–60). For an ethnography of the Revival in Lebanon on the Shiʿi side, see Deeb (2006). For a way to explain the Revival, see Asad (2007). For a slightly dated bibliography, see Haddad and Esposito (1997).

23. Following Asad (1986), I use *Islamic tradition* in the sense of a living, vibrant dialogue with foundational texts, where participants make truth-claims about their interpretation, which is why I still speak of Islamic tradition and Islam (rather than Islams). See my exposition of Asad's intervention (Moumtaz, 2015, 126–29).

24. For studies that describe and analyze some of these transformations, see Eickelman (1992), Bowen (1993), and Messick (1993).

governance" (Hallaq 2009, 361). New law schools replaced madrasas; lawyers, Muslim jurists; and European codes, *fiqh* (Islamic law). The madrasas themselves transformed into shariʿa colleges that adopted many of the pedagogies of modern schooling (Messick 1993). Even more, Islam has been put into the service of the modern state (Skovgaard-Petersen 1997; Starrett 1998). Many aspects of Muslims' lives are governed by different imperatives than living a good life according to the Islamic tradition. Actually, the very states where Muslims live are oriented to very different kinds of ideals, like freedom and the (economic) well-being of the nation, as I elaborate below. These transformations show the strong ruptures in the Islamic tradition.

Yet, ruptures are not always destructive or obliterating. A rupture can cause a tradition to become incoherent or even to disappear, but some traditions are robust enough to absorb a fracture.[25] A rupture can also produce new possibilities. Crucially, ruptures are never neat; older practices continue to exist through practitioners, discourses, spaces, and material objects. Shariʿa continues to operate as a discursive practice enacted by those who privilege older methods of teaching and forms of authority and who attempt to live their lives based on shariʿa, as described in many accounts of the contemporary Islamic Revival (for example, Mahmood 2005; Pierret 2013). Furthermore, contemporary Islamic practices still contribute to a project different from and irreducible to liberalism. Many Muslim reformists have different aims from liberal ones—a national nonsecular modernity (Shakry 1998)—and some even want to put the modern state to the service of an Islamic society (Osanloo 2006). Some scholars have questioned the rupture altogether and have placed many of these non-liberal reformists within the fold of Islamic tradition, arguing that they draw on and build on existing discourses and practices in the Islamic tradition (Haj 2011; Ayoub 2016). However, I maintain that, despite this very different project that non-liberal reformists are invested in, one needs to be attentive to the effects of these changes, independently of the projects and discourses of their authors, because liberal concepts, discourses, and practices have come to inflect contemporary Islamic tradition (Deeb 2006; Silverstein 2011; Schielke 2013), so that even revivalist groups share with modernizers and secularists common epistemological assumptions and understandings of history, time, and religion (Iqtidar 2011; Quadri 2013).[26]

To better understand these deeper changes of Islamic tradition in its encounter with the modern state, I suggest paying attention to the grammar of concepts (Asad 2003, 25) and to styles of reasoning in the tradition. I use the term *grammar* in the

25. For those familiar with the history of the shariʿa, one can conceptualize the Sunni synthesis, for instance, as a rupture because it inaugurated a new way of deriving law (a legal methodology) that is neither just that of the Traditionalists nor that of the Rationalists, and it was followed by an effervescence of the tradition rather than its obliteration.

26. A possible explanation for these effects is that technologies are not simply neutral tools but come with particular epistemologies (see Hallaq 2013, 155, for a parallel between the modern state and Aristotelian logic).

late Wittgensteinian tradition, as "rules for the use of a word" (Wittgenstein 1974, I:§133). The word *rules* in this tradition does not refer to syntactic rules, rules that, for example, determine word order or declination in a sentence. Grammar here is about semantic rules; it is about meaning. Wittgenstein's concern with meanings has different motivations from those of a lexicographer—namely, overcoming philosophical confusion (Schroeder 2017, 254). The meaning of many words for Wittgenstein consists in their use in the language (Wittgenstein 2009, §43); we learn the meanings of these words by using them in particular activities, which are among what Wittgenstein calls language-games, whereby a word's meaning derives from its role and place in the activity (grammar is like the rules of a game). Furthermore, despite his affirmation of the presence of rules, Wittgenstein suggests that such rules can be implicit (but known to practitioners), piecemeal, and changed and improvised upon.

My project as a historical anthropologist differs from a philosopher's but, as scholars of Wittgenstein note, grammar is not just about language but can be expanded to a "specific form of discourse, or, more generally, to a certain set of activities or of some institutionalized form of life" (Schroeder 2017, 267, for example)—in my case, the Islamic tradition. Analyzing the grammar of concepts—their meaning in use—at specific moments allows us to better understand continuities and ruptures in the tradition between these moments.[27] Although one grammar might be dominant at a certain time, other grammars might still be perpetuated by different communities or in particular practices. What makes a concept the same despite possible radical changes in its understanding is that it is anchored in the tradition; it is a practice that produces similar effects in the quest for the good life—for example, bringing founders closer to God, in the case of waqf. Because grammar calls for attention to the meaning of a concept in use, I focus on the institution and practice of waqf and analyze the meaning in use of waqf at different temporal junctures in order to examine ruptures and continuities across these moments. I show, for example, how waqf came to denote a subject, a nonprofit, like the human-rights waqf, rather than a revenue-bearing object, while also tracing the persistence of these older practices of waqf as object through practitioners and artifacts. I thus highlight particular meanings in particular settings rather than sweeping rules or grand theories about Islamic tradition in the absolute.

A focus on the grammar of waqf requires us to pay attention to the structure and larger practices in which waqf operates, which I call "architecture" (the language-game and forms of life in Wittgenstein's terms).[28] I find the term

27. Although he does not frame it as grammatical analysis, Reinkowski makes a similar argument for the need to analyze the "words in their specific contexts and elucidates the change of meaning these terms have experienced" to understand the way Ottoman political vocabulary changed in meaning over the nineteenth century (2005, 198).

28. To show how grammar determines use, Wittgenstein likens grammar to the bed of a river, and use to the water that flows in the bed (Forster 2004, 10). We can say that the language-game is the geography that limits how that bed can change.

architecture useful when talking about the context of use because it reflects a certain solidity and fixity that determines movement and use—that is, grammar. One imagines these relations between state, law, and religion to constitute a complex construction, which can be remodeled and rebuilt but that recedes into the background in daily life while determining much of the possibilities of the use of space/concepts. This architecture is not an implicit part of the rules of grammar; it is what allows the following of these rules in the first place. If these structures were different, these specific rules of grammar would not make sense. Without stairs, the idea of walking up and down stairs would not be meaningful. In Ottoman Beirut, waqfs were part of the system of the shariʿa and shariʿa-defined practices[29] of living the good life of a Muslim, which existed within a particular architecture of state, law, and religion. With the advent of modernizing and modern states, waqfs became subject to state law, discussed under legislation on property, inheritance, and personal status, and even subjected to new state legislation. Waqfs also fell under the discipline of political economy and, later, economics, where they became conceptualized as real estate wealth.

A grammatical analysis also requires us to bring to the fore and examine the constellation of concepts with which waqf is used. Waqf is used in conjunction with the concepts of intent, family, and benefit, and thus the grammar of waqf is very much tied to the grammar of these concepts. For instance, while early nineteenth-century juridical discussions of the concept of the waqf's benefit involved the concepts of necessity and stipulations of founders, the benefit of the waqf came to be wedded to the "religious benefit" of the Muslim community throughout the twentieth century. I determine the grammar of each of these concepts by examining the weft of legal texts, legal theory, and court documents *in use*. However, as discussed above, I do not simply analyze language (and texts) but remain attentive to practices that were tied to institutions (courts, schools, offices), because these concepts make sense only within a system and context of use.

THE NOVELTY OF THE MODERN STATE: PROGRESS, ECONOMY, AND THE USES OF LAW

I locate the determinant of the current architecture of state, law, and religion under which waqf operates, which gives contemporary waqf its particular grammar, in the modern state. In Lebanon, I trace this formation to the Ottoman state and the modernizing reforms undertaken in the empire, especially during the long

29. I use *practices* in this work in the Aristotelian tradition as defined by philosopher Alasdair MacIntyre as "any coherent and complex form of socially established cooperative human activity through which goods internal to that activity are realized in the course of trying to achieve those standards of excellence which are appropriate to, and partially definitive of, that form of activity, with the result that human powers to achieve excellence, and human conceptions of the ends and goods involved, are systematically extended" (1984, 83).

nineteenth century. These reforms, which started with military reforms in the late eighteenth century and continued with fiscal, administrative, and legal reforms in the nineteenth century, sought to address the military defeats and economic challenges posed by Russia and European powers.[30] Historians of the Ottoman Empire have long debated the origins of these reforms, including whether these ideas of reform and progress were internal to an Ottoman-Islamic paradigm or whether they were imported from Europe via state functionaries trained in Europe and interpellated by European notions of progress (Davison 1963; Berkes 1998; Abu-Manneh 1994; Ayoub 2016). Scholars have also considered likely agents of change, including Istanbul and its reformers, Western ideas, and the world economy (Pamuk 1987; İslamoğlu-İnan 1988; Owen 1993), with more recent scholarship suggesting instead an essential role for provincial elites in initiating these reforms (see, e.g., Hanssen, Philipp, and Weber 2002; Hanssen 2002). Furthermore, these historians have considered the periodization of these reforms: their exact beginning and the characteristics of various periods (Westernization, a more Islamic idiom, and abandonment).[31] While these are important questions, in this study I am interested in the deep structural changes that these reforms have initiated, independent of their origins or agents. These reforms introduced "fundamentally new governmental powers," instating a paradigmatic shift in the early nineteenth century (Salzmann 1998, 38). This was a point of no return, so to speak, that transformed forever how government was approached, whether rule was constitutional or autocratic, "Islamic" or "Westernized."[32]

Following Asad (1992, 334) who builds on Foucault (1991), I take the particularity of the modern state and the center of its practices to be articulated around the concept of the nation's economy and its increasing wealth and progress. The distinctiveness of the modern state does not lie in bureaucracy (à la Weber), in centralized government (à la Hobbes), or in class domination (à la Marx), all of which were found in premodern states. Instead, progress tied to the economy constitutes the distinguishing feature of the modern state as compared to its Old Regime predecessor. A new "type of intervention characteristic of government" arose: "intervention in the field of economy and population" (Foucault 1991, 101). While one could argue that the aim of a non-modern (Ottoman) Islamic state was

30. The literature on Ottoman reforms is enormous, although the earlier literature is marred by nationalist and secularist ideologies that took Western Europe as the end of history. For a good, more recent introduction, see Hanioğlu (2008). Classics include Davison (1963), Ortaylı (1983), and Findley (1980). In the context of the Levant, the classic remains Maʿoz (1968).

31. For a review of the historiography of the late Ottoman Empire, on which I rely here, see Emrence (2007).

32. In that I concur with Ariel Salzmann (1999), who argues that this was modern governmentality independent of the "liberal franchise" of the 1839 reform edict. For an article that adopts a similar approach and traces the new idioms and their continuities across these periods through charitable giving and the public sphere, see Özbek (2005).

"public benefit" (Fadel 2017, 66), this benefit was not measured in terms of continuous progress and growth and was concerned with the afterlives of subjects.[33]

One can trace the implanting and blossoming of the idea of progress in the Ottoman context in the reforms starting in the late eighteenth century: whether in a liberal or an Islamic idiom, they were driven by alarm over the "decline" of the Ottoman Empire and the progress of Europe and were concerned with how the empire should initiate its trajectory towards this natural path of ever-improvement (Mardin 1962, 135, 319–23). In that project, I will show, waqfs became conceptualized as abstract objects of administration, part of the nation's wealth, its "economy," having its own patterns, distinct from the sum total of the individual acts that made up the economy. Waqfs needed to be attended to and made to grow. This approach differed from earlier Ottoman policies, where waqfs were surveyed during land censuses with an eye towards imperial revenues (Shaw 2000, 94) rather than towards governing them to make them prosper and contribute to the nation's economy.

Progress necessitated the whole remaking of society, a break with the past. Modern power's distinctive "point of application" is on the conditions that shape the lives and bodies of subjects, rather than directly on their bodies. Indeed, enlightenment reason necessitated the uprooting of superstition and prejudice by eliminating the conditions that produced them and installing new conditions based on "clear, sound, rational principles".[34] Similar rationalities and principles operated in the Ottoman Empire, where the "idea was that the old institutions and ways should be entirely destroyed as they were replaced" (Shaw 2000, 93). And indeed, many of the reforms did destroy old conditions, despite other readings of these reforms as aiming to "restore Sultanic power" or instate "virtuous" rule (Abu-Manneh 1994, 182). One can cite here for instance the destruction, in 1826, of the Janissary corps, the elite slave infantry corps that was the cornerstone of the Old Regime, and the Sufi order that was affiliated with it. This does not mean that the destruction of old conditions was complete or that older institutions did not survive, but the impulse to eliminate them was there.

33. Fadel argues that Muslim jurists conceived of the positive law of the state as the "result of the deliberation of an idealized agent acting to further the rational good of his principal" and not the result of an engagement with the foundational texts of the tradition (2017, 49). These laws cannot contradict divine law as expressed in the *fiqh* (making permissible what is not permissible, for example), but they can make obligatory an act jurists consider only optional, or even reprehensible. Yet, whether his reading would have been accepted by jurists remains to be historically examined. The rejection by Ottoman provincial scholars of many Ottoman state laws (*qānūn*) that do not necessarily make permissible the impermissible suggests that state legislation in the name of public benefit was not as acceptable to jurists as Fadel suggests. Rapoport (2012), examining attitudes of jurists toward Mamluk sultanic intervention in the administration of law, notes that some thought it was necessary and lauded it as ensuring justice; others completely rejected it; and still others distinguished between just and unjust state intervention.

34. The notion of a "point of application" of power is Foucauldian but elaborated in this context by David Scott (1999, 32–33).

To remake society and make progress possible, law was crucial. "In a modern state, laws are enacted not simply to command obedience and to maintain justice, but to enable or disable its population. . . . It is more than merely an instrument. . . . In the modern state, law is an element in political strategies—especially strategies for destroying old options and creating new ones" (Asad 1992, 335). As political and legal theorist Samera Esmeir (2012) elaborates, modern positive law eliminates such old options by making the present the ground of the law. Indeed, positive legal codes only refer to themselves rather than relying on the authority of tradition; they are self-authorizing. It is no wonder that the Ottoman reforms were so heavily characterized by a "new juridical foundation for the government" (Salzmann 1999, 42): new legislative and judicial bodies, new legislation, and the extension of governmental reach into emerging spheres of urban life such as the press, international commercial relations, and industrial relations. Many historians usually take the promulgation of an imperial edict in 1839 as the beginning of the reforms known as the Tanzimat. The 1839 edict was followed by another edict in 1856 and the Constitution of 1876, as well as a massive amount of legislation: a penal code in 1840, a commercial code in 1850, a land code in 1858, and a maritime code in 1863 (many based on French codes) (Örücü 1992). Also, a project of codification of Islamic law begun in 1868 appeared as the Mecelle-i Aḥkâm-i ʿAdliyye (Mecelle, henceforth).[35] The new codes provided the law of new courts, both commercial and penal, that were added to the long-existing shariʿa courts.

Despite the importance of the modern state for the transformations I describe, I do not take it as the ultimate locus of power but as a major field defining possibilities and rationalities. I approach the state with an awareness that government involves much more than the state and is much more diffuse. I also walk the avenues opened by anthropological approaches to the state, as in the works of Mitchell (2006 [1999]), Trouillot (2001), and Gupta (2006). Instead of analyzing the state as a "distinct, fixed, and unitary entity," I take such a conception of the state as an "*effect* of practices that make such structures appear to exist" (Mitchell 2006 [1999], 180; emphasis mine). The "state effect," the appearance of the state as an external structure, is not an illusion or ideology; it is the very real effect of practices. In recognition of the reality and the power of the state effect and of the term's importance for my interlocutors, I still refer to "the state." I analyze the mobilization of this model, the processes of distinguishing the state from other institutions, and the consequences of this model on the operation of power in society (Gupta 2006, 8). In this way, I emphasize the constant work involved in the production of the state and particularly in the claims to legal sovereignty, a crucial discourse in competition with the shariʿa and in the restriction of shariʿa to the new category of family law, as we shall see. In this context,

35. This was not the first attempt to codify Islamic law. See the examples discussed by Fierro (2014).

jurisdictional politics, the conflict between different legal forums and authorities (Benton 2002, 10), plays a crucial role in the creation of the state effect.

Waqf participated in the making of the state effect when waqf administration was subjected to new practices of "good administration" under a state ministry instead of being the personalized administration of particulars, including high dignitaries. Already in 1826, the newly founded Ministry of Imperial Waqfs (Nezâret-i Evḳâf-i Hümâyûn), the ancestor of the contemporary Directorate General of Islamic Waqfs, took over the supervision and administration of some of the major waqfs traditionally held by high officers of the imperial court (Barnes 1986). The ministry, like other state bodies, was now hosted in a fixed location. The centralization and reform of waqf administration is far from novel, whether in various periods of Islamic history or various parts of the Muslim world. The year 1826, however, marks a turning point because of the techniques of government introduced: uniform practices of accounting, reporting, and supervision produced the effect of a state structure governing waqf as real estate wealth.

This modern transformation of the approach to waqf also shifted the meaning of essential elements of waqf practice: (public) interest, family, and intent. I turn now to an understanding of these concepts under the modern state. I hint at some of the effects of these changes in meaning to the grammar of waqf as associated with each of these concepts, which I will then elaborate in the chapters.

PUBLIC INTEREST

The modern state had its particular art of government, governmentality—adopted by the Ottomans (Salzmann 1999) and applied in Beirut (Hanssen 2005, Abou-Hodeib 2017)—whose object was the population and whose aim was specific purposes associated with the objects governed. Starting in the late eighteenth century, this art of government displaced (but did not eradicate) sovereignty, whose object was territory and whose aim was "common welfare," "salvation for all," and "public utility" because no *good* sovereign "is entitled to exercise his power regardless of its end" (Foucault 1991, 94). Under a sovereign power, the common good is obedience to (divine or natural) law and respect for the established order—that is, submission to sovereignty. Before the reforms of the nineteenth century, sovereignty was the model of rule of the Ottoman Empire, because preserving and expanding territory was essential to its finances and because the empire, ruling as a Muslim power, aimed at the well-being (*maṣlaḥa*) of the population, through ensuring the application of Islamic law. If Islamic law was a "non-state, community-based, bottom-up, jural system" (Hallaq 2009, 549), it commanded a certain degree of willing obedience, and so it was the instrument that allowed obedience to law and ensured the common good.[36] Justice and the good, in the eyes of

36. This does not mean that the Ottomans always had legitimacy among the populations they governed, many of whom were Christians, or that there were no rebellions or attempts at toppling

Muslim jurists, consisted in obeying the law because it was a divinely ordained (albeit humanely derived) law that aimed to ensure the well-being of humankind (Darling 2013).

With the new art of government, the objects, means, and aims of government changed: from territory to population, from law to disposition of things and people (the conduct of conduct), and from a common good to "public benefit" (Fr: *intérêt public*; Ar: *maṣlaḥa ʿāmma*), which became associated with "plenty" rather than with power or the preservation of the sovereign's realm (Gunn in Hirschman 1977, 37).[37] For Foucault (1991, 95), the objective of this mode of governing is a whole series of specific finalities, a plurality that reflects the specific aim for each thing governed (such as growing wealth or enough subsistence for all). When the Ottoman state started adopting governmental tactics, the question of common welfare remained salient especially in discussions of "public benefit," as we will see in chapters 2 and 5, but it was now associated with the welfare of the population. In the case of waqf, the specific finality sought was its "good administration" to allow its flourishing.[38]

FAMILY

The emergence of the population as the object of modern state government—a population that had its own reality and regularities (rates of death, epidemics), uncovered through statistics and political economy—transformed the family. "Economy" in European political theory had been associated with the "wise government of the family for the common welfare of all," and the new art of government introduced the economy into the running of the state (Foucault 1991, 92). At first the family was the model of government, but with the creation of the population, the family became a segment of the population, internal to it, and (most importantly) the main instrument of governing the population. As Donzelot shows with regard to French working-class families, the family was transformed from a domain of sovereignty for the head of the family (who could decide the fate of family members) to one of discipline and biopower, becoming the "nexus of nerve endings of a machinery that was exterior to it . . . with the help of the norm, against patriarchal authority, organizing—in the name of the hygienic and

---

the dynasty, but the longevity of the empire points to a degree of legitimacy. (Gerber goes as far as claiming that "the Ottoman state was on the whole highly legitimate" [2002, 67].) See, for example, Abou El Haj (1984). Whether these rebellions used the same idiom of a legitimate Muslim rule would be of particular interest but is outside the scope of this project.

37. For a genealogy of the rise of the term *interest* itself in European political thought, see Hirschman (1977).

38. Foucault proposes in his lectures in *The Birth of Biopolitics* that interest is pluralized, "a complex interplay between individual and collective interests, between social utility and economic profit, between the equilibrium of the market and the regime of public authorities, between basic rights and the independence of the governed" (2008, 46).

educative protection of these members—the depletion of parental authority in general, and placing the family under an economico-moral tutelage" (1979, 91). The family in the modern state was becoming governmentalized. Waqfs, many of which used to sustain relations between family members and various other entities (God, the deceased founder, many times a patriarch acting as an administrator, and family beneficiaries) based on the founder's will, had to then also be extracted outside the sovereign power of the founder to allow for that governmentalization of the family.

While the family became the main instrument of governing and was heavily regulated biopolitically, it was also paradoxically mapped onto the space of the "private" in its legal regulation. What Janet Halley and Kerry Rittich (2010) term "family law exceptionalism," arising in the nineteenth century, distinguishes the family and family law (and the religious) from the market and contract law (and the secular). According to this distinction, while "contract was individualistic, market-driven, affectively cold, and free, the family was altruistic, morality-driven, affectively warm, and dutiful" (758). However, family and market are not naturally existing spheres, and as Katherine Lemons argues, "*labor* [is] required to separate an ostensibly private sphere of family, home, and religion from an ostensibly public sphere of politics and exchange" (2019, 8). And that labor, as she shows in divorce cases in contemporary India, is often accomplished through litigation (rather than prior to it) and by fora outside state institutions. That labor helps produce and reproduce the private as the realm of culture and religion and the public as the realm of universal reason and economy. In this dichotomized world, waqf, which now consisted of both "religion" and "economy," became a problematic practice in the eyes of French colonial officers and in the eyes of today's waqf founders. This was even more the case for waqfs dedicated to families, as charity became tied to an "abstract public utility" (Birla 2009, 78–79). Indeed, as Birla demonstrates, colonial law on the economy "distinguished between legitimate forms of capitalism and local ones embedded in kinship, between practices that directed capital to circulate for the benefit of the public or to be hoarded in what were considered 'private' extended family networks" (2009, 3). So, family waqfs became a threat both to the family as a sphere of emotion, because they brought the economy into the family, and to the economy, because they tied up wealth in "private" kinship networks and eventually were heavily restricted by law.

THE MODERN SUBJECT AND INTERIORITY

These changes to the notion of the public interest and the family and the latter's overlay on the reconfigured private sphere were also accompanied by changes to the conceptualization of the subject. As Charles Taylor and others have noted (Taylor 1989; Burckhardt 1921), the idea that we have inner depths that are the locus of the true self is characteristic of modern subjectivity.[39] This conceptualization then raised the question of the relation of that inner self to its outward expression—that is, the question of sincerity and authenticity—and indeed such questions have figured prominently in discussions of modern subjectivity. This is not to say that sincerity is a modern concern or that there was no sense of interiority before then, as Taylor himself notes (1992). In the Islamic tradition, sincerity, in the sense of the absence of dissimulation or feigning, is very much present in the Qur'an with references to hypocrisy (*nifāq*) and to people who say one thing to the Prophet's face but do other things behind closed doors, or who dissimulate what is in their hearts. In Sufi disciplines of the self, disciples practice vigilant observation (*murāqaba*) of the sincerity of their intent behind ascetic practices lest the lowly desire of self-glorification creep in.[40] However, in these discussions of sincerity, the concern is for purposeful deception and for failure at training one's lowly self rather than truthfulness to one's essence.

The novelty of the modern self consists in its detachment from outward action and its lodging in the inner depths; it is through an exploration of the self from a detached perspective that one can find one's self and develop as a human being (Taylor 1992). In this context of a new form of subjectivity, one would not be surprised to hear that the real intent of waqf founders, as reflecting their innermost aims, became open to suspicion: were founders really making waqfs with the proper intent of getting closer to God? I will show that this suspicion and concern about true motives developed in relation to material conditions and became an important way to perpetuate new property and debt regimes. When waqfs founded by debtors stood in the way of foreclosures as newly instated by the Ottoman commercial courts, suspicion of the founder's charitable intent provoked legislation that restricted waqf foundation.

The modern concern for sincerity is predicated upon a dissociation between the private self, which is sincere, and the public image, which is theatrical, a separation that strongly affected the understanding and practice of religion (Targoff 2001). In the context of early modern England, the state (or the queen) did not care to "make windows into men's hearts and secret thoughts," as Francis Bacon famously put it (quoted in Targoff 2001, 2). This adage is usually explained in the context of church attendance: as long as worshippers came to the legally required

39. The narrative of the rise of a modern interior self has been questioned. See, for example, Martin (2004). Yet, as Taylor (1992) explains, it is not the idea that we have an interior self that is modern, but rather that we can stand in self-reflexive disengagement from ourselves to uncover the true self and that this inner perspective is privileged as the only way to achieve certain capacities and to develop as a human being. One can contrast that vision with the Islamic disciplines of the self that aim not so much at uncovering a true self but at developing the proper dispositions and virtues in the self through practices.

40. See, for example, the discussion of *murāqaba* in Keeler's discussion of *adab* in early Sufism (2017).

Sunday services, they could believe what they wanted in their hearts. This maxim brings to the fore the place of law in the distinction between actions and internal states and beliefs; it seems to confirm another dictum, that "law is concerned with external conduct [and] morality with internal conduct" (Morris 1976, 1). Nonetheless, law is not unconcerned with intent, as we know from definitions of burglary and murder (*mens rea*). Yet, law is not concerned with mental states *alone*; "for law there must be conduct" (Morris 1976, 4). The question then becomes how these mental states are accessed in law when they are considered an essential element of an action. And it is here that the modern sciences introduced a court expert for intent, as Brinkley Messick notes: the legal psychologist who performs "'depth' analyses" that attempt to determine a person's subjective intent (what they really think) (2001, 177), based on an assumption that such a state of mind is both known to the subject and knowable to others. In the context of the modern "buffered self," the individual who is separated from the worlds of gods and spirits (Taylor 2007), it thus became even more important to discover waqf founders' true intent, especially that it cannot simply be left to God as the ultimate judge in the hereafter.

A GENEALOGICAL ANTHROPOLOGY: THE NOTEBOOK, THE ARCHIVE, THE LIBRARY

After this description of the modern state setting and the changes in understandings of public interest, family, and intent, let me turn to my methods of analysis and my sources, for these matters are essential to the questions I ask and the answers I propose.

An analysis centered on grammar is facilitated by the work of economic and social historians. In the case of Beirut's nineteenth-century waqfs, Aurore Adada (2009) answers many crucial substantive questions of waqf founding: Were founders mostly men or women? What did they endow and for whom? Whom did they name as administrators? Answers to such questions arise through a compilation of series, extracting data from documents and analyzing them in order to narrate a social and economic history. While this book relies on such works, it is neither an economic nor a social history; grounded in the political, economic, and social setting of Beirut, it is closer to a conceptual history in its attempt to unearth different understandings of religion, property, and charity. Yet, as an anthropology, the attentiveness to different understandings of the same concepts aims not to better comprehend the past but to unsettle the present, to parochialize contemporary waqf practices and concepts. In this way, the project complicates an anthropological trope that takes a spatial other to render unfamiliar the familiar, where the familiar is that of the Euro-American anthropologist. Indeed, as a native anthropologist who hopes to produce knowledge that is useful in Lebanon, my interest lies in historicizing and making unfamiliar the apparently intractable sectarianization of waqf, in order to open up a more radical potential for future waqf practices. Furthermore, contemporary waqf practices, as partly products of the modern state, do not represent a radical alterity to liberal charity. However, because they are defined in the Islamic tradition, they have a telos that differs from liberal traditions of giving—even if the Islamic tradition has been in conversation with other religious and social traditions since its inception.

Not only does my subject matter differ from that of historians, but so does my approach to documents. While I read many of the same shariʿa court documents (waqf-foundation deeds, appointments of administrators and functionaries, waqf-exchanges) as historians like Adada, I read them in order to probe their logic and grammar and their unspoken assumptions.[41] I center my analysis on cases and incidents that most starkly demonstrate these grammars, which I derived from reading hundreds of documents and from the process of transcription during my research. These cases are neither extraordinary nor exceptional; they are usually generic, representative of the "normal," the taken-for-granted, so readers will not find many colorful characters or entertaining stories but rather the humdrum of the everyday. But they will find assumptions and conceptions that might be unexpected or even repulsive.

Moreover, the questions I asked of the documents during the writing process—on the importance of sincerity in founding waqf, the ethic of the family, and the meaning of the notion of public benefit—arose in the dissonances and resonances between my historical research and my ethnography, which I refer to metonymically as "the notebook." It includes my physical notebooks and digital notes where I recorded my conversations with some forty waqf founders, lawyers, and activists; the oral histories of the family waqf I collected; and observations in the archives of both Beirut's Sunni shariʿa court and the Directorate General of Islamic Waqfs. The notebook also includes physical copies of waqf documents and images plus documents as well as newspaper articles about waqf, waqf regulations, and images of material objects.

Finally, I read these historical documents against and in conjunction with legal manuals (see appendix A). As an anthropologist, and like social historians, I analyze Islamic "practices" through observation and court records; however, I supplement these sources with a serious engagement with the texts of the Islamic tradition, usually the domain of Islamic legal historians who study "theory." Such a methodology is informed by my approach to Islam as a tradition, where foundational texts are constantly interpreted and inform practices, which in turn allow for the reinterpretation of texts. Thus, following the footsteps of Brinkley Messick (1993), Zouhair Ghazzal (2007), and Martha Mundy and Richard Saumarez Smith (2007), I bring together what Messick (2018) has termed the "archive" and the

41. This concern for deep discursive formations is also shared by Ghazzal (2007) in his study of court records and Islamic law in fin-de-siècle Beirut, although we start from different premises as to the adaptability of the Islamic legal tradition and its difference from modern formal rational legal systems.

"library," "two distinct discursive modalities of a juridical culture" (22). The library is doctrinal works, authored books that could circulate widely across the Islamic world, penned without much reference to their context, time, and place, in a formal register, usually of Arabic. The archive denotes "applied genres," the realm of the document (or register), drafted by scribes, that specifies time and place and names, that can include a variety of linguistic registers, and that usually remains in a locale or with the people to whom the documents refer.

The "archive" I use is housed in the drawers and coffers of Beiruti families but also, fundamentally, in today's Beirut's Sunni shariʿa court and Ottoman state archives. Not many family waqfs remain in Beirut, and many that do exist do so because of long-lasting lawsuits between family members or with the Directorate General of Islamic Waqfs. It is because of such disputes that I was drawn to these families. "Have you encountered documents pertaining to this family's waqf in the archive?" friends of family and friends of friends would ask.[42] "We are looking for this *waqfiyya*," they would say, and so I was introduced to the case and the family, and eventually its collection. In this book, because of the type of analysis I favor, where cases are not read as representatives of patterns and facts but rather for their unspoken assumptions, I concentrate on one of those families—the Qabbanis, who are connected to my own family in Beirut. I had not heard of their waqf before starting my research, or maybe I had heard without listening. Nonetheless, after I started the research, I attempted to collect the documents scattered throughout the family due to war, deaths, and feuds. Because of this, my archive of the family documents is incomplete and will always remain so. I also had the opportunity to talk about the case with various members of the family and to hear them quarrel in family reunions or our meetings, so the family's personal collection was supplemented by the oral histories that I collected in my notebook.

My archive also contained documents from state archives. These include litigations brought to the central Ottoman state and housed at the Prime Ministry Ottoman Archive in Istanbul; orders from Istanbul addressed to the provinces; letters of appointment to offices in Beiruti waqfs from the Waqf Directorate Archive in Ankara; waqf foundations, litigation, and administrative appointments from the qadi[43] court of nineteenth-century Beirut (now housed at Beirut's Sunni

42. A gendered phenomenon, which I did not get the chance to investigate, was the fact that it was always women of the proverbial certain age who were engaged in these odysseys of "recuperating" their family waqf. They were the living archive of the waqf, always incomplete, about to disappear.

43. In discussions of the Ottoman Empire, I use *qadi*, not *judge*, because the duties of a qadi went far beyond what we assign today to judges, adjudication. Qadis also served as public notaries and were consulted on administrative issues, among other duties. Qadis' sessions were not originally housed in a special location but happened wherever qadis were, usually in their own house (Hallaq 1998). The nineteenth century saw the creation of "court locales" independent of the judges themselves. The courts where they adjudicated became the "shariʿa courts" of today. Some scholars of Ottoman courts have argued that they should be referred to not as "shariʿa courts" but rather as "qadi courts" during

shariʿa court). Nineteenth-century Beirut was an Ottoman city, and the Ottoman official jurisprudence followed the Ḥanafī school of Islamic law.[44] The court archive contains many "types" of registers: minutes of court proceedings, marriage registers, powers of attorney, and divisions of inheritance. The most extensive collection, the main collection, holds those registers spanning from 1843 to the present and consists of summaries and copies of original documents, short and very formulaic, being instantiations of legal instruments and requirements. They contain a plethora of waqf cases: foundations, rentals, appointments, exchanges, acquisition of property for waqfs, and modifications in stipulations. Under this pile of different yet similar cases emerge litigations, particular and unique cases, usually around the choice of rightful administrators and beneficiaries. These cases differ from the more formulaic instruments in that they usually tend to be longer and include legal opinions that refer to the legal texts and manuals supporting the opinion its authors favored.[45] It is from these citations that I gathered the titles of the doctrinal works that I use. In the archive, we can get a glimpse of the library.

The library, despite its cosmopolitanism, is always localized: it denotes the common library of scholars engaged in the tradition at a certain point in a certain place. It does not constitute the library of a particular scholar, even if it certainly is partially so. The "sources" noted in opinions represent the library of these Ottoman scholars: the books they have studied, the tradition in which they were schooled, and the dialogues in which they were engaged. Reading its books against the "cases" of the archive, this library allowed me to sketch a picture of the Ottoman late Ḥanafī tradition.[46] These waqf litigation cases cite three types of legal manuals. First are waqf treatises (*rasāil*), which are solely concerned with waqf regulations (usually titled with a variation of "Waqf Regulations"), some of which are short and address a single issue. Second are *shurūḥ* (sing., *sharḥ*), or commentaries, which are explanations and elaborations on a core text or legal manual, known as *matn* or *mukhtaṣar*. Sometimes, these commentaries are the subject of supercommentaries or glosses. The *matn* is physically inscribed and differentiated

---

the Ottoman period because they applied much more than the shariʿa, including sultanic laws known as *qānun*.

44. In Sunni Islam, there are four major schools of law, or *madhhabs*: Ḥanafī, Shāfiʿī, Mālikī, and Ḥanbalī. The fact that the Beirut court was Ḥanafī does not mean that the other schools did not exist in Beirut or that their opinions do not appear in the court cases of the Ḥanafī court.

45. Muftis, learned religious scholars who were sought out for legal opinions (fatwas), were required to cite the sources they used to support their judgments as early as the sixteenth century (Heyd 1969, 45), perhaps a particularity of the Ottoman Empire and its attempt to create an Ottoman canon of Islamic law (Burak 2015).

46. As Ayoub (2014) shows, late Ḥanafī (*al-mutaʾakhkhirūn*) is a category used by Ḥanafī jurists themselves, starting in the eleventh century, to distinguish their opinions from the school's earlier opinions. The category became particularly prominent in the early modern period in the Ottoman Empire.

in the commentary by being put in parenthesis in printed versions (or written in a different color of ink in manuscripts), thereby allowing one to read the text of the *matn* in the commentary by reading only the text in parenthesis (or differently colored text). As commentaries, which are actually reinterpretations of an original text, these *shurūḥ* elaborate on waqf legislation, taking the original very short few sentences on waqf and expounding on them with the various opinions held for each issue, based on previous explanations, the waqf manuals cited above, and fatwas. Fatwas are legal opinions that can be answers to actual questions addressed to the jurist by any subject or simply be abstracted from particular people, times, and places to a general point of legal theory.[47] The third type of books in the library are fatwa collections, which constitute the most recent of the titles cited in terms of opinions and developments in waqf regulations.[48] The dissonances and consonances among library, archive, and notebook triggered the questions I asked.

WHAT LIES AHEAD

In order to better trace changes in grammar in the Islamic tradition, I opt for thematic chapters that follow certain concepts. Each chapter, and the book more broadly, takes a *longue durée* approach to uncover changes in waqf practice that would not be apparent in a microhistory or an ethnography. Despite the importance of the epistemological break and the rupture of the modern state, the story that I tell is not simply a story of before and after, of old versus new, of the religious waqf that becomes the secular waqf. It is a story of both ruptures and continuities, of slight shifts that are imperceptible except over time, of discourses that persisted and continue to resonate, and of old terms that acquired new meanings. The transformation that I describe unfolds in moments, snapshots exemplary of the changes each of these moments represents. While the modern state introduced a rupture in the manner of government, which affected the waqf, this government operates differently under different forms of rule—imperial, colonial, national. Thus, every chapter starts with the Ottoman late Ḥanafī tradition, then moves into the moment of the Tanzimat, then the French colonial moment, and finally the postcolonial moment. As the reader will notice, the postcolonial moment does not always unfold immediately after independence in the 1940s and the 1950s. It is a suggestion of this book that postcolonial waqf law and practice continued or, even

47. On the Ottoman fatwas, their form, length, and citation requirements, see Heyd (1969). The relation between fatwas and the short epistles is worth investigating as some epistles seem to address in depth issues that arose often as questions for fatwa.

48. Studies of Islamic law ascribe a particular importance to fatwas as an interface between theory and practice, and the location where "change" in positive law occurs (Hallaq 1984; Masud, Messick, and Powers, 1996). Building on ethnographic work at the fatwa council in Egypt, Hussein Ali Agrama (2010) emphasizes a different way to understand fatwas: as ethical practices. This is a particularly important insight as to the contemporary usage of fatwas, but it does not take away from the importance of fatwas as answers to questions of law.

more, brought to their conclusion many of the reforms that the French colonial state had introduced. Indeed, while many Muslims were wary of these reforms as undermining Islamic tradition, they adopted them after independence under the banner of progress and modernization of the waqf. Therefore, many of the post-colonial shifts that I describe happened after the end of the 1975–1990 civil war, with the rise of the Islamic Revival and a new division of power that reshaped the political landscape.

Part I, "Architectures," introduces the waqf and the change in its practice and main form (chapter 1) and the architecture of state, religion, and law under which waqf operated during the period under study (chapter 2). Part II, "Grammars," delves into the transformation of the grammar of three concepts. The chapters here are organized by scale, moving from the most intimate to the more general, as each scale opens new possibilities for the following scale: from the subject of property relations and charitable intent (chapter 3), to the kind of social relations these forms of property and charity sustain, especially with the family (chapter 4), and their relation to public benefit (chapter 5).

Chapter 1 analyzes the transformation wrought on the understanding and practice of waqf starting in the second quarter of the nineteenth century and leading to the transformation of the waqf from an object to a subject in property relations. I start with the debates in the Ottoman late Ḥanafī tradition around the effects of God's ownership of the waqf in terms of its perpetuity and inalienability and show that the perpetual inalienable waqf became the standard waqf. In all these definitions, a waqf is a pious act that is not divorced from economic activity. To the contrary, when they were not mosques or schools, waqfs often needed to generate rent in perpetuity. In waqf, charity then was not a one-time donation and had to be sustainable. This chapter thus reverses the assumption often found in studies of charitable giving, which posits that before the dominance of development discourses, charity emphasized the here and now and was not geared towards sustainability. Nonetheless, the chapter also delinks sustainability from progress, as the waqf's perpetuity was geared towards the relief of poverty (but not its eradication) and towards the eternal rewards it brings to its founder. I then show how new state-issued waqf law along with a private property regime that took God out of the "persons" involved in property relations opened the possibility for new waqf practices, such as the waqf nonprofit, transforming the main use of waqf from an object to a subject of property relations. In that process, the waqf came to have an explicit legal personality, whereby it "owned" assets, and the economic activity that allowed it to finance its purposes became external to the act of charity.

Chapter 2 dwells on the relation of waqf and state throughout the period under study, through the administration and supervision of waqfs. I analyze how the techniques of control of waqfs and their revenues contributed to the creation of the modern state-effect. In addition, I argue that because of its control over Islamic waqf law, the state became a coveted site of authoritativeness and thus an arena of struggle between different Sunni groups. In this process of state control, I show how certain waqfs were reconceptualized as real estate wealth that could be developed through new accounting methods, statistics, and uniform methods of administration, thus beginning waqfs' journey towards the newly created sphere of the economy. Furthermore, with the French Mandate, the waqfs were reconceptualized as the religious property of the Muslim community, becoming an essential space for the instantiation of that community in relation to the other communities (Maronite, Greek-Orthodox, Druze). Indeed, while under the Ottoman state, the Muslims had been the unmarked group that dominated the state, the French sealed a political regime of minorities in Lebanon, transforming the Muslims into one community among others. The book argues that the waqf was essential to the production of the new way Muslims imagined themselves, because it mobilized them as a community in order to fend off French control of the waqfs.

After part I has set up the architecture of state, law, and religion in Beirut in this period, chapter 3 moves to the waqf-making subject and the way waqf practices became an important site for the instantiation of a new grammar of the self and its intent. The nineteenth-century transformation of the debt regime from one that privileged debt forgiveness to one based on foreclosure (creditors taking ownership of mortgaged property) made waqf a practice that stood against foreclosures. With the rise of foreclosures, the question of the "true intent" of founders and whether their actions were truly charitable became urgent, whereas beforehand it was limited to fulfilling legal requirements regarding charitable beneficiaries. This entailed a shift in the way that true intent was conceived and could be assessed, which was an important change in the basis of one's subjectivity. Indeed, up to the middle of the nineteenth century, the waqf subject's true intent was accessible to others, particularly in the judiciary, only through actions. This shift, I suggest, participated in the introduction of a new kind of subject whose intentions are disembodied from actions and are a distinct object of scrutiny and suspicion that is accessible to the expert. Thus, the book contends that the requirements of capital accumulation not only contributed to reshuffling control of the means of production and of social relations but also left a mark on the conception of the person, the inner self and intent, in the Islamic tradition.

This new notion of the self became the foundation for a new way to distinguish truly charitable waqfs. Chapter 4 first shows that before this new emphasis on true intent, waqfs, whether dedicated to families or to general charitable purposes like the running of mosques, produced and reproduced the family bond as the central mode of social relation, questioning the distinction between the self-serving family waqfs and the truly charitable, public waqfs. It then shows how French reforms, with their emphasis on limiting charity to "public" beneficence, encouraged the creation of citizens who kept the family in the private sphere and became individual citizens in public. The devaluing of family beneficence and its association with nepotism in the public sphere has become the dominant grammar of family, but the chapter ends with some ethnographic observations of the practices and debates that still challenge this order of things. This chapter shows that this devaluing of family waqfs was done through the introduction of a new statistical style of reasoning into the Islamic tradition, in combination with a changed notion of public benefit.

Chapter 5 then moves to examine that notion of public benefit through the relation of individual waqfs and their specific purposes to state rationality. It analyzes the transformation of the grammar of the concept of "public benefit" (Ar: *maslaḥa ʿāmma*; Fr: *interêt général*) with the rise of the modern state and its associated architecture of law and religion. The notion of public benefit, essential to modern states, has been almost completely assumed in contemporary Islamic discursive tradition and practice, becoming the basis of all kinds of reform, anachronistically projected back onto the concepts and practices of the tradition by both contemporary Muslim thinkers and academic scholars of Islam. Using exchanges of waqf during expropriations at three different moments (Ottoman, French Mandate, and contemporary), I show how the grammar of "public benefit" transformed from one defined by the goals of the shariʿa and embodied in each waqf—and thus used in conjunction with the notions of the "waqf's benefit," the stipulations of the founder (as to the administration of the waqf and its beneficiaries), and necessity (of the exchange)—to one defined by the state and directed towards growth and progress. Public benefit, understood in this context as the opening of roads and city planning in a process of "creative destruction," gradually displaced the preservation of individual waqfs' objectives. Even so, this chapter also traces ways in which the old grammar of public benefit endures through claims against the elimination of waqfs in the latest expropriation scheme.

PART I

Architecture

1

Waqf, A Non-Definition

I was sitting in Hajj Tawfiq's office at the Imam Awzaʿi Islamic Studies College, in Tari' el-Jdide, the Beiruti Sunni bastion par excellence. Within a stone's throw were the Beirut Municipal Stadium, home of the (Sunni) Ansar football team, and the Beirut Arab University (BAU). As ʿIsam al-Huri, the director of the university's board of trustees, had told me a few hours prior, BAU was one of the first private higher education institutions developed shortly after independence within an Arab nationalist agenda to counter the American and French universities founded by missionaries in the nineteenth century. This meeting was my first encounter with Hajj Tawfiq, but as soon as I entered, and without much by way of niceties and introductions, he started asking *me* questions about waqfs: "So, what do you know about the difference between an association and a waqf?" I was not ready for the question, so I tried to deflect by talking about the nineteenth-century waqfs I had encountered in my historical research in the past year, but he retorted: "These are not waqfs." I was very confused: how could these Ottoman waqfs, which I had assumed were the model for the waqf revival, not be waqfs? And without much explanation or time for me to follow up, he followed closely with another question, with a hint of a smile on the corner of his lips: "Do you know the waqf of al-Birr wa al-Ihsan?" This was a trick question because it was the much less familiar name of the waqf behind the BAU, as I had just learned from ʿIsam al-Huri. My Beiruti credentials confirmed, we launched into a discussion of that waqf.

Hajj Tawfiq explained the circumstances of the foundation of the waqf of al-Birr wa al-Ihsan and how he and a few members of the board of trustees of the BAU had gone to the shariʿa court and founded the waqf some twenty-five years after the establishment of the university. Using a grammar of waqf that I had become familiar with by reading legal texts and tens of Ottoman waqf deeds, I asked what "objects" they had made into a waqf: was it the university buildings? He laughed at my question and replied enigmatically: "We waqfed words."

"But that is not a waqf, if it does not start with an object that is moved from the ownership of a person to the ownership of God!" I thought to myself. I then remembered the "note to self" that I had made in my notebook early in my research: "I am being too normative about what waqf *is*. I should be much more attentive to what people all over think waqf is when I tell them that I am working on waqf." Putting my anthropologist hat on, I stopped and tried to understand how Hajj Tawfiq approached waqf. But I was caught, as usual, between my research and my practical concerns with the politics of waqf—in this case, how the legal form of the waqf mattered and how a deed that did not follow legal conventions could be seized by the Directorate General of Islamic Waqfs (DGIW). That day, I was not able to get deeper into the conversation with Hajj Tawfiq. But in a later discussion, he explained to me, like many others would also do, that the waqf deed of al-Birr wa al-Ihsan created a moral person rather than transferring the ownership of an object to God and dedicating its revenues to some charitable purpose. The waqf of al-Birr wa al-Ihsan became the owner of the BAU, shielding it from the supervision of the Ministry of Interior, which had overseen the association of al-Birr wa al-Ihsan since its foundation in Tari' el-Jdide in 1937.

The story of the waqf of the BAU encapsulates what I learned through various encounters in Beirut between 2007 and 2013: the decline of waqfs as objects and their rise as subjects in property relations between the nineteenth and the turn of the twenty-first century. This transformation has been noted by Gizem Zencirci (2015) in Turkey and Mona Atia (2013) in Egypt. Zencirci relates this change to development discourses, showing that in Turkey, from the founding of the republic to the 1960s, economic nationalism and state-led development encouraged a conceptualization of waqfs as "national treasures tasked with financing state-led projects" (2015, 534). Starting with the neoliberal development in the 1980s, she shows that waqfs were reconceptualized as nonprofits or, as they are known in Lebanon, nongovernmental organizations (NGOs).[1] However, Lebanon experienced these same changes in waqf understandings without a similar development discourse. (Lebanon did not witness much state-led development, as Gaspard [2004] shows.) I therefore suggest that these changes in the understanding and practice of waqf were first made possible because of novel definitions of a legal person,[2] or "moral

1. Nongovernmental organizations (NGOs) are one kind of association (*jam'iyya*) among other forms of associations like political parties, cultural clubs, youth clubs, and religious organizations. In the United States, they are more commonly known as nonprofits. In the book, I will use the Lebanese appellation (NGO or association).

2. Other terms for the same concept include *juridical person, artificial person, juridical entity,* or *juristic person* (*Black's Law Dictionary*, thelawdictionary.org). I use the variation *moral person* to indicate the commonsensical ascription of personhood to corporations independent of the recognition of

person" (*personne morale*) in French legal nomenclature: entities or beings whom the law regards as capable of rights or duties and who are distinct from human beings, known legally as natural persons. The rise of the waqf as a moral person, then, reflects the ascendance of a private property regime and the notion of a moral person, as well as transformations in notions of charity in Beirut, such as their restriction to religious purposes.

This transformation of waqf from object to subject was also made possible by a private property regime that expunged God from the actors involved in property relations. It is thus an essential part of the secularization of land, an important process in the instatement of a private property regime and its assumptions regarding the individuation of people, the clear separation of people and things, and disenchantment.[3] Anthropologists have demonstrated that such a conception of property is a Western native category (Hann 1998) whose assumptions do not hold true in other places and times (Humphrey and Verdery 2004). Furthermore, these assumptions do not reflect the complexity of the private property regime itself, for even in the West, people and things are not stable categories, but are constantly made and remade. Corporations, for example, straddle the line between being objects and subjects in property relations. Body parts become "things" sold, and rivers become people who can sue for pollution.[4]

By attending to the way that the waqf was remade from an object to a subject, this chapter demonstrates that the making of people and things in line with the private property regime—autonomous people, separate from things—is not a matter of the past. It is a reminder of the new practices that arise with this transformation and the older notions that continue to exist. Concurrently, I show that the transformation of waqf into a moral person during the waqf revival rendered the practice of waqf as charity less tied to a revenue-bearing object, thus contributing to the dissociation of charitable acts from "commercial" endeavors and perpetuating the idea that waqf making involves the creation of mosques or other religious institutions rather than ensuring their funding. Yet, at the same time, the idea of

this personhood by law, a point highlighted by Maitland (2003, 63), which was the case for waqfs in the nineteenth century; they were treated as moral persons before they were recognized as such in the law. Bashkow (2014, 297) also notes that universities, businesses, and nonprofits are personified in everyday discourse, whether they are incorporated or not, suggesting that corporate personhood is produced discursively and socially. I use "legal person" to emphasize recognition in law.

3. Anthropologists and historians have argued that despite claims to the immanence of property, the private property regime is "rooted in the transcendence and violence of the state, sworn to with the authority of the Holy Bible at hand" (Klassen 2014, 181).

4. For different understandings of people and things, as well as the relation between people and their environment, see, for example, Weiner (1985), Strathern (1988), and Nadasdy (2002). On the transformation of body parts into objects, see, for example, Scheper-Hughes and Wacquant (2002), Sharp (2006), and Hamdy (2012). On corporate personhood, see the special issue of *PoLAR* (Benson and Kirsch 2014). On rivers being granted legal personality and the distinctions between nature, person, and deity, see Alley (2019).

a waqf as a revenue-bearing object continues to persist through practitioners and things that embody and perpetuate this logic.

OTTOMAN LATE ḤANAFĪ WAQF: WAQF AS OBJECT

To understand the origin of my assumption that waqfs should involve an object, I will start with the practice of waqf in the Ottoman late Ḥanafī tradition as described in the legal manuals of the "library" of that tradition, which I collected from the references cited in the legal opinions used in litigations around waqf (see introduction and appendix A).

Definitions: Abu Hanifa versus His Students

Waqf, linguistically speaking, is a noun, the gerund (*maṣdar*) of the verb *waqafa*. In common usage, *waqf* means "halting, stopping." In legal parlance—at least for the Ḥanafi school to whose founder, Abu Hanifa (d. 770 CE), the following definition is ascribed—a waqf is

> the confinement of a *ʿayn* [the corpus of a specific object, *res* in Roman law, the principal in endowment terminology] to the ownership of the waqf-founder, and the gift of its *manfaʿa* [yield or usufruct] to some charitable purpose. (al-ʿAyni, *Ramz*, 1:343)

Here, waqf is the enactment of an owner's decision to dedicate the usufruct of his or her property to some charitable purposes while retaining ownership—the right of alienation, or the right to buy, sell, gift, mortgage, and bequeath the object. The usufruct could take the form of rent, taxes, bread, shelter, returns on money, and even shade. However, what does the "confinement" of an object to the ownership of its owner mean exactly? The question elicited internal debates among Ḥanafī scholars. Some jurists argued that since the founder owns that property, the action of confining ownership to the owner is a tautology, a nonaction; it just confirms the ownership of the owner. Mamluk jurist Ibn al-Humam (d. 1457 CE)[5] objected to Abu Hanifa's use of "confine" (*ḥabs*). He argued that since the ownership remains in the hands of the founder, the act of founding would not have changed any of the owner's rights that come with ownership: the rights to sell, gift, and bequeath. Waqf founding then, he argued, does not include any confinement: it is simply the will of the founder to gift the usufruct to a pious purpose (Assaf 2005, 13). While gifting the usufruct to some charitable purpose, the owner retains full property rights and can revoke the waqf. Hence, for Abu Hanifa, a waqf is not necessarily binding.[6] This is the reason why certain explanations compare Abu

5. The Egyptian jurist credited in the Ḥanafi school for having accommodated existing land practices of state ownership of land with Ḥanafi *fiqh* based on individual ownership (Johansen 1988).

6. A waqf based on Abu Hanifa's definition becomes binding in two cases: if a judge rules on it or if the founder makes it part of his or her will.

Hanifa's waqf to the gifting of usufruct or to interest-free loans (*ʿāriya*);[7] the owner can retract the gift of the usufruct. The waqf is not a gift (*hiba*)[8] because the ownership of the object and with it the rights of alienation remain with the founder. In addition, after the death of the founder, the waqf reverts back to his or her estate and is divided according to inheritance law. Hence, for Abu Hanifa, a waqf is not necessarily inalienable either.

Abu Hanifa's definition was questioned by two of his prominent students, Abu Yusuf (d. 798 CE) and Muhammad al-Shaybani (d. 805 CE), for whom waqf is "the confinement of the corpus [of a specific property] (*ʿayn*) to the ownership of God" (al-ʿAyni, *Ramz*, 1:343). The students' innovative definition stemmed from a hadith (a tradition attributed to the Prophet Muhammad) supposedly unknown to Abu Hanifa. Had this tradition been known to Abu Hanifa, the students claimed, he would have espoused their position. This may very well be true, but the authority that the students' definition acquired cannot be explained on such grounds only, since Abu Hanifa also builds his argument on the basis of a hadith. As Peters (2012) has argued, the authoritativeness of the students' definition can be related to the changing socioeconomic and military conditions of the Islamic world at that time.[9] Contrary to Abu Hanifa, who confines the ownership of the waqf to the waqf founder, the students confer it to God. The conceptualization of waqf as God's property (*milk allāh*) thus dates to these very early debates. In this definition, human ownership of the waqf—and its most important prerogative, the right of alienation (*al-tamlīk*)—ceases to exist (*yazūl*) (al-ʿAyni, *Ramz*, 1:343, 345). Here, then, waqf is inalienable. Furthermore, since the only subject who can dispose of an object is its owner, the waqf becomes binding. Thus, as we have seen, even within a single law school, there was major disagreement on the essential characteristics of waqf: its inalienability and its bindingness. Yet, as all commentators explain, it was the students' definition that became authoritative.

Waqf as Object

The definitions of Abu Hanifa and his students share commonalities in addition to their differences in terms of perpetuity and bindingness. In both of them, a waqf is a pious act that is not divorced from profit-making economic activity. Founding a waqf is an act that brings its founder closer to God, but it is also a revenue-generating endeavor. A waqf object generates either rent that is dedicated to a pious purpose or has a use that is itself a pious purpose. In the latter

7. "Tamlīk al-manfaʿa bilā ʿiwaḍ."

8. "Tamlīk al-ʿayn bilā ʿiwaḍ."

9. The questions of why and when the students' definition became more authoritative are worth investigating as they would give us insight into the socioeconomic determinations of the law, but I have not found works that answer them. During the lifetime of the students, their teacher's definition still held currency. Abbasid Caliph al-Mahdi (r. 775–85) appointed to Egypt a judge who subscribed to Abu Hanifa's definition and attempted to revoke many waqfs (Abu Zahra 2005, 12–13).

category, founders built mosques, fountains, libraries, and madrasas as waqfs.[10] These would later, in the nineteenth century, be referred to as charitable organizations (*müessesât-i hayriyye*) (Hilmi 1909: Article 17). In the former category, an array of land, shops, and houses were made into waqf, so that their revenues went to the running and upkeep of these waqf mosques, fountains, and madrasas.[11] In fact, most waqf foundations of mosques and other charitable institutions also included rent-producing assets. Similar rent-producing objects could also support other pious purposes, like the indigent in one's family or the poor. Thus, while providing a way to be closer to God, waqf was also a way to finance a multitude of public amenities and provide public services and relief for the poor, especially at a time when these services were not conceived as rights a state owed its citizens, and poverty was not yet conceptualized as a problem to be eradicated.[12] Thus waqfs, even if they were founded at a particular time and place, were perpetual because their ultimate recipients, the poor, were deemed eternal.

Both these definitions also emphasize waqf as an action, a process that transfers and then confines the ownership of an object. That is why I will sometimes use *waqf* as a verb, as in "she waqfed a shop." The word *waqf* is also used to refer to the objects whose ownership has thus been confined, as attested by legal texts: "The waqfed object is also widely known as waqf, so one says 'this house is a waqf'" (Ibn ʿAbidin, *Ḥāshiya*, 3:357). Following this usage, instead of saying "the waqfed house" or "the house made into a waqf" (*al-dār al-mawqūfa*) to describe a house or any object whose ownership belongs to God (as per the dominant practice in the court, following the students' definition) and whose usufruct belongs to specified subjects, I will refer to it as the house-waqf. This usage appears in court records of my archive. *Waqf* there is used as a qualifier of an object (a shop, house, or parcel) to describe its legal "status." It is mostly used when identifying a parcel of land through a description of its limits: it can be bordered "on the east by a shop-waqf of al-Hamra Sufi lodge," on the west by "a house-waqf of the Great Mosque," or on the "*qibla*[13] by the waqf of the priests."[14]

The archive, however, also points to a different usage of the word *waqf*, which the library books deny: that waqf is beyond a process or an attribute of objects, that it is akin to a person. In the shariʿa court records, numerous documents record sales and purchases for the waqf. For instance, a purchase records the administrator of

10. In Ḥanafī fiqh, mosques become automatically waqf; one cannot open a space for prayer and then change one's mind (Ibn ʿAbidin, *Ḥāshiya*, 3:369).

11. These revenue-bearing waqfs might remind the reader of trusts and endowments for universities in the United Kingdom and the United States. As I mention in the introduction (footnote 1), some scholars (e.g., Gaudiosi 1988) have advanced that the British trust has its origins in the waqf.

12. See Mine Ener (2003) for the transformation of attitudes towards the poor and the role of the state therein in Egypt in the nineteenth century; and Fleischacker (2004) for a historicization of notions of redistributive justice and the eradication of poverty.

13. The *qibla* is the direction of the Kaʿba. In Beirut, it is almost south.

14. MBSS.S3/32/4, and MBSS.S3/35/4, respectively.

the Hamra *zāwiya* (Sufi lodge) buying shares of a shop for the *zāwiya* "from the funds [*māl*] of the aforementioned *zāwiya*."[15] Here, the waqf owns assets and possesses money and can buy real estate; it is close to a moral person that can acquire rights around objects. In accounting records, waqf expenses beyond the revenues generated by the waqf's assets are often noted as a debt that the waqf owes to the administrator. The accounting of the mosque of the Hamra zāwiya for the years 1256–58 [1840–42], for example, ends with around 9,000 qurush in the red, which is recorded as "a debt of the aforementioned mosque to the administrator."[16] In these examples, the waqf emerges as a moral person, distinct from its administrator and able to enter into commercial transactions.

These practices differ from the explicit conceptualization of the waqf's moral personhood in the fiqh library. There, the notion of a moral person can be found in the doctrine of the *dhimma*, "generally defined as a presumed or imaginary repository that contains all the rights and obligations relating to a person" (Zahraa 1995, 202). It embraces both religious and financial obligations and rights. The question then becomes whether the waqf has a dhimma. All commentaries repeat the same statement: "The waqf does not have a moral personality" "laysa li'l-waqf dhimma" (e.g., Ibn Nujaym, *Baḥr*, 5:210). Despite this absence, jurists allow transactions that end up treating the waqf "as if" it had a dhimma. For instance, the absence of a moral personality would prevent the waqf from borrowing money because a debt is held against one's personality, based on analogy (*qiyās*). Yet, based on necessity, jurists allow administrators to borrow for necessary expenses like repairs after they take permission from the judge, with the debt being held against their own dhimma, but they can then recover that debt from the waqf revenues (Ibn Nujaym, *Baḥr*, 5:210; also in Ibn ʿAbidin, *Ḥāshiya*, 3:419–20). While this procedure constantly interposes the administrator's own dhimma between the creditor and the waqf, the administrator is not personally liable for these debts.[17]

Islamic legal and economic historians, based on the explicit statements of jurists in law manuals, have claimed that moral personhood does not exist in Islamic law (Schacht 1964, 125; Kuran 2005). However, as seen in the examples above, and as historian Doris Behrens-Abouseif argues, the waqf has "attributes of a legal personality" (2009, 56): it outlasts its founder; it has the capacity to buy and sell; its assets cannot be foreclosed for the personal debts of the beneficiaries or the administrator; and its administrator, as an agent acting in good faith, is not liable for losses of waqf revenues, making the waqf have effectively limited liability. The waqf is therefore a moral person even if jurists do not articulate a concept of "moral personality."

15. MBSS.S2/45, dated 15 C 1263 [30 May 1847].

16. BOA.EV 11192/56.

17. The practices that administrators could do for the waqf (borrowing, buying, etc.) according to jurists certainly effect the *dhimma* of the waqf and are worth a much lengthier discussion but are unfortunately outside the scope of this study.

A Waqf Deed from the Archive

In light of the debate in the library on the definition of waqf, we can turn to my Beiruti archive (the shariʿa court records and some deeds from the family archive) to analyze the various practices of waqf and their relation to the different legal definitions described above.[18] Abu Hanifa's students' definition forms the backbone of the waqf cases recorded in the Beirut registers. Indeed, foundation deeds draw on and invoke the terms of their definition, mentioning the perpetuity and inalienability of waqf, as I will illustrate based on one of the earliest foundation deeds of the nineteenth century registered in the court.[19] A waqf foundation deed describes the original owner and founder of the waqf, the object to be made into a waqf, the beneficiaries, and various stipulations as to administrators, length of lease, and anything else the founder might deem necessary or desire.[20]

In this particular example, Darwish ʿAli Agha al-Qassar surrendered the ownership of a shop he owned in the main square inside the walled city and dedicated its rents to himself during his lifetime and then to the shrine and tomb (*al-maqām wa al-ḍarīḥ*) of Sayyid Ahmad Badawi (1200–1276 CE) in Tanta, Egypt, and to the mosque housing it, and if these beneficiaries became extinct, to the Haramayn, the sacred sanctuaries of Mecca and Medina.[21] Darwish stipulated that the revenues should first go to the repairs of the shop, that the shop should not be rented to someone powerful or for more than three years, and that the administrator should receive six qurush for his services.[22] He appointed himself the administrator; after his death, his cousin Mustafa; and after him, the most upright of his children.

In this example, the shop waqf founded by Darwish al-Qassar sustains forever a Sufi shrine and the sacred sites of Muslim pilgrimage, sites that allow the perpetuation of Islamic ways of life. In the future imagined by the founder, Muslims would always be doing similar things: visiting Sufi saints and going on pilgrimage. Other waqfs were dedicated to the poor, which jurists take as one of the surest values in terms of providing a perpetual charitable recipient. Such waqfs' revenues

18. Note that different locales had different relations to the library, and the typical waqf deeds exhibited slight variations.

19. MBSS.S3/157, dated 29 L 1233 [1 September 1818]. The waqf deed was copied "letter by letter" in the court register based on the request of its administrator in order to preserve it and confirm it in Shawwal 1268 [July-August 1852]. The administrator also registered another waqf of the same family, dedicated to the repair of a water fountain in Beirut, dated 8 M 1098 [24 November 1686].

20. Ghazzal (2007, ch. 6) describes the various parts that I describe below, but we have different purposes in our endeavor: my aim is to show the multiple definitions indexed; he is concerned with fictitious litigations and the way they allow for avoiding some of the requirements of contract law.

21. On Sayyid Badawi, see ʿAshur (1966) and Mayeur-Jaouen (1994). The shrine remains a major site of visitation up to this day.

22. I have not stumbled upon any litigation where the question of a "powerful" tenant comes up, while the question of the length of the contract is central in the debates in the library and has led to innovations in the archive that have found their way back to the library. See, for example, Hoexter (1984, 1997); Knost (2010); and Güçlü (2009).

were geared towards the relief of poverty, not its eradication, and were built on the assumption that the poor would always be there. In both cases, these waqfs sustain a future of the same rather than the better. This is charitable giving that provides what the literature on development would term "sustainable" income for this shrine, distinguished from one-time handouts of food and money, which are often depicted in this literature as a quick fix, a "Band-Aid," that does not solve any need in the long term and instead creates dependencies. This alignment with notions of sustainable development allows the conscription of the waqf by the United Nation's ESCWA (Economic and Social Commission for Western Asia) as a local model of sustainable development (ESCWA 2013). Yet, such waqf practices delink sustainability from progress because they reproduce the same practices rather than improve or eradicate them. They remind us that progress and the eradication of poverty are not a hallmark of sustainability but of a time-horizon characteristic of our modern age.[23]

Darwish's waqf deed records first a speech act, because for most Ḥanafī jurists, the mere utterance of "I made into a waqf" or an equivalent expression is sufficient to create the waqf (Austin 1962).[24] A founder does not need to go to court for the legal effects of the foundation to take place. The registration of the waqf deed in court serves a different purpose, as I describe below. We first encounter waqf as eternal in the verb forming the speech act of the foundation. After describing the founder, the waqf deed registers the founder's actions: "he made into a waqf, eternalized, confined, dedicated and gifted to charitable purposes" ("waqafa, wa abbada, wa ḥabbasa, wa sabbala, wa taṣaddaqa").[25] In this particular foundation, the verbal nouns derived from these verbs are then added at the end of the sentence (*waqfan ṣaḥīḥan sharʿiyyan wa taʾbīdan dāʾiman sarmadiyyan, wa ḥabsan mukhalladan marʿiyyan*), a rhetorical move that intensifies the effects of the speech act. The waqf deed sometimes mentions the consequences of the perpetuity of the waqf, mostly in terms of its inalienability. Expressions like "cannot

23. As such, waqfs question the assumption in the literature on charitable giving that religious *charity* is about one-time handouts that create dependency, since waqfs most often provide regular and sustainable income. Amira Mittermaier (2019) addresses another side of this assumption (that one-time handouts are bad) by showing the radical politics that one-time charitable handouts framed as "giving to God" allow in Egypt and beyond. For a great discussion of assumed distinctions between charity, development, and humanitarianism in terms of temporality, agency, motivation, see Scherz (2014, 5–7).

24. In many fiqh manuals, the discussion sometimes uses direct quotations by switching to the first person when explaining the words necessary for the performativity of the speech act. Sometimes, as in the waqf deed on the cover of the book, the deed starts with a section that describes the importance of charity in the tradition and the desire of the founder to do good and get close to God. However, this section does not have any legal effects, but it is one of the few places where judges do not follow prescribed formulas, providing particularly valuable information as to the conceptualization and presentation of such acts of charity.

25. MBSS.S3/157.

be gifted, inherited, pawned, owned, appropriated, transferred, or transmitted, in all or in parts, to anyone" can follow the waqf object and further confirm the use of the students' definition of waqf. Nonetheless, the use of the verb *eternalize* and the description of the inalienability of the newly found waqf are not requisites in the waqf deeds, and many of the documents of the Beirut shariʿa court skip these rhetorical devices altogether. In fact, most of the waqf deeds actually do not refer to the students' definition in this part of the deed that contains the speech act and the description of the waqf objects, beneficiaries, and stipulations.

The next section of the waqf deed, termed by jurists "Delivery and Receipt" (Taslīm wa Tasallum), describes first the founder who "took the waqf out of his ownership [*milk*] and transferred it to the ownership of God." The reference to the students' definition is here completely unambiguous. The founder then delivers the waqf to a person whom she names as a co-administrator or sometimes as the sole administrator (*mutawallī*).[26] That action of delivery and receipt points to a debate among Abu Hanifa's students on how ownership can become extinct. They disagree as to whether the utterance is performative. For Abu Yusuf, as for most other scholars of all schools (*jumhūr al-ʿulamāʾ*), arguing based on the analogy to manumission of slaves, the utterance suffices to enact the waqf and transfer ownership from the founder to God. For al-Shaybani, the waqf remains in the hands of its owner and is thus revocable until the handing of the *ʿayn* to the administrator, because all ownership ultimately belongs to God, so the forfeiture of ownership only occurs through delivery (al-ʿAyni, *Ramz*, 1:344). It is because of the need for delivery that, for al-Shaybani, the founder cannot be the administrator, whereas for Abu Yusuf she can. The waqf deed in question, in the delivery and receipt section, enacts the forfeiture of ownership in accordance with al-Shaybani's opinion and thus avoids any challenge to the waqf; it renders the waqf binding because the waqf has now left the possession of the founder.

With the delivery and receipt, the second part of the waqf deed reaches an end. The third and last section introduces further action into the waqf deed, which transforms from a forfeiture of ownership to a litigation. The section almost always starts with the statement: "Then, after the finalization of the waqf . . ., it occurred to the founder to revoke his waqf." This sudden change of heart appears at first puzzling from a founder who has buttressed the foundation deed with every possible locution that renders the waqf unquestionable and binding. In fact, the supposed revocation is a "procedural fiction" or "fictitious litigation," a stratagem based on the tenet that a qadi's ruling is final (res judicata), and is yet another way to make the waqf deed binding. This fictitious litigation indexes the possibility of another definition even before it is brought up by actual litigants. This fictitious litigation is part of the model legal instrument developed by jurists to enforce what had become the dominant opinion of Abu Hanifa's students and to stop potential

26. Many times, the section also includes a "threat" (*tarhīb*) to anyone who changes the waqf.

heirs and interested parties from coming to court, conjuring Abu Hanifa's definition, and arguing that a waqf ends after the death of the founder and that therefore the waqf should revert back to their ownership. This part of the foundation was probably not uttered by the founder. This fictitious litigation is used in every single foundation deed in Beirut and unfolds in the following manner: After the founder changes her mind, an administrator, who is often temporary, steps in as the trustee of the waqf and argues that the students' opinion does not allow revocation. The qadi then rules in favor of the administrator, and the founder dismisses the temporary administrator. Because a judge has ruled in a litigation in favor of one of the opinions, the waqf deed becomes binding.

Consequently, waqf deeds, like the one I use here, even if they are based in and actualize the students' definition of waqf, point to another definition of waqf (and different requirements for bindingness) that very much inform the content of the document. The use of this fictitious litigation indexes these early debates and the constant possibility of a challenge to the irrevocability of the waqf. Abu Hanifa's definition appears in the shadow, as a threat to the perpetuity of the waqf. Thus, the debate over bindingness and inalienability does not simply belong to a theoretical fiqh debate of the library; it makes itself apparent in the archive as it structures the documents recorded at court.[27]

LATE NINETEENTH-CENTURY WAQF: THE QUESTION OF THE WAQF AS LEGAL SUBJECT

Thus were the general contours of waqf practice that appear in the archive in Beirut: a definition of waqf that privileged perpetuity and inalienability, with the definition of waqf as temporary lurking in the background, where God belonged to the cast of characters involved in property relations, and the hereafter figured in the practice. Waqf was mostly an object around which property relations were formed, and charitable practices were not divorced from economic profit. I turn now to the reforms of the nineteenth century and, rather than investigate their origins or aims, I turn to what actually remains of these reforms: the work they did and the effect they had on contemporaneous practice.

The new state-endorsed and exclusive Ottoman legal codes of the nineteenth century did not provide a definition of waqf. The 1858 Land Code did not define

27. The aim of the fictitious litigation is not simply to register the deed at court as a form of public registry, because public registry would not necessitate this collusive litigation (sale contracts registered at court are not accompanied by such litigation). The fact that even waqf deeds drafted by qadis but not registered at court contain the same fictitious litigation points to the possible challenges by heirs that need to be shut down by a judge's decision in a litigation. Other legal schools that do not share these differing opinions as to the inalienability do not use litigation. See, for example, Müller (2008, 74–75), who describes how Shāfiʿis in Mamluk Jerusalem notarized waqf deeds at court through a certification process that involved witnesses only.

waqf, for that belonged to the jurisdiction of the shariʻa.[28] The codification of the shariʻa in the Mecelle had not reached a section on waqf when the new sultan Abdülhamid II interrupted its publication in 1876.[29] The books of the library along with various state-issued regulations remained the main sources for individual judges to make decisions on the most appropriate rulings for the founding and administration of waqfs.

However, in the late nineteenth and early twentieth centuries, new types of manuals dealing exclusively with waqf started appearing. It was my notebook that alerted me to these new manuals, rather than the archive, keyword searches at university libraries, or the bibliographies of works on waqf.[30] I had not encountered these manuals until one day in the summer of 2009, when an employee at the DGIW pulled a photocopied bilingual Ottoman-Arabic edition of Ömer Hilmi Efendi's *İthâfü'l-Akhlâf fî Mushkilâti'l-Evkâf* (1890 [1307]) from a shelf behind him, as he was trying to figure out the legal requirements of a particular contract. Such manuals are still used at the DGIW, where they are not arcane Islamic legal manuals that have been supplanted by postcolonial waqf legislation, a reminder of their lasting effects and their authoritativeness. Besides Ömer Hilmi Efendi's book, which appeared in French in 1895, in Arabic in 1909, and in English in 1922, these manuals include Muhammad Qadri Pasha's *Qānūn al-ʿAdl wa al-Inṣāf fī al-Qaḍāʾ ʿalā Mushkilāt al-Awqāf* (1311 [1893]), which was published in Egypt and appeared in French in 1896; Hüseyin Hüsnü's *Aḥkâmü'l-Evkâf* (1310 [1892]); Elmalılı Muhammad Hamdi Yazır's *İrşâdü'l-Akhlâf fî Aḥkâmi'l-Evkâf* (1330 [1912]); and Ali Haydar's *Tertîbü'ṣ-Ṣunûf fî Ahkâmi'l-Vukûf* (1340 [1922]). The last three Ottoman-language manuals do not seem to have had any translations and are the least available of the five books. Muhammad Hamdi's manual was recently "rediscovered," and a critical edition in modern Turkish was published in 1995.[31] These new manuals, as I discuss further below, opened up new possibilities for waqf practices while foreclosing others.

These five manuals diverge in their audience or purpose: the first two manuals (Ömer Hilmi Efendi's and Muhammad Qadri Pasha's) seem to have been targeted at lawyers and judges, while the last three are lecture notes or textbooks intended for use in the new law schools producing future lawyers and judges. Together, nonetheless, these two types of manuals indicate the way the reforms of the legal

---

28. The Land Code originally applied only to *miri* lands and not to *milk*. The literature on the Code is voluminous, but for an introduction and excellent summary of the state of the field, see Mundy and Smith (2007, 3, 45–48).

29. According to Aydın (2003) in the *İslam Ansiklopedisi* entry on Mecelle-i Ahkâm-ı Adliyye. Öztürk (1995, 3) provides 1868–1889 as the window during which the Mecelle was published. Shaw and Shaw (1976, 119) advance 1866–1888.

30. This is the case because most of these studies are historical and end before the nineteenth century. Hoexter (1997) cites them and relies on them as "semi-official Ḥanafî *waqf* manuals" in use in Algiers.

31. See also Çilingir (2015) for a study of Elmalılı's views on waqf.

system became inescapable realities: the coupling of the adoption of the new codes as the exclusive law of the state with a new education system that familiarized the bureaucrats, lawyers, and judges-to-be with the new laws and made the ʿulamaʾ's independent reasoning and traditional madrasa education much less central to the development and practice of law.

All these manuals share nonetheless a common format, introduced by the Mecelle: "the code" or general rules presented as articles and arranged thematically in sections. This form of waqf manual was structured very differently from the dialogical waqf manuals of the third century AH/ninth century CE and the topical discussions of al-Tarabulusi's compilation. The novelty of the code form and its "thinning out" of shariʿa have been the subject of much debate (Peters 2002; Fierro 2014; Ibrahim 2015; Ayoub 2016; Burak 2017), with the recent conclusion that codification is not inherently contrary to Islamic law. Nonetheless, the more important question is not about codification and its effect on the shariʿa but rather about the place of the code in the legal system and the role of law in society and in relation to the state: what happens to the shariʿa when it is used in a modern state where law serves to produce disciplined and self-governing citizens by changing the conditions of their lives (Asad 1992; Rose and Valverde 1998), rather than being an expression of God's will for how to live a good life in light of the hereafter? The new waqf manuals and code-like works of the nineteenth century came to exist in different legal universes than the late Ḥanafi fiqh books.[32]

Projects and Agents of the State

Muhammad Qadri Pasha's and Ömer Hilmi Efendi's manuals, although not adopted as legal codes by the Ottoman state, were almost as authoritative as state law. Qadri Pasha's codification was only published posthumously in 1893 through the efforts of his son, who edited the three copies into the present volume after the Ministry of Education deemed the three manuscript drafts an unfit format to review (Siraj 2006, 30). Despite being under British occupation, Egypt was still under Ottoman rule, and Qadri Pasha's son navigated the Ottoman state bureaucracy to publish the manual. The Ministry of Education sent the manuscript to the Egyptian grand mufti, who represented the scholarly community, for review. The mufti observed that the book "misquoted its sources" and did not recommend it for publication (Siraj 2006, 30). Eventually, two fiqh teachers at the newly founded schools, and thereby embedded in the state modernizing project, edited the manuscript.[33] Following that edition and upon the recommendation of the shariʿa court inspector, the Ministry of Justice bought and endorsed the

32. Arguing from a different perspective, Samera Esmeir (2012) shows that these legal textbooks and positive codes create a rupture in the conception of time and authority. By abstracting law outside of tradition and by their self-referentiality, they introduce a presentist temporality.

33. One of them was an al-Azhar graduate (on al-Azhar see footnote 36 below); the other I could not locate.

book and printed a first edition (Siraj 2006, 31). The purpose of the book therefore was not to participate in a scholarly debate within the tradition, which the mufti recognized. It was instead targeted to courts, judges, and lawyers, who recognized its value as such. The preface to the 1936 French annotated translation (when Egypt had become a monarchy under British "influence") presents the endeavor of Qadri Pasha as an educative one, "for the edification of his contemporaries" (Qadri 1942, i), but then mentions that the Egyptian government commissioned its translation. The unofficial endorsement of the manual appears unquestionable, despite the preface's claim that the manual was simply about education. The translation almost transformed the manual into a code, its translators claim. They note, nonetheless, the controversial nature of the book, as some lawyers considered it to be highly authoritative and others relegated it to a haphazard compilation of opinions.

Ömer Hilmi Efendi prepared his manual in the context of his position as a member of the Mecelle Committee, where he was assigned the codification of waqf law (Özcan 2007). The book was published posthumously in Istanbul in 1889 [1307].[34] Twenty years later, the Arabic translator of Hilmi Efendi's manual emphasized its comprehensiveness, including its fiqh contents, but especially recent developments in waqf practice and their customary treatments. He advanced that Hilmi Efendi's book had become indispensable to any "judge, president of a court, waqf employee, civil court member and scribe, law student, waqf administrator, supervisor, collector, beneficiary, and mosque staff, claimant, defendant, and lawyer, and anyone related to waqf" (Hilmi 1909, 3). These two manuals come close to being, in the minds of their authors and the practices of the courts, an Ottoman-state-endorsed code on waqf.

The authors of these two manuals came from quite different backgrounds, yet they shared a common path into state bureaucracy, and it was their work for the state that brought their manuals together and allowed the traditionally schooled scholar and the modernly educated one to overlap in their approaches and their projects. Born in 1821 to a Turkish bureaucrat who settled in Egypt, Qadri Pasha (1821–1888 CE) followed a course of studies typical of the century.[35] He started with the memorization of the Qur'an, then attended a small local school, after which he joined the School of Languages (Madrasat al-Alsun) in Cairo, which had been founded in 1836 and headed by the leading modernizing educator Azharite Rifaʿa al-Tahtawi; "both Islamic and European branches of learning . . . [like]

34. It was not until 1977, through an initiative of the Directorate General of Waqfs (Vakıflar Genel Müdürlüğü), that the book was transcribed into modern Turkish and republished, showing the effects of the secularizing reforms of the Turkish state, which eradicated waqfs and made all such manuals irrelevant until the revival of the practice.

35. The biography is based on the introduction to the 2006 Arabic edition of his book (Sira 2006) and on Iskarus (1916). Iskarus mentions that Qadri Pasha's father came from Anatolian town Vezirköprü (which he calls Vezirköprülü).

French, English, Italian, Turkish, Arabic, mathematics, history, and geography" were taught by "a staff of European and native teachers . . . [including] several well-known Azharites"[36] (Heyworth-Dunne 1939, 966). Qadri Pasha seems to have worked in Arabic, French, and Turkish, and upon his graduation he occupied various governmental offices as a translator in Cairo, Damascus, and Istanbul. He returned to Cairo and was appointed successively as an advisor to the mixed courts,[37] a minister of justice, a minister of education, then once more a minister of justice. He was a member of the committee working on a new civil code and new criminal legislation. He was also commissioned by the Ottoman sultan Abdülaziz to participate in the revisions to the Ottoman constitution. Qadri Pasha was also heavily involved in the process of translation and codification occurring at the time in the Ottoman center and peripheries. He not only translated into Arabic the French penal code in 1866 [1283], as well as the civil code used in the Mixed Courts of Egypt, but also codified personal status law (Abu-Odeh 2004, 1101; Cuno 2015, 158–84), as well as pecuniary transactions and waqf.

Ömer Hilmi Efendi (d. 1889 CE) was born in 1842 in Karinabad (Karnobat, Bulgaria) and followed a more traditional education for a Muslim scholar. He belonged, like his father, to the *ilmiye* (the religious class in the Ottoman Empire) rather than the new class of bureaucrats.[38] After memorizing the Qur'an, Ömer Hilmi studied under various 'ulama'. He read the two classical hadith collections, *Ṣaḥīḥ Muslim* and *Ṣaḥīḥ Bukhārī*, and received his license to further transmit them (*ijāza*) from the *kazasker* (chief judge) of Rumeli. He started teaching at the Fatih Mosque in Istanbul before pursuing a bureaucratic career in the various bureaus of the Office of the Fatwa and the Waqf Ministry. He received the honorary ranks associated with the judgeships of Jerusalem and the Haramayn (Mecca and Medina) as well as that of Istanbul, considered the highest of all. He joined the Committee of the Mecelle in the early 1870s and played a critical role in the preparation of the last four books of the Mecelle. First a member of the Court of Appeal, he became its head in 1888 and taught at the newly established law school.

In the still common distinction between modernist scholars trained as lawyers and traditionalist scholars classically trained in madrasas (for an early formulation,

36. Azharites are graduates of al-Azhar, which was then and remains today one of the leading madrasas in the Muslim world, even though it adopted many modern methods of teaching in the nineteenth century. On al-Azhar's modernization, see, for example, Gesink (2009).

37. The courts existed only in Egypt, which at the time had gained some autonomy from the Ottoman Empire under the rule of Muhammad Ali and his successors. For more on the question of Egypt's sovereignty and its relation to the Ottoman Empire, see Fahmy (1998) and Hunter (1998). On the legal system in Egypt at the time, see Brown (1995) and footnote 56 below.

38. This biography is based on the *İslam Ansiklopedisi* entry on Ömer Hilmi Efendi (Özcan 2007). He held a professorship (*müderrislik*)—the grade of *müderris* is the highest in the Ottoman religious hierarchy (see Akiba 2004). He also acted as a lecturer (*dersiâm*) in Karinabad.

see Schacht 1964, 105; for recent usage, see Zaman 2012), Qadri Pasha would be placed among modernists and Ömer Hilmi Efendi among traditionalists. Such a categorization would lead one to assume that Ömer Hilmi Efendi, as part of the "old guard," opposed reforms that undermined the reproduction of the system that produced him as a scholar. The fact that he did not, but was instead an active reformer, points to the two men's convergence through their common careers in the state bureaucracy. Their position as agents of the state can better explain why they produced this form of fiqh manual.

Exclusivity of Legislation

While the form of these manuals as codes might not have been in and of itself a novelty and while the codes of Qadri and Hilmi mostly reproduced the dominant opinions in the Ottoman late Ḥanafī tradition, these codes operated differently than code-like manuals in the tradition.[39]

We can see these differences from the waqf definitions that both Qadri Pasha and Ömer Hilmi Efendi provide. *Waqf* according to Qadri Pasha is

> the confinement of a ʿ*ayn* from the ownership of any human being, and the gift of its *manfa*ʿ*a* to the poor, even if [the poor is only one beneficiary] among others, or to a charitable purpose. (Qadri 2006: Article 1)

According to Ömer Hilmi, however, it is

> the confinement of a ʿ*ayn* so as to give its *manfa*ʿ*a* to humans and to prevent its ownership and transfer, so it is tantamount to being in the ownership of God. (Hilmi 1909: Article 1)

If these manuals are comparable to the genre of *mutūn* (core texts) in terms of their conciseness, then the provision of a single definition is not unusual. *Al-Kanz* provides one definition, for instance, even if Timurtashi's *Tanwīr al-Abṣār*, the *matn* of Ibn ʿAbidin's *Ḥāshiya*, provides both Abu Hanifa's and his students'. Upon closer scrutiny, however, a few differences between these codes and the mutūn start appearing. The definitions used here combine definitions from different commentaries. Qadri Pasha's definition, for instance, combines parts of the commentary on Timurtashi with others from *al-Fatāwā al-Hindiyya*. In addition, the authors do not attribute these definitions to any authority; these definitions stand as absolutes, contrary to the way they do in the mutūn, since both the *Kanz* and the *Tanwīr* refer

39. Analyzing Qadri Pasha's codification of the personal status law, Kenneth Cuno makes similar arguments about the changes that codification introduces, from the elision of alternative opinions to the creation of a "definitive statement of the legal rules as a guide for legal practitioners" (2015, 173). Because the personal status code, unlike waqf, has parallel sections in the French Civil Code, Cuno can also trace the way Qadri organized the fiqh to conform to the order of the French code.

to the definitions as "for him" (*ʿindahu*) or "for them" (*ʿindahum*). The definitions in these new manual codes are presented as definite and absolute.

Form is emblematic of deeper changes within the whole structure of the judiciary and the realm within which these waqf manuals were to be used. The original mutūn did not stand on their own except as textbooks, and their meanings could not be understood without the commentaries that qualified the concise definitions provided. Here, the commentaries on these manuals (and more broadly on the Mecelle) do not bring out the debates in the tradition but, rather, clarify various interpretations and fine points of the articles, supplementing the articles with court decisions. The inclusion of higher court decisions, which displays the use of the doctrine of stare decisis, or precedent, requires the judges to follow these decisions on disputed matters. The new manual codes were written to be the sole source of the "law" of waqf among lawyers and judges, supplemented only by court decisions that further delimited these codes.

The articles following the definition further delimit the consequences of the definition of waqf with regard to the main element of controversy in the shariʿa, irrevocability, and its two effects, perpetuity and inalienability. Here, both Qadri Pasha and Ömer Hilmi Efendi adopt the students' definition with its emphasis on forfeiture of ownership and hence irrevocability. Irrevocability is the first characteristic that Qadri Pasha's code states (Article 3), after stating that the mere utterance of a waqf enacts it. Qadri Pasha and Ömer Hilmi Efendi consequently take the same position when they actually tackle perpetuity. Ömer Hilmi Efendi's Article 73 simply states: "A waqf has to be eternal. The temporary waqf is not valid." Article 13 of Qadri Pasha's manual echoes this requirement: "The meaning of perpetuity is a necessary condition for the validity of waqf." Both Qadri Pasha and Ömer Hilmi's works then codified the most authoritative opinions in the Ḥanafī school.[40] Yet, the mixing of opinions from various manuals and privileging a single definition without referring it back to a scholar or placing it in the shariʿa debates on waqf severed the codes from the Ḥanafī tradition and presented these rules as absolutes, while commentaries linked them to court decisions that now became binding.

Formulating Waqf as a Moral Person

The use of waqf in this transformative period retains many of the features earlier discussed (namely, being an object in property relations and a revenue-generating object for charitable purposes), even though a new formulation of the waqf as a moral person starts to make its appearance in the commentaries of these new manuals, rather than only in the archive as shown in court records.

40. All the articles of Qadri Pasha's manual can be traced to seven canonical books of the Ḥanafī tradition (Siraj 2006, 36–37).

Waqf remains an object in the 1858 Ottoman Land Code, which divides the lands of the Ottoman Empire into five types: *memlûke*[41], *mîrî*[42], *mevkûfe*[43], *metrûke*[44], and *mevât*.[45] Except for the *mîrî*, all the structures of the adjectives are passive participles (*mafʿūl bih*): they are the objects of actions. Waqf, while recognized in the Land Code, was not yet formulated as a subject of land rights. Ömer Hilmi also makes explicit the practice, which we noted above from the court records, of calling the object made into waqf, the waqfed object, waqf. In his second article he points to the practice of calling the *mevkûfe* lands "waqf." The new code then formalizes the use of the term *waqf* as a designation for the object made into a waqf, in addition to the process of alienation and dedication.

Despite these continuities, the new waqf manuals and legal codes paved the way for new framings of the waqf as a moral person. The various commentaries on that innovation continued with the assumption that, before this time, moral persons did not exist in Islamic law. For instance, the commentators on the French edition of Qadri Pasha's first article note: "The main legal effect of the constitution of a waqf is taking out the ownership of the *biens* [possessions] made into a waqf from the patrimony of the founder and its transfer into the ownership of the moral person called waqf" (Pace and Sisto in Qadri 1942, 1: Article 1.6). As can be seen in comparison with the definitions provided above, this formulation contradicts any formulation of the ownership of the waqf, whether by Abu Hanifa or his students—or any school or Muslim jurist prior to the end of the nineteenth century, as a matter of fact. According to these late Ḥanafī fiqh definitions, the

41. Property held in *milk*, freehold. Scholars, especially legal scholars who emphasize the translatability of legal idioms across traditions, argue that *milk* owners have rights similar to private property owners today (they can sell, exchange, gift, lease, loan, pledge, and bequeath it), and so they can "physically use or enjoy it to the fullest extent consistent with the public interest." Furthermore, the *milk* owner's ability to "immobilize the property interest in perpetuity, making it forever inalienable," through waqf, is proof to these authors that the owner has complete rights of ownership in his property and is not subject to any other limitations (Debs 2010, 20). However, Ottomanist historians might disagree with this understanding of *milk* as absolute ownership including the rights to the land. Instead they present it as an "entitlement to tax revenues which, like other types of revenue grants, the grantee held by virtue of an official document from the ruler" (İslamoğlu 2000, 290). The *milk* owner had the right to sell, bequeath, and endow this entitlement, yet, as Huri İslamoğlu points out, these rights were not conceived of as absolute ownership. A hint to the limits placed on *milk* rights in Ottoman practice is that, in rural areas, a *milk* owner had the duty to cultivate his land and pay taxes, and if he did not do so, the ruler could rent out the land or even sell it (Mundy and Smith 2007, 14).

42. Lands owned by the state.

43. Waqfed land. The Code distinguishes between two kinds of waqfs, which eventually come to be known as waqf *ṣaḥih* (valid waqf) and waqf *ghayr ṣaḥiḥ* (invalid waqf). The former is the waqf discussed by jurists. The latter is founded on land that belongs to the Treasury and thus does not fulfill an essential condition of the object in the foundation: that it is the *milk* of its owner. Jurists have allowed such waqfs. See Cuno (1999) for these *ghayr ṣaḥīḥ* waqfs known as *murṣad* in Egypt.

44. *Mîrî* land for public use, such as roads and communal lands, akin to public domain.

45. Literally, "dead." Young renders it as "*terrains vagues*," abandoned, uncultivated usually because they are too far away from inhabited regions (a distance is given in miles, time, and audibility—from where "one cannot hear a loud voice") (1905, 6:74, translation mine).

ownership of the waqf belongs either to God or to the founder, not to a juristic entity called waqf. The *legal formulation* of the waqf as being a moral person is completely novel.[46] These European commentators who were part of the Egyptian legal system aligned the waqf with their understanding of corporate personality. The terse definition of Qadri Pasha, which did not mention the owner of the waqf and did not report the debates on the new owner in the Ḥanafī tradition, allowed new interpretations of the waqf as having a moral personality to make their way into the law. While Hilmi retained God in its definition, the enshrinement of the waqf as a moral person and the permanent expulsion of God from property relations happened by way of the property regime and its categories.

FRENCH MANDATE: WAQF AS SUBJECT

After the end of World War I and the dismantling of the Ottoman Empire, the project that the codification of Qadri Pasha and Ömer Hilmi had begun took different trajectories in various areas of the Ottoman Empire. In the Turkish Republic, the project was halted as the state eradicated waqfs through their sale at auction, appropriation by different ministries, and reversion to private property (Çizakça 2000, 86–90). In Egypt, the codification of waqf law initiated by Qadri Pasha continued and was issued as state law, the 1946 Law of Waqf.[47] This law severely curtailed and even abolished waqf outside mosques and charitable institutions (Abu Zahra 2005, 40–41).[48] In what became Lebanon, however, the French Mandate state adopted a much more careful policy—informed by the French colonial experiments in North Africa and the strong opposition of the Muslim population to their Mandate in the Levant.[49]

French Colonial Experiments

The French came to Lebanon with extensive experience with waqf from their colonial enterprise in North Africa, an experiment that has been well documented and analyzed.[50] Algeria, occupied in 1830, was the first site of French experimentation

46. As discussed above, the waqf could borrow, via the trustee, without incurring the trustee's liability. Yet, this change "in the letter of the law" was felt during the French Mandate, when waqfs started having bank accounts without the intermediary of the trustee, for example.

47. These two countries became models, especially in terms of legislation, for many of the newly founded nation-states. See footnote 56 below.

48. I will discuss the arguments behind these measures in chapter 4. Turkey reversed its position in 1967 with a new and "modernized" law of waqf, marrying American trust law with the shariʿa (Çizakça 2000, 90–110).

49. On that opposition, see Johnson (1986, 22–26); and Khoury (1987, 5–6). On the appropriation of the Ottoman politics of notables by the French to co-opt the Sunnis who were opposed to the Mandate, see Eddé (2009).

50. For Algeria, see Ruedy (1967, 6–8, 67–79); and Saidouni and Saidouni (2009), which includes an extensive survey of studies of French intervention in waqf in Algeria. For Tunisia, see Hénia (2004); and Cannon (1982, 1985). For Morocco, see Luccioni (1982); and Kogelmann (2005). Finally,

with waqf legislation. Waqf was not particularly conducive to French interests in Algeria as a settler colony, insofar as waqf lands could not be sold as freehold to settlers.[51] Ernest Zeys, chair of Islamic law at the École de Loi d'Alger, writes that France found half the "land immobilized, outside any transaction. She could not accept such a situation. We did not conquer such a vast and rich territory to live there precariously, without settling longer term" (quoted in Shuval 1996, 56). Also troubling for colonial power was the sale of these waqfs to European settlers by some beneficiaries or speculators who then reclaimed them on the basis of their inalienability (Powers 1989, 540). In a revisionist account that reminds us that colonial policy was not as farsighted and planned as many studies have assumed, Saidouni and Saidouni (2009) argue that French attitudes towards the waqf in the early years of the colonization of Algeria oscillated between the eradication of waqf and its reform to serve French interests.

Eventually, French legislation along with Orientalist knowledge produced about the shari'a radically transformed what waqf was and could be in French Algeria.[52] By 1843, legislation had integrated all "public waqfs" into the public domain (Ruedy 1967, 75) and made waqf alienable when Europeans were involved in long rents or sale contracts on waqfed assets (Pouyanne 1900, 96). In 1859, the provision of alienability was extended to all transactions on waqf. In practice, waqfs that were not religious buildings became alienable.[53] French waqf legislation in Algeria drew on and influenced studies of waqf in the school that came to be called French Algerian law.[54] These studies were elaborated by members of the "colonial school," Frenchmen intimately connected to and invested in the colonial

---

see Powers (1989) for a comparison between the French-Algerian and English-Indian policies and approaches to waqf. Even though the majority in Algeria followed the Mālikī *madhhab*, they established waqf based on the Ḥanafī *madhhab* (Hoexter 1998a, 9).

51. The percentage of waqf-land is difficult to ascertain. Shuval estimates that 25–30 percent of the city was waqfs (1996, 56). Ruedy mentions that "the greater part of urban *milk*" was waqfed, whereas in rural areas at least 26,000 hectares and possibly even 75,000 hectares were waqf (1967, 8). Rural waqf constituted only 4.5 percent of the "total domain made available to colons" (1967, 67).

52. In their accounts, historians have emphasized strong ruptures in waqf in Algeria, but as this study will show, older notions and practices were not completely eradicated.

53. Bleuchot (1999) notes that these are developments in the North and that the waqfs of the South had a different trajectory, even if they were also almost obliterated.

54. Note that these were not the first Orientalist studies on waqf, as some had been written from the Ottoman Empire. One can cite here Belin (1853), an annotated translation of two waqf documents from the court of Galata. Although written by an Ottoman-Armenian subject, Ignatus Mouradgea d'Ohsson, the massive eighteenth-century *Tableau général de l'empire ottoman* had a "clear intent to explain the Ottomans to the outside world" (Findley 1999, 3). In addition, the French consuls in Istanbul had been following closely the development of waqf reforms and regulations in the Ottoman Empire. Thus, reporting to the Ministry of Foreign Affairs in June 1867, the French ambassador in Istanbul forwarded a new law on the lease of waqf properties, translated as "law of the reform of waqfs." He seems apologetic but also hopeful: "This law still has some restrictions on the complete assimilation of waqf to private property, but it is understood that these will be eliminated soon after" (Documents Diplomatiques 1867, 163, quoted in Deguilhem 2004, 402, translation mine).

project: colonial officers, judges, and professors.[55] The work of these Orientalists "campaigned to discredit the institution among the Algerians themselves" (Powers 1989, 536). These studies permeated and transformed the very thinking and meaning of shariʿa, and waqf in particular.

The "colonial attack" on waqfs in Algeria did not go unresisted. Strong opposition from the muftis and religious scholars led to the exile of both the Ḥanafī and the Mālikī muftis (Saidouni and Saidouni 2009, 15, 25n90), and French reforms could move forward only after the protestors had been exiled (Ruedy 1967, 68). Tenants stopped paying rent and waqf administrators rented for very low prices, even passing off waqfs as private property, because they feared that "the properties were heading straight into the hands of the infidel government" (Ruedy 1967, 70–71).

The French adopted a much less radical policy towards waqf in Tunisia and Morocco, which left waqfs under Muslim administration with French supervision, in line with the new indirect-rule system of the protectorates. While no studies document the reasons behind the shift in policy, a lessons-learned explanation was put forward by Jean Terras (1899, 164), in addition to the already dominant private property regime in Tunisia. The new strategy is a source of pride for Terras, as it involves self-ascribed skillful maneuvering of the French administration. He writes: "Our administration, through a series of wise [*avisé*] regulation, modified this institution to the point of making it compatible with our juristic ideas and with our practical needs, without offending the mores and beliefs of a foreign people" (1899, 4). This strategy would also prevail in Syria and Lebanon.

Transmission of Colonial Knowledge to Egypt and the Levant

The discourses, debates, and arguments around waqf and its reform that were first formulated in French Algeria informed and influenced those in Egypt[56] and the Levant, through the circulation of both texts of French Algerian law and people in colonial offices. Leonard Wood (2016), in his history of Islamic legal revivalism in Egypt between 1875 and 1952, demonstrates that Orientalist knowledge circulated between Algeria and Egypt as teachers moved between schools in those countries, and Egyptian manuals penned by Muslim authors were modeled after Orientalist manuals of Islamic law (following their order and format). Furthermore, writings in Arabic, in Egypt particularly, during the debate on waqf

55. See Powers (1989) for details on that school.

56. Egypt constitutes a key interlocutor for Lebanon for two main reasons. First, its legal codes provided the blueprint of many, if not most, of those of the Arab world (Brown 1995, 106). Second, it was a place where the French refined their experience with waqf. Egypt had acquired a semiautonomous status from the Ottoman Empire after Muhammad Ali's successful challenge to the Ottoman sultan, a challenge that the Ottomans were able to contain and repel only with the help of the British. Legal reforms in Egypt had started at the beginning of the nineteenth century, but the creation of Mixed Courts in 1876 introduced a code based on the French Code Napoléon. French and Belgian judges staffed these courts alongside Egyptian judges. Despite their growing presence, the British could not anglicize the legal system because of strong local opposition (Brown 1995).

reform in the 1910s and up to the 1940s show that Orientalist discourses circulated widely and informed deliberations, especially about the abolition of family waqf that took center stage in Egypt twenty-five years after it happened in Algeria (as I demonstrate in chapter 4). Between 1924 and 1928, several doctoral dissertations by French and Egyptian lawyers studying at the University of Paris's law school investigated various aspects of waqf from the perspectives of both shariʿa and the civil law tradition.[57] Waqf reform projects in French Syria and Lebanon, mostly centered on the abolition of the family waqf, were contemporary to those in Egypt and, here again, we find pamphlets penned by Muslim jurists engaging the Egyptian debate.

Colonial knowledge and discourse on waqf were also transmitted through colonial officers who moved between the various colonies and mandates, and officers were aware of the waqf experiments in Algeria. For instance, in one of the first yearly reports to the League of Nations, required by the League from mandatory powers, the section on waqfs notes how the "enemies" of the French tried to depict any French interference in waqfs as a "return to our olden misguided ways in Algeria, when we incorporated, due to our ignorance of this special issue [of waqfs], the immovable waqf assets into the public domain" (Haut Commissariat de la République française en Syrie et au Liban 1921, 195). The probable author of this section is the delegate of the High Commissioner on real estate matters, Philippe Gennardi, who had links to French North Africa because he had served in Morocco in World War I.[58] Gennardi represented a style of administration common to French officers of the Moroccan protectorate, epitomized by its Resident General, General Lyautey: these officials were well-versed in the languages of the area and less forceful and more shrewd in their strategies than their colleagues who ruled colonies like Algeria, exploiting "the strengths and weaknesses of Moroccan society and its respect for native religion and customs" (Burke 1973, 176). Gennardi knew Arabic and Ottoman, and even married a Beiruti woman in 1921. His personnel file indicates that he was "well-informed" about Muslim matters and had a deep knowledge of Islam.[59]

"What Is Waqf?": French Interpretations

In Lebanon and Syria, the French mandatory powers did not "define" waqf or issue a comprehensive waqf law, like they did with real estate, commercial, and criminal law. In some ways, then, the project of the state adopting a single definition of waqf and having a single body of laws about waqf appears as a project that can be

57. For example, Bidair (1924); Massouda (1925); Cotta (1926); Delavor (1926); and Saad (1928).

58. As Kupferschmidt (2008) mentions, Gennardi's near absence from histories of the Mandate contrasts sharply with his heavy trail in the French archive of the Mandate in Nantes: report after report on waqf between 1922 and 1940 bear his signature.

59. MAE20/72. I would like to thank Elizabeth Williams for her generosity in taking pictures of the Gennardi file for me, since the file arrived after I had left Nantes.

pursued, even as an ideal, only under certain conditions. The Muslim suspicion towards the French mandatory powers and their intentions in Lebanon towards the Muslim population rendered French maneuvering on waqf more delicate and more prone to providing ammunition to Muslim opposition to the Mandate. The various waqf codes of Qadri Pasha and Ömer Hilmi, with their definitions of waqf, did not become or inform state law in Lebanon.

The French faced an old problem when defining the waqf and determining jurisdiction over it. Firstly, it was a problem of classification inherent in law. It was further compounded by the confrontation of two legal systems, primarily because waqf, developed in Islamic law, did not have an obvious civil law equivalent—or so French jurists argued.[60] Is waqf a real right? Is it a personal right? This debate represented, at its core, "jurisdictional politics"—that is, "conflicts over the preservation, creation, nature, and extent of different legal forums and authorities" (Benton 2002, 10). Part of the colonial legal order was the division between personal status (*statut personnel*)[61] and real status (*statut réel*),[62] which fell under the jurisdiction of different courts and followed different codes. These disputes over jurisdiction were crucial, Benton argues, because they embodied "cultural boundaries" between settlers and natives, between the civilized and savages. While Muslim jurists also debated whether waqfs were worship acts (*ʿibādāt*) or pecuniary transactions (*muʿāmalāt*),[63] their conclusion that waqf was a mix of both did not cause such a jurisdictional problem because both worship and transaction laws were elaborated by the same jurists and were part of the same "divine law." Conversely, in French Mandate Lebanon and Syria, where real estate property was governed by French-promulgated civil codes and personal status was governed by religious law devised by legally autonomous religious sects, the classification of waqf opened space for jurisdictional politics.

French mandatory powers considered waqf to be both a personal and a real right. The preamble to Decree 753/1921, organizing the administration of waqfs in Lebanon, notes: "The administrative and case law applied on waqfs are taken from religious shariʿa, which differs considerably from the laws that are applied in other governmental offices." Jurisdiction over the foundation of waqf belonged to

60. "It does not have any equivalent in our codes; it is not a will, nor a gift, nor a substitution per se," a jurist exclaimed (Robe in Mercier 1899, 5).

61. On the creation of this new category of "personal status" in Arabic, see Asad (2003, 231fn55). In the definition of the commentators of Qadri Pasha's manuals: "We understand by personal status, the sum of natural or familial states that distinguish among individuals and that are the sources of rights and obligations. One can cite for example the state of being male or female, of being married, widowed, or divorced, father or legitimate son, possessing legal capacity or minor" (Commentary 37 to Article 1 in Qadri 1942, 3).

62. "All questions related to patrimony pertain, in principle, to real status" (Commentary 37 to Article 1 in Qadri 1942, 3).

63. For further elaboration on this distinction, see chapter 2.

the religious courts that applied the shari'a.[64] In the 1930s, the power to legislate on waqfs was given to the Supreme Waqf Council (later renamed the Supreme Islamic Legal Council). However, French regulations also considered waqf as partly real estate and thus regulated by the Real Estate Code, and various laws pertaining to real estate and certain legal ordinances around waqf exchange were issued by the French high commissioner. These codes regulated waqf without tackling its definition, creating contradictory effects as to the waqf's essential characteristics of alienability and irrevocability.

The 1930 Real Estate Code, for example, defined land categories parallel to those in the 1858 Ottoman Land Code: *milk*, *amīriyya*, *matrūka*, and *mawāt*. The title of the code, however, indicates a different approach to the environment: it is the "real estate" code rather than the "land" code, transforming "land," a part of the environment, into real estate and signaling the rise of a private property regime where land is mostly a financial asset.[65] Furthermore, compared to the 1858 code, the 1930 code displaced waqf lands from the "categories" of land. Instead, it classified waqf as a right on real estate property, dealt with in Articles 174 to 179. Rather than being a kind of ownership, divine ownership, that differs from state ownership or private ownership, waqf became a right one can have on private property. However, unlike the rest of articles tackling various rights (like possession, usufruct, etc.), the articles on waqf rights do not begin with defining them and the rights and duties they create. Indeed, Article 179 of the Real Estate Code specifies that "the regulations concerning the founding of a waqf, its validity, aim, division [*qisma*], rental, and exchange are specified in the special regulations pertaining to it." We see here how the jurisdiction over waqf was split between civil and religious laws and courts.

Waqf in these various laws was sometimes alienable and sometimes inalienable. The first article of the section on waqf in the 1930 code states: "It is not permitted to sell, dispose of, transmit through inheritance, or mortgage a waqfed immovable[66] but it is possible to exchange it, and to establish a dual tenancy or a long rent[67] on it" (Article 174). Waqf is here inalienable. However, other articles in the same code and other legislation on waqf make waqf alienable and revocable. In the same section of the code, special lease contracts on waqf known as dual tenancies and

64. The jurisdiction of shari'a courts was defined in Article 14 of the 1942 Legislative Decree no. 241 on the Organization of Sunni and Jaafari Shari'a Courts and included this: "the waqf: its qualification [*ḥukm*], bindingness [*luzūm*], validity, conditions, beneficiaries, and division [*qisma*]."

65. This does not mean that there was no speculation earlier, as I explain further in footnote 11 of the introduction. These changes in humans' relationship to land are one of the main factors in the waqf transformations I describe.

66. I use *immovable* as a noun in lieu of *immovable property* or *immovable possession* to reflect the Arabic *ghayr manqūl* and the French *immeuble*, both of which are nouns classifying property.

67. These are types of leases that give tenants long-term inheritable rights of use and usufruct on the waqf, against an original lump sum and small yearly or monthly installments afterwards. For example, see Hoexter (1984; 1997) and Baer (1979).

long rents are defined, discussed, and codified in terms of the rights they give, the duties incumbent upon their possessors, and the way they can be conveyed and voided. Holders of both these types of leases can buy out the right of alienation (*raqaba*) of the waqf (Articles 181 and 196) and therefore end the waqf, a process that makes waqf alienable. Other legislation also rendered waqf alienable. Legislation on the exchange of waqf (Decision 80/1926) allowed and sometimes forced the exchange of waqfs against cash and the reversion of waqfs to the ownership of beneficiaries and therefore effectively made waqf alienable and revocable, also here without tackling its definition as such.[68]

Creating Waqf as a Moral Person

According to the 1930 Real Estate Code, waqfs were valid only upon their registration in the real estate registry (Article 176), and not just in the shariʿa court. This registration requirement redefined waqf and allowed its existence as a moral person in the civil legal tradition. The new property regime with its new categories introduced a new grammar of waqfs, where the subjects and objects of waqf were differently configured, creating a fair amount of confusion and opening the door for the dispossession of some rights holders to the advantage of others, including the state. Let me illustrate with the Qabbani waqf, which I was able to follow in some detail because the family was still in disputes with the DGIW over the waqf and held on to the documentation of the lawsuit. Indeed, the lawyer of the waqf in the previous generation of beneficiaries, Rushdi Qabbani (1885–1974), was one of these beneficiaries and he had kept a file for the waqf, which his daughter had shared with me after pulling it from a box lodged in her bedroom closet.

Based on its waqf deed, the waqf of sitt el-ʿeish, as the family called it, was founded in 1854 by an Ottoman merchant, Mustafa Agha Qabbani, who dedicated a part of his garden in the up-and-coming extra muros neighborhood of Zuqaq al-Balat to his daughter ʿAʾisha.[69] His third daughter from his first marriage, ʿAʾisha was married to Muhammad al-Mufti al-Ashrafi. In the waqf deed, Mustafa Agha allowed his daughter to build whatever she pleased on the land, and it would be her own.[70] Between 1854 and 1905, when she died, ʿAʾisha Qabbani in

68. Whether the exchange was forced or optional depended on the rights that existed on the waqf. The law required the eradication of certain types of rights.

69. The waqf deed, pictured on the cover of this book, bears the seal of the Sayda judge. The document does not state whether the deed was drafted in Sayda or by the qadi in Beirut, but based on the witnesses' family names, one could make a guess that the deed was drafted in Sayda. Beirut at the time was attached to the province of Sayda and was the provincial capital. Mustafa Agha was surely well connected, renting out some of his waqfs to the dragoman of the province. Based on the oral histories I have collected from the family, Mustafa Agha lived in Beirut but went to Egypt to fight with the Ottomans against the Napoleonic invasion (1798–1801). The family thought he was dead, but he reappeared, even though he seems to have been wounded. On Zuqaq al-Balat, see Gebhardt and Hanssen (2005).

70. The founder also stipulated a yearly stipend of 50 qurush for Qurʾanic recitation, paid to the scholar Abd al-Qadir Jamalzade and posthumously to his progeny in perpetuity.

turn, through a long-term rent agreement, allowed her husband to build on the endowed land a house, a guesthouse, and a few other small structures. Since her husband had built these objects using his own money and with ʿA'isha's consent, he had various rights to dispose of them, including selling them, as long as he paid the land rent owed to the waqf. In 1875, ʿA'isha's husband relinquished the ownership of the trees and houses to God and dedicated their yields to his wife and, after her death, to their children, and, if they had no children, to his six brothers and sisters. ʿA'isha's husband died before her, and she became the administrator and beneficiary of the waqf he had created. However, when she died, she left no sons or daughters; therefore, the beneficiaries of her husband's endowment became his brothers and sisters, while the beneficiaries of her father's endowment became her heirs—that is, her brothers and sisters.

At first impression, property relations around that piece of Mustafa Agha's garden seem far from common understandings of "private property" today. Here is a piece of land that has been endowed for a certain beneficiary, whose houses and trees belonged to a different person and were then dedicated to yet another set of beneficiaries. How could one "own" trees and buildings but not the land on which they exist? In fact, this scenario is not so far from contemporary property relations in the West. In the United Kingdom, where the queen remains a very important landowner through the Crown Estate, ground leases allow developers to build and sell anything from shopping malls to apartment buildings (Shoard 1997, 124–25). This is a very similar scenario to the buildings of Muhammad al-Ashrafi on ʿA'isha's waqf, which he could build, use, sell, or waqf after paying yearly ground rent. If one shifts the language of analysis from "ownership" to "rights," the description of the endowments in the garden of Mustafa Agha offers less of a conundrum. ʿA'isha had the right to the usufruct of the land and transferred that right to him. He originally had the right of alienation, usufruct, and use of the house he built. He then surrendered this right of alienation to God and transferred the right of usufruct and use to ʿA'isha and then his heirs.

This twice-waqf illustrates the Ottoman property rights regime where the same parcel was claimed for multiple functions, with rights of use, revenues, and alienation (e.g., the right to cultivate, right to a portion of the harvest, right to taxes, right to sell) dispersed among various people (İslamoğlu 2000). While the Ottoman Land Code of 1858 introduced individual and absolute ownership, such understandings were hotly contested (as detailed by İslamoğlu 2000, 35–39). Furthermore, in Jordan, as Martha Mundy and Richard Smith masterfully show, while the new codes individualized the subject of ownership, they did not yet manage to "detach the object 'land,' to which individual rights were attached, from the social forms of its mobilization in production" (2007, 235). Similarly, this process in Beirut had to wait for the cadaster, with the French occupation after the parceling of the Ottoman Empire, when a new land registry and land code were instated. These rearranged the various rights and provided new categories that the parties had to use, changing the grammar of waqf.

The new land registry (Decrees 186,188, and 189, dated 15 March 1926), whose novelty lay in being based on maps and a cadaster, did not explicitly modify the Ottoman categories in use at the time.[71] It allowed, therefore, the preservation of certain "facts," while opening the possibility of their recategorization and rearrangement. A certified copy of the delimitation report (*maḥḍar al-taḥdīd*), also preserved in the family archive, reveals a protracted and contested process of registration, because new laws allowed beneficiaries to claim ownership of waqf, end the waqf, and revert it to private property, setting the two families of beneficiaries (of the land waqf and the house waqf) against each other.

The delimitation report consists of three pages, the first of which is a printed one-format-fits-all table containing rows and columns with headlines based on a private property regime. The two following pages have a heading (one page in French, the other in Arabic), "Ruling of the Land Surveying Commission," summarizing the lengthy lawsuits that pitted the two families against one another.

The original delimitation report table, dated 6 February 1928, registered the details of the various rights on the parcel, now identified as Parcel 340. In the row for the "legal type of parcel" (*nawʿuh al-sharʿī*), the surveyor had written "waqf." This notation continues the categorization of lands in the Ottoman Code, where waqf is a type of land. However, in the row for the "name of owner" (*ṣāḥib al-milk*), "the waqf of the deceased Muhammad al-Mufdi al-Tarabulusi [sic] and his heirs" was jotted down, and the row titled "name of the waqf, type of right, amount of deferred rents [*muʾajjalāt*], lump sum rents [*muqāṭaʿāt*], and tithe [*badal al-ʿushr*]" was filled with "family waqf." In the miscellaneous-details row, we learn that "the land on which the house is built is private [*khāṣṣ*] to the heirs of ʿAbd al-Qadir Qabbani, and the built-up areas to Muhammad Mufdi Tarabulusi [*sic*], the waqf founder." The various facts noted in these records (that it is a waqf, that the land belongs to the Qabbani waqf, and that the built-up areas were part of Mufti-Ashrafi waqf) correspond to the different rights that I described above.

In this regime, noting "God" as the owner would be nonsensical, and thus, during real estate registry, God was evicted from the characters involved in the waqf, and the waqf itself became the "owner" of the newly created Parcel 340. Furthermore, important characters in waqf, like the "administrator" and "beneficiaries," could not be identified as such by the surveyors who had to subject the information to the space and structure of the table. In addition, the multiple waqfs could not be registered, and the title of "owner" fell upon the waqf of the family that was inhabiting the house at the time, the Mufti-Ashrafis. The rights the Qabbanis held were relegated to the fine points around the parcel—the Qabbani name was not even mentioned in the decision of the Commission.[72] With its single table per parcel, the new property registry did not allow for the multiplicity of rights to be

71. However, changes would follow, as we saw above with the 1930 real estate code.

72. The registry decision was challenged by the Qabbanis, who were able to marshal their knowledge of the French legal system to get a decision to annul the Mufti-Ashrafi waqf as invalid and have the land registered as the waqf of ʿAʾisha Qabbani.

concomitant: it hierarchically classified these rights to give one of the rights holders the title of "owner." The waqf became the "owner," a person, transformed from being mostly an object around which property relations are articulated to a subject in these relations.

Thus, legal reforms paved the way for the transformation of the understanding and practice of waqf. By recategorizing and sometimes even erasing the main characteristics of Ottoman waqf practices and making "waqf" a person—that is, the "owner" of the parcel—the new property regime opened the way for the use of waqf as a "moral person" that could buy, sell, and enter into various transactions. Let me turn now to explaining how the intersection of the French Mandate's classification of waqf as a person with historical contingencies and practitioners familiar with the tradition, like Hajj Tawfiq, opened the legal possibilities to both revive the waqf and make the waqf as moral person a common practice today.

POSTCOLONIAL WAQF PRACTICES: WAQF AS MORAL PERSON

The Making of a Waqf Revival and the Waqf as a Moral Person

I came to Hajj Tawfiq through a winding road. The lawyer of the human rights waqf I mentioned in the introduction traced his exposure to waqf to a workshop titled "Waqf and Collective Duties" (al-Waqf wa Furūḍ al-Kifāya), led by Abu Samah of Jam'iyyat al-Irshad wa al-Islah al-Khayriyya al-Islamiyya (the Islamic Charitable Association for Guidance and Reform). When I followed up with Abu Samah, he pointed me to Hajj Tawfiq, who, he said, "was interested in the private waqf [*al-waqf al-khāṣṣ*]." Abu Samah explained that a booklet that Hajj Tawfiq had self-published, *The Private Waqf*, had opened the window of waqf before them. The booklet, he remarked, contained all the documents and procedures necessary to transform an association into a waqf.

I was puzzled by the notion of the "private waqf" because *private* is a notoriously ambiguous adjective, even here: it could mean waqfs dedicated to private, named persons rather than a wider public, like the poor. That was the dominant meaning in current legislation, which equated charitable waqf with public and family waqf with private (discussed in chapter 4). But *private* could also indicate that the waqf (even a mosque) was privately administered by a named individual or board, outside the supervision of the DGIW. When I got hold of the thirty-page booklet published in 1989 through Hajj Tawfiq, I noticed that it was in fact titled *The Islamic Charitable Waqf*. Following the contemporary legal classification of waqfs, these charitable waqfs would be public (benefiting a section of the public—unspecified members of the public writ large, such as "Muslims"). Even so, Abu Samah's calling the book *The Private Waqf* reflects the essential characteristic of these waqfs for those engaged in this revival: They were neither administered nor supervised by the DGIW. Instead, they were run by an administrator that the founder could designate and were nominally under the supervision of the religious courts and their judges, which did not have any mechanism in place for such oversight, perpetuating the lack of actual supervision by nineteenth-century shariʿa courts. Abu Samah did not use the term that the Ottomans used to describe these waqfs—"exempt waqfs" (*awqāf mustathnāt*), which I discuss next chapter—signaling the near-eradication of such waqfs during the French Mandate waqf administration.

Abu Samah credited Hajj Tawfiq for the revival of the idea of waqf in the mid-1990s.[73] Similarly, ʿIsam al-Huri, the head of the BAU board of trustees, mentioned that had it not been for Hajj Tawfiq, the BAU would have never become a waqf. Hajj Tawfiq, he explained, belongs to an "older generation" who had closer encounters with the waqf and a religious disposition (*tawajjuh dīnī*). Hajj Tawfiq himself framed the idea of using waqfs instead of NGOs, or of transforming existing NGOs to waqf, in such a "religious idiom": it was a God-sent inspiration (*ilhām*). Hajj Tawfiq's familiarity with the waqf was not only the result of his religious disposition but also, as he explained, of his engagement with the Palestinian cause, which taught him the importance of the waqf in the resistance to Israeli dispossession of Palestinians.[74]

The presence of practitioners like Hajj Tawfiq intersected with a historical conjuncture that allowed waqf as a moral person to exist as a practice in the 1980s, long before the "waqf revival" that Kuwait initiated in the 1990s. For Hajj Tawfiq, the momentous event that planted the seed of the waqf was the Israeli invasion of Southern Lebanon in 1978. Suddenly, resistance to Israeli dispossession seemed as much a Lebanese necessity as a Palestinian reality. In 1982, when the invasion reached Beirut, he recounted, General Security revoked the permits of seven Islamic and five Christian associations because they were related to parties opposing Israel. This move brought to the Hajj's mind uncanny resemblances to the Israeli strategies in Palestine and crystallized the idea that "political factions could use the power of the state to threaten the operation and existence of opposing parties, and even silence them." Along with the fear of state intervention in associations, the experience of waqf in Palestine forwarded the waqf's sanctity as a way to found Islamic organizations without such a threat. In 1979, Hajj Tawfiq and some associates founded the Islamic Center for Education as a waqf. Yet, it took a few years, the Israeli invasion of Beirut, and the massacres of Palestinian Muslims at the hands of the Israeli Defense Forces and the Lebanese right-wing Christian militias in 1982 before he could convince the board of trustees of al-Birr wa al-Ihsan association, of which he was a member, to convert the association and

73. The first "new" waqfs were founded in the 1980s, but the waqf revival would not blossom until the mid-1990s.

74. For more on Hajj Tawfiq, his connection to Palestine, and the Imam Awzaʿi Islamic Studies College, see Rougier (2007, 203–28). For waqf in Palestine, see references in footnote 19 of the introduction.

all of its schools and university campuses into a waqf. Waqf, explained the Hajj, allowed for the preservation of property from the intervention of political power (*al-sulṭa*).[75]

Because waqf revival came from Muslims familiar with and active in social and educational work through associations and NGOs, the new waqfs adopted much of the format of NGOs: they have internal regulations instead of founder stipulations and an administrative board in lieu of an administrator. The name that Hajj Tawfiq's booklet gives to these waqfs is "charitable waqfs of public benefit" (*al-awqāf al-khayriyya dhāt manfaʿa ʿāmma*), an amalgamation of the category of "charitable waqf" defined in the 1947 Family Waqf Law and the adjective "of public benefit" of the 1977 Legislative Decree on Associations of Public Benefit. Hajj Tawfiq's booklet provides sample documents to be presented to the shariʿa court for the transformation of associations into waqfs. One addresses the judge with a letter attesting that "the Board of Trustees [of the Association] has decided to make into a waqf all the institutions of the association and its movable and immovable possessions" (1989, 10). Notice that the object that is made into waqf, which both fiqh definitions (outlined earlier in this chapter) require to be a well-defined, usufruct-bearing object, movable or immovable, becomes here an institution.[76] For instance, in the waqf of the Islamic Center for Education, the phrasing is "made into an Islamic charitable waqf all that is related to the Islamic Center for Education, immovables or movables, present or future." There were no revenue-bearing immovables that were clearly defined; the waqf deed was a performative that created a moral person.[77] I realized later that this is why Hajj Tawfiq had told me, tongue-in-cheek, that they waqfed words.

The dominance of the idea of a waqf as a moral person can be seen in the grand mufti himself approaching waqf as a such, especially in the case of the ubiquitous but extremely opaque Waqf al-ʿUlamaʾ al-Muslimin al-Sunna. I first encountered that waqf (because indeed it was a moral person) in a conversation with the lawyer of the DGIW, when asking him about the waqfed parcels that were under the supervision of the DGIW. He showed me a list, but told me that this list did not include the parcels of Waqf al-ʿUlamaʾ. Waqf al-ʿUlamaʾ was originally a waqf like the hundreds of waqfs noted in the courts of Beirut. In its structure, its waqf deed followed exactly the structure I described above based on the students' definition. It would have easily passed unnoticed, unremarkable were it not for its eminent founder, the Ottoman governor of the province at the time, Nassuhi bey, who in

75. This discourse echoes scholarly analysis of historical waqf (for instance, under the Mamluks) and how founders used waqf to escape confiscation of property (Petry 1983). I will demonstrate in the next chapter how "escaping political power" is a much more complicated issue than appears here.

76. Jurists consider a waqf that does not specify the object made into a waqf to be invalid (Ibn ʿAbidin, *Ḥāshiya*, 3:373), as in contracts, because it leads to uncertainty. See the discussion on *gharar* (uncertainty) and *jahāla* (lack of knowledge) in Hallaq (2009, 244).

77. The use of cash brings these foundations more in line with fiqh requirements, even if the cash is not used as revenue-bearing principal.

1895, surrendered the ownership of an 875-square-meter parcel to God and dedicated its revenues to the students of legal religious sciences (*al-ʿulūm al-dīniyya al-sharʿiyya*). The founder divided the revenue among teachers and students, and dedicated two-fifths of one-third of the revenue to the administrator of the waqf, which he assigned to the mufti of Beirut.[78]

At the end of 2006, the grand mufti addressed a judge of the Beirut Sunni shariʿa court asking for a new foundation deed. The mufti spoke in his capacity as the administrator of the ʿUlamaʾ Waqf, which was not under the administration or supervision of the DGIW.[79] The process itself is unusual but could be analyzed in a tradition of renewing waqf deeds and restating waqfs in order to preserve them. It was a practice that sultans sometimes carried out upon their ascension. It was a practice I even encountered in the archive, as with the Qassar waqf discussed above, an older deed copied in the registers for confirmation. However, the reason behind the grand mufti's request was different. In his note, he described how various muftis before him bought "parcels for the ʿUlamaʾ Waqf" and registered them under the name "Muslim Sunni ʿUlamaʾ Waqf administered by the grand mufti." The current grand mufti followed his predecessor's lead in buying for the waqf, and notes in his memorandum that these parcels "have become appended to the principal (*aṣl*) of the waqf." Therefore, he argued, it was necessary to document this waqf with a new waqf deed that notes the new "name" that the waqf has acquired and its new objects. The mufti requested the new waqf deed to explicitly state and consider the "Muslim Sunni ʿUlamaʾ Waqf administered by the grand mufti" a "charitable waqf having its own moral personality that is completely independent of the DGIW, since the day of its foundation by Nassuhi bey." In this request, the transformation of the waqf from an object to a moral person becomes particularly stark as the grand mufti seeks to subject the old foundation deed to the new understanding of waqf, asking for a rewording of the original foundation deed that would have been unutterable in the late nineteenth century, when the deed was drafted.

The reader may recall from the opening vignette of this chapter that in my first encounter with Hajj Tawfiq, I was not ready for his question on the difference between a waqf and an association. The reasons might now be clearer, given that most of the waqfs I had encountered before my ethnographic research were parcels of land and shops whose revenues supported charitable purposes, as I described above; the connection of waqfs to associations had not been obvious to me. Thus, *waqf* conjured in my mind a building or a piece of land, while an association

78. The position of Mufti of Beirut became the Mufti of the Lebanese Republic, or Grand Mufti (as I explain in further detail in chapter 2), making the grand mufti the administrator of the waqf.

79. Quotes in this paragraph are from this memo. The mufti's independent administration of the ʿUlamaʾ Waqf stirred controversy, especially under mufti Hasan Khalid. As some of my interlocutors narrated, Khalid was accused of using the funds of the DGIW (and inciting people to donate to this waqf rather than the DGIW) to buy parcels for the ʿUlamaʾ Waqf that was not under the supervision of the DGIW, particularly because this waqf carried the stipulation of a revenue percentage that went to the mufti personally.

conjured executives, meetings, fundraisers, and volunteers doing things. Perhaps I was too literal, because historians of waqf, particularly in the Ottoman Empire, have argued that waqfs, especially smaller ones, "constitute a major example of the autonomous working of civil society and the public sphere in the Ottoman Empire" (Gerber 2002, 77; see also the essays in Hoexter, Eisenstadt, and Levtzion 2002; Isin and Üstündağ 2008), a place of civic engagement outside the state, which is what associations today provide. In some ways, these historians' analyses seems confirmed by current waqf practitioners in Lebanon, like Hajj Tawfiq, who consider the waqf an alternative to associations. Yet, this coincidence hides some modern transformations that made this convergence possible: centering the waqf on its purposes and stripping it of its assets and rent-producing function.

Separating Religion and Economy

Discussing these transformations with Hajj Tawfiq, we concurred that the new waqfs were indeed different from the old ones. But not only were they different, he insisted, the new waqfs were *better*. He explained that in older times, waqf was not thought of as dynamic (*ḥarakiyyan*); civil work (*al-ʿamal al-ahlī*) used to take a specific shape and a fixed one—a building, a shop. He credits himself and his association with the introduction of the concept of the "agile waqf" (*al-waqf al-mutaḥarrik*) in Beirut, a waqf that is based on institutions. For Hajj Tawfiq, then, the anchoring of waqf in particular revenue-bearing immovables to finance institutions *fixed* the "flexibility" of movement that markets allowed. Hajj Tawfiq's view of the pre-modern waqf as unchanging very much echoes modernist arguments (discussed further in chapter 3) that waqf was outside the market and thus incompatible with development (Klat 1961). This view remains prevalent, even in Hajj Tawfiq's discourse. For Hajj Tawfiq, the waqf as a moral person, an NGO, which is not an object but can itself be the subject of property relations and own property, allowed such organizations to "escape" this predicament.

The making of the waqf into a moral person, which secularized waqf by removing God as an actor in property actions, coincided with a different kind of secularization as well: the continual quest to separate religion and economy. Waqfs that serve Muslims through providing worship spaces and religious education came to denote what is considered a pious purpose, while the activities that fund them came to belong to the realm of the economy.

The stripping of the economic from the religious and their production as two distinct spheres appeared in the process of emptying mosques of their "non-religious" functions during the reconstruction of Beirut's city center at the end of the civil war. Older buildings, like the ʿUmari mosque, stood as an embodiment of the older logic of waqf. The mosque was invisible except for its main arch-door, as it was hidden behind an office building and shops, all of which were waqfs that supported it (Rustom 2011, 3). During renovations, the mosque became a space of struggle between older understandings of waqf that included revenue-bearing assets and newer ones that considered religious space and commerce separate. The latter vision won over, and shops and office buildings affixed to the mosque were destroyed, while all commercial space was assigned to functions and programs not geared towards profit—a library, a conference center, a reception hall (for condolences usually), and an Islamic museum. Religion was thus "purified" to worship. As a former director of the DGIW explained, having shops and commerce around the mosque was not "proper" (*mā bilī'*) for such religious buildings. This was a process that transformed the 'Umari mosque into a "*religious* monument," in contrast to the integration of religious practice into the community's daily life and its imbrication with the economic activities around the mosque through networks of support via waqf shops and offices.[80]

This separation of religion into its own sphere also appeared in my conversations with founders. As appears above, in my discussions with the founders of these new waqf NGOs, the "Islamic character" or "pious purpose" of waqf was not a central topic of conversation. The transformation of waqf into a moral person seems to have ousted God from charitable endowments. New waqf actors seemed very matter-of-fact and pragmatic about the decision to create waqfs: it was about the legal advantages that they provided. But this would be too hurried a conclusion.

God was very much present, but outside these property relations. When I asked one of the founders of the Waqf of Social Affairs why they thought about founding a waqf and if they had an example in mind, she did at first mention a practical consideration: that a judge in a court in the outskirts of Beirut allowed cash waqfs, which was the main form of waqf-NGOs (waqf-ing a little money to create a moral person). But then, as if stating the obvious, she backtracked: "What *first* encouraged us to found a waqf is that waqf is *qurba* to God, *ḥisba* for God; it is a *ṣadaqa*." All three terms signify, without the need for much explanation, actions "for God's sake," with *qurba* clearly expressing the desire to be close to God in the hereafter. Similarly, the booklet that al-Irshad and al-Islah distributed to visitors and members to encourage them to donate to the waqf library started with this hadith: "When a man dies, all but three of his deeds come to an end: ongoing charity [*ṣadaqa jāriya*], knowledge that benefits [humans], or a virtuous descendant who prays for him." This was by far the most ubiquitous hadith in my notebook, especially among founders of mosques, and was also one of the main hadiths used in waqf deeds in Ottoman Beirut. The continuing circulation of this hadith highlights the persistent importance of the otherworldly rewards of waqf founding, even when utilitarian discourses occupy discussions of the legal form of waqf.

80. Not all mosques in Ottoman Beirut and beyond were enmeshed in the urban fabric around them. Around the mid-eighth century, mosques were sometimes surrounded by an empty space known as the *ziyāda*, although the exact purpose of the space is unknown. Was this a "monumentalization" of the mosque? What did it say about religion and its place? I hope to pursue these questions in a later project.

Despite the dominance of conceptualizations of waqf as a moral person and the waqf as a mosque or religious institution, we find traces of old understandings of waqfs as revenue-yielding assets from practitioners familiar with these older practices. One such trace appears in ʿUmar al-Fahl's waqf, founded in 2003. This was a piece of land endowed for the charitable purposes of creating an Islamic center, which included a mosque and various shops to support the operation of the center.[81] The founder was carrying out the will of his grandfather, and also namesake, whose piety was legendary, to create such a waqf. One can surmise that the elder ʿUmar al-Fahl's exposure to Ottoman waqfs under the Mandate translated in a new waqf that carried that same logic of a revenue-bearing, self-sustaining project, allowing for the older waqfs as objects to continue to exist in buildings and typologies that embody this logic.

Yet, the al-Fahl waqf and its revenue-bearing assets were not always legible as waqf. Hajj Tawfiq commented that this waqf was problematic precisely because the founder "wanted something between a waqf and something commercial." For Hajj Tawfiq, then, the idea of a waqf as a process that could be charitable while seeking the creation of profit was contradictory. This tension or even conflict that Hajj Tawfiq identifies between waqf, a charitable endeavor, and a commercial enterprise is a very modern one, partly arising from the dominance of the waqf as a moral person, since it dissociated waqf from these revenue-bearing objects.

Furthermore, Hajj Tawfiq's vehement rejection of profit-making in waqfs may also be due to the migration of discourses from the convergence and equivalence of waqf with associations. Indeed, the purpose of an association in Lebanese law is defined in opposition to profit-sharing (Article 1 of the 1909 Associations Law): it is a group of people who aim to advance purposes other than profit-sharing.[82] The comparability of waqf to associations for Hajj Tawfiq exacerbated the process of separating rent and profit-producing activity from waqf, which was already under way through the transformation of waqf into a moral person.

I also witnessed the lingering approaches to waqfs as revenue-bearing objects among family waqf beneficiaries. On a glorious sunny July Sunday in the mountains, my mother had organized one of her enormous annual family lunches. On the balcony overlooking Beirut, covered in a haze of humidity and pollution, her aunts were huddled together with some of their cousins. As much as I tried to enjoy my time with family, as always, questions of waqf were continually on my mind. So at the first lull in their conversion, I found myself imprudently asking about the family waqf and what the DGIW intended to do with it. My grandmother kept quiet as usual, but Tante Alia, Tante Asma, and Tante Inʿam

81. MBSS.H 2003/134.

82. Lebanese law distinguishes and has separate legislation for profit-seeking corporations, known as companies (sing.: *sharika*, pl.: *sharikāt*), and corporations not aimed at profit-sharing, known as foundations (sing.: *muʾassasa*, pl.: *muʾassasāt*). Anglo-American law calls both corporations and distinguishes the nonprofits through taxation. Because not all nonprofits in the U.S. serve public benefit, they are not all completely exempt from taxation.

erupted in a loud discussion. "The mufti is saying that he's going to make it into a mosque," said Tante Alia. Tante In'am added that a soup kitchen is also part of the plan. They started to argue about what the best plan for the waqf would be. Tante Asma was not opposed to the mosque and soup kitchen proposal, since the waqf's charitable recipients were the poor of Beirut. But Tante In'am insisted, "What is the use of the kitchen for the poor of the Muslims? One should not just do something to feed them, but something more productive." When I shyly asked her what *productive* means, she answered, "Look at the Christian waqfs and how they have all these schools to educate their poor." In this statement, Tante In'am echoed critiques of handouts (by both academic and development-oriented institutions) as insufficient, arguing instead for an intervention along the lines "teach a man how to fish," which would help eliminate the need for a kitchen and thus "truly" help the poor. But she then continued, "I once told the DGIW director, 'Forget about this mosque. This land—just make it into a parking lot [Beirut is infamous for its parking shortage], and then spend that money on the poor.'" Everyone laughed and nodded in agreement. In such moments, practitioners like Tante In'am carry forward ideas of the waqf as a revenue-bearing object.

The idea that waqf is associated with profit-producing enterprise is nowhere better represented than by the DGIW itself, because it operates almost like a real estate developer in seeking rent, even if it does not the reinvest these rents but spends them on charitable purposes. For instance, in the past thirty years, it has developed a few waqf parcels that it administers in downtown Beirut into shops and offices, through a financing model of design-build-operate-transfer. A 1982 report of the DGIW resembles a building portfolio. The opening remarks of the grand mufti are entitled "The Development of Waqf Resources [*al-Mawārid al-Waqfiyya*] Is Our Means to Energize Islamic *Da'wa*." The creation of revenue-bearing projects on waqfed land is key in such a development, as the revenue generated goes to finance the work of mosque personnel, "religion" teachers in public schools, scholars, administrators, and *da'wa* more broadly. The grand mufti called for "stirring the wheel of waqf development in order to provide a fixed revenue [as opposed to needing to constantly collect donations] for a budget that can support such an effort" (al-Mudiriyya al-'Amma li'l-Awqaf al-Islamiyya 1982, 3). One can see that even when waqf is linked to sustainable income, its revenue is spent on "energizing Islamic *da'wa*" and revitalizing Islamic tradition, rather than on improvement, accumulation, or more building projects.

CONCLUSION

In this chapter, we have seen how the late Ḥanafī Ottoman waqf was an object in property relations, mediating connections between God and founders and among humans, in a horizon bound by the hereafter. Even though waqf was then used as a moral person *in practice*, and both its administrator and beneficiaries had limited liability, it was not legally theorized as such in the Ottoman late Ḥanafī library.

Waqfs usually involved an immovable whose ownership founders surrendered to God and whose use and usufruct they dedicated to particular people, groups, or institutions. To engage in a rent- and profit-producing economic activity whose revenues went to a charitable cause was an act of charity that not only benefited humans but also brought founders closer to God in the hereafter. In Ottoman waqf, the horizon of property relations was not simply one's lifetime or that of one's offspring; the hereafter, an unknown future of accountability, guided action in the here and now. Calculations for one's well-being in this far-off future and the desire to please God suffused property relations. While waqfs were certainly important material assets that connected the family of the founder or a class of people, their owner was God. Waqfs were thus distinguished from other forms of voluntary charitable gifts like food or other consumables that are present-centered or bound by the lifetime of the recipient. Yet, the future in the temporality of tradition is not one of progress and improvement, of increasing wealth and eradicating poverty, but one of common patterns and cyclical time: human beings procreating, living, worshipping God, always divided into rich and poor. In late-Ottoman Beirut, waqf was part of a property regime that included not only an object and the claims of individuals and the collectivity but also God's claims and the desire to please him.

Today, waqf has mostly become a moral person in property relations. The transformation of waqf into a legal subject was made possible by modern legal reforms during Ottoman rule but especially in the French Mandate, which formalized the notion of a moral person, sought to concentrate various property rights with a single owner, and subjected property, NGOs, and people to different jurisdictions. Yet, it was only during the civil war that these legal openings came together to initiate a revival of the waqf as a moral person. Today, God is not named as the owner of the immovable in the real estate registry; it is rather the waqf as a moral person that is. With the waqf a moral person, it came to own assets, and God exited the network of entities involved in property relations, which are now limited to people, groups, and institutions. Less present in the legal definition of waqf in the Real Estate Code, God stands on the side, in a more abstract way, separate from the hustle and bustle of property relations and economic activity of leasing, building, or fructifying the land. The economic activity and profits that financed the waqf became external to the act of charity. Even more, as historian of South Asia Ritu Birla concisely put it, starting in the 1880s, charity came to be conceived in the law as "the corrective to profit," with the introduction of the private/public distinction in tax law (2009, 55).[83] To please God, waqf founders chose instead to do explicitly religious projects like mosques and Islamic centers.

83. In the Islamic tradition, obligatory alms purified wealth (Hallaq 2009, 231); see also Mittermaier (2013) for an ethnographic account of different economic theologies of charitable giving. Yet, wealth lawfully acquired and purified through taxation did not have the guilt that is associated with it in certain Christian traditions, as in Matthew 19:24: "It is easier for a camel to go through the eye of a needle than for someone who is rich to enter the kingdom of God." On the problem of wealth in early Christianity, see, for example, Brown (2012).

Yet, the understanding of waqf as an (inalienable) object continues to loom over contemporary waqf practices. It is carried through practitioners who have experienced waqf as an object in property relations and who then reinscribe and perpetuate this practice in new material objects and allow for these older ideas of charity mixing "economy" and "religion" to pervade the built environment and to act as reminders that things could be otherwise. The continuity of understandings of waqf as an object is also possible because of what one of my interlocutors called the "*flou*" of the law, its indeterminacy, as well as the multiple jurisdictions over waqfs in the Lebanese state. We turn in the next chapter to these indeterminacies and complexities borne out of the changing architecture of state, law, and religion, which we will discuss in the relation of the state to waqf administration.

2

State, Law, and the "Muslim Community"

I arrived early at Dar al-Fatwa, the official Sunni authority in Lebanon, housed in a small complex in Beirut.[1] In the lobby under a Lebanese flag, a police officer in uniform sat behind a table with a register. The officer took down my name and that of the person I was meeting, then asked me to pass through a metal detector. These various signs—the flag, the police, the security—signaled that I was entering a state building. It was one of my earliest meetings with the head of the Directorate General of Islamic Waqfs (DGIW). As I was discussing my project with him and asking for permission to conduct research there, he tried to convince me that a worthy project would be collecting all legislation pertaining to waqf for my dissertation.[2] Coming from the second highest authority on waqf after the grand mufti, this suggestion took me by surprise. Indeed, the DGIW is represented in the legislative council in charge of many of these laws, the Supreme Islamic Legal Council (SILC), so I was puzzled that there was no such collection at the DGIW itself.[3]

1. Dar al-Fatwa, or literally "the house of fatwa," is the complex that houses the grand mufti and the institutions of official Sunni Islam. The term is used figuratively to refer to official religious Sunni Muslim authority.

2. The gendered aspect of such advice, which I received time and again, should not escape the reader.

3. Note how the Sunnism of these institutions is unmarked. For instance, the Supreme Islamic Legal Council is the Sunni one, but the Shiʿi one is qualified with *Shiʿi*. I will discuss the reasons of this unmarkedness in this chapter.

The director then handed me a SILC decision published in 2003 in the *Official (Legal) Gazette of the Lebanese Republic.*[4] The decision required the DGIW to be named the administrator of any new mosque or prayer hall, even if a private individual or an association had funded its construction and upkeep.[5] That was even more puzzling to me because attempts at state control of waqfs, in the form of administration and supervision, had a long history—starting with the Ottomans, before Lebanon even existed as a nation-state—as I knew from reading the literature on waqfs and from various documents I had collected at the Ottoman archives. That the SILC still needed to issue laws to assert the DGIW's control over mosques suggested that the Ottoman project of state control of mosques and waqfs was still not realized two hundred years later in contemporary Lebanon. What do these paradoxes—the DGIW's apparent ignorance of all waqf-related legislation and the continued need to reassert state control of waqfs despite two hundred years of such attempts—tell us about the nature of the modern state and its use of law and about shariʿa-originating practices like waqf in contemporary Lebanon?[6]

This chapter traces these paradoxes to the nature of the DGIW as a part of the modern state and as a new actor added to the cast of characters involved in the administration of waqf before the long nineteenth century. Indeed, this encounter with the director, duly noted in my notebook with plentiful exclamation and interrogation points, drove me to dig into the history of the DGIW and of those in charge of administering and supervising waqfs. I started to look at both library and Ottoman archive anew: Who appointed administrators? What was the procedure for such appointments? What was the role of qadis in these appointments? Before the reforms of the nineteenth century, which affected Beirut waqfs in the 1850s, three main individuals were involved in the administration of the waqf: the founder, the administrator, and the qadi. Under the supervision of the qadi, each waqf was individually administered according to the founder's stipulations as noted in its foundation deed or according to customary practice when no such document existed. Yet, the qadi's supervision was only nominal and there were no audit procedures: qadis interfered only when beneficiaries and administrators filed lawsuits. Centralized waqf administration and supervision was created in 1826 with the foundation of the Waqf Ministry in Istanbul, among modernizing reforms. The genesis of the DGIW in the modern state explains some of the

4. In the legal hierarchy, decisions (*qarārāt*) are at the lowest end of the scale, followed by legislative decrees (*marāsīm ishtirāʿiyya*), laws (*qawānīn*), the constitution, and international conventions.

5. This requirement differs strikingly from the lax *fiqh* requirements with regard to waqf foundation for mosques: if someone builds a mosque, the act of prayer in it makes it into a de facto waqf without the requirement of delivery to an administrator or the ruling of a judge (Ibn ʿAbidin, *Ḥāshiya*, 3:369).

6. I urge the reader not to assume that this lack of control is due to the "weakness" of the Lebanese state, as I explain below. On the effects of the trope of the weak state in Lebanon, see Kosmatopoulos (2011). For a broader review of the anthropology of the state in the Middle East, which addresses the weakness and absence of the state in popular discourse there, see Obeid (2015).

contradictions of the DGIW's (and before it the Waqf Ministry's) lack of control over waqfs and waqf law. I show how intra-state and intra-institutional competition rooted in secular questioning perpetuated the impossibility of the DGIW "controlling" both waqfs and legislation of waqf. Waqf founders and administrators regularly resorted to "jurisdictional politics," conflicts among different state institutions over jurisdiction of waqf, to find the authority most sympathetic to their cause.

At the same time, the specific shape jurisdictional politics takes is historically contingent on the different configurations of the state, law, and Muslim (Sunni) community in the Ottoman, colonial, and postcolonial periods. Therefore, I turn the spotlight on three significant moments in the administration of waqfs in Beirut (1850, 1921, and 2003) to illuminate how these different configurations allowed for different possibilities for the state's administration and supervision of waqf. In some ways, then, the chapter also contours what I called *architecture* in the introduction—the "context" and state configuration (particularly the relation of the state to the shariʿa) under which individual waqf founders operate and which determine the possibilities of waqf practices.

I show how, when an Ottoman Islamic state attempted to take over the supervision and administration of some Beiruti waqfs—what I refer to as "state control" in this chapter as a shorthand—through an 1850 imperial decree (*firmân*) (VGM300.82) and attach them to the Waqf Ministry that had been founded in 1826, it drew on arguments from within the Islamic tradition but also advanced a new ideal of "good management." Most of the regulations the Ottoman state introduced ushered in techniques of micromanagement with standardized procedures of accounting and calculation, or regulations rather than laws, making waqfs a resource to be managed and developed. Such techniques required many innovations: new officials in the peripheries, new chain of approvals, new standardized registers, new offices, and new archives. These requirements produced the effect of a state that now stood apart from society and from these practices (Mitchell 2006). Because this effect is dependent on practices, their continued performance is necessary to maintain it; this chapter suggests that the repeated attempts at regulation are not a failure of the state or a weakness thereof but are a product of what one of my interlocutors called the "*flou*," the blurriness, of waqf law and administration. The *flou* is what necessitates further intervention and practices that seek to reproduce the state effect.

The French colonial power took over the state apparatus and claimed supervision of these same waqfs through a 1921 law that created the General Waqf Supervision to replace the Ottoman Waqf Ministry. The techniques through which waqfs were governed and their conceptualization as "real estate wealth" remained the same; these are modern techniques of government. However, the French Mandate introduced new arguments and a new arrangement for administration reflecting the new architecture of state, law, and religion. In this new architecture, sometimes termed the dual legal system of personal status law and civil law (Thompson 2000, 113–15), the "Muslim community,"[7] now conceived of as one sect (*ṭāʾifa*) among the eighteen recognized by the state, had jurisdiction over the personal status of its congregants. Because the various communities were independent legal entities with financial autonomy, the state itself defined the waqf directorate as an independent public authority. It remained under the umbrella of the state, in an ever-ambiguous independence, at the "margins of the state."[8] Triggered by the secular questioning that subjected waqf to a legal regime that differentiated between religion and economy, the Mandatory power placed some waqfs within the domain of the religious and created waqf as a patrimony that the "Muslim community" owns, administers, and regulates collectively, dividing jurisdiction over it between shariʿa courts and the General Waqf Supervision. This transformation of waqf into the religious property of a sect is what I call its sectarianization. Yet, concurrently, because waqfs also involve real estate, they fell under the jurisdiction of civil courts. This attempt to fit waqf into these legal categories and jurisdictions contributes to the *flou* of waqf law in the Lebanese Republic, and in fact applies to much of law, making these observations about institutions at the margins of the state much more central to the modern state. This blurriness allowed waqf practitioners to engage in jurisdictional politics, triggering the constant need for the assertion of state control through regulations like Decision 42 of 2003.

OTTOMAN LATE ḤANAFĪ WAQF ADMINISTRATION: INDIVIDUALIZED AND QADI SUPERVISED

The Interplay of the Founder's Will and the Law

Let us first turn to the library and the way its manuals envisage the administration and supervision of waqfs under an Islamic state that implements the shariʿa. The administrator, along with the founder and the qadi, form the main cast of

7. Early French archival documents on waqf use *Muslim community* to include both Shiʿi and Sunni waqfs. It was not until 1926 that the Shiʿa were recognized as a sect with their own shariʿa courts (Weiss 2010, 100–108), and the term *Muslim community* came to be the unmarked designation of the Muslim Sunni community instead of encompassing the Sunnis and the Shiʿa as an unrecognized unorthodox sect. However, in my discussions of French waqf legislation, I continue to use the term *Muslim community*, as used in the law, because the question remains as to how long waqf supervision remained applicable to both Sunnis and Shiʿis and when it came to mean just the unmarked Sunni waqf. Max Weiss's work shows that Shiʿis started to use the Shiʿi courts for disputes over waqfs, but it is unclear whether any of the Shiʿi mosques and shrines were considered seized or semiautonomous by the Ottoman Waqf Ministry and thus fell under the jurisdiction of the new French waqf administration. 1967 Law 72 and Decision 15, which created and organized the Supreme Islamic Shiʿi Council (SISC), also mandated the formation of a General Waqf Committee in the SISC.

8. I borrow this expression from the title of an edited volume of essays on anthropology of the state (Das and Poole 2004).

characters in the library's discussions of waqf. A large part of the chapter on waqf in *fiqh* books of the Ottoman late Ḥanafī library serves to determine jurisdiction: the rights and responsibilities of the founder, administrator, and qadi involved with the waqf. What does each of these characters stand for with respect to the waqf?

As the original owner, the founder of the waqf is the highest authority in decision-making concerning the waqf—guided ultimately by the shariʿa. In the foundation deed, the founder can specify the manner of administration up to the smallest minutiae. As long as these stipulations do not contradict the law (*sharʿ*),[9] they form guidelines that the administrator needs to follow. As the famous dictum goes, "The stipulation of the founder is like God's law" ("sharṭ al-wāqif ka-naṣṣ al-shāriʿ") (Ibn Nujaym, *Baḥr*, 5:245). However, Ibn Nujaym expands on the limits of this statement as a rule, quoting from other scholars in a "consensus of the *umma*" (*ijmāʿ*) that some of the stipulations of the founders are valid and can be followed, while others are not. He follows another scholar's explanation that the dictum is true in "its meaning and guiding principle, and not in its necessity" ("fī al-fahm wa al-dalāla lā fī wujūb al-ʿamal") (*Baḥr*, 5:245). This qualification implies that the text of the founder is understood to be a felicitous representation of the founder's desires and thoughts, and that the language of the text represents common understandings. The administrator and the qadi can go back to the text (*naṣṣ*) of the foundation and use it as an accurate representation of the will of the founder. Contra Ibn Nujaym, Ibn ʿAbidin, writing in the nineteenth century, uses the same phrase, with three positive injunctions: the dictum is true in "its meaning, signification, *and* necessity." This is not to be taken to mean that the stipulations of the founder apply even if they are contrary to the law, but that they are necessary when they do not contradict it. However, if these stipulations contradict the law, the qadi and the administrator have the right or even the duty not to follow them. For instance, an administrator who breaches fiduciary duty (*khāʾin*), whether the administrator is the founder or named by the founder, is to be removed from his position "*even* in the case that the founder has stipulated he should not be removed—that is, that the qadi and the sultan should not remove him—because this is a stipulation that is contrary to the *sharʿ*" (al-ʿAyni, *Ramz*, 1:347, italics mine).

The stipulations of the founder nevertheless occupy a central part in running the waqf. While Islamic law provides general rules on the jurisdiction of the administrator (and that of the qadi), these apply only when the founder has not stipulated particular conditions. For instance, Ibn Nujaym discusses at length when officeholders who receive a share of the revenues of the waqf for the fulfillment of a certain function (like imams, callers for prayers, teachers, and

9. *Sharʿ* shares the same root verb as *shariʿa* and is often used as a synonym. However, when authors of fiqh manuals refer to God's law in its varying appearances and interpretations (like the laws they are producing), they use *sharʿ* rather than *shariʿa*; therefore I tend to use it.

students) forfeit their share: the acceptable length of their absence, the reasons for the absence, their location. However, the section ends with a caveat: "But, if the founder has stipulated conditions [contrary to Ibn Nujaym's recommendation], they shall be followed" (*Baḥr*, 5:227). When the stipulations do not contradict the law, they acquire priority in the running of the affairs of the waqfs over the laws of jurists in commentaries and fatwas. In the presence of founder stipulations, waqfs should be treated not according to their general aims but according to the particulars laid down by the founders. For instance, if a waqf's revenues support stipends of fiqh teachers and students at a particular school, they cannot be spent on these teachers and students if they do not attend this school—even if they are engaged in teaching and learning somewhere else. In the Ottoman canon, the administration of the waqf is very tightly bound to the stipulations of the founder, even if the administrator, as we shall see, takes care of the general benefit of the waqf. The benefit of the waqf is not an abstract good to be achieved as the administrator sees fit. Rather, it is achieved by fulfilling the stipulations of the founder as long as these do not contradict the law.

The Role of the Administrator

The second major character in waqf administration is the administrator, which legal manuals refer to interchangeably as *mutawallī* (administrator), *nāẓir* (supervisor), and *qayyim* (superintendent),[10] even if in practice, one of these terms might be more dominant in a certain area.[11] With the founder no longer an owner, it is the administrator who then makes decisions for the waqf and is responsible and will

10. This multiplicity is reflected in the archive, where the wording of the appointment of an administrator is "[the judge] appointed and assigned him *nāẓiran mutawalliyan* and *qayyiman* who can speak [*mutakalliman*] for the waqf," conflating the three different words for *administrator* (MBSS. S03/160). The structure of the sentence, apposition and alliteration, using parallel phrases (*nāẓiran mutawalliyan* and *qayyiman mutakalliman*) that rhyme, emphasizes the equivalence of these terms. In addition, the document refers to the position of the administrator as "*naẓar wa tawliya*." At the Haṣṣeki Sultan soup kitchen in Jerusalem, Amy Singer distinguishes between a supervisor (*nāẓır*); the chief white eunuch at the Topkapı Palace in Istanbul, who had "ultimate responsibility for its [the waqf's] proper functioning"; and a local administrator or "general manager" (*mutawallī*) (2002, 54–55). It is possible that in Jerusalem as in the rest of the waqfs administered by the chief eunuchs (and other key officials like the grand vizier or the *şeyhülislâm*), the supervisor and administrator are not two separate positions, but that the administratorship held by the chief eunuch is farmed out or delegated to a local administrator. For a similar explanation of these different persons as delegates, see Eychenne's (2018) description of the administrator of the waqfs of the Umayyad mosque in Damascus in Mamluk times.

11. In Egypt, *nāẓir* seems to have been the most common term (ʿAfifi 1991, 86–94), whereas in the Beirut court record *mutawallī* seems to be more prevalent, even though *nāẓir* is also used. Note also that the legal manuals speak of the administrator in the singular when the size of the waqf might necessitate a managerial team with various specialists (ʿAfifi 1991, 83). In Beirut, most waqfs had one administrator, or two at most.

be accountable and liable for any problems due to the administrator's negligence.[12] Indeed, the person whom the founder appoints as an administrator is actually the founder's agent (*wakīl*) (al-Khassaf 1999, 23, 168) and is responsible for carrying out the wishes of the founder as spelled out in the waqf deed. As an agent, the mutawallī, or the *waliyy* in al-Khassaf's terminology, stands in the place of the founder[13] (al-Khassaf 1999, 168). This designation gives the administrator executive power in managing the affairs of the waqf as an agent represents the principal who delegates power to that agent to act on his or her behalf. A similar description of the administrator can be found in Ibn Nujaym's discussion, when he advances that "the mutawallī is the agent [*wakīl*] of the founder" (*Baḥr*, 5:242), and "the nāẓir is either a guardian [*waṣiyy*] or an agent [*wakīl*]" (*Baḥr*, 5:241), where *guardian* and *agent* are used interchangeably because they both act on behalf of another person.[14] What are the duties and areas of jurisdiction of the administrator over waqf affairs? What are the administrator's rights?

The tasks of the administrator fall into three main categories: caring for the waqf (repairs),[15] exploiting the waqf (renting or planting), and fulfilling its purpose (distributing revenues to beneficiaries) (Ibn Nujaym, *Baḥr*, 5:243–44). The general duty of the administrator is to attend to the benefit of the waqf (*yaqūm bi-maṣāliḥ al-waqf*). However, the administrator's duties are not set in stone; they vary with custom (*bi-ḥasab al-ʿurf*), argues Ibn Nujaym, with support from al-Khassaf: "What the founder assigns to the mutawallī does not have fixed limits, but it is determined according to custom and practice [*mā taʿāraf ʿalayh al-nās*]" (*Baḥr*, 5:243). The administrator is not required to do more than what other administrators do. Some of an administrator's duties can be taken up by specific individuals stipulated by the founder: a rent collector (*jābī*) can gather rents and taxes from tenants, and a treasurer (*ṣayrafiyy*) can check and weigh the money (*Baḥr*, 5:244). It is the administrator's responsibility to sue tenants (e.g., if they do not pay rent). All these functions and actions give the administrator privileges and rights to

12. The extent of his or her responsibility is represented in the framing of his holding of the waqf as a *yad amāna* (possession that does not incur liability except for negligence) rather than as a *yad ḍamān* (possession that incurs liability).

13. The administrator also becomes the founder's testamentary executor (*waṣiyy*) if the founder extends the appointment after his or her death.

14. Ibn Nujaym reports a discussion in al-Khassaf's *Adab al-Qāḍī* where he distinguishes between a guardian (*waṣiyy*) and a (waqf) superintendent (*qayyim*). For al-Khassaf, "the guardian is delegated preservation [*ḥifẓ*] and management/taking action [*taṣarruf*] whereas the superintendent is only delegated preservation without prerogative of action" (Ibn Nujaym, *Baḥr*, 5:243). According to this distinction, the waqf superintendent does not have the prerogative to take decisions and actions for the waqf, but simply follows rules. However, Ibn Nujaym establishes that the jurists of this time and place see that the duties of both guardians and caretakers necessitate spending (*infāq*) and therefore they have equal responsibilities, and so the terms are interchangeable and that is the authoritative opinion.

15. In order to produce revenues that will allow the fulfillment of the charitable purpose of the waqf, taking care of the waqfed assets through repairs and renovation is absolutely necessary. Jurists put repairs as a priority even if it is not stipulated by the founder (al-ʿAyni, *Ramz*, 1:346).

waqf revenues, usually in the form of a wage. These rights arise from the labor the administrator puts in as a caretaker for the waqf. If the care of the waqf does not require any labor, the administrator does not have any right to the fee. Ibn Nujaym illustrates this condition with the example of a mill whose beneficiaries take their shares directly from the mill's long-term tenant. In this case, the administrator does not receive any fees, because "what he receives is by way of wage, and there is no wage without labor" (*Baḥr*, 5:244).

The labor of the administrator varied greatly depending on the size and the type of the waqf. In an imperial soup kitchen, supported by dozens of waqf villages and feeding hundreds of poor people daily, the administrator had to coordinate personnel, provisions, and revenues and supervise the functioning of the kitchen, which might require a fair amount of labor (Singer 2002). In large waqfs, like those in Algeria dedicated to Mecca and Medina, known as the Haramayn, which accumulated many smaller waqfs, a board of four members with an average of a five-year tenure was in charge of administration (Hoexter 1998). In smaller waqfs, the administrator acted as a landlord and was responsible for securing tenants, collecting rents, and taking care of repairs. Most administratorships did not constitute full-time jobs in the way we understand them today, since they mostly involved collecting rents for a few assets. Yet, even in larger waqfs, administrators held other functions, such as belonging to the military-administrative class (Singer 2002, 104–5). Small waqf administrators could be merchants, artisans, clerks, imams, or mothers at home. Given that their fees were mostly nominal, one would be hard-pressed to call them a "rentier" class. The administrators of mosque-waqfs, especially a town's congregational mosque (like the ʿUmari Mosque, with its assets and the mosque itself to manage), would have more work than those of small waqfs.

The Role of the Qadi

If the administrator has such wide agentive powers on the waqf, why then is the qadi so present in Islamic legal discussions about the role of the administrator? In what capacity does the qadi intervene with the administrator and within the affairs of the waqf, and what areas fall under the qadi's jurisdiction? The question is especially important given the maxim that Ibn ʿAbidin describes: "The particular jurisdiction overrides the general one" (*Ḥāshiya*, 3:381).[16] Therefore, the functions of an administrator appointed by a qadi with general jurisdiction on waqf as part of the shariʿa cannot be fulfilled, reversed, or superseded by the qadi when the administrator is present, even if the qadi himself appointed the administrator. It would be useful to go into some detail here on who the qadi is, in what capacity the qadi is appointed, and by whom.

16. The maxim is extracted from Ibn Nujaym's classic legal maxims manual, *al-Ashbāh wa al-Naẓāʾir* (1999), and cited by Ibn ʿAbidin (*Ḥāshiya*, 3:381).

The sultan delegates qadis, who thus derive their power from him. The qadi, then, stands in for the sultan in the capacity to administer justice, including in waqf affairs. The sultan, however, retains the "power to do justice in person" (Tyan and Káldy-Nagy 2012), which explains the occasional designation of the ruler—sometimes with a qadi, sometimes not—as a possible player in waqf affairs. For instance, the sultan himself can appoint an administrator.[17] It is also because of this retained power that al-ʿAyni names both the qadi and the sultan as authorities with the power to dismiss an administrator who breaches fiduciary duty (*Ramz*, 1:347). Nonetheless, in this case too, the legal maxim that the particular trumps the general jurisdiction prohibits the sultan from dismissing and reversing a "just" decision by a qadi he appointed. This is the core of the delegation of power.

Yet, Ibn Nujaym finds it necessary to stop his discussion of the administrator's appointment in order to warn about which qadi has the right "to nominate a guardian (*waṣiyy*), a mutawallī, and to supervise waqfs" (*Baḥr*, 5:233). A long discussion ensues about whether any qadi, unrestricted or unqualified, can unconditionally deal with the affairs of the waqf. Ibn Nujaym argues that a qadi can supervise waqfs only if the qadi's appointment letter specifies this domain to be under his jurisdiction. Only the *qāḍī al-quḍāt*, the chief justice, can automatically deal with any and all waqf affairs because "obviously such an appointment is like describing these domains of jurisdiction in the appointment letter" (Ibn Nujaym, *Baḥr*, 5:233). This is obvious to Ibn Nujaym because the chief justice is the highest judiciary authority, to whom all judiciary power is delegated and who has the right to appoint delegates. This quibble over which judges have jurisdiction over waqf arises at the historic conjuncture when Ibn Nujaym is writing because of "well-known" instances of corrupt judges annulling waqfs. It presents an attempt to restrict the actions of regular judges with regard to waqf by making the chief justice the sole authority on waqf.[18]

As delegates of the sultan and his power to administer justice and apply the *sharʿ*, qadis can intervene in the actions of the founder and the administrator.

17. Political theory manuals that define the jurisdiction, authority, and power of the sultan place the supervision of waqfs under the sultan's direct justice (*wilāyat al-maẓālim*) (on the *maẓālim*, see Tillier 2015). It is the duty of the sultan to inspect public (*ʿāmma*) waqfs, which in this context means waqfs serving a broad public, and to make sure that they are serving their purposes based on their waqf deed. In the case of waqfs dedicated to particular individuals and groups, the sultan can interfere only if a lawsuit is brought to him: see Hoexter (1995); and Meier (2002). The Ottomans did not have special courts where sultans administered justice, but one can interpret the sultan's initiatives at accession like inventory and confirmation of public waqfs as a continuation of this jurisdiction.

18. See the discussion in chapter 5 when this issue arises with regard to exceptional substitutions (*istibdāl*) of ruined waqfs. See also van Leeuwen's discussion of a treatise from eighteenth-century Damascus about such exchanges and the power of judges (1999, 59–65). Van Leeuwen notes that substitutions appear only in the registers of the chief justices, showing that the authority of delegate judges was restricted. In Beirut there was only one judge, making it impossible to confront the library with the archive.

The jurisdiction of the judge regarding waqf includes appointing the administrator, making sure the administrator follows the *sharʿ*, and if not, dismissing the administrator or revoking any of the administrator's decisions, which could include appointments to offices, leases, and other affairs of the waqf.

The qadis' jurisdiction over the appointment of administrators vary according to the stipulations of founders. Many times, administrators are appointed by the founder or based on the founder's stipulations. In this case, and when there is no contention over the administrator, there is no need for an official appointment by the qadi. The appointment of an administrator falls under the qadi's jurisdiction in four cases: if the founder dies without having nominated an administrator;[19] if the administrator appointed by the founder dies after the death of the founder; if the administrator does not fulfill his or her duties towards the waqf; or if the administrator declares to the qadi the wish not to be an administrator anymore (Ibn Nujaym, *Baḥr*, 5:232–35). It is therefore when there is no clear administrator that the judge appoints one.

These pronouncements of the jurists on the role of the qadi in the late Ottoman library are echoed in the archive. The appointments of administrators recorded in Beirut's shariʿa court in the first half of the nineteenth century confirm these roles of the qadi; very few appointments for family waqfs exist in the records, as these were usually chosen from the family of the founder or following founder stipulations. In the few appointments that do exist (e.g., MBSS.S02/03, MBSS.S03/160, MBSS.S36/77–8/1052, MBSS.S36/78–9/1055), claimants to the position of administrator brought forward trustworthy community members whose reports confirmed their claims (that the foundation deed gives them the right to be an administrator, and that they are morally upright, and so on). Upon hearing these reports, the judge appointed the claimant as an administrator, urging the claimant to care for the benefit of the waqf, to follow the stipulations of the founder, and to fear God in all the claimant does. All these summaries mention that the position had been vacant, signaling a conflict, which might explain the reason for the few appointments: when there is agreement and transmission of the position from father to son, as is the case for most waqfs, a judge is not involved.

19. Ibn Nujaym is here again much more cautious. He qualifies the absoluteness of this rule with some very pragmatic considerations. If some beneficiaries of a waqf, renowned for their virtue and righteousness, name a mutawallī in the absence of a stipulation, Ibn Nujaym considers this appointment not only valid without the approval of a qadi but also even commendable. Indeed, in "our age, given what is known about the greed of qadis towards waqf property [*amwāl*]" (*Baḥr*, 5:233), such an appointment would uphold the interests of the waqf better. This sidelining of judges continues the attempt discussed above to restrict judges' authority over waqf by allowing only the chief justice to have such jurisdiction. Pragmatic considerations of the character and practices of contemporaries are worth investigating further in terms of the legal reasoning and the weighing of opinions, but they are outside the scope of this book. See van Leeuwen (1999) and Ayoub (2014) for discussion of jurists incorporating arguments about "our present time" in their reasoning.

Whether or not the qadi directly appointed the administrator, a second responsibility of the qadi is supervising the administrator. The qadi makes sure the administrator is trustworthy, renting as required, repairing the assets of the waqf, and distributing the revenues. The qadi does so as a representative of the sultan for the administration of justice, but also as a representative of the poor and the orphans. "The qadi is delegated with looking after the poor and the dead" (Ibn Nujaym, *Baḥr*, 5:246–47). If the administrator stands for the founder, the judge stands for those who are many times the ultimate beneficiaries of the waqf: the poor and the orphans, those who cannot represent themselves (the poor because they are a collectivity, the orphans because they are minors). In both these capacities, the judge supervises the administrator.

The manuals of the library, while making supervision of the administrator a qadi's duty, do not provide a standardized process (like requiring individual administrators to submit accounting records periodically) through which a qadi could discover if an administrator is acting in the best interest of the waqf or breaching fiduciary trust. It seems that the choice of an *upright* administrator was taken to guarantee the care of the waqf and its best interests. One of the rare instances where we get a glimpse of the process through which a judge comes to know about the mismanagement of the waqf is the case of an administrator renting waqf assets below market rate. Ibn Nujaym mentions that the "inhabitants of the neighborhood" (*ahl al-maḥalla*) cannot be excused for remaining silent on such an abuse (*Baḥr*, 5:235). In his example, moral and communal mechanisms reflect a commitment to live as good Muslims, which ensures the good administration of the waqf, rather than a strict process of accountability.[20] Thus, the *administration* of waqf remained in the hands of individual administrators, and the state/imperial *supervision* of waqfs via qadis was limited to contentious appointments and lawsuits rather than being a regular practice that reinscribed the state's sovereignty.

THE 1850 DECREE: WAQF AS REAL ESTATE WEALTH AND THE BEGINNINGS OF STATE ADMINISTRATION

The nineteenth century witnessed a change in this order of waqf administration, one that is most often described as a transition to "imperial control" over waqfs

20. Hoexter (1995) argues that the silence of the fiqh on these issues stems from the fact that waqfs involve rights of God, which are upheld by the state under *siyāsa*. Therefore, the ruler has the prerogative to issue detailed administrative laws about supervision, auditing, and the like. However, this manner of administration would apply only when the waqfs have reached their final eternal charitable beneficiaries. Furthermore, as Hoexter notes, even waqfs that devolved to state administration continued to follow the shariʿa, except with regard to the distribution of income (1995, 151–52). Based on her extensive research on the Haramayn waqf, whose patrimony is mostly constituted of hundreds of small waqfs whose particular beneficiaries have been extinguished and which reverted to the poor of Mecca and Medina, Hoexter found that a fixed amount, rather than all the funds, were sent to the poor of the Haramayn and that income from the Haramayn waqf was also allocated to other endowments.

(Barnes 1986, 3). Indeed, in 1826 the Waqf Ministry was created,[21] and slowly, through a protracted process, imperial orders like the Sultanic Decree (*firmân*) of 1850 [1266] seized various waqfs in the center and the provinces and put them under the administration and supervision of the Waqf Ministry.[22] It is important to note that I am not arguing that this was the first time a central waqf administration or a "waqf bureaucracy" existed in the Ottoman Empire or in an Islamic state.[23] Rather, I am more interested in the types of arguments advanced for such an intervention, how they resonated with the production and administration of law in modern states, and the consequences they had on the ways scholars invoke authority. We will see how, by distinguishing between administrators (mutawallīs) and supervisors (nāẓirs)—terms borrowed, then resignified, from the Islamic legal tradition—the Waqf Ministry, a new organ of the Ottoman state (and not an office like that of the chief eunuch, which kept with individualized administration), inserted itself in the fiqh mix of founder, mutawallī, and qadi, stripping qadis of many of their powers *and* jurists of their legislative power on waqf matters. Although before the creation of the Waqf Ministry, there was no "supervisor" separate from the qadi, following its creation, the ministry became exactly such an institution. This bureaucratization and institutionalization of waqf administration, however, had its limits: it was not a clearly formulated project that was simply applied, but a product of multiple rounds of legislation and revisions that were challenged and intermittently followed.

New Distinctions: Administrators versus Supervisors

In the codified waqf manual written at the end of the nineteenth century, which we encountered in the first chapter, Ömer Hilmi Efendi, writing in Istanbul, starts by defining the various key words associated with waqf, including *nāẓir*, *qayyim*, and *mutawallī*. He begins with the latter and provides a description similar to al-ʿAyni's earlier one: "He who is appointed to take care of the affairs of the waqf and to look after its benefit according to the stipulations of the founder in his founding document" (Article 8). According to Hilmi Efendi, *qayyim* is synonymous with

21. For the details of the foundation of the Waqf Ministry, see Barnes (1986).

22. VGM300.82. See Meier (2002) for a description of the reactions of the Damascus Provincial Council to the order to seize Damascus mosques.

23. In Egypt, where the Shāfiʿī and Mālikī schools dominated and a good example because it is densely studied, a waqf council (*dīwān al-aḥbās*) had existed since Umayyad rule (seventh century CE) if not earlier. Behrens-Abouseif (2012) mentions that in the Abbasid period, the judges inspected waqfs monthly and collected all incomes and gave them to the council, which spent them on charitable purposes independently of the will of the founder. This latter practice seems very jarring to a student of late Ḥanafīs who consider respecting the wishes of the founder especially as to expenditures to be paramount. It is difficult to know whether this was an exceptional measure in exceptional times or whether flexibility in expenditures was more common in the early doctrine or in other *madhhabs*. In Mamluk Egypt, the waqf council was in charge of the administration of *rizaq aḥbāsiyya* (treasury lands dedicated to particular people for charitable reasons) (Amin 1980, 108–12), and the Shāfiʿī judge managed the charitable waqfs (known as *awqāf ḥukmiyya*) (Amin 1980, 113–16).

mutawallī. The nāẓir is "the person appointed to supervise [*naẓāra*] the actions of the mutawallī and to be a reference [*marjaʿan*] for the mutawallī regarding the affairs of the waqf" (Article 11). Hilmi remarks however, that, in certain regions, the word *nāẓir* denotes the mutawallī. While the caveat is certainly correct, it is worth noting that the mutawallī of the imperial waqfs was called *nâẓir-i evkâf-i hümâyûn*—showing that even in Istanbul the distinction between *mutawallī* and *nāẓir* was not as entrenched at this moment as Hilmi's definition suggests.

Even a history of the Imperial Waqf Ministry written in Istanbul in 1917 by one of the premier scholars of the late Ottoman Empire, İbnüelmin Mahmud Kemal,[24] with another "man of knowledge," Hüseyin Hüsâmeddin,[25] declares that "the administration of waqfs is called supervision [*naẓar*]" (Ibnülemin Inal and Hüsâmeddin Yasar 1917, 5). However, the section continues and describes a *new* development: "Lately, the nâẓir to whom the administration of the affairs of the waqf has been conferred by the authority (*waliyy al-amr*) has been called the mutawallī of the waqf, whereas the title of nâẓir has been used more generally. Consequently, the title of nâẓir has been specifically given to those who have been checking the affairs of the mutawallī and to those who have supervised the general administration of Muslim waqfs" (5–6). Unlike İbnüelmin and Hüsâmeddin, Hilmi does not present this development as a historical one.[26] He separates and clearly distinguishes the positions of nāẓir and mutawallī, thereby naturalizing it. Article 303 of Hilmi's waqf manual, for instance, prohibits a single person from being both an administrator and a supervisor of a waqf.[27]

This new distinction between supervisor and administrator served the Waqf Ministry in Istanbul well by increasing its revenue, as waqfs now administered by the ministry had their incomes forwarded to the Ottoman state. Before the creation of the ministry, all waqfs in Beirut were administered by administrators and (nominally) supervised by qadis. The Waqf Ministry introduced a separate office of a "supervisor," distinct from the qadi. The administration/supervision distinction that is normalized rather than historicized for Hilmi (and for the Ottoman state) represents the attempt of the state to take over the jurisdiction of qadis for certain waqf matters. This distinction couches a new arrangement in the old terms of Islamic law and hints at the reorganization of the production and administration of law, and the role of the state in this process as well as in the life of its citizens.

The new Waqf Ministry started as the administrative body for many endowments of Mahmud II (r. 1809–1839) and his father. Because of their size, these endowments required more than a single administrator. However, Mahmud

24. See "Ibnüelmin" in *İslâm Ansiklopedisi*.

25. See "Hüseyin Hüsâmeddin" in *İslâm Ansiklopedisi*.

26. As I argued in chapter 1, this might be traced to his position as an agent of the state.

27. Writing from a semiautonomous Egypt, Qadri Pasha does not incorporate these changes in his manual, which continues with the fiqh terminology, using *mutawallī* and *nāẓir* interchangeably (see, for example, Article 145).

II started to bring more waqfs under the administration of the Waqf Ministry (Barnes 1986, 72–83). After the creation of the Waqf Ministry, waqfs could be classified into three categories depending on their administration and supervision by the Waqf Ministry: seized, semiautonomous, or autonomous. The "seized (or annexed) waqfs" (*awqāf maḍbūṭa*) had the Waqf Ministry as both their administrator and supervisor. This meant that, instead of an individual administrator for these waqfs, an employee of the ministry took charge of renting, collecting the rents, and paying the beneficiaries. That employee was accountable to the ministry and would send the Waqf Ministry in Istanbul accounting documents and any remainder of the revenues of the waqfs after paying the beneficiaries. Second, the "semi-autonomous waqfs" (*awqāf mulḥaqa*) continued to be administered by local administrators according to the wills of their founders, but here too, the administrators had to report to the ministry, which also claimed the remainder of the revenues. Last, the "autonomous (exempt) waqfs" (*awqāf mustathnāt*) did not provide any accounting or remainder of revenue to the ministry, were administered by their own administrators, and remained under the supervision of local qadis. Because the project of the Waqf Ministry was not to reorganize waqfs but arose from individually targeted seizures of waqfs, autonomous waqfs remained the main baseline of waqf administration.

Arguments of the Decree

This new distinction between nāẓir and mutawallī, which takes the appearance of an old one, allowed the Waqf Ministry to legitimize its jurisdiction over certain waqfs, particularly those classified as seized or semiautonomous. The 1850 decree advanced arguments for the Waqf Ministry seizing (Tr: *zabt*, Ar: *ḍabṭ*) *some* mosques in Beirut and Sidon—effectively sacking their current mutawallīs. In the same register, a very similar decree follows, concerning some of the mosques of the city of Tripoli. It appears, therefore, to be very much a formulaic order and part of the Ottoman state's (latest wave of) efforts to claim control over waqfs. But this scripted quality provides insight into the general order of arguments advanced for the claim to seize the administration of some waqfs.[28] Rhetorically, the *firmân* uses repetition, particularly with the aim of discrediting the current mutawallīs and therefore justifying their dismissal. Every time the decree refers to the current mutawallīs, it uses a variant of "those who *claim* to be mutawallīs" ("mütevellîliğî

28. The Ottoman state's decision to examine all waqfs in the sultanate and assess whether their administrators were following the founders' wills, and whether they were fulfilling their duties is itself not a new idea. It is part of the duties of the sultan, as described by political theory manuals like al-Mawardi's *al-Aḥkām al-Sulṭāniyya*, as mentioned in footnote 17. As Barnes elaborates in a short chapter (1986, 60–66), such ideas circulated at various times. Barnes describes the advice of a bureaucrat, Koçi Bey, to Sultan Murad IV (1623–40) to examine all foundations for their validity, proposing that only waqfs that supported mosques and shrines were to be allowed to exist, while nullifying all "family waqfs" (1986, 63). Koçi Bey was mostly concerned with increasing the income of the treasury.

iddiʿâsinde bulunân kesâne"). The first time the decree refers to those holding mutawallīship, it laments that these waqfs have been passing from hand to hand ("şûnun bûnun eyâdîsine geçerek"), a brusque dismissal of the legitimate claims these mutawallīs might have had to their appointments. The decree does not base its claims on slander, however; it draws on Islamic law and bases the legitimacy of its arguments or conclusions on familiar arguments from Islamic legal manuals and fatwa collections in order to justify the dismissal of current mutawallīs.

The three main arguments for dismissal are embezzlement, the absence of official appointment letters in the hands of the administrators, and the neglect of waqf properties and their maintenance. Each one was sufficient for proving the breach of fiduciary trust of the mutawallī. Let us first turn to embezzlement or, as the decree terms it, "ḥâṣilâtlerî ṣarf-i meʾkel." One of the few characteristics of the mutawallī that is explicitly specified in Islamic legal texts is trustworthiness (*amāna*) (al-Khassaf 1999). Therefore, a mutawallī who appropriates and spends waqf revenues contradicts the very definition of a mutawallī, who is supposed to take care of an object entrusted to him or her. Ibn Nujaym, for instance, allows a qadi to change the untrustworthy persons (*ghayr maʾmūn*) in a group of mutawallīs appointed by the founder (*Baḥr*, 5:227). By accusing various mutawallīs of Beirut mosques of embezzlement, the *firmân* therefore creates the legal (*sharʿī*) ground to dismiss them. The decree does not stop here, however. The mutawallīs and other officeholders, the decree claims, do not have in hand founding deeds or official appointment letters. In addition, no record of their appointment exists in Istanbul. The decree argues that these are necessary for appointments, because where an original founding document is missing, the founder's stipulations cannot be known, including whether the founder named an administrator. The absence of an official appointment document opens the mutawallī to dismissal. The last argument that the decree advances concerns the repair, upkeep, and maintenance of the waqf assets (*taʿmîrât ve tanẓîfât esbâbî*), or rather the absence thereof. Here again, the argument draws on one of the most important responsibilities of the mutawallīs in Islamic legal manuals of the library.

Ḥüsn-i Idâre: *A New Understanding of Administration*

While the 1850 Decree justifies state annexation of waqfs based on Islamic law, like saving the waqfs from embezzlement and disrepair, it also advances a more general principle that uncannily resonates with analyses of modern state power: *ḥüsn-i idâre*, or good management.[29] As discussed in the introduction, the nineteenth century saw the rise of governmentality as a form of power, whereby the population (and not territory) becomes the object of government. Economy, then, or "the

29. I surmise that the development of such a mode of government in the Ottoman Empire is not simply an uncanny coincidence but is the result of the transfer of knowledge through the education of Ottoman bureaucrats in Europe. This takes us back to the debates discussed in the introduction about Western influences versus Islamic roots of these reforms.

correct manner of managing individuals, goods and wealth," becomes essential to political practice (Foucault 1991, 92). This governing of people is linked to the governing of things because the things governed (wealth, resources, means of subsistence) are connected to the population and its well-being (Foucault 1991, 95).

The term *ḥüsn-i idâre* appears earlier than the 1850 Decree and in many documents relating to waqf (Öztürk 1995b, 74).[30] The use of the term signals a new conceptualization of waqfs as real estate wealth, which has a reality of its own greater than the sum of its individual parts—each and every waqf—that needs to be developed and whose administration is an area of expertise for bureaucrats. Indeed, whereas records of most waqfs had been kept since the Ottoman conquest (see chapter 4), it was only with the foundation of the Waqf Ministry and its seizing of administration and supervision that uniform methods of administration, statistics, and new accounting methods entered into use. These new methods defined good administration and regulated in greater detail the theretofore sparse fiqh requirement that "the mutawallī aims in his actions for the care of the waqf and its well-being"[31] (Ibn Nujaym, *Baḥr*, 5:235), with the individualized care based on founder stipulations that it presupposes. Good administration and management, in the form of uniform standards scaled up and applied to a large number of waqf objects, create a new reality, making various waqfs equivalent when seen through the lens of their revenues and expenses. Let us turn to the way the decree rearticulated the responsibilities of the mutawallī and the qadi and the practices of good management (*ḥüsn-i idâre*) it introduced.

The Bureaucratization of Mutawallīship. The decree's main consequence and innovation is to claim, for certain waqfs, the position of mutawallī for the Waqf Ministry, thereby bureaucratizing the previously less-rigid mutawallīship by defining the position, salary, and the location out of which the mutawallī operated. Whereas waqf administration outside of Istanbul had been regulated through imperial orders since 1841 [29 Z 1256], controlling administration was not smooth or simple; it involved experimentation, trial and error, and pushback from the provinces. It took several iterations of the regulations—in 1841, 1842, and 1845—before the 1863 Waqf Administration Regulations (Nizâmât-i Idâre-i Vakfiyye, 19 C 1280)[32] delineated the manner of waqf administration and supervision outside

30. The expression *ḥüsn-i idâre* appears in the Gülhane Edict and, therefore, is part of the language of the Tanzimat. Although it is outside the scope of this book, I would be interested in further investigating whether good government carries over from the Islamicate genres of public law/ political theory and mirror for princes and the notion of the circle of justice therein. Linda Darling (2013) mentions "good administration" in the earliest circle of justice elaborations but argues that the form of this good administration differs in different periods.

31. "Yataḥarrā fī taṣarrufātih al-naẓar li'l-waqf wa al-ghibṭa."

32. In Düstûr (Turkey 1872, 2:143–69).

Istanbul.[33] The mutawallī ceased to be that individual whom the founder named or the qadi appointed, someone known for trustworthiness, soundness of mind, and maturity.[34] Administration shifted to a bureaucratic state apparatus, where the individual bureaucrat was replaceable. This shift signals a change from individualized administration to a uniform state policy applied to all seized waqfs.

While earlier mutawallīs mostly held their positions on the side, even in the larger waqfs, the new administrators followed a "career path" as waqf administrators. This was signaled in the change of the title of administrator from a mutawallī to an *evkâf memuru/müdürü*, a waqf employee/director in the very "state-bureaucratic" meaning of employee/director. The *memurs/müdürs* received from the Waqf Ministry a fixed monthly salary according to the hierarchy of provincial waqf directors,[35] 5 percent of the collected waqf revenues for their services,[36] and a uniform fee (Article 47). This bureaucratization also manifested itself in the location from which these mutawallīs operated: earlier mutawallīs probably did their duties as mutawallīs from their home or workplace. The new waqf directors held meetings in the provincial council's building, where the seals and accounting books were kept, signaling that these were tied to the position and not to the individual. With the seizing of many waqfs and their placement under the Waqf Ministry, waqf administration turned into a *service* that the state provided, replacing the three main tasks of the mutawallīs—repairing, leasing and collecting rents, and distributing revenues—and subjecting administration to uniform policies. These practices of administration of many large waqfs in the empire therefore created the state effect, the modern state as an entity independent of those who occupied it, with buildings and bureaucrats' offices, archives, and laws. It created one standard of management for various elements of administration.

The first objects taken by the new management were the accounting techniques of the newly appointed waqf director (*evkâf memuru/müdürü*). Accounting became a "governmental discourse" (Yayla 2011, 11); the 1863 Waqf Administration Regulations contained three long articles describing the way accounting was to be done, from the type of registers to be held to the type of information to be recorded. In total, the waqf director prepared and maintained six types of registers

33. The trial-and-error mechanism, also discussed above in qadi jurisdiction, shows us that there was a necessary process of negotiation between center and periphery. The new system of administration was definitely not a smooth and clean rupture, but a protracted one. As Meier notes, in Damascus, "the old system of control was not replaced all at once, but . . . the reforms were introduced in small steps that led to the coexistence of different controlling agencies" (2002, 215). As this book shows, the new system could not eliminate all previous conditions and practices.

34. This is not to say that administration was always in the hands of a single person, as discussed above, but each waqf was managed differently.

35. According to Öztürk's table of waqf employee salaries (1995b, 101) based on an 1879 revision, Beirut's waqf director, who belongs to grade 1, received a salary of 1,750 qurush (almost double his older salary of 1,000 qurush), while his secretary's salary decreased to 300 qurush (from 400).

36. Except for the Baghdad waqf director who received 10 percent of the revenues.

(a daily register, quarterly registers for revenues and expenditures, a yearly register, a register for seized waqfs, and a register for semiautonomous waqfs, detailing their assets and their beneficiaries). The maintenance of the accounting required a significant amount of labor by the waqf director.

I had gotten a hint at this systematization through my notebook. I was keeping notes during my work at the archive, and as I was ordering the various accounting registers in the Evkaf Defterleri (EV; Waqf Registers) series at the Ottoman state archive in Istanbul, I noticed a variety in the shapes of the accounting books sent from Beirut to Istanbul: most did not amount to more than a few pages, but they were each different in size, type of paper, covers, and binding. No two were alike, but they were never bigger than a large notebook, even if some were tall and skinny. But starting in 1880 (BOA.EV 25057), the registers were printed with fixed column widths and headings. They were truly huge registers (almost 1 m wide and 60 cm tall), which made for long discussions with the staff at the archive on how to make copies as they were extremely inconvenient to handle and were outside the range of the digitizing technology in use (cameras), leading certain sections of the digital copy to be blurry. These new registers were the delayed result of the 1863 regulations in Beirut, which specified that all six types of registers had to follow a sample that the treasury would send (Article 4). It was a new kind of "disciplinary writing technique" (Yayla 2011, 14) where the scribe-cum-bureaucrat was forced by the logic of the register to help create uniform administration, fashioning the bodies of the bureaucrats to the needs of the modern state.[37]

The long list of Beirut accounting records that shows up in the Evkaf Defterleri series at the Ottoman Prime Ministry Archive is a testimony to the productivity of these practices of good management. However, looking more carefully at the registers, one realizes that the regularity and uniformity that good management sought to produce did not materialize as expected, necessitating further instructions and regulation. Thus, despite the over one hundred registers sent from Beirut, covering the sixty-five years of administration by the Waqf Ministry (1850–1914), it is hard to find a series of accounts that is uninterrupted for a few years, particularly with the required trimestrial accounting.

By appending the administration of some waqfs to the Waqf Ministry, the decree also subsumed the collection of revenues to the new ministry, which changed revenue collection both in Istanbul and in the provinces. In the imperial center, instead of a supervisor (like the chief black eunuch) farming out various administratorships, the Finance Ministry employed new waqf collectors (*muaccalât nâẓirî*,

37. The scribes who were at the service of the Porte before the Tanzimat also went through training that subjected them to uniform ways of writing and notation. Looking at a pre-Tanzimat series at the Ottoman archive, like the Mühimme Registers, reveals a consistency in style. As Messick argues in the case of Yemen, in the older order the form of the registers was dictated by the content, because the writer organized the blank pages of registers and registered their writing and authority: "The text was suffused with the human presence" (1993, 240).

or, later, *muaccalât müdürü*) to collect the waqf revenues. In the provinces, instead of the administrators themselves collecting rents, taxes, and various revenues owed to the waqf and then paying beneficiaries and expenditures, salaried collectors took over. The collectors took out taxes (the tithe, *ʿushr*),[38] paid the functionaries of the waqfs, and delivered any remainder to the Finance Ministry, which was to direct that money to the Waqf Ministry—an aim never fulfilled.[39] Instead, it was spent as the Finance Ministry saw fit. Revenues went to modern state building and consolidation needs, like the expenses of a modern army.[40] More importantly, revenues of all waqfs were consolidated into a single fund and spent as necessary, independently of the wills of founders.

The language of the 1850 Decree presents annexation as a way to rid waqfs from treacherous mutawallīs whose negligence appears in their neglect of one of their most important tasks: the repair of waqf assets. Four times, the decree repeats that the seizure will "save the waqfs from ruin" ("awqâf-i şerîfe khayrâtlerînin kharâbiyyetten . . . qûrtârılması") and that the new directors will "complete the necessary repairs and cleaning" ("lâzimgelen taʿmîrât ve tanẓîfât esbâbinî istikmâlî"). The 1863 regulations, however, do not dictate any inspection duties for the waqf director, but they go into great detail about how and when money should be spent on repairs, which underscores the decree's concern about "embezzlement" but also confirms the interpretation of the waqf seizure as an attempt to seize resources to finance the modern state's growing bureaucracy and army (Barnes 1986, 83). The details of the procedure for repairs show a deep concern for the possibility of false claims where the sought-after repair money would go into the pockets of administrators or waqf directors. The state now tightly controlled repair expenses through approval by the provincial council for any repair above 500 qurush, and through approval by the imperial treasury for any repair beyond 2,500 qurush. In such cases, the waqf director was to present a written report to the council, which would send a member with the waqf director and with experts (master builder and waqf experts [*ehl-i vuqûf*]) to inspect the locale to check if it actually needed the described repair. The inspection procedure would continue, from examining the number of repairs to verifying their execution and quality and the payment of the contractors (Article 20). The rest of the section on repairs includes very detailed descriptions of various scenarios (such as assets in faraway places and the amount of repairs) and acceptable expenses and compensation.

38. Contrary to the often-repeated claim that waqfs were exempt from taxes, the accounting registers show that waqf administrators paid taxes.

39. Barnes describes at length petitions from the Waqf Ministry demanding that the Finance Ministry forward waqf revenues (1986, 108–9).

40. Öztürk pushes the argument further and claims that even the necessary repairs, maintenance, and restoration became secondary to these state expenses, contrary to the jurists' requirements. This decision, according to Öztürk, was a deliberate one aimed at eliminating waqfs (1995b, 299).

The other task that mutawallīs used to fulfill and that now fell on waqf directors was the leasing of waqf assets, which afforded an easier avenue for standardization. This change is apparent in the standardization of rent contracts for the seized (*mazbūṭ*) waqf assets: these are mostly printed annual contracts, with particular details filled out by hand for each case (Gerber 1985, 190). This is not to say that these contracts were no longer negotiated, but it does indicate that the dominant mode of operation became the standardized procedure, and that such a project of uniformization was being undertaken. The regulations about waqf administration lay out in detail the manner of renting, the fees to be charged and to whom they will be forwarded, bookkeeping requirements, the hierarchy of approvals, and the penalties for infringing on rules. Without going into the details of the policies, the regulations sought to limit certain types of contracts and practices prone to giving permanent rights to tenants on waqfs. They also sought to ensure maximum rents (through public auction and strict liability of tenants). The waqfs were no longer left under the care of individual administrators; the state interfered in the manner of administration and exploitation, seeking to increase waqf revenues. They mattered not only because the sultan's duty was to protect the rights of the poor and follow the stipulations of the founders and the shariʿa, but also because of the revenues waqfs produced. Such uniform practices then produced the waqfs as a totality, a part of the national economy, real estate wealth.

Redefining the Jurisdiction of Qadis. After discrediting the older mutawallīs, the decree did not turn to the qadis. It did not direct them to apply the *sharʿ* and replace allegedly corrupt mutawallīs with more trustworthy ones. It gave these prerogatives to the Waqf Ministry. The ministry took over many of the tasks that jurists assigned qadis (appointing, auditing, and supervising administrators) long before it took over the administration of the seized waqfs in 1850 in Beirut.[41] As early as 1841, it made its presence felt in the provinces by creating Waqf Departments (Evkaf Dairesi) there, composed in the case of Beirut of a waqf accountant, a head secretary, a secretary, and a collector (Çelik 2010, 57).

From that early date, the Waqf Ministry requested audits of all charitable waqfs (*khayrāt*) in the city,[42] instituting a procedure for the vague supervision jurists assigned to the qadi. The Waqf Registers series, mentioned above, includes such accounting registers from Beirut starting in 1843 [1256] and recording revenues and expenditures from 1839—the year before the Egyptians surrendered the control of the city back to the Ottomans. In the first iteration of the Waqf Administration Regulations in 1841, the qadi was still in charge of drafting an accounting register based on documentation brought by individual waqf administrators. The archive here mirrors this state of affairs: the 1842 register [17 Ca 1259] in the Waqf

41. Astrid Meier (2002) describes a very similar process of sidelining judges in Damascus.

42. Based on BOA.EV 11192, because the register includes accounting for thirty waqfs, many more than those that would be seized by the Waqf Ministry eight years later in the 1850 decree.

Registers series, summarizing the accounting of Beirut's waqfs for the years 1839–1841, was ratified by the administrators of the various waqfs each with his seal and ended with "penned by" followed by the name and seal of the qadi (and seal of the waqf employee).[43] The summary at the end of the register also notes that, based on a sultanic decree (*firmân*) and regulations (*lâyiḥa*), all remainders from these waqfs (after repairs and payment of employees), were delivered to the waqf employee so that they could be sent to the Waqf Ministry and so that the Treasury could take its dues (BOA.EV11192/40B). The Waqf Ministry seems to have then claimed the remainders of Beiruti charitable waqfs even before some were seized.

The results of this first reorganization were deemed unsatisfactory and blamed on the qadis, who were "too busy to take appropriate care of waqf affairs" (Öztürk 1995, 82), leading to a new proposal by the Waqf Ministry to sideline qadis in audits and mutawallī supervision.[44] Indeed, a new configuration in 1842 handed supervision to the provincial rulers (governor, treasurer, and military commander): the local governor appointed a waqf director from local public and customs employees. The qadi was missing from this new arrangement. The new waqf director was responsible to the provincial council and Waqf Ministry, and not to the qadi (Öztürk 1995, 82). This new organization and restriction of the qadis' jurisdiction on supervision of mutawallīs is confirmed in the archive. In the 1847 [1263] accounting record sent from Beirut to Istanbul (BOA.EV 12403), the qadis are not present at the ratification of the register drafted by the waqf employee.[45] The 1850 decree mentions the audits of 1846 and 1847 [1262 and 1263] and requires the waqf director to send his accounting to the Waqf Ministry once every year in registers detailing the yearly revenues and expenditures for each waqf. By 1863, auditing had increased fourfold to a quarterly basis. The decree, therefore, not only took away the qadi's supervisory jurisdiction over waqfs but also created a procedure that systematized supervision.

In addition to supervision, the Waqf Ministry took over another area from the jurisdiction of qadis: the appointment of mutawallīs and various officeholders in waqfs. Indeed, as John Robert Barnes shows, this particular jurisdiction of qadis over waqf affairs had been limited by 1837 [1253], thirteen years before the 1850 decree. This occurred as a consequence of a report on Izmir qadis who were allegedly appointing the highest-paying candidates, rather than the most-qualified

43. The still crucial role of the judge in waqf supervision is also apparent in my archive. The shariʿa court register of Beirut for that year, which happens to be the earliest register preserved in the archive of Beirut's shariʿa court, contains lists of these same waqfs and their properties (sometimes coupled with the amounts of their monthly rents). These lists seem like notations done during the preparation of the register sent to Istanbul.

44. Öztürk (1995b, 82) does not specify the author of the document discussing these accusations, even though he mentions that there were many experts who testified to this state of affairs.

45. Unlike the earlier accounting register, the accounting here uses the *siyaqat* script, the script used by the treasury, confirming that it was not the judge who drafted it but the waqf officer who now belonged to this specialized group. The mutawallīs of the various waqfs were still present at the provincial council and ratified the draft summary accounting register (BOA. EV 12403/20).

candidates, to vacant waqf offices (Barnes 1986, 103). The qadi's registers in Beirut reveal that qadis did not appoint officeholders to seized waqfs, but did so to the semiautonomous waqfs administered by mutawallīs but supervised by the Waqf Ministry.[46] MBSS.S9/151, for example, is a copy of a letter requesting the Porte for an official appointment letter (*berat*), confirming the qadi's appointment. The details of the entry reveal that officeholders first went to the waqf accountant and took exams that certified their competence. The role of the qadi was limited to the formal appointment, while the actual process to determine eligibility was outside his jurisdiction.

The 1850 Decree subjected all seized waqfs to similar procedures of administration and accounting. By centralizing their revenues and distributing them independently of the stipulations of the founders, the new administrative protocols produced waqfs as an aggregate that had one budget. Instead of individual waqfs individually administered, waqfs grouped together became an important part of the national economy that needed to be well managed and developed. This administration and supervision sidelined qadis in their duties as upholders of the shariʿa.

Under the banner of "good management," the Ottoman state introduced techniques of government that helped produce the state effect. The Ottoman Empire had had a bureaucracy for a long time, and there were surveys, reconfirmations of deeds, accounting and appointment requirements, but they were much more dispersed and not regular enough to create the state effect. So, it is not bureaucratization per se that created the state effect, even if bureaucratization did help in the case of waqf, but these novel methods of accounting and "good management" that did. Uniform practices of accounting, reporting, permission requests, and supervision produced the effect of an overarching structure dictating the way waqf administrators and beneficiaries dealt with waqf.

DECISION 753 OF 1921: WAQF AS "RELIGIOUS" PROPERTY OF THE "MUSLIM COMMUNITY" AND STATE SUPERVISION

The Allied Forces' occupation of the Ottoman Levant at the end of World War I ruptured the connection between the Ottoman Waqf Ministry and the waqfs under its jurisdiction in Beirut. Waqfs were instead attached by the administrators of the occupied territories to the Ministry of Justice (Haut-Commissariat de la République française 1921, 192). In a "note" on the possibilities of organizing waqfs in French Mandate Lebanon and Syria (MEA/251.1/Dossier Arrêté 753/1, 1921), the delegate of the high commissioner on real estate matters, Philippe Gennardi, explained that there were two interpretations of Article 6 of the Mandate's regulations commanding that the "control and administration of wakfs shall be exercised

46. In addition, officeholders who had appointment letters from Istanbul sometimes registered them with the qadi (e.g., MBSS.S3/142), using the qadi as a notary.

in complete accordance with religious law and the dispositions of founders" (Longrigg 1958, 377). The first interpretation of ensuring administration according to religious law would be to protect these waqfs from new legislation aiming to "secularize waqf or to modify its character" without actually interfering in the actual business of administration. Although Gennardi does not elaborate on what "secularizing waqf" means, we can infer from the French experience in Algeria that this referred to the state moving waqfs to the public domain. The second interpretation would be for the Mandatory power to ensure that religious law and the will of the founder are applied, and thus to interfere in waqf administration.

Highlighting that both options do not contravene the shariʿa, Gennardi nonetheless notes that that the second option serves best "our own interests" and those of the territories under Mandate. Indeed, being in charge of waqf administration

> will allow us to exert a direct action over 4,000 religious employees, more than 30,000 beneficiaries and approximately 100,000 people who depend to a certain degree on waqfs. It will also allow us to control strictly the revenues so that they are not used to xenophobic and anti-French ends especially since they are a powerful means of action as we can estimate their revenues to 15 million francs. (MEA/251.1/Dossier Arrêté 753/1.2, 1921)

This was quite a financial resource given the tattered state of the French economy at the time and the budget of the Mandate state, which reached 235.8 million francs (Casey 2019, 93). Gennardi also underlines other advantages of Mandatory control, like restoring monuments without any cost to the state and extending education and public assistance. He notes that such supervision would allow "the regular operation of cultural, charitable, and education works, and prohibit the squandering of their resources" (MEA/251.1/Dossier Arrêté 753/1.2, 1921).

It was this last point, saving charitable waqfs, rather than the other more "self-interested" ones discussed above, that the French Mandatory powers used in their report to the League of Nations to justify the need for their supervision. The report (most likely penned by Gennardi) described the situation of waqfs under occupation as dire:

> Given the absence of any competent person because of the suppression of all control bodies . . . waqfs have been left completely abandoned. There was more and more dilapidation of their revenues and abusive operations. The registers had disappeared in part. Legal injunctions had been contravened. Real rights [quasi-ownership rights] have been constituted on waqfs. (Haut-Commissariat de la République française 1921, 192)

By arguing for the necessity of Mandatory control over waqfs, French powers thus claimed the institutions and the place of the Ottoman state. Among the early pieces of French legislation was Decree 753, on the administration of Islamic waqfs. Its full provisions remained in effect from 2 March 1921 until 22 December 1930, when Decree 157 replaced many of its regulations. Decree 753 created a General

Supervision of Islamic Waqfs (Muraqaba ʿAmma li'l-Awqaf al-Islamiyya) for both Syria and Lebanon. The apparatus of the directorate consisted of three organs: the Supreme Waqf Council[47] (the legislative and administrative apparatus), the General Waqf Committee[48] (an advisory apparatus), and the General Supervisor of Waqf.[49] The decree extended many of the changes introduced by the 1826 Ottoman Waqf Ministry, particularly control of administration through the issuing of multiple regulations and the supervision of waqf administration by the General Supervision of Islamic Waqfs instead of the judges. However, the decree moved waqf administration to the margins of the state: While it remained directly attached to the high commissioner or his representative,[50] the General Supervision was not a ministry, staffed by civil servants paid by the state and with a budget coming from the state treasury. Many institutions all over the world, especially those defined as authorities, share this marginal location in modern states and thus provide an entry point into the production of the state effect. These margins make the work of producing the state effect even more visible because they require constant assertion and negotiation.

Analyzing the preamble of the 1921 decree will show us how its arguments differed considerably from the language of the Ottoman 1850 Decree. However, its effects were more ambivalent: one the one hand, it continued the centralization of the production of waqf law in the state, but, on the other, it initiated the sectarianization of the Muslim waqf and its secularization.

Arguments of the 1921 Decree

Because the Ottoman state took the application of the shariʿa as one of its responsibilities and sources of legitimacy, the arguments of the 1850 Decree for seizing the administration and supervision of waqfs were articulated from *within* Islamic jurisprudence. The French Mandatory powers introduced a new architecture of state, law, and religion, as they had a different relation to the shariʿa

47. Conseil Supérieur des Wakoufs, or al-Majlis al-Aʿla li'l-Awqaf. The council decides on the manner of administration in and outside the center (Article 6.2 and 6.3); on beneficiaries of increases of waqf revenues (Article 6.4); on the ways to rehabilitate Islamic waqfs, increase their revenues, and ameliorate their administration (Article 6.6); and on the number and salaries of the directorate's employees. One of the council's "financial" duties is the auditing of the accounting of the directorate.

48. Commission Générale des Wakoufs, or al-Lajna al-ʿAmma li'l-Awqaf. Even though Article 10 starts by describing the commission as the "highest administrative power," in effect its role was very vaguely defined beyond the discussion of the budget: "it discusses . . . all issues related to the interest of the waqf that the waqf council or the local councils bring to it" (Article 10). It was dissolved in a later revision of the decree.

49 Contrôleur-Général des Wakoufs, or Muraqib al-Awqaf al-Islamiyya al-ʿAmm. The general supervisor runs the daily business of administration. He is the only executive power, takes decisions on administration issues that are beyond the powers of local administrators, and collects fees and rents (Badr 1992, 20). He suggests the budget, the committee discusses it, and the council approves it.

50. A similar setup had been successfully tried in in Tunisia and Morocco, as mentioned in chapter 1.

and a different understanding of their role in the fulfillment of the aims of waqfs and their administration and supervision. The preamble to Decree 753 of 1921 explains the reasoning behind the decree and the role of the French Mandatory power in administration. Its language introduced new concepts, like "religious," "public utility," and "Muslim community."[51] Instead of arguments from the fiqh, the decree used "public utility" as the essential reason behind the supervision of waqfs. The decree placed waqfs in the private affairs of the Muslim community.[52] In so doing, it created a complex situation whereby the state constructed and acknowledged a "religious law" outside a state whose sovereignty resides in its exclusive production and administration of law. It thus became necessary for the state to endorse and authorize certain now-called "religious" laws of waqf; in fact, the decree delegated the creation of waqf law to an "independent" organ "representing" the Muslim community and its most authoritative opinions.[53] Such a policy of state control of waqf falls in line with the Ottoman centralization of the production of waqf law in the state. The way it is achieved, however, necessitates a very different maneuvering and operates distinctly from the Ottoman precedent. While one might assume that this solution would actually leave the production of the so-called religious law undisrupted, we will see how the creation of such a "Muslim" legislative body rearticulates the field of law and knowledge production among Muslim scholars, effectively secularizing the law.

Such state logics are reflected in the argument of the preamble (*asbāb mūjiba*), which begins with the premise that waqfs have a "purely religious Islamic character" ("awqāfuhum hiya dīniyya islāmiyya maḥḍa") and can be administered only by Muslims. The preamble then presents a sketch of waqf administration under Ottoman rule particularly during the Great War. It follows with the principle that "the government [*ḥukūma*] has the right [*ḥaqq*] to supervise the communities [*ṭawā'if*] and the duty to preserve their interests [*maṣāliḥ*]." However, it continues, waqf follows laws taken from religious law (literally, "religious shariʿa" [*al-sharīʿa al-dīniyya*]), which are notably different from those of the state. Therefore, it concludes, the supervision of waqfs is required only for the necessities of great public benefit ("mā taqtaḍīh al-manāfiʿ al-ʿumūmiyya al-ʿuẓmā").

The tour de force of the preamble and the premise allowing the complex maneuvering that gives the supervision of the waqf in the final instance to the French

51. The preamble mixes this argument with concepts borrowed from the fiqh, such as "the waqf's interest" but uses them in a different grammar. I will analyze this new grammar in chapter 5.

52. In these discussions of French laws, I continue to use the term *Muslim community*, as I explain in footnote 7 above.

53. The same body is also responsible for the production of "personal status" legislation, which is then ratified as state law. In this process of ratification, the production of the shariʿa is subsumed under the modern state's legislative process. The logic is exclusive state law on certain issues, but because some of these are acknowledged as "religious" and "private" and at the same time the state cannot leave these to decide for themselves because of legislative sovereignty, the state creates a process through which these religious laws are then endorsed by Parliament. See Méouchy (2006) for a discussion of the way various communities thought about themselves as nations claiming extraterritorial authority.

Mandatory state consist in the characterization of waqfs as "religious." According to the preamble, "Since waqfs, established by Muslims intending beneficence and piety [*al-khayr wa al-taqwā*], have a purely religious Islamic character, they can only be administered by Muslims." Assigning the adjective *religious* to these waqfs is not a characterization I had seen in any of the juristic discussions of waqf, and it is very much tied to the particular architecture of state, law, and religion, in this case, the secular configuration of Lebanon.

Although the juxtaposition of waqfs with *religious* was novel, I do not intend to suggest that the modern term for *religion*, *dīn*, was not used in pre-modern discussions, nor that there was no attempt to classify waqf within a certain category of practices. The modern Arabic translations of *religion* (*dīn*) and *religious* (*dīnī*) gloss over the varied meanings that the Arabic term held prior to the modern era.[54] To give a few examples of these earlier uses, *dīn* appears in the Qur'an in the sense of judgment and retribution, as in *yawm al-dīn* (the Day of Judgment), and in meaning of cult/worship/the law (Karamustafa 2017, 164). According to an often-quoted hadith known as the hadith of Jibrīl, dīn consists of faith (*īmān*), the practice of submission through the performance of required worship acts (*islām*), and the interiorization of faith (*iḥsān*). *Dīn* also signifies habit or custom (*al-ʿāda*) and worship (*al-ʿibāda*) (Firuzabadi 1863). In short, the "Muslim concept [of dīn] denotes above all the Laws [and ethics] which God has promulgated to guide man to his final end, the submission to these laws (and thus to God), and the practice of them (acts of worship)" (Gardet 2012). Dīn encompasses all the ways one should live one's life as a Muslim.[55]

Despite an all-encompassing conception of dīn, Muslim scholars distinguished between matters and sciences of dīn and those of *dunyā*, with the latter broadly referring to worldly matters: "arithmetic, engineering, astronomy, and the rest of the crafts [*ḥiraf*] and skills [*ṣināʿāt*]" (Abbasi 2020, 208). Scholars also discussed the dīnī and the *dunyawī* advantages of certain actions, or whether the Prophet's authority extended to *dunyawī* matters in addition to dīnī ones (Abbasi 2020, 202–5). Most importantly, all worldly actions can become dīnī if done with the right intent, in submission to God. Furthermore, Muslim scholars attempted to classify

54. As Karamustafa notes in a short chapter on Islamic dīn, there have been very few studies of the concept beyond the Qur'anic text (2017, 164). He picks a few examples of the variety of meanings the term has in the legal, theological, and mystical traditions; in literature, philosophy, historiography, and science; and in practice—to show that the concept was polysemic and cannot be reduced to the meaning of "religion." A more thorough examination of the pre-modern use of *dīn* remains necessary.

55. In the chapter on Islam in his classic *The Meaning and End of Religion*, W. C. Smith is more concerned with whether *dīn* connotes "religion," noting that the Qur'an sometimes uses *dīn* in the contemporary Western sense of *religion*, implying both personal piety, as well "a particular religious system, one 'religion' as distinct from another'" (1964, 76). However, he continues his analysis to argue that that word is mostly used in the Qur'an to speak of religion as *īmān* and *muʿmin*—that is, faith—and that *islām* is a verbal noun meaning "obedience . . . the willingness to take on oneself the responsibility of living henceforth according God's proclaimed purpose" (1964, 103), arguing that the meaning of *dīn* as a reified entity, a "religion," is a later development.

acts, waqf included, between "liturgical acts or acts of worship [*ʿibādāt*] and 'transactions' between particulars [*muʿāmalāt*]" (Johansen 1999, 60). The former are devotional acts to God, usually discussed in commentaries in five sections on ablutions, prayer, fasting, almsgiving, and pilgrimage. They deal with the relation of man and God and are part of the "claims of God" (*ḥuqūq allāh*), while the *muʿāmalāt* deal with "claims of men" (*ḥuqūq al-ʿibād*), including sales, rents, inheritance, marriage, and divorce. Waqf founding falls in both these categories. Done with the aim of getting closer to God (*qurba*), it involves a human being's relation to God. As a nineteenth-century jurist and teacher of the law of waqf argued, waqf "can be said to be like worship" (Yazır 1995, 250). However, it also creates relations between men. The translator of Hilmi's codified waqf manual foregoes the worship act of waqf-making and calls the waqf the "transaction of waqf" (Hilmi 1909, 5). This did not mean that the waqf did not belong to the category of dīn anymore. Both *ʿibādāt* and *muʿāmalāt* fall within dīn. Concurrently, it does not mean that waqf does not have *dunyawī* advantages, like the preservation of property from fragmentation. In this older grammar, describing waqfs as *religious possessions* would highlight their value as acts of worship that bring rewards in the hereafter.

A characterization of waqf as religious under the particular architecture of state, religion, and law instated by the French Mandate in Lebanon—namely, secularism—produces a different meaning. Using the term *religious* to describe waqfs as possessions places them in the "sphere of religion" and therefore as part of the "private" affairs of the community to be managed by the community according to its own laws (which also become characterized as religious); here the classic secular scheme of privatized religion makes itself visible through the proclaimed "autonomy" and "independence" of the various religious communities in the running of their "properly religious" affairs. As mentioned above, Article 6 of the 1921 Mandate regulations states: "Respect for the personal status of the various people and for their religious interests shall be fully guaranteed. In particular, the control and administration of wakfs shall be exercised in complete accordance with religious law and the dispositions of founders" (Longrigg 1958, 377).[56] This article grants "the entitlement to difference [and] the immunity from the force of public reason" (Asad 2003, 8), an essential aspect of secularism. Notably, however, it is the state that provides such an immunity, a state that presents itself as outside these religious communities, as a civil state. The state, the preamble declares, is the "guardian" of the various religious communities (Ministère français des Affaires étrangères 1922, 334).[57] Concurrently, this description obscures both the Catholicism of the French Republic and its use of this Catholicism to secure a connection with and present

56. The 1926 Constitution enshrines this right in Article 9: "La liberté de conscience est absolue. En rendant hommage au Très-Haut, l'État respecte toutes les confessions et en garantit et protège le libre exercice, à condition qu'il ne soit pas porté atteinte à l'ordre public. Il garantit également aux populations, à quelque rite qu'elles appartiennent, le respect de leur statut personnel et de leurs intérêts religieux" (Ministère français des Affaires étrangères, *Rapport*, 1926, 202).

57. "L'état, tuteur légal des collectivités."

itself as a protector of the Maronite Christians, whose existence was a significant reason for France's presence as a Mandatory power.[58] Yet, this private immunity only goes so far. Since it is granted by the state, the immunity is not absolute, as the preamble points out: public benefit might require the intervention of the state, even in these "religious" possessions.

Because of the religious character of waqfs, the "Muslims" acquired the right to administer "their" waqfs according to "religious" shariʿa. This right entailed the creation of the Muslim community as one among many others within the Lebanese nation-state,[59] a conceptualization that was different under the Ottoman Empire, which remained an Islamic state. Nonetheless, one might argue that the Muslim community already imagined itself as a community, as an "umma." *Umma*, like *dīn*, has a multiplicity of meanings both in the Qurʾan (e.g., the group [*jamāʿa*], followers of prophets, dīn, a righteous man that can be a leader) and in various later writings, but it was not necessarily restricted in the Qurʾan to a "religious" community nor to the Muslim community in particular (Sayyid 1986, 44–47). It had the potential to include all of humanity in its surrendering to God, in all of the world becoming Muslim. It is pregnant with the potential reunification of humanity in "a single human world in the name of Islam" (Sayyid 1986, 41). That Muslim-human world umma was, however, imagined and projected as a universal and all-embracing community through, among other things, property: the common ownership of land and bounty (Sayyid 1986, 83).[60] Therefore, the French Mandate's linking of property and community, as in the preamble's statement "waqfs are like the religious private property of the Islamic community" ("al-awqāf hiya bi-mathābat milk al-ṭāʾifa al-islāmiyya al-dīnī"), is not a novelty. Yet, this analogization of the waqf to the private property (*milk*) of the Muslim community here again displaces God as the owner of waqfs and assimilates waqf into private property, albeit owned by a new entity (the Muslim community). If each individual waqf has a legal person who is its owner, the totality of waqfs belongs to the Muslim community.

Nonetheless, the shape and form of the Muslim community under the French Mandatory nation-state of Lebanon differed radically from the religious imaginary of the umma. It was one community *among others*, outside the state and

58. The presentation of secularism as a universalism severed from particular (Christian) traditions is one of its characteristics; for examples, see Asad (1993; 2003); and Jakobsen and Pellegrini (2008).

59. While I speak of the creation of the Muslim community *as a community*, this concept is tied to that of minorities, which was also produced during the French Mandate, as historian Benjamin White (2011) shows.

60. While in the first Islamic conquests, booty and land were divided among Muslims, later on the first caliph was said to have made certain types of conquered land into waqf, with all Muslims as beneficiaries of the right of use, so as to allow the Muslims of later times access to these lands. However, such waqf was not a legally constituted waqf, but rather a use that indicates a fiduciary relationship, whereby the state is a trustee (Debs 2010, 12). "The ownership of *kharaj* land passed to the Muslim community as a whole" (Cuno 1995, 123–24).

circumscribed within the nation. The French advisor on waqf, Gennardi, was very much aware of the transformation required for such a manner of administration. Indeed, in his explanation of the two options (discussed above) for the Mandatory state to exert its control over the waqfs, the direct and the indirect, Gennardi argues that the choice of the particular setup should depend on the conception of the Muslim "milieux." In places with a non-Muslim majority, where the "Muslim community is starting to distinguish its own personality from that of the state," as was happening in Beirut, Tripoli, and Saida in Greater Lebanon, indirect control should be favored. The Muslims in these places, according to Gennardi, were joining non-Muslim communities, which already thought of themselves as separate communities in the Ottoman nineteenth century because they were *millets*, self-administering groups.[61] This was not an obvious development among Muslims, as Elizabeth Thompson shows (2000), because many Muslims, both populist and secularist, did not want a sectarian republic and fought it. The Muslim community was finally becoming a "sect," Gennardi was pleased to report, even though many Sunni Muslims contest their designation as a sect up to this day (as is seen in the erasure of all references to the Muslim Sunni "sect" of Decree 18/55 in 1967).

The notion of the Muslim community advanced in such French Mandatory documents differs substantially from the Muslim community as an umma. The umma includes the whole community with a single leader whose duties reflect his leadership of the *Muslim* umma: "guarding the faith against heterodoxy, enforcing [Islamic] law and justice between disputing parties, . . . [protecting] peace in the territory of Islam and its defense against external enemies, . . . receiving the legal alms, taxes" (Madelung 2012).[62] The French Mandatory state divorced the Muslim community in Lebanon from the larger Muslim umma and from the state. It created for it (and for each non-Muslim community) a different "official" leader and representative to the state, the mufti (and the patriarch),[63] whose duties became restricted to the "spiritual well-being" of the congregation and to what came to be defined as "personal status," which includes waqf.[64] Such a restriction of

61. MAE251.1/Dossier Arrêté 753/1.4, 1921. Note, however, that the regime of sects cannot be seen as an extension of the *millet* system of the Ottoman Empire. As Abillama (2018, 150–51) explains, building on Méouchy (2006), the French-instated political sects were based on a secular sovereign power of legal recognition that the state granted to any group that met certain criteria, whereas in the Ottoman Empire the status accorded to communities were the result of privileges and immunities granted to "people of the book" as long as they had a particular relation to the Muslim rulers.

62. The Ottoman Empire was majority Christian until the conquest of Syria and Egypt in 1516–1517, and so their legal recognition as a community was not theorized under the majority-minority assumption that we take for granted today. On the *millet* system and the need to historicize it in the late Ottoman Empire, see Braude (1982).

63. For the institutionalization of these different sects through the creation of an official leader representing the community to the state, see Henley (2013).

64. Whereas I focus on the Sunni Muslim community, Max Weiss examines the way the Shiʿi community was produced as a sect in French Mandate Lebanon (contrary to the dominant narrative

religion to "spiritual well-being" and its confinement to the private sphere is part of the secularization of religion and waqf more specifically.

By doing so, the 1921 Decree actually straddles a difficult line. It places the law of waqfs in the hands of the Muslim community, as a "religious" and therefore private (outside the state) matter, while one of the state's claims to sovereignty stems from its exclusive production and administration of law. The handing of jurisdiction to the Muslim community over these affairs represents a delegation of legislative power to the Supreme Waqf Council, whose decisions are then ratified as state law by Parliament. The creation of such a council thus concentrates the production of law on issues like waqf not in the hands of the Muslim community and its many jurists wherever they may be, but in the members (at first appointed, but then elected) of the Supreme Waqf Council. The waqf was then subsumed under the Lebanese republic's architecture of state, law, and religion, which transformed the Muslim community into a "sect;" it had been sectarianized.

State Production of Waqf Law: The Supreme Waqf Council

The 1921 Decree officially consecrated the modern Ottoman nineteenth-century transformations in state and law: taking the bulk of legislation on waqf matters out of the hands of the scholarly community of jurists and placing it in the hands of the Supreme Waqf Council, which became the highest legislative and administrative authority for the supervision of the waqfs (Article 5). The council was therefore made responsible for legislative changes (pertaining particularly to financial matters). It decided on the "ways that local directors and waqf administrators should follow in the administration of public and family waqfs" (*al-awqāf al-ʿumūmiyya wa al-ahliyya*) (Article 6). Therefore, while the article still assumes and concedes that some waqfs are administered by their own administrators—persons distinct from the director or the directorate and its various local delegates—the laws these independent administrators are to follow were now issued by the council. The council and the directorate more generally assumed the responsibility of legislating on all waqf affairs and for all waqfs; the council decided on "the amendments to be introduced, according to the shariʿa, on the laws particular to Islamic waqfs" (Article 6.1).

Such a statement supposes that the "legislating" members of the council are familiar with the shariʿa. It also assumes a single law for waqf and that the council is the single waqf lawmaking body. If the only enforceable waqf law is the one produced by the council, the legislative efforts of other jurist-scholars become much less central to the production of waqf law. It will be recalled that Ottoman waqf law

that it became so after independence through its marginalization and then mobilization by Imam Musa al-Sadr) especially through the Jaʿfari (Shiʿi) court and its "re-organization and the re-imagination of the relationship between Shiʿi community and the state, the institutionalization of Shiʿi law through the Jaʿfari court" (2010, 30). In chapter 4 especially, he shows how the practice of going through the Jaʿfari courts to adjudicate religious patrimony (especially waqf) transformed the Shiʿa into sect.

was elaborated in a whole body of literature by jurists, with sultanic orders settling particularly controversial issues. The relevance of this body of literature becomes much less evident when the state adopts a particular opinion from this corpus or even other legislation elaborated by the council (which included some jurists) as "the" law of waqf administration comes to be applied to all waqfs. Yet, as I show later, waqf law produced outside the bounds of the council can still make its way into state-sanctioned waqf law, and the boundaries between state and non-state scholars are not as clear as they appear to be from such an article.

Refiguring Jurisdiction over Supervision

Decree 753 does not stop at extending legislative power over all waqfs to the directorate; it also expands the jurisdiction of the General Waqf Supervisor to include the supervision of all waqfs, without exception. Article 21 states: "As the General Waqf Supervisor, he can supervise the actions and management of the administrators of general and family waqfs [*al-awqāf al-ʿumūmiyya wa al-ahliyya*] and the directors of charitable Islamic associations whatever their purposes are. He also works to force the [above-mentioned] administrators and directors to comply with the rules of the codes in effect and the founding documents of the associations." He had the right to audit and examine the work of these administrators and directors. This article therefore extends the jurisdiction of supervision of the so-called exempt waqfs to the General Supervision, obliterating the category of exempt waqfs and fusing it with the semiautonomous waqfs. All waqfs are now supervised by the General Supervision.[65] The judges lost any jurisdiction they had over the supervision of waqfs. However, the decree does not specify the process through which this auditing is to happen. The audit process therefore remains unsystematic and unenforced unless a particular director, waqf, or case comes to the fore, either because of zeal, disputes, or complaints. Although the absence of systematic auditing might appear as a lack of actual enforcement, such blurriness, or "*flou*," is actually productive, allowing space for maneuvering around waqfs and people, as we will see.

Even though the decree placed the production of waqf law and waqf administration in the hands of the General Supervision, effectively, the French High Commissioner still had the final decision-making power. In general, the opening articles and definitions of the new directorate did not hide the High Commissioner's role in the administration. Indeed, the Directorate General of Waqf is directly attached to the High Commissioner or his representative[66] (Article 2), who appoints the General Supervisor and can dismiss him at any time (Article 24). Hence, the General Supervisor and his decisions are at the mercy of the High Commissioner.

65. Article 23 shows this extension of jurisdiction by making the supervisor of waqfs the legal representative of both "public and family waqfs."

66. A similar setup had been successfully tried in Tunisia and Morocco, as mentioned in chapter 1.

Examining how members of both the Supreme Waqf Council and the General Waqf Committee were chosen, how often they met, and how they operated also shows that their powers became much more limited. Both council and committee emerge as peripheral to the functioning of the directorate, especially since the council met twice a year and the committee once. The council totaled ten members, six of whom were ex officio members.[67] It also had a "representative of the Muslim community [*ṭā'ifa*]" (Article 9.2) in each of the four cities appointed (not elected) by the local government after consultation with the local Muslim community of scholars (*'ulamā' al-islām*). The members of the General Waqf Committee were the same as those of the council with the addition of local waqf directors, a representative of each of the (local) committees of the counties and districts.[68]

Representatives on all boards were therefore appointed directly or indirectly by the High Commissioner. In addition, all bodies were to report to him or to his representative. The council was to inform the High Commissioner of anything illegal (*mughāyiran li'l-qānūn*). Only the High Commissioner could decide on an extraordinary council meeting. Decree 753 also makes the High Commissioner's representative, his advisor on real estate matters, the only means of communication between the General Supervision and all other state administrations during the Mandate. This was in line with the general manner of French administration, where Lebanese directors-general holding executive power were supposed to be the right hand of the governor of Lebanon, but "real power in the administration lay in the hands of the French 'advisers'" (Traboulsi 2007, 88; see also Longrigg 1958, 114–15, 260). Finally, and most importantly, no decision taken by any of the bodies of the General Supervision could be effective unless the High Commissioner ratified it.

While the newly created General Supervision appears to replace the Ottoman Waqf Ministry and to continue and even further the changes that the ministry had introduced, the actual setup and functioning of the General Supervision shows a very different relation to the state. The ministry was part of an Ottoman Islamic state whose attempt at waqf administration, supervision, and waqf lawmaking was couched in the language of the Islamic tradition, even if the arguments and techniques of administration introduced innovations. If the sultan could remove waqf supervision from the hands of judges, it was because their supervisory power emanated from him. In fact, he could make an argument from within the tradition for such a restriction of jurisdiction. The French-created General Supervision is an *independent* authority, which transfers waqf administration, supervision, and waqf lawmaking to the Muslim community. However, because the sovereignty of the French Mandatory state rested partly on its exclusive production and

67. The members are the director of the General Supervision and the highest shari'a judges in Beirut, Damascus, Aleppo, and Latakia and the shari'a judge of appeal (all of which are positions to which judges are appointed after examinations).

68. These committees take on the local administration of waqfs in smaller towns and remote areas.

administration of law, it effectively retains the power to ratify all decisions of the General Supervision. In addition, based on claims of "public utility," it reserves the right to oversee the work of the General Supervision. French supervision was so tight that it almost amounted to French Mandatory state administration, supervision, and legislation over waqfs.

DECISION 42 OF 2003: CLAIMING THE STATE, CONTROLLING WAQFS

Given this history of the ever-tightening grip of the state on the administration and supervision of waqf through the General Supervision, the reader might now better understand my surprise at Decision 42 of 2003, which required any new mosque to have the Directorate General of Islamic Waqfs (DGIW), the heir of the General Supervision, as its administrator, even if a private individual or an association had funded its construction and upkeep. Both the General Supervision and the DGIW, as public authorities, had an ambiguous relation to the state. The DGIW was born out of resistance to Decision 753 of 1921 and reversed some of the advances of that decision, thereby splitting jurisdiction over waqfs and creating more *flou*. This ambiguity allowed waqf founders and administrators to play various agencies and state actors against each other.

Decision 753 had given the Muslim community nominal control over Islamic waqfs, which proved controversial and was heavily contested in the Sunni milieu. Gennardi complained, for example, that "the Beirut mufti refuses to work with the local waqf committee and thwarts the collection of waqf revenue" (quoted in Kupferschmidt 2008, 103). Opponents of the decree and of French control in Damascus, Aleppo, Beirut, Tripoli, and other Mandate cities gathered and organized the Waqf Congress in 1930 in Aleppo, which created a Waqf Defense Committee. As a result, the Supreme Waqf Council issued Decision 10 in 1930 (ratified by the High Commissioner as Decree 157) to reorganize the waqf administration and hand over administration to the "Muslim community" by eliminating the High Commissioner's supervision and transferring the task of administration to elected boards.[69]

The effects of Decision 10 were twofold. On the one hand, it split jurisdiction over waqf supervision between two state apparatuses, the Directorate General of Islamic Waqfs and shariʿa courts. The latter regained jurisdiction over waqfs that were once exempt under the Ottomans. This division has persisted and continues to cause jurisdictional debates and competition between the courts and the DGIW and between the chief justice of the Beirut Sunni shariʿa court and the grand mufti. On the other hand, Decision 10 created *elected* administrative and scholarly councils

69. Decision 10 also separated the administration of waqfs in Lebanon and Syria.

with extensive executive powers, instead of appointed ones, dwarfing the power of the appointed director.[70] To elect members of these councils, Decision 10 created the Islamic Electoral College, representing the Muslim community—a council that came to acquire a major role, especially after independence, in the election of boards and, most importantly, the appointment of the mufti himself.[71] These administrative and scholarly councils took most of the executive authority in waqf administration, replacing the single-handed administration of the director, who retained a modicum of power in "small" decisions.

The handing of waqf control to the Muslim community—one of the aims of Decision 10—did not sever the DGIW's relation to the state, as can be seen from its designation as a public administration (*idāra ʿāmma*) and its budget. When characterizing the DGIW as a public administration, the *state* needs to acknowledge that mosques and waqfs are *public utilities*[72] which should not be left to individual initiatives and enterprises and that they are best served if administered independently (Yakan 1963, 128).[73] The question then becomes whether waqfs dedicated to worship and Islamic education are a public utility. In other words, is religion a public benefit? In the Lebanese constitution, it is—because the state "assumes the obligations of glorifying God, the Most Exalted" (Article 9), highlighting religion as an important good for the state to promote. Furthermore, because a religious

70. As the directorate fulfills the role of administrator for seized waqfs, there is a rationalization and differentiation of waqf administration such that the decree now distinguishes between the different tasks of the administrators and hands them to two different councils: administrative and scholarly. The administrative council's duties fall mostly under a financial umbrella (Article 24)—from the supervision of the budget and of the expenses to renting out waqfs—under the aegis of caring for the "interest of the waqf" (see chapter 5). The scholarly council's main task is the examination of candidates for the religious positions and their appointment, and also ensuring the shariʿa compliance of the decisions of the administrative council. The decree also creates a "classification committee" whose purpose is to inventory and classify all religious buildings and all their employees, from mosques to schools to charitable foundations, with the aim of standardizing and "rationalizing."

71. The Islamic Electoral College comprised all Muslim members of Parliament and some thirty-two members representing Muslims in liberal professions (lawyers, engineers, pharmacists, etc.), scholars, waqf administrators, official Islamic charitable associations, and the highest Muslim officials: judges, the mufti, the waqf director, and the representative of the descendants of the Prophet Muhammad. The Islamic Electoral College, following very strict rules for its meeting and voting, elects the members of the scholarly council and then those of the administrative council. This structure was retained after independence, but the composition of the Islamic Electoral College is subject to constant debates, especially before the election of the mufti. The Islamic Electoral College represents a modern interpretation of those who are supposed to represent Muslims who matter for consensus (*ijmāʿ*). See, for example, Zaman (2012, 50), for a discussion of Muhammad ʿAbduh and how he widened the definition of consensus to include politicians.

72. Public utilities are a public good or a public need that should be satisfied, and not for profit. On the construction of public utility in opposition to profit, see Birla (2009, 99–100).

73. There are other legal theories on whether it is public utility that defines administrative law, which Yakan outlines (1963, 144–54).

trust that benefits a group or a section of a community is considered to benefit the larger public,[74] concerns that these waqfs benefit only the Muslim community do not arise.[75]

The French Mandatory power also saw waqfs as a way to fulfill public utilities like education. As the 1923 *Report to the League of Nations* notes: "General waqfs, because of their universal character as charitable acts, can provide revenues for increasing public assistance works" (Ministère français des Affaires étrangères 1924, 333). The DGIW can therefore be supervised by the government (approving decisions or auditing accounting) (Yakan 1963, 208) and can also be dissolved if the state decides that the public utility provided is not needed anymore. Thanks to this classification, the DGIW acquired privileges of state institutions (tax exemptions and some salaries paid out of the state budget). This was especially contentious given the DGIW's confessional character and the state's supposed equidistance from all sects.[76] Furthermore, reflecting Ottoman practices of delegating and selling tax collection to individuals, many waqfs in the early Mandate received "fixed amounts from the transmission of the tithe [land tax] and other public revenues dedicated to waqfs . . . and tithes and other public revenues given as freehold to waqfs" (Articles 1.2 and 1.4 of Decision 167 on Waqf Revenues, 22 March 1926). This amounts to earmarking revenues from taxes of citizens for the budget of the DGIW, revealing the myth of DGIW's financial independence, since the Ministry of Finance owed some citizen-paid taxes to the DGIW.[77]

Summoning the DGIW as a State Apparatus

Within these fuzzy relations between the DGIW and the state, Decision 42 of 2003 and its attempt to take control of the administration of new mosques becomes less puzzling. If "state control" of waqfs began as a project for the Ottomans, who could justify it in the ruler's jurisdiction over Muslim waqfs, it became more contradictory in a secular state. Indeed, in the indirect control option enshrined by Decision 10, the waqfs were supposed to be under the administration and supervision of the "community," and waqfs could retain founder-named individual

74. This approach to religion as part of public benefit diverges from the French anticlerical approach, which considers religion a private good that should be left private and which treats any support for religion as an exception (see, for example, Asad 2006).

75. See, for example, Atiyah's (1958) discussion of whether a trust to entertain police is considered a public benefit. Because entertaining police is not a public benefit, one could argue that such a trust is not for the public benefit. However, one could argue that entertainment of police renders them better at their job, which serves the public benefit.

76. For early contestations, see the description in al-Hut (1984, 106–9). For a recent critique of all these exemptions, which the author terms "budgetary and fiscal sectarianism," see Haddad (2015). Law 210/2000 extended various tax exemptions to other sects under a call for equal treatment. Particular exemptions are constantly debated under new proposals. For the latest, see ʿAqiqi (2017).

77. These yearly amounts were eventually settled through one-time payments that amounted to the Ministry of Finance buying out the waqf's share.

administrators.[78] In these contests between individual waqf administrators and the DGIW, the DGIW's director's handing me a copy of Decision 42 was a performative act that restated the DGIW's control over all new mosques. In the decision itself, the DGIW mobilizes the authority of the state to project the DGIW's location within the state apparatus. Decision 42 appeared in the official gazette of the Lebanese Republic, after being endorsed by the grand mufti of the Lebanese Republic. It appeals to previous state regulations to authorize itself but makes three innovations with respect to the process of mosque building and waqf administration. First, anyone who desires to build a mosque or prayer hall needs to first request written approval from the DGIW for the plans and building permit documents and then make the DGIW the administrator (Article 1B). Second, founders also need to make the plot or the part thereof where the mosque/prayer hall stands into a waqf (Article 1D). Finally, no organization, institution, association, or similar organism can take any existing or new mosque or prayer hall as its headquarters, base, address, or private waqf (*waqfiyya khāṣṣa*),[79] from whichever private party (*jiha khāṣṣa*) and for whatever purposes, subjects, or activities (Article 1H). Despite these allusions to an overarching control over Muslim bodies, systems, and institutions, the DGIW's self-proclaimed authority was challenged by other organs of the state, as well as by individuals within and outside it.

Challenges to the DGIW as a Public Authority

The Circulation of Waqf Objects among Various State Apparatuses. The Mandate debates over the authority responsible for waqfs continued in the postcolonial period. The claim that mosques are a public utility does not necessarily imply that the DGIW should be responsible for their administration, as Decision 42 asserts. Indeed, two other state apparatuses can compete for the task: shariʿa courts and the Ministry of the Interior. The competition between the DGIW and the shariʿa courts over waqfs is partly a result of Article 17 of the Organization of Shariʿa Courts of 1962 (Tanzim al-Qadaʾ al-Sharʿi al-Sunni wa al-Jaʿfari), which describes the jurisdiction of these courts as including "the waqf, its rules, bindingness, validity, necessary conditions, beneficiaries" (Article 17, no. 14). The issuing of the waqf-foundation deed is under the jurisdiction of the shariʿa courts. Any waqf deed, in order to be legally valid, needs to be drafted by a shariʿa judge and registered at the shariʿa court. Shariʿa court judges have many responsibilities: they appoint administrators of family waqfs (Article 17, no.15) and fire them, audit the administrators of both family and exempt waqfs (whether they are 'charitable' or family), approve their expenses (Article 17, no.16), give permission to the

78. This contest between individual and central supervision happened in the various Christian denominations, and individual churches were able to keep administering their waqfs. See Mohasseb Saliba (2008).

79. "Taking a mosque as . . . a private waqf" is a strange formulation. I assume it means founding a mosque as a private waqf.

administrators of "pure" (*maḥḍa*) family waqfs, and draft and record waqf deeds in conformity with regulations (*uṣūl*) (Article 17, no.18). Whereas the DGIW is the administrator of seized (*maḍbūt*) waqfs, it is not involved in the supervision of family or associations' waqfs—that is the responsibility of the shariʿa courts. The administration of the DGIW and that of shariʿa courts are actually separate; they are housed in different buildings, in different parts of town. In addition, the shariʿa courts report directly to the prime ministry and do not fall under the purview of the mufti. Even more, these two state apparatuses do not have an official bureaucratic procedure that requires communication and information sharing.[80]

Another contender for the supervision of mosques is the Ministry of the Interior. It oversees most Islamic organizations, which are not waqfs but rather nongovernmental organizations (NGOs), like al-Irshad wa al-Islah. Instead of registering the mosques they create as waqfs in shariʿa courts, these Islamic NGOs could use the jurisdiction of the Ministry of the Interior over NGOs and have mosques as their headquarters without going to the shariʿa court or the DGIW to register these mosques as waqfs. Indeed, in the late Ḥanafī legal tradition, any space that one opens up to public collective prayer becomes a waqf without the need for a waqf-founding act or deed (Ibn ʿAbidin, *Ḥāshiya*, 3:369). Yet, Decision 42 specifically supports the decision by citing "the most authoritative Ḥanafī opinion" (*arjaḥ al-aqwāl min madhhab Abī Ḥanīfa*), which requires a mosque to be registered as a waqf. When NGOs make mosques their headquarters, neither shariʿa courts nor the DGIW have supervisory power. Decision 42 attempts to restrict this possibility by prohibiting any association from having a mosque for headquarters.

The Circulation of Persons between the State Apparatus and "Private Entities" (Jihāt Khāṣṣa). By prohibiting associations from taking mosques as headquarters, Decision 42 paints the DGIW as part of the state apparatus distinct from such private associations. In my notebook, however, that distinction was not as clear-cut. The DGIW does not have the resources to staff all mosques from the graduates of its shariʿa schools.[81] It cannot control the political and ideological affiliations of its religious staff—even if it has the power to dismiss them because of misconduct,[82] and even if it specifies in its regulations that they cannot join any political parties or unions (as defined in Article 35 of the Administrative Regulations of the DGIW, 3 April 1980). Therefore, many of the religious staff and employees of

80. Hajj Tawfiq recounts how he sent a list of the waqfs of al-Birr wa al-Ihsan to the DGIW when Marwan Qabbani was its director, and how Qabbani replied, "Thank you very much, but this will sit on a desk and will not be useful," because the DGIW does not have jurisdiction over such waqfs. Employees of the DGIW complained about the lack of coordination between the DGIW and the shariʿa courts.

81. These schools are Kulliyyat al-Shariʿa and Azhar Lubnan.

82. See for example the case of Mustafa Malas, who was dismissed from his duties as an imam at the Minya mosque in Tripoli (al-Siddiq 2007).

the DGIW belong to the very associations whose activities in and administration of mosques Decision 42 attempts to restrict. Conversely, many private organizations have official employees on their boards. Let me illustrate with two examples from my notebook.

Sheikh Muhammad is the resident imam at one of the Beiruti mosques administered and supervised by the DGIW. He is beloved by the worshippers. One of them, Samer, explained, "He keeps the sermon short and to the point, does not ramble, and does not rebuke constantly—preaching to the choir, us who go to the mosque to pray." Samer was very surprised to hear that Sheikh Muhammad was an active member of the Jamaʿa Islamiyya (Islamic Group). Very closely associated with the Egyptian Muslim Brotherhood since its inception in the early fifties, the Jamaʿa Islamiyya laments the state of Muslims in the world and in Lebanon in particular: fallen prey to materialist desires, abandoning Islam, and lured by the West and its values. It took upon itself to spread the message of the Qurʾan and organize Muslims in a society where "Islam would be the measure of the individual's actions."[83] Implicit in the Jamaʿa's discourse is a critique of the official representatives of the Muslims, the mufti and Dar al-Fatwa, because, had they done their work properly, Muslims would not be in their present condition. Therefore, while the association to which Sheikh Muhammad belonged was critical of the DGIW and Dar al-Fatwa in general, he was able to secure himself a position at a mosque the DGIW administered. Negotiation between the DGIW and "private organizations" then seems to happen on an individual basis, rather than the two being mutually exclusive. When the DGIW mobilizes such a trope of independence and opposition between the DGIW and private organizations, it is to make a claim on the control of mosques and to try to silence some of the groups challenging its authority and criticizing its fulfillment of its duties as the religious head of "the Muslims." By laying claim to these mosques, the DGIW can then staff them and appropriate the platform these mosques provide through Friday sermons and other public educational activities.

The flip side of members of private organizations circulating in the corridors and mosques of the DGIW are state employees staffing the waqf boards of various "private" organizations. Both the chief justice at the Beirut Sunni Shariʿa Court (the "boss of all these judges," according to Hajj Tawfiq), and the Attorney General at the Supreme Shariʿa Court at the time, are on the waqf board of al-Birr wa al-Ihsan. The reader may recall from chapter 1 that this is an NGO that converted itself to a waqf, whose main purpose is the provision of education. The new campus of the Arab University in Dibbiyye, part of the waqf of al-Birr wa al-Ihsan,

83. From its website (http://www.al-jamaa.org, "who are we?" section). The Jamaʿa distinguished itself from its sister organization, Jamaʿat ʿIbad al-Rahman, by its political positions and its military actions: supporting transnational Islamic struggles and the Palestinian cause. Until the early 2000s, for instance, it was very much in line with Hizbullah's positions, especially in Parliament.

includes a mosque that is not under the administration of the DGIW or any formal state apparatus. As a prominent member of the organization rhetorically asked me: "Who is going to stand against us, unless there is a reason?" If it is the very people who are requesting mosques to be administered by the DGIW who are administering some of the mosques outside the DGIW, the constructed opposition in the administration of mosques is not, as the language of the Decision might imply, an opposition between private organizations and the DGIW control of mosques, but one between particular organizations and those dominating the DGIW.

Decision 42 embodies a mobilization of the state and an appeal to its stability and authority by a certain group in order to silence the challenges it is receiving. Telling in that regard was the statement of an advisor to the grand mufti when I asked him about the reasons behind the Decision. He answered, "It was different movements, associations, and parties [*qiwā ḥizbiyya*] producing sheikhs and students, each on their own, without approval, and challenging the authority of the Dar." Such challenges pushed the mufti to try and put an end to the "chaos" (*fawḍā*) the challenges were producing. This veiled explanation referred to the inter-Sunni struggle in the early 2000s, with various associations critical of the official representative of the community taking over the imamships at mosques and using them as platforms for critiques of Dar al-Fatwa. This struggle became especially protracted in the attempt of the Association of the Muhammad al-Amin Mosque to build Beirut's biggest mosque in the city center.[84] Following in the footsteps of the Ottomans, the DGIW used state legislation to silence these various groups. Instead of using epistemic and moral authority to counter the claims of other groups (as the latter do to challenge the DGIW and official Islam), the DGIW used state law to suppress them.

Marshalling Arms and Legs of the State

The human rights waqf I mentioned in the introduction is Al-Karama (Dignity) for Human Rights (http://ar.alkarama.org/), an international human rights organization based in Geneva. According to its website, al-Karama was founded as an association (*jamʿiyya*) in 2004 and became a Swiss foundation (*muʾassasa*) in 2007. Lebanon is but one of eighteen Arab countries where the organization combats arbitrary detention. As the lawyer of the organization narrated, al-Karama's main founder is a Qatari sociologist whose personal experience with arbitrary detention drove him to organize against it. He used to be close to the Qatari emir, Hamad bin Khalifa Al Thani, but was imprisoned without a sentence for a few years because of a criticism he had voiced about Shaykha Muza, the emir's second wife, a highly public and active figure. The reformist Salafi sociologist was released only after pressure from the United Nations. He became convinced of

84. For a discussion of these rivalries and the construction of the al-Amin mosque, see Mermier (2015, 91–119) and Vloeberghs (2016).

the need to create a system to monitor infringements of freedom of speech and to have international connections that could enforce international regulations about such abuses. After a failed attempt at an alliance with secular groups, he eventually founded al-Karama through a collaboration with a group of European-based North African Islamist political refugees who contributed their experience with the human rights machinery. They selected Lebanon to create a waqf that was a human rights organization.

The lawyer of the organization told me that the waqf foundation I had seen served not only for the Lebanese branch but for the whole organization. Indeed, he explained, in Arab countries, nongovernmental organizations cannot be established except in "a very official manner." In Lebanon, foreign organizations need the approval of the cabinet. There are also restrictions, he continued, like the fact that 75 percent of the founders have to be Lebanese, which makes it very difficult for an *international* human rights organization to get a license without political backing. Most international human rights organizations in Lebanon, the lawyer maintained, operate without permits. He explained that the Lebanese state easily hands out permits for international NGOs concerned with women's and children's rights but is very wary of those that are "overtly political."

Faced with these legal restrictions to founding an international NGO, the choice fell on founding a waqf. A senior member of a different association which founded a few waqfs explained that "a waqf is the easiest way to start something like an association because you can do it with $50 and you can start working. It is less than the fees you pay for registering an NGO!" In addition to the ease of founding a waqf and its low cost, the waqf provided al-Karama a different kind of protection as well: it is supervised by the shari'a courts rather than the cabinet (which it would have been if it was registered as an international NGO).

This supervision by shari'a courts is also an advantage for *local* organizations registered as waqf, which could have more easily registered as an association for public benefit (sing.: *jam'iyya dhāt manfa'a 'āmma*) or an NGO (sing: *jam'iyya*), forms that have their advantages. An association for public benefit can profit from tax cuts and various kinds of exemptions and reductions on phone rates as well as access to funding from the Ministry of Social Work, even though such associations are required to have at least five founding members to hold elections.[85] A local NGO can be operated through a simple public notice (*'ilm wa khabar*), even though it is required to have internal regulations.[86]

85. See Decree 87 on Public Benefit Associations of 1977.

86. See the 1909 Ottoman Law of Associations, still in effect. There is a disagreement between the Ministry of Interior and various social activists about the way an association is founded: whether it needs prior authorization or whether a public notice suffices. The 1909 Ottoman law requires only a public announcement, while a decree issued in 1983 (contemporaneous with the Israeli invasion, converging with the analysis of Hajj Tawfiq regarding the freedom of association and its curtailment) requires prior authorization (*autorisation préalable*). Even though the decree was abrogated in 1984,

Both kinds of organizations, however, are ultimately accountable to an organ of the state—respectively, the cabinet or the Ministry of the Interior—which can dissolve them if they constitute a threat to national security.[87] In the lawyer's discourse, the state appears to be using its power of regulation and protection of national security (in the form of the threat of dissolving NGOs) to produce a "civil society" that does not hold it accountable.[88] Civil society is not a haven outside the control of the state.

Distinct from this kind of accountability, "charitable" waqfs, as I described above with the French Mandate, were left to the Muslim community to regulate as part of its "religious affairs". Furthermore, as al-Karama's lawyer mentioned, waqf law is currently *flou*, and this blurriness afforded al-Karama's founders room for maneuvering. Founders and experts explained to me that since shariʿa judges are not bound by a codified law and rule based on the most "authoritative" (*al-arjaḥ*) view of the school, each can exercise their own interpretation, reading, and assessment of the various opinions prevalent in the fiqh, regardless of school.[89] Judges can decide what they think are acceptable objects to waqf, as well as what constitutes charitable purposes. Some, for instance, accept founding "cash waqfs," like al-Karama, while others refuse.[90] One must find a judge who supports such a waqf. Waqfs cannot legally be dissolved without the will of their administrators or beneficiaries. The judge can hold accountable the administrators of the waqf only in the case of misuse of funds or purpose. Many founders assume that judges of the shariʿa court share their own political leanings or that they are not as politically motivated as possible governments that might come to oppose Muslim institutions more broadly. Furthermore, as Hajj Tawfiq writes: "Waqfs have their sanctity [*ḥurma*], and their legal personality [*dhimma*] independently of the state; they cannot be confiscated or sold; they can only be exchanged for another parcel or for a monetary equivalent" (Huri n.d., 4). Founders also bank on that sanctity to deter judges from interfering in these waqfs.

---

the Ministry of the Interior insists on authorization. The Constitutional Court ruled against the practice in 2003. See Moukheiber (2002) and Report of the Parliamentary Commission on Human Rights (Lajnat Huquq al-Insan al-Niyabiyya and UNDP 2008).

87. The influence of such jurisdictional politics and differing regulations for associations, foundations, and waqfs on the creation of such institutions also plays out in Egypt, albeit in a different configuration (see Atia 2013).

88. Reports regarding freedom of association note the illegal administrative practices of the Ministry of Interior that flipped the meaning of public notice to one that the ministry delivers. See Moukheiber (2002, 18–19).

89. This is not exactly the case, as Clarke (2012, 109) explains, since the president of the court can discipline those decisions through the appeals court.

90. Unlike Ottoman cash waqfs, where a significant amount of cash is waqfed so that its revenue (interest from lending or profit from investing it) could actually be significant enough to support a charitable cause, the $100 of al-Karama is a pro forma "object" to create the waqf. The revenues necessary for the operation of the waqf are collected through donations held by the waqf.

While it appears that al-Karama's founders used waqf to escape the control of the modern state, whether exercised by the Ministry of the Interior or the cabinet, they were instead switching to the control of a different organ of the state, the shariʿa courts. Furthermore, the shariʿa courts themselves turn out to be much less uniform in their stance than first appears: different judges at court can hold different opinions and sanction certain waqfs their colleagues would not accept. Not only did "the state" itself disintegrate into various directorates and ministries competing over jurisdiction, but the unity of these various entities themselves fragmented as individual functionaries turn out to have the discretionary power to uphold different rules and conflicting regulations. We see founders navigating ambiguities of authority and jurisdiction between the grand mufti, the chief justice of the religious courts, the judges, the Ministry of the Interior, and the prime ministry around waqf, even creating a new entity, the "charitable waqf serving public benefit." An attempt by the grand mufti to control the possibilities allowed by these multiple jurisdictions by ordering judges to get final approval from him for every new waqf was impossible to enforce. It also exacerbated tensions between the chief justice of the shariʿa court (particularly in Beirut) and the grand mufti because shariʿa court judges are legally accountable and responsible not to the grand mufti but to the chief justice.[91] Yet, at the same time, the attempt of these founders to escape control of "the state" through the religious courts is itself a result of the modern state that separated some of the administration and legislation on waqf into an entity separate from the courts.

CONCLUSION

In this chapter, by focusing on three moments in the administration of waqf, I have attempted to bring forth the fundamentally different logics of modern state power but also to point at the incompleteness and the contradictions this new order engenders. It is not that waqf administration and supervision have been taken over by the state, but that this is an always-incomplete project that forever calls for new attempts at control. The modern state project is always so: a project. While modern power appears to have an overwhelming logic, when examining it in one particular area—here, waqf administration—its ambiguities and contradictions come forth. What surfaces, as the various moments illustrate, are constant rearticulations with changing conditions.

By tracing the manner of administration of waqf, I have drawn a picture of the architecture of state, law, and religion in the three different moments. Under an Islamic polity like the Ottoman state, many waqfs were seized by the Waqf

91. Back in 2009, rumors abounded that the chief justice of Beirut, ʿAbd al-Latif Diryan, was eyeing the grand muftiship, threatening the then grand mufti, and creating tension. These rumors were confirmed in 2014 when Grand Mufti Qabbani (unrelated to the Qabbani waqf) was forced to resign and Diryan replaced him, following a protracted political crisis in the midst of Dar al-Fatwa.

Ministry and subjected to new regulations and uniform, regular methods of accounting and administration. This process helped to create the state effect and to make the state the primary location for the production of waqf law, competing with its Muslim scholarly production.

With the transformation of the state—from an Islamic polity that granted privileges and immunity to some non-Muslim religious communities to a civic state equidistant from the eighteen recognized religious sects having legal sovereignty over various personal status matters—waqf administration exemplifies the way the Muslim community and waqfs became "sectarianized," while bearing vestiges of the earlier dominance of the Sunnis in the state. The new conceptualization of waqfs made by Muslims as the "property of the Muslim community," rather than individual endeavors now occupies pride of place in general discussions of waqf as an institution. It appeared in the campaign of the DGIW to unify all its property titles in the real estate registry in the early 2000s under the name "Directorate General of Islamic Waqfs—The Waqf of the Sunni Sect". This process of registration was also yet another attempt by the DGIW to produce its authority over these waqfs, indexing the persistence of the connection between particular waqfs and their founders and the localization of waqfs in their neighborhoods.

This sectarianization of waqf was made possible by and further reproduced secular understandings of religion and its place in society: religion now belonged in the private sphere and needed to be separate from economy and politics. Indeed, the new legal regime introduced by the French Mandate differentiated between personal status under religious law and real status under civil law. The making of waqf as "religious" property under religious law is thus a secularization of the waqf. This secularization is a continuous project that incites sovereign control and produces the state-effect. Indeed, carrying over Ottoman state supervision of waqfs through the Ottoman Waqf Ministry and the shari'a courts, Muslim waqfs remained connected to the state with the DGIW and the shari'a courts as state institutions splitting jurisdiction over the religious aspects of the waqf. Muslim actors thus employed jurisdictional politics in their waqf practices, necessitating constant reassertions by these different state institutions of their control over waqf.

After this long detour into the context that determines waqf practices, we can now turn to these practices and how their transformations with the modern state opened ways to instantiate new grammars of self, family, and community.

PART II

Grammars

3

The Intent of Charity

While doing archival research at the Başbakanlık Osmanlı Arşivi (BOA) in 2008, I encountered the kind of "file" that historians and historical anthropologists dream of: a thick collection of documents and correspondence that extended over many years and included original documents from Mount Lebanon sent as a result of an investigation. The trigger for the investigation was an 1875 inquiry from Mount Lebanon's governor,[1] Rüstem Pasha, to the highest official religious-legal authority in the Ottoman Empire, the office of the *şeyhülislâm*, the chief imperial mufti,[2] about some waqfs. "Some inhabitants of the 'Mountain' [Mount Lebanon]," he noted, "have been founding waqfs with the intent [*qaşdıyla*] of escaping the sale of these properties in fulfillment of debts." He asked, "Are these waqfs legally valid?" (BOA.ŞD.MLK 2271/66/9).

At the time, the question did not particularly puzzle me, as suspicion about founders and their use of waqf for various self-serving purposes lined up with scholarly analyses of waqf that emphasized founders' ulterior motives. The question arose at a time of vast changes in the Ottoman property regime, including a new land code, an attempt to bypass tax farmers in favor of direct taxation of titleholders, systematic foreclosure for debt, up-front ownership by foreigners, and

1. Since 1861, Mount Lebanon (known as the Mountain [*al-jabal*]) had been a semiautonomous Ottoman governorate (*mutaşarrifiyya*), whose governor was appointed by and responsible to the Ottoman Porte. While the inhabitants of the Mountain were mostly Maronite Christians and Druze, civil transactions followed the official Islamic legal school of the Ottoman Empire, the Ḥanafī *madhhab*.

2. The *şeyhülislâm*, the mufti of Istanbul, sits at the top of the Islamic scholarly hierarchy in the Ottoman Empire. For more details on the office, its functions, and development, see Repp (1986).

increased security of usufruct rights in *miri* (state-owned) land. In such a tumultuous landscape, the attempt to escape some brutal effects of these changes did not come as a surprise. However, when I sat down to start writing, after having gone through most of my qadi court archive, the formulation of the question began to intrigue me. In the qadi court records I had never encountered any such inquiry or lawsuit regarding the sincerity of founders. The governor's question became even more puzzling as I started reading about law and intent in Euro-American legal theory and encountered the maxim that "law is concerned with external conduct, [and] morality with internal conduct" (quoted in Morris 1976, 1).

This question of intent sent me down my notebooks, pressing Ctrl+F and searching for some keywords: "intent" in English, and "*niyya*" and "*qaṣd*" in Arabic.[3] They appeared in a few places. I read the sections around them. Long-forgotten conversations and episodes in my ethnographic research started coming back to me, and I started seeing them differently. I remembered a mufti describing people using waqfs as NGOs, and thus endowing a little money or in one case a few computers. From his description of "five computers from here, five computers from there," I had assumed that he was suspicious, but as he began to elaborate, he had stopped himself mid-sentence and changed topics. I now realized that he perhaps did not want to attribute bad intent to these founders. It took an encounter in the archive for me to question my own common sense, to realize that my deep suspicion of the DGIW, the DGIW's suspicion of waqf founders, and the more generalized suspicion of people's intent in charitable giving was circumstantial. I started wondering whether that concern with the sincerity of acts of charity was a reflection of the modern grammar of interiority, especially the idea that we have inner depths that are the locus of the true self, as Charles Taylor (1989) and others have noted (e.g., Burckhardt 1921). But if state officials were worried about the intent of subjects, the records of my qadis showed the qadis were not.

Concerns with interiority are not new to Islamic law (T. Asad 2003, 225), and the intent of getting close to God is essential to the making of waqf as an act of charity. Furthermore, the question of the waqf-making ability of indebted individuals is not new in the Ottoman Ḥanafi fiqh. However, as this chapter demonstrates, in the earlier elaborations, intention was structured along this-worldly effects and otherworldly effects and was always tied to action and expression. The question of waqf-making now introduced a new grammar of intent that opened the inner self and its intentions to scrutiny beyond its outward expressions and introduced suspicions about ulterior motive, contrary to the cultivated abstinence from subjecting intent alone to scrutiny in the Ḥanafi school. This new grammar, along with a changing relation between the family and charity as discussed in the next chapter, was used to legally question the validity of family waqfs as charitable

3. The words *qaṣd* and *niyya* both indicate intent, but *niyya* is the one that jurists use more often to discuss intent in the abstract, whereas *qaṣd* indicates intent behind an action. For a discussion of the use of these two words in the Islamic legal tradition, see Powers (2006, 3–4 especially).

acts. This further ensured the dominance of the new property regime and the foreclosures it enshrined, restricting the challenge that waqf, as an instrument of ownership devolution, posed to that dominance.

The chapter starts with a snapshot of the grammar of intent in the Ḥanafī tradition, especially around waqf-making requirements. Using legal manuals and historical court records of loans from the Beirut qadi court, I analyze the way loans were secured in Ottoman legal practice prior to the Tanzimat. Waqf was not perceived as a threat to enforcing debtors' claims because of a regime of debt that emphasized forgiveness. In the second section, I outline some of the Ottoman legal reforms that expanded and systematized foreclosure and show how they destabilized the debt regime promoted in the Ottoman canon. I then turn to the political-economic and social situation in Ottoman Mount Lebanon to understand why such a question on the use of waqf to escape debt arose. I argue that the answer given by the office of the şeyhülislâm enshrines a minority opinion formulated in the early sixteenth century during the price revolution, which rendered intent an object of suspicion and scrutiny. In the third section, turning to the French Mandate, I show how systematic foreclosure, introduced by Ottoman reforms, was expanded by French regulations, which instated it as a real right independent of mortgage contracts. Suspicion about the intent of founders and debtors continued to appear in both legal texts and queries from French advisors. In the last section, I scrutinize my conversations with various practitioners involved in waqf today and observe how the old grammar of intent continues to arise among practitioners of the tradition, despite the generalized suspicion around waqf foundation and charitable intent today.[4]

OTTOMAN ḤANAFĪ SUBJECTS OF WAQF BETWEEN INTENT IN ACTION AND DEBT FORGIVENESS

On Intent in the Ottoman Legal Canon

How was the legal subject conceived in the Ottoman fiqh?[5] What is the role of intent in the validity of his or her actions? Is the legal subject's intent accessible

4. For a similar but much more expansive and complex account of the transformation of debt regimes between the late eighteenth and early twentieth centuries in the Indian Ocean, see Bishara (2017).

5. A previous version of this section and the following appeared in Moumtaz (2018c). The Hanafi fiqh was the dominant framework for civil and criminal law in Mount Lebanon, especially after the eighteenth century. Touma (1972) describes two phases in the organization of the judiciary in Mount Lebanon up till 1861. In the first phase, which starts around 1450, before Ottoman rule, and continues into the eighteenth century, before the reign of Bashir II (1789–1840), the Ottoman governor of Damascus (or whichever province Mount Lebanon was attached to) confirmed a Druze judge, the Shaykh al-Shuyukh (according to Touma, these judgeships were hereditary), who applied Islamic law not only among the Druze but also among Muslims, Christians, and Jews of the Mountain (Touma 1972, 474). This function was eventually taken up by the governors of the districts and/or a judge they themselves nominated. In parallel, there were Druze and Maronite judges who applied Druze and Maronite law

to scrutiny, and, if it is, how is intent examined? In a monograph on intent in Islamic law, Paul Powers asserts, "Aside from religious faith itself, intent is arguably the most important subjective or 'internal' component of the action prescribed, proscribed, and evaluated by Muslim legal scholars" (2006, 1). The importance of intent articulates what Brinkley Messick calls foundationalism in Islamic law, where the "site of authoritative meaning-generation" is in the heart, internal, within the self, "beyond direct observation" (2001, 153). Testifying to the importance of intent in Islamic law and practice, most *qawāʿid* (legal maxims) manuals start with the maxim "[The qualifications of] deeds are determined by their intentions" ("innamā al-aʿmāl bi'l-niyyāt").[6] In Ibn Nujaym's canonical Ḥanafī version of the manuals, the discussion on intent is longer than any other maxim and includes ten subtopics like the essence of intent, the reason behind its legislation, and its sincerity, timing, and location. Ibn Nujaym reports the legal definition of intent as the "aim [*qaṣd*] of obedience and drawing close to God in performing an act [*fī ījād al-fiʿl*]" (Ibn Nujaym, *Ashbāh*, 24). The proper intent is then *qurba*, becoming close to God. The purpose of requiring intent, explains Ibn Nujaym, is to distinguish worship acts (*ʿibādāt*) from mere habitual acts. For instance, the intent of submitting to God makes fasting a ritual rather than a weight-loss strategy. Intent then also becomes unnecessary in certain worship acts like remembrances (*adhkār*) or reciting the Qur'an, acts that are unmistakably aimed at worship. Even more, intent fixes the legal determination of certain acts. Here Ibn Nujaym gives the example of slaughtering an animal: an act considered permissible or recommended if intended for eating; an act of worship if intended for ritual sacrifice; and a prohibited act if intended to celebrate the arrival of a prince.

Beyond the technical definition of intent as obedience and *qurba*, the discussion of the legal maxim uses the understanding of intention as "what one really meant," what in American law is known as "subjective intent." There, for Ibn Nujaym, the general rule is that "if intent in the heart differs from its expression 'in the tongue,'

---

in family matters. In the second phase, starting in the eighteenth century, the rulers of the Mountain abrogated the functions of the judge appointed by Damascus or by district governors and those of the Maronite judges responsible for family law. This system culminated under Bashir II, who appointed and dismissed the judges himself and applied Ḥanafī law to all the Mountain and its subjects. Both Bashir II and his predecessor nominated a Sunni judge as the head judge of the Druze community. With the founding of the *mutaṣarrifiyya* in 1861, a new system of tiered courts under the control of the governor and tied to the central government was instituted by the Réglement of Mount Lebanon and refined and revised by the successive governors based on their on-the-ground experience (for details, see Akarlı 1993, 132–46).

6. In Ibn Nujaym's manual, the discussion on intent is split between two rules: "There is no reward except through intent" and "Matters are evaluated according to their purposes." Wensinck in *EI2* (2012) translates the latter as "Works are only rendered efficacious by their intention" (*EI2*), while Powers renders it as "Actions are defined by intentions" (2006, 1). I base my translation on Ibn Nujaym's explication that the intended meaning of actions (*al-aʿmāl*) is the qualification of actions (*ḥukm al-aʿmāl*).

true intent is the one in the heart" (*Ashbāh*, 39). However, how can a judge know what is in the heart? This dilemma raises the question of the role of expressions and their performativity in arenas other than worship (since judges do not interfere in worship), as in pronouncements of divorce, manumission, and oaths. The main issues arise around the effects of expressions that depend on intent, where the effects can be this-worldly and legal, or otherworldly. For instance, what is the effect of saying, "I divorce you" as a joke? Ibn Nujaym here uses a key distinction to judge the effect: *qaḍāʾan* and *diyānatan*: whether the decision concerns and occurs in the "domain of adjudication, which is enforceable in this world" or in the "domain of conscience," which affects only the "relationship between the believer and God" and is subject to God's justice in the hereafter (Peters and Bearman 2014, 2). Even though intent is always accessible to God, humans and judges can know it only through the *ẓāhir*, or "manifest signs and forms of legal expressions" (Messick 2001, 153), such as words and writing. Thus, a joking pronouncement of divorce has legal effects in this world but would not be counted among one's reprehensible actions in the hereafter. Another example is that of a man who swore not to lead group prayer. He gets up to pray. Another man then arrives and prays behind him. For the purpose of his relation to God, he has not broken his oath. However, if he had promised his wife to divorce her if he leads prayer, and she takes him to the judge, then the judge bases his judgment on the manifest (*al-ẓāhir*), which is that he led another man in prayer—unless he can show proof that he has expressed such an intent not to lead in prayer. We see here the dominant grammar of intent in the Ḥanafī tradition (and one could say in Islamic law generally) as tied to its exterior signs (Ibn Nujaym, *Ashbāh*, 25).

Another meaning of intent—that of ulterior motive—arises in the discussion of the sincerity of intent or devotion, *ikhlāṣ*, a Qurʾanic term that denotes purity.[7] In worship, in acts of submission to God (*ṭāʿāt*), sincerity is opposed to "making show" (*riyāʾ*) (according to the dictionary *Lisān al-ʿArab*). A large part of Ibn Nujaym's discussion on *ikhlāṣ* is about the effects of "making show" and the

7. Interestingly, the English term *sincere* has similar connotations. Trilling traces the early uses of the adjective *sincere* in English to the Latin *sincerus*, when it was used in the literal sense of "clean, or sound, or pure" (2009, 12). So, one spoke of "sincere wine" to say that it has not been adulterated and of "sincere religion" to imply that it had not been "tampered with, or falsified, or corrupted. . . . But it soon came to mean the absence of dissimulation or feigning or pretence" (Trilling 2009, 13). This latter sense of sincerity is very much present in the Qurʾan as well, as discussed in the introduction. Although outside the scope of this chapter, one can perhaps link that development in meaning to the social change ushered by the rise of Islam, as Trilling does for modern Europe. Indeed, Trilling argues that the new conception of the self as the sincere individual arose in the sixteenth century with the beginning of feudalism's demise and increasing social mobility and with it, the anxiety around people who are in places where they should not be. According to Trilling, the concept of sincerity seems to acquire saliency in periods of social reordering: for England and Europe, it applies to people moving across classes, above the station to which they were born; in early Islam, it could apply to people moving across religious and class divides.

absence of reward for worship acts performed to please others rather than God. In pecuniary transactions, the problem of ulterior motive arises with legal transactions whose effects are illegal, such as a sale that eventually allows charging interest and circumventing the prohibition on usury. This is the problem of what Powers, following philosopher of language John Searle, calls complex intention or the accordion effect (2006, 15). The dominant Ḥanafī position with regard to pecuniary transactions is a formalist one whereby "subjective states have no effect unless made overt" (Powers 2006, 115). Ḥanafīs prioritize intent in-action rather than complex prior intention and do not consider context in order to ascertain ulterior motive.[8] "When the ultimate aim of the contracting party is not apparent either from the terms of the contract or from the prevalent usage of the object under contract, the Ḥanafīs . . . ignore ulterior motivation, which has no legal effect on the validity of the transaction" (Arabi 1997, 215). Given the number of legal stratagem (*ḥiyal*) manuals in Ḥanafī fiqh, this position is not surprising.[9] Nonetheless, such contracts require particular expressions because clear words for the Ottoman Ḥanafīs are considered performative in the Austinian sense: they make things happen in the world even if the intent is not there.[10] It is only when the words are ambiguous that there is an attempt to figure out intent, and here again through its outward expression.

Waqf is a pecuniary transaction, but its charitable purpose makes it also an act of worship, as discussed in chapter 1. To be valid as a worship act, waqf necessitates the intent to get closer to God, or *qurba*. Intent was then not alien to discussions of waqf founding even in the late Ḥanafī Ottoman canon. The question, however,

8. This is the opinion of Abu Hanifa, whereas his students sometimes take into consideration indirect evidence, such as the dominant intent in the majority of cases (such as that musical instruments are used for entertainment), and if that intent is illegal, then they deem these contracts invalid (see Arabi 1997, 213–14).

9. The Mālikī and Ḥanbalī schools of Islamic law give more weight to intentions (see, for example, Powers 2006, 116–18; Arabi 1997), as can be seen in cases of *tawlīj*, when a parent uses a lawful contract of sale, acknowledgment of debt, or gift to one or some of his or her heirs in order to escape inheritance law. Mālikīs consider the contract valid unless there is direct evidence that it was illegal (witnesses to the parent admitting to fraud) or circumstantial evidence pointing "unequivocally to its fraudulent nature" (Powers 1996, 100). For more on *tawlīj*, see Powers (1996).

10. J. L. Austin demonstrates that utterances do not always "'describe' or 'report' or constate anything at all," but can, under certain conditions, also "do things" in the world, as in the pronouncement "I name this ship the *Queen Elizabeth*" (1962:5). The use of outward expressions to determine intent becomes a particularly thorny issue when such outward expressions are "*alfāz al-kufr*" (utterances of unbelief) that are used to determine that a Muslim has renounced Islam, which has very grave consequences (execution). Unlike a joking expression of divorce, whose legal consequences are immediate, the effects of these expressions are mitigated by a questioning of real intent and giving the accused the chance to give context or, deny unbelief, or to repent (Omar 2001, 93–94). Late Ḥanafīs had a very extensive list of what constituted utterances of unbelief. This became an issue during the Safavid-Ottoman conflict, when strict enforcement of the law would have led to the execution of many subjects of the Empire. For the solution to this dilemma, the "renewal of faith," see Burak (2013).

is whether intent was actually available to the scrutiny of judges and how they could uncover it. In the Ottoman canon, because "intent is subjective—invisible, silent, 'internal'—Muslim jurists must establish some legally recognized means for discerning it, such as deciding which objective indicants point to which subjective states" (Powers 2006, 3). In the case of waqf, intent and the validity of the waqf as a charitable act were determined by actions and expression; they were determined by the fulfillment of conditions with regard to the founder, the expressions used, the object endowed, and the beneficiaries. The founder had to have the legal capacity (*ahliyya*) to act; he or she had to be a sane adult free person. He or she had to use certain expressions that denote waqf. The objects endowed had to be his or her *milk*. Finally, the beneficiaries had to belong to a class of acceptable recipients to ensure the *qurba* purpose and the perpetuity of the waqf. Thus, as long as the waqf founder fulfilled these conditions of waqf-making, the waqf was valid. His or her action and expression were the indicants of his or her intent. Was there a concern with *ulterior motive* in and of itself, be it escaping inheritance law, confiscation, or debt repayment, as was posed in the question of the Ottoman governor of Mount Lebanon?

The question of waqf and debt arises from the earliest waqf manuals up to the latest codified manuals of the nineteenth century. Al-Tarabulusi (d. 1516), for instance, declares that the waqf of an indebted person "who is not under interdiction is valid *even if he intends by founding the waqf to harm his creditors* because their rights are established in his legal personality (*dhimma*) and not the object" (al-Tarabulusi 2005, 10, italics mine). The ruling on the validity of such a waqf shows that ulterior motive does not have a legal effect. Even more, it makes clear a fundamental aspect of debt contracting in Ḥanafi law: that it does not give rights to any object but is instead "an incorporeal right existing in the *dhimma* of the debtor" (*EI2*, *dhimma*). The particular phrasing of al-Tarabulusi in terms of intent to harm and not to pay back debts is very rarely mentioned, because the crux of the issue in discussions of indebtedness is the latter's effect on the legal capacity of the founder. Because indebtedness and even insolvency do not impact the legal capacity of founders ("li'ann al-waqf tabarruʿ wa lam yashtariṭ liṣiḥḥatih barāʾat al-dhimma min al-dayn al-mustaghriq bi'l-ijmāʿ"), they can still make waqfs—unless they are imprisoned for nonpayment (Ibn ʿAbidin, *Tanqīḥ*, 1:218).[11] Similarly, even if they have secured the loan through an immovable property, they can make a waqf of another property they possess.[12]

11. I more systematically discuss the effect of indebtedness and insolvency on the donative capacity of founders below.

12. There is a further ruling that "the waqf of an insolvent [*muflis*] *rāhin* is invalid," but the texts are unclear whether the ruling concerns the waqf of the security or whether it applies to another property that is not a security. In the *Tanqīḥ*, Ibn ʿAbidin uses this ruling after a question regarding the waqf of the security itself.

There is, however, another reason why the intent to escape foreclosure does not arise in the same way as it does in the question of the Mount Lebanon governor: the Ottoman Ḥanafī debt regime and its enshrinement of an ethic of forgiveness rather than foreclosure.

On Debt in the Ottoman Fiqh Property Regime: Forgiveness and Equity

A loan according to Ottoman Ḥanafī law does not require a security for it to be valid. It can be just noted down; a Qur'anic verse enjoins the worshippers to keep record of debts (2:282).[13] However, a voluntary act *(tabarru')* of giving an object as a security that serves only to increase the guarantee of the right (*ziyādat al-ṣiyāna*) can be offered by the debtor (Ibn Nujaym, *Baḥr*, 8:237). This is the *rahn* contract, translated as pledge or a security (Hallaq 2009, 267), and defined as the "detention of an object because of a right, like a debt, that can be satisfied by the object" ('Ayni, *Ramz*, 2:287). Here again, part of a Qur'anic verse is at the root of the obligation to transfer the object (2:283, *farihānun maqbūḍatun*) (Ibn 'Abidin, *Tanqīḥ* 2:408). When the object moves to the possession of the creditor (or an agreed upon third party), the voluntary pledge becomes irrevocable. The transfer of possession does not imply any transfer of the rights of usufruct and use ('Ayni, *Ramz*, 2:289), or the right to sell the object to the creditor. These rights remain in the hand of the debtor. However, none of the rights on the object can be exercised by the debtor or the creditor, for the purpose of the rahn is simply the confinement of the object, which therefore can only remain detained ('Ayni, *Ramz*, 2:289). The creditor cannot "rent" back the rahn (also used in the sense of the object pledged) to the debtor but can lend it back, allowing the debtor to still use the property (Ibn 'Abidin, *Tanqīḥ*, 2:408). While a similar contract called *bay' bi'l-wafā'* (similar to the *bay' al-khiyār* described by Bishara 2017, 90–99) developed, and was much more commonly used in Beirut, to allow using and deriving usufruct from the rahn, the new contract did not transfer ownership to the creditor, who could not sell the property. The rahn contract provides security because it gives the creditor priority in acquiring his or her debt from the estate of the debtor when the latter dies, before other creditors who do not have a rahn and before the division of the estate among heirs (Ibn Nujaym, *Baḥr*, 8:231).

13. The first part of Muhammad Asad's translation reads:

> Whenever you give or take credit for a stated term, set it down in writing. And let a scribe write it down equitably between you; and no scribe shall refuse to write as God has taught him: thus shall he write. And let him who contracts the debt dictate; and let him be conscious of God, his Sustainer, and not weaken anything of his undertaking. And if he who contracts the debt is weak of mind or body, or is not able to dictate himself, then let him who watches over his interests dictate equitably. And call upon two of your men to act as witnesses. . . . And be not loath to write down every contractual provision, be it small or great, together with the time at which it falls due; this is more equitable in the sight of God, more reliable as evidence, and more likely to prevent you from having doubts [later]. (1964, 75–76)

Given that a rahn involves confining the property and withholding any transactions by the debtor or creditor, one would expect the waqf of a rahn to be invalid. Yet jurists appear to allow some leeway when it comes to waqf, most probably because of its provision of various public goods, from early on (e.g. Khassaf 1999, 244). The waqf of a rahn by a (solvent) debtor (whose debt is not yet due) is valid, according to Ibn al-Humam, if the rahn is redeemed (*in iftakkah*) or if the founder dies after paying the loan. However, if the founder dies without having paid off the debt, the waqf is invalidated and the rahn sold. Other jurists like al-Tarabulusi are more stringent with affluent indebted founders: the judge forces them (*ajbarah*) to pay off their debts if they want to waqf a rahn. Insolvent debtors, for their part, cannot make a rahn into a waqf; the judge is to annul the waqf and sell the rahn to pay off the debt (all in Ibn Nujaym, *Baḥr*, 5:190; also quoted in Ibn ʿAbidin, *Tanqīḥ*, 1:218).

Comparing rahn with kin concepts in European law (whether in the common law or civil law traditions) highlights the particularities of the understanding of debt in the Islamic legal tradition. It also helps us see the novelties introduced in the Ottoman property regime around debt and rahn in the nineteenth century, based on European laws and codes, as these laws became more salient in the Ottoman Empire, especially with foreigners in the empire being subject to their national laws because of the capitulations.[14] The object of the rahn could be movable or immovable in civil law language, and chattel or real estate in common law language, obliterating the European legal distinction between pledge/pawn and mortgage (Gatteschi 1884, 51). To further push the comparison, one needs to look at forced sales, which were key in guaranteeing the "full usefulness and efficacy" (1884, 60) of these pledges according to nineteenth-century Orientalists like the Italian lawyer residing in Alexandria, Domenico Gatteschi.[15] "According to our laws, . . . forced sale [of the object pledged/collateral], or foreclosure, is an inevitable consequence of the pledge, or mortgage," whereas in Islamic law, Gatteschi notes, the existence of a pledge is not "enough to produce the forced sale of the object pledged" (1884, 60). The above analysis makes the concepts of *usefulness* and *efficacy* the criteria for evaluating these laws. But why did Gatteschi reach the conclusion that systematic forced sale was not present in Islamic law? Are the criteria of usefulness and efficacy what determine the operation of forced sale in the Ottoman Ḥanafī canon? Let us examine the logic and the place of foreclosure for debt for Ottoman Ḥanafīs in the fiqh and in legal practice.

14. The Ottoman capitulations are clauses attached to treaties done at the height of the empire's power in the sixteenth century, granting privileges to some European powers as diplomatic tools to create alignments with the Ottomans in their incursions against other European powers and to facilitate commerce. Later, with the rise of European power, these privileges, especially the commercial and legal ones, became a way that Europeans gained economic advantage and interfered in the Ottoman Empire. See İnalcık (2012) for this classic view, and Özsu (2012) for a revisionist account that highlights these instruments as sites of contestation.

15. For more on Gatteschi, see Wood (2016, 103–4).

In the Ottoman Ḥanafī canon, when a debtor defaults on payments, the creditor can request the debtor's imprisonment until the debtor fulfills his or her debt, in whatever way the debtor wishes—not necessarily by selling the object mortgaged. The first purpose of imprisonment is to allow the judge to determine whether the debtor is affluent or in financial hardship. Indeed, imprisonment aims to instigate "the boredom of the heart and then the payment [of the debt]" (ʿAyni, *Ramz*, 2:87), because the prison does not have a bed or a mattress, and the detained cannot have guests, nor go out for a Friday, the hajj, a funeral, Ramadan, holidays, or even the death of a near of kin. Imprisonment is also a retribution (*jazāʾ*) for injustice, here delaying payment due by an affluent person (ʿAyni, *Ramz*, 2:288), independently of the presence of a security (rahn). Affluent debtors can be imprisoned for life or until they pay their debt, according to a minority view.[16] At first hand, then, forced sale does not appear to be the standard procedure prescribed in the Ottoman Ḥanafī fiqh, or the inevitable consequence of the rahn contract, as wished for by Gatteschi.

Nonetheless, forced sales are not unheard of. First, the rahn contract can include a stipulation to give the creditor the power to sell the object in case the debtor fails to pay the debt by the time specified in the contract (for example, MBSS.S 04/101, 9 Feb 1857 [15 C 1273]). So, while the rahn contract does not stipulate foreclosure for debt, such a clause can be included in the contract. Second, if the debtor becomes insolvent (*muflis*)—his or her debts exceed his or her assets (cash, personal property, and real estate)—but has assets, the creditors can request his or her interdiction (*ḥajr*), and the payment of the debts by the judge on behalf of the debtor, first using cash, then selling personal property, and finally real estate (ʿAyni, *Ramz*, 2:224; Ibn ʿAbidin, *Tanqīḥ*, 2:149). Finally, if the imprisoned affluent debtor stubbornly refuses to pay (*mutamarridun mutaʿannitun*) after a judge orders him to do so, the judge can sell enough of the debtor's property on the

16. Such an approach to debtors' prison is very different from the French ancien régime debtors' prison (known in French as *contrainte par corps*), which allowed merchants to secure debt through the body of the debtor, when this debtor did not have immovable property—the main store of value and signifier of wealth and honor at the time—that could serve as a collateral. In that economy, mobile wealth was suspicious and dangerous. In addition, in France, debtors' prison was tied to the commercial code, and the ability to put debtors in prison was one of the privileges accorded to a certain class of people. Merchant courts, backed by guilds, were founded based on "Old Regime corporate ideas of jurisdictional authority" (Vause 2014, 655). After the French Revolution, with the enshrinement of the principle of equality and state sovereignty, state law came to govern all citizens equally. Nonetheless, because of the failed experiments of the Terror government with paper money, apprehension about the free market and mobile wealth led to the re-establishing of the *contrainte par corps*. Proponents of debtors' prison "affirmed the ideal that a government dependent on mobile wealth was morally and economically feasible, as long as creditors and debtors were themselves virtuous" (Vause 2014, 672), and the *contrainte* was what was going to ensure this virtuousness. In that scenario, merchants were not simply self-interested agents, they were "servant[s] of public welfare engaged not so much in profit seeking as in the management of an important sector of the national interest" (Shovlin, quoted in Vause 2014, 657). The *contrainte* was finally abolished in 1867.

debtor's behalf and settle the debt (*al-Fatāwā al-Hindiyya*, 3:419–20). Forced sale in this case and in the previous one is the view of the students of Abu Hanifa (Shaybani and Abu Yusuf), contrary to Abu Hanifa's view that the affluent debtor should be imprisoned forever, or until he or she pays, as noted above.[17]

Both imprisonment and forced sale of the assets of a solvent debtor for fulfilling debts have a very important caveat: the debtor must have the means (cash, movables, immovables) to pay; he or she must be affluent (*mūsir*) or insolvent having property. Both measures are suspended when the debtor is in financial hardship (*mu ʿsir*).[18] This ruling originates from the Qurʾanic injunction that "if, however, [the debtor] is in straitened circumstances, [grant him a delay] until a time of ease; and it would be for your own good—if you but knew it—to remit [the debt entirely] by way of charity" (2:280).[19] It is this very verse that Ibn ʿAbidin uses in an answer to a question about the validity of imprisoning a debtor who has legally been proven to be in duress (*Tanqīḥ*, 1:547).

While the penniless and propertyless debtor is set free, the insolvent debtor who possesses movables or immovables whose value would not suffice to pay off the debt as established by a judge falls under a different rule. His or her property is sold to pay off the debt, but jurists here use the concept of *ijtizāʾ* (sufficiency) to determine the legitimacy and extent of forced sale. Jurists debate what is essential property to be exempt from distribution to debtors. They distinguish between movables, personal items (clothing, tools of the trade, fiqh books) and immovables, especially one's home. Al-Ramli summarizes the possessions that debtors in hardship can keep: the clothes that they need, a cauldron (*dast*) or two, and the home that is not excessive (Ibn ʿAbidin, *Tanqīḥ*, 1:546). As importantly, sustenance of the debtor's family (like a wife's maintenance) takes precedence over the rights of creditors. The creditors can take back the debt in installments by taking whatever remains from a debtor's earnings after ensuring his livelihood and his family's ("[mā] yafḍul ʿanh wa ʿan nafaqat ʿiyālih") (Ibn ʿAbidin, *Tanqīḥ*, 1:546). Jason

17. Abu Hanifa does not allow such forced sales because, in his view, interdiction is an offense that humiliates debtors and brings then to the level of animals, which is a public harm (*ḍarar ʿāmm*) that cannot be made to compensate for a private one (*ḍarar khāṣṣ*) (ʿAyni, *Ramz*, 2:224).

18. Mālikīs distinguish two forms of *i ʿsār*, or financial hardship: destitution (*i ʿdām*) or scarcity (*iqlāl*). The destitute (*al-mu ʿsir al-mu ʿdim*) do not possess any cash, movables, or immovables. The impoverished (*al-madīn al-muqill*) do not possess money at hand but might possess movables or immovables whose value does not suffice to pay off their debt and whose sale would cause them duress, like selling the house that serves as a shelter to their family. Destitution makes imprisonment, forced sale, and even the demand for payment prohibited, an injustice and a grave sin (*kabīra*) (al-Salami 2010).

19. While there are reports that this verse addresses Muslims who had engaged in usury (*ribā*) before their conversion and thus applies only to *ribā*, Qurʾanic commentators interpret the verse as a more general injunction that applies to debt more broadly (see, for example, Tabari 2003, 5:57–63). In his commentary, Ottoman şeyhülislâm Ebüssuʿûd explains the verse as just a general injunction (Abu al-Suʿud 1990, 1:314).

Kilborn summarizes the guiding philosophy, following al-Marghinani, as "[the debtors'] indispensable wants precede the rights of his creditors" (2011, 354).

For instance, a question in the chapter on interdiction in Ibn ʿAbidin's super-commentary on *al-Fatāwā al-Ḥāmidiyya* (*Tanqīḥ*, 2:257) revolves around the case of an insolvent impoverished debtor who does not possess anything but a dwelling that answers his or her needs, and whose needs would not be fulfilled without the house. Ibn ʿAbidin answers that such a sale is illegitimate, but continues with an analogy to clothing, which has been discussed by earlier scholars: if the debtor possesses more clothing than he or she needs, he or she is to sell it all, buy a garment to wear, then pay off some of the debt with the money from the sale. Ibn ʿAbidin's solution, as "our scholars" say, is then to sell the house only if it exceeds the needs of the debtor, buy a smaller house that is more appropriate to the debtor's new social status, and use the remainder of the money to pay back the creditors.[20] Forced sale therefore brings criteria (like need and sufficiency) that are socially constructed while also taking into account the social financial status of the debtor and bringing a moral imperative to give time to a debtor in duress. Here the concept of an "absolute" right of the creditor to recover a debt is superseded by an emphasis on what kind of person one (both creditor and debtor) should be and the life one should be leading.[21] That is because the subject, even in pecuniary transactions, is morally constructed.

The concept of duress and its influence on requests of debt payment do not remain in the books of the library, but come through in the archive. For the existing record in Beirut between 1842 and 1885,[22] the cases of claims of financial hardship (*iʿsār*) (for example, MBSS.S5A/23/3, 5A/20/3, 7/125/3, and 7/172/2) reproduce the arguments discussed above for or against the collection of a debt. All cases are articulated as lawsuits (*daʿāwā*) and follow a similar blueprint, as is the case with most judicial decisions and contracts.[23] The document copied on the page of the court *sijill* represents a summary of a process that did not happen in a single court session. The lawsuit, most likely, happened over the course of a few days, if not a few weeks, as it involves finding witnesses, imprisonment, and bringing witnesses to court. The lawsuit starts with a creditor who claims that a debtor owes him (*fī dhimmatih*) a certain amount of money, and requests the debtor to pay it

20. I have not found a discussion of the fate of a bankrupt debtor who had made his only house into rahn: should the judge sell the house? Given that the wants of the debtor take precedence over the creditors' rights, I imagine that it is not sold.

21. Many dues (like child and spousal maintenance [*nafaqa*], dower [*mahr*], etc.) are defined in the fiqh based on the norms of a certain class in a certain time and place, rather than in absolute terms. See, for example, Hallaq (2009, 279) for maintenance.

22. The record starts in 1842. Lawsuits about foreclosures stop appearing in the registers in 1885 (MBSS.S27 is the last register containing entries about debt, with the exception of debts owed from the estate of a deceased); that is the date when they must have been moved to the Nizamiye Courts.

23. This is no surprise as model documents for many contracts and legal transactions were included in manuals known as *shurūṭ*. See entry on *sharṭ* in *EI2*.

back. The debtor acknowledges the debt and claims to be in financial duress. The burden of proof falls here on the creditor who is claiming that the debtor is affluent and has the means to pay off his debt, because poverty is the "*aṣl*," the "natural state of affairs" (Ibn ʿAbidin, *Ḥāshiya*, 4:318).[24] If the creditor is able to summon witnesses to attest to the prosperity of the debtor, the judge requires the debtor to pay off the debt. If the creditor cannot summon such witnesses, the debtor needs to take an oath as to his duress, because he cannot summon witnesses himself to deny the claim of prosperity since testimonies are only valid as a confirmation, not as a denial ("bayyina ʿalā al-nafī . . . lā tuqbal") (ʿAyni, *Ramz*, 2:87; Johansen 1999, 37). Such a testimony (denying affluence) can only be a supplement to an original proof, which here is imprisonment (ʿAyni, *Ramz*, 2:87), as the willingness to stay imprisoned is taken as a proof of duress. The judge then orders the debtor to be released and the creditor to wait for the debtor to be in a "state of affluence" (*maysara*).

In these lawsuits, what are the arguments used to counter the right of the creditor? Why isn't it treated as an "absolute" right? What types of rights and values do the jurists and the law prioritize and in what circumstances? In all cases of hardship, there is no dispute about whether the creditor has a rightful claim: she does, as the debtor owes her money. Debtors acknowledge this claim. To counter this right, debtors advance an argument based on capability. They always make the claim that they are currently in "financial hardship, unable to pay off their debt" ("muʿsir lā qudra lah ʿalā īfāʾihā").[25] In hardship, the debtor is unable to provide his necessary food ("lā qudra lah ʿalā taḥṣīl qūtih al-ḍarūrī"), let alone pay his debt, as one debtor claimed. He also may not have any immovables or movables (*ʿaqār* and *manqūl*), as some witnesses testify. When duress is proven, examining how the judge weighs arguments for or against collection becomes crucial to understanding the reasoning behind the administration of justice. The judge's decision states: "I ordered the creditor to grant him a delay until the debtor becomes in a financial ease" ("amartuh bi-inẓārih ilā maysara"). This decision follows verbatim the Qurʾanic verse mentioned above,[26] a verse that is sometimes quoted and used as a justification for the judge's decision (MBSS.S5A/20/3). In the hierarchy of proofs, a Qurʾanic injunction trumps other proofs, and one can say that quoting the injunction to wait also serves as moral admonishment, most likely bringing to the creditor's mind the second half of the verse: "It would be for your own

24. The burden of proof falls on the plaintiff who is arguing against the "natural state of things" or "appearances" (Johansen 1999, 437). So, if A is in possession of a piece of land, and B claims that this land is his or her *milk*, it is up to B to prove that claim. The judge assigns the role of plaintiff and defendant, a crucial task as it affects the burden of proof (see Schacht 1964, 190–92).

25. In some of the cases, in addition to financial hardship, a debtor claims he is insolvent (*muflis*) (MBSS.S7/172/2, Ah5A/20/3). Abdullah bin Nasir al-Salami says that "every *muʿsir* is insolvent but not every insolvent is *muʿsir*." Therefore, mentioning that they are insolvent seems redundant.

26. "If, however, [the debtor] is in straitened circumstances, [grant him a delay] until a time of ease; and it would be for your own good—if you but knew it—to remit [the debt entirely] by way of charity" (Qurʾan 2:280).

good—if you but knew it—to remit [the debt entirely] by way of charity." The injunction for patience, and even debt forgiveness, seems to be a major consideration in the rulings into the late nineteenth century.

In Beirut's shariʿa court records, sale for fulfillment of debt was not unknown, but it certainly was not a generalized clause. Gatteschi was not wrong, then, in ascribing a "lack" of systematic foreclosure for debt in Islamic law. Nonetheless, examining the articulation of rights and duties and their fulfillment in Islamic law, here with regard to debts, shows that this "lack" originates from a different logic of negotiation, fulfillment, and enforcement than Gatteschi's concern with the *efficacy* of pledges. In this logic, the notion of justice is not separated from a moral assessment of rights; it is "a moral logic of social equity, rather than a logic of winner-takes-it-all resolutions" (Hallaq 2009, 166). Even though the creditor has a right, the debtor's conditions, especially the consequences of enforcing the creditor's right, are taken into account. A different kind of ethic regarding debtors appears: charity, forgiving debts, and forbearance inform decisions. These conclusions about the connection between debt and morality seem to confirm David Graeber's insight in *Debt: The First 5,000 Years* (2011) that debt regimes in non- or less-monetized economies were regimes of trust, built very much on cycles of credit, where foreclosure was not fully enforced.[27] People did lose land and valuables but not on the scale to come after the enshrinement of forced sale in the law.[28] It was with the monetization of the economy and the rise of European finance capital that nonpayment of debt started to become criminalized, and that we moved towards an insistence on foreclosure for debt. Let us see how this happened in Ottoman Mount Lebanon.

TANZIMAT FORECLOSURE FOR DEBT AND THE NEW LEGAL SUBJECT: SCRUTINIZING INTERIORITY

A New Debt Regime

The middle of the nineteenth century saw the rise of a new debt regime in the Ottoman Empire. Nonetheless, the different codes and regulations governing different subjects and land categories created a complex and variegated legal terrain, despite widening the foreclosure net.[29] New regulation on "mortgage" was included

27. The Ottoman Empire had a monetized economy, but it did not encompass all transactions and areas. A discussion of debt in Mount Lebanon will follow in the next section.

28. In that regime, waqfs were outside the domain of foreclosures: waqf objects could not be used as a security for a loan since *rahn* could be done only to *milk* objects.

29. The main regulations on mortgage can be found in *Düstur*, 1. Tertip (1289 [1873]); Ongley and Miller (1892); and Young (1905); and in the Mecelle (Haydar 2010). Ongley and Miller's translations are a bit convoluted and unclear; Young's are much clearer. The regulations are the Land Law of 1858 [7 N 1274] (Articles 115 to 118); the Tapu Law of 1859 [8 J 1275] (Articles 25 to 29); the supplement to the Tapu Law in 1861 [26 S 1278] (Ongley and Miller 1892, 135); the Irade of 1860 [Ra 1279], on the sale

as early as 1850 in the Code of Commerce, which was based on the 1807 French commerce code. The code established systematic foreclosure for debt, stating, for instance, that "the judge can authorize the trustees of the bankruptcy to proceed to sell the immovables or the merchandise of the insolvent" (Piat and Dahdah 1876, 588). The code was first used in mixed commercial courts that settled disputes between Ottoman and foreign merchants, as well as among Ottoman merchants themselves (Rubin 2011, 26). Through its application at the Beirut Commercial Court in the 1850s, the Code of Commerce reached the inhabitants of Mount Lebanon, as all commercial litigation in the Mountain, in addition to civil litigation involving foreigners, was placed under its jurisdiction (Akarlı 1993, 132–33).

The extension of foreclosure on *milk* in Nizamiye Courts was enshrined through the Mecelle in 1871. The civil code modified the Ottoman Islamic legal regime of forgiveness that is described above, allowing systematic foreclosure on rahn. Indeed, Article 757 clearly states: "If the debt comes to term and the debtor does not fulfill it, the judge orders him to sell the mortgaged property and to pay off his debt. If he refuses [to do so], the judge sells the mortgaged property and pays off the debt." Ali Haydar, in his six-volume commentary on the Mecelle, notes that the last part of the article follows the *madhhab* of the students of Abu Hanifa and, as discussed above, that their teacher does not allow forced sale by the judge, who can imprison the debtor only until the latter pays off the debt by selling the mortgaged property or by other means. Furthermore, Ali Haydar brings up some of the debt relief measures discussed in the fiqh and explains that they do not hold when there is a rahn involved. "This mortgaged property is sold even if it is the residence of the debtor, and even if he (or his heirs if he passes away) do not have any other house they can reside in, because the right of the creditor is attached to it" (Article 757). When there is no rahn involved, the same exemptions for the needs of the debtor apply (Article 999). Gone were considerations of poverty and need, of sufficiency and destitution. The Mecelle instated a debt regime for *milk* lands, where foreclosure on mortgages was enforced independently of the state of the debtor and its effects on him or her.

The foreclosures allowed by the Code of Commerce and the Mecelle did not apply to all kinds of land. Both waqf and *miri* land could not be mortgaged, based on Ḥanafī law, since the possessor of these lands did not possess the right of alienation, *raqaba*. And indeed, the Land Code of 1858, which applied to *miri* land, reiterated positions similar to the Ottoman late Ḥanafī debt regime discussed above. Article 116 confirms that waqf and *miri* could not be mortgaged. However,

of the land of certain debtors for payment of debt; the Law of 1869 [23 N 1286], on the forced sale of *miri* and *mevkûfe* lands, and the *müsakkafât-i* and *mütsaghallât-i vakfiye*, along with its 1871 annex [21 N 1288] (Ongley and Miller 1892: 216–17); the Irade of 1871 [21 R 1287], on the procedure of mortgage; the Law of 1871 [15 L 1288], concerning the sale of immovable property for debt. Mecelle Articles 118 (*bayʿ biʾl wafāʾ*), 119 (*bayʿ biʾl-istighlāl*), and the whole of Book 5: Rahn (Articles 701–63) and its 1871 addendum [26 S 1288] deal with mortgage and foreclosure on *milk*.

the code allows the contract of *ferâğ bi'l-vefâ* (the equivalent of *bayʿ bi'l-wafāʾ* for lands that are waqf and *miri* since one cannot sell them), whereby "the holding is registered as sold to the lender but with the right of redemption by the debtor on full payment of debt" (Mundy and Smith 2007, 46). As Mundy and Smith note, this permission in practice introduced a "form of mortgage" on *miri* (2007, 46). The Land Code also restated that foreclosure was not possible without a rahn or *ferâğ bi'l-vefâ* (Article 115). As in the Ḥanafī fiqh, at the death of the debtor, creditors with debts guaranteed against land through *ferâğ bi'l-vefâ* had to receive the amounts owed to them before the heirs could inherit the land (Article 118). Nonetheless, if the debtor died without heirs, the land would revert to the state, making it impossible for the creditor to recover his debt (Article 118). Both during the lifetime and after the death of the debtor, the creditor could not sell the land—unless the debtor expressly gave her that right, as in Ottoman late Ḥanafī requirements. However, an exception was granted to the Treasury in an Irade issued in 1862 [Ra 1279], and *miri* land could be sold without permission from the debtor by the judge to fulfill debts due to the Treasury even during the lifetime of the debtor.

The restrictions of the Land Code on the foreclosure of *miri* and waqf were, however, relaxed starting in 1869, fulfilling earlier unfulfilled promises to promulgate laws describing procedure and process of foreclosure. Indeed, the Tapu Law of 1858 had already noted that an 1858 imperial ordinance [9 N 1274] had allowed a creditor to sell mortgaged *miri* land to recover his debt, "solely because of public benefit" ("mücerred menfaʿat-i ʿâmme için") (*Düstur* 1289, 205). Laws published in 1869 [23 N 1286] and in 1871 [15 L 1288] specified foreclosure procedures during the lifetime and after the death of the debtor. Article 2 of the 1869 law, for instance, does not leave it up to the heirs to fulfill the debt of a deceased debtor in order to inherit the land; it allows the sale of the mortgaged property if the deceased's estate does not suffice to cover the debt, when it is guaranteed by a piece of land.[30] Foreclosure is also rendered possible on *miri* and waqf for a debt (when used in a contract of *ferâğ bi'l-vefâ*) established in court, even during the lifetime of the debtor (Article 1 of the 1871 law), by the judge and without the permission of the debtor. The extension of foreclosure on *miri* and waqf thus made these different categories much closer to *milk*, the forced sale of which the Mecelle allowed in 1871 (Article 757), pushing towards what Mundy and Smith term a "unified field of property law" where "formerly different categories" were unified (2007, 51).[31]

30. Nonetheless, if the debt is not guaranteed by that piece of land, or if that piece does not suffice to cover the debt, the creditor cannot pursue other properties of the debtor (Law of 1869, Article 4).

31. For a discussion of the entrenchment of the rights of usufructuaries on waqf (and therefore its assimilation to *milk*), see Güçlü (2009). Mundy and Smith (2007) propose that the use of the term "immovable property" (*emvâl-i ghayr-i menkûle*) in the title of the 1871 law on foreclosures [15 L 1288] testifies to this unification of property law. The argument is appealing, even though the variety of terms used in the laws on mortgage show that the effort to unify had a long way to go—for instance, *arâzî* in 1858, *emlâk* in 1867, *arâzî -yi amîriye ve müsakkafât-i ve müstaghallât-i vakfiye* in 1869; *emlâk* in 1870, *emvâl-i ghayr-i menkûle* in 1871.

Despite these advances in foreclosures, the new legislation kept many of the brakes that existed in the fiqh, while adding some others, thereby protecting debtors from becoming "free workers" in the sense of being dispossessed of any land and therefore having to sell their labor power on the market (Marx 1992, 272–73).[32] Thus, as early as 1862, the Irade that allowed foreclosures for debts owed to the Treasury also stated that the lowest-valued house of the debtor was to be left to the debtor. This provision was again reaffirmed in 1869 and 1871, enshrining this rule even after the death of the debtor. Article 7 of the Appendix to the 1869 law, dated 1871 [21 N 1288], thus states that if the heir does not have a house, "a habitation sufficient for him to live in shall not be sold, and if the maintenance of the deceased debtor depended on agriculture, sufficient land for the maintenance of his [household] will not be taken from his heirs" (Ongley and Miller 1892, 217). The codes also required various processes of clearance and registration in order to recognize the mortgage and to initiate the process of foreclosure (Article 26 of the Tapu Law of 1858 [8 C 1275]; Irade of 1870 [21 R 1287]). Most articles of the Law of 1871 only serve as caveats to restrict foreclosure: if there is an appeal, foreclosure cannot proceed; if the debtor proves that his revenues for the coming three years will pay off debt and interest, he can be exempt from selling the land (Article 2); public notices of the foreclosure need to be posted in the newspaper and public spaces (Article 8). Finally, foreclosure does not touch all the assets of a debtor, but only those used as securities in contracts of rahn or *ferâğ bi'l-vefâ*.

To add complication to the factors affecting the operation of debt and foreclosure (from type of land to person), different courts handled different cases. The Code of Civil Procedure (1879) clearly delimited the jurisdiction of each court. The Nizamiye Courts dealt with civil and criminal law and shariʿa courts with personal status law and waqfs (Rubin 2011, 63). Rubin notes that waqf, nonetheless, presented one of the gray areas, which allowed for "forum shopping" (2011, 64). He describes waqf cases that were brought to the Nizamiye Courts and suggests that litigants and courts took for granted that waqf cases could be tried in Nizamiye Courts (2011, 65). In a couple of the waqf cases he discusses, the Court of Cassation in Istanbul annulled the decision of the Nizamiye Courts for lack of jurisdiction. However, in one case, it did not, and Rubin sees in this case a possible confirmation of the difference between the everyday use of courts and the letter of the law. However, I would like to suggest that this might be due to the fact that jurisdiction is not always clear-cut: was a foreclosure involving waqf to be enforced in the shariʿa courts or in the Nizamiye Courts? How were the shariʿa courts to know whether a piece of land was the subject of a mortgage before allowing a waqf foundation? Such indeterminacies made waqf a possible threat to or reprieve from the new debt regime and its foreclosures.

32. One can read in these measures confirmation of the analysis of the Land Code as a way to "maintain rural stability and continuity" (Quataert 1997, 858).

These changes to the property and debt regime could not but affect the approaches to intent in these codes and beyond. Indeed, as Arabi (1997) reveals, there is an intimate connection between approaches to intent and approaches to pecuniary transactions. The permissibility of certain contracts depends on the approach to intent of the legal school (formalist like the Ḥanafīs or subjectivist like the Ḥanbalīs and Mālikīs). Discussing stipulations in contracts, Arabi explains that for the Ḥanafīs, most stipulations that are agreed upon by the contracting parties to the benefit of one of them (like stipulating the use of a sold house for a year before delivery) are invalid because they incur a profit without compensation ("ziyāda lā yuqābiluhā ʿiwaḍ") or "an increment with no countervalue" (1997, 38), which is the definition of usury, *ribā*. Thus, because Ḥanafīs do not investigate ulterior motive or real intent, anything that "looks like" usury is considered unlawful. Arabi explains that, to the contrary, Ḥanbalīs who judge "the legality of a transaction by the legality of its underlying motives" (1997, 38) are not as suspicious of a stipulation that "looks like" usury, since they can investigate the intent behind this contract.[33] For Ḥanbalīs, for instance, selling grape juice and knowing that the buyer will be making wine out of it is an illicit act, even if the buyer never expressed that intent.

Given that contract law is intertwined with the approach to intent adopted by the legal system, changes in contract law in Ottoman legislation of the nineteenth century were accompanied by changes to the approaches to intent. Thus, while the Mecelle opens with a series of legal maxims based on Ibn Nujaym's *al-Ashbāh wa al-Naẓāʾir* (Haydar 2010, 10), beginning with the usual "[The qualifications of] deeds are determined by their intentions" (Article 2), it proceeds then in a different direction. Article 3 contradicts the main tenet of the Ḥanafī approach to intent in contract law, its formalism, as it states: "What matters in contracts are intents and meanings, not expressions and structures; therefore the [contract of] bayʿ bi'l-wafāʾ follows the qualifications of rahn." Granted, this rule actually formalizes the way the Ottoman state dealt with the contract of bayʿ bi'l-wafāʾ as a contract of rahn even though it is called a sale (*bayʿ*). However, its framing as a general rule that prioritizes intent over expression directly seems to be in contradiction with other articles of the Mecelle, particularly the continuous illegitimacy of stipulations that do not benefit one of parties (Article 189). Such stipulations are considered invalid on the grounds of, as Arabi explains, "semblance of usury" (1998, 41). Given this

33. Arabi (1998) argues that this approach to intent liberates contracts from conditions on stipulations, since Ḥanbalīs allow any contracts and conditions to which the contracting parties agree, as long as the contract is not expressly prohibited in Islamic law. Nonetheless he warns that the liberation of stipulations does not imply a Ḥanbalī liberation of contract (Arabi 1998, 43). As Powers explains (2006, 119–20) with regard to the stringency of Ḥanbalī law about legal devices to escape usury, this emphasis on intent actually opens the door to challenges of many contracts and thus limits freedom of contract. Arabi (1999, 44) maintains that the Ḥanbalī liberation of stipulations is a step forward to the freedom of contract in Islamic law.

heightened concern with intent, it is perhaps then not a surprise that it arose in the question of the Ottoman governor of Mount Lebanon to the *şeyhülislâm*.

Debt and Foreclosure in the Governorate of Mount Lebanon

In the first letter he had addressed to the Porte, the governor, Rüstem Pasha stated that it had been brought to his attention that some Ottoman subjects of Mount Lebanon had founded waqfs with the purpose of escaping foreclosure and sought advice on the legality of such a practice and on the course of action. The Porte's response was to request further investigation and to demand copies of all waqf deeds, instigating a memo[34] from Rüstem Bey to the various subgovernors of districts of Mount Lebanon to that effect. The request yielded forty-six waqf foundation deeds established between 1866 and 1877.[35] The waqf foundations reveal that fifteen of the founders were Druze and twenty-four were Maronites, and most importantly that twenty-five out of the forty-six founders were men and women of a certain status, the various honorific titles preceding their names (shaykh, amir) placing them within the old notable tax-farming families of the area (Arslan, Hamadah, Shihab).[36] Rüstem's suspicion brought these foundations to light and linked them to foreclosure for debt. But perhaps, following qadi practices, we should not assume that these individuals were indeed intending to escape debts or that such a practice was indeed extant. Nonetheless, the inquiry does point to a problem of indebtedness and recovery of debts. Why was debt causing so much anxiety? Who was indebted and to whom?

Before the nineteenth century, debt had been part and parcel of the life of both peasants and landlords in Mount Lebanon; it was, as Bishara (2017, 51) demonstrates for the Indian Ocean and as Graeber puts it, "the very fabric of sociability" during a period when cash was limited (2011, 329). Between the sixteenth and the eighteenth centuries, despite the production of marketable crops sold in the Syrian interior for cash, barter was the main means of exchange between the inhabitants of the Mountain (Saba 1976, 2), and it remained an important one until the 1930s. Indeed, Latron (1936, 46) describes how peasants within villages avoided costly debts by relying on barter and deferring in-kind payments. Within a village, he advances, the total amount of cash available was always "derisory," or ridiculously little. Did the production of cash crops in Mount Lebanon, where silk monoculture dominated in the nineteenth century,[37] lead to the creation of large estates

34. The memo is reproduced in the document with waqf foundation deeds issued by the Shuf court in response to the memo (BOA.ŞD.MLK 2271.66/5/12A).

35. The deeds were distributed in the Mountain as follows: one from Zahla, two from Batrun, two from Kisrawan, three from Jizzin, nineteen from the Matn, nineteen from the Shuf (based on my count of the deeds reproduced in BOA.ŞD.MLK 2271.66).

36. On the tax-farming families of the Mountain, see, for example, Makdisi (2000, 31–32).

37. Starting in the early 1800s, so much of Mount Lebanon was cultivated with mulberry trees that inhabitants needed to import food and cattle for subsistence (Owen 1993, 30). Firro (1990, 152) gives

from lands of dispossessed peasants in repayment of debts? What was the role of debt in the local economy?

Discussion of indebtedness in the nineteenth-century Ottoman Empire usually centers on peasant indebtedness due to the commercialization of agriculture leading to foreclosures of small peasant holdings to moneylenders, most of whom were wealthy merchants or notables who then become the possessors of large estates (for a general survey espousing this earlier view, see Owen 1993). The need to produce for the market arose even for small peasants after the Tanzimat because of the new tax regime, which created many new cash-based taxes while continuing the old in-kind tithe (*ʿushr*)[38] (Owen 1993, 37). However, the teleological narrative of large, landed estates (*çiftlik*) producing cash crops to meet the increasing demand from Europe has been questioned (see, for example, Gerber 1987; Keyder and Tabak 1991). Quataert argues, "Large commercial estates . . . were unusual and economically unimportant except in Moldovia, Wallachia, and the Çukurova plain, much of the Iraqi regions, and in the Hama area" (1997, 863), and small holdings accounted for 82 percent of the total arable land in the Ottoman Empire in both 1859 and 1900 (1997, 863–64). Small landholders and peasants produced surpluses that went to the world market. Furthermore, Quataert argues, the development of large landholders came from the dispossession of tribes whose lands were considered *mevat* (Quataert 1997, 874). Moreover, in a study on peasant indebtedness based on debt registers for two towns in Western Anatolia, Aytekin (2008) shows that debt was actually much more cyclical and permanent as it worked to transfer some of the surplus that the peasants were producing to a class of wealthy merchants who had the cash to lend them—without indebtedness necessarily leading to foreclosures. This is not to say that these are the new consensuses about the effects of the commercialization of agriculture, but rather that we need to be more attuned to the particular social and political-economic milieux in order to understand the effects of the commercialization of agriculture in various parts of the Ottoman Empire.

The nineteenth century in Mount Lebanon saw the rise of a silk monoculture in Mount Lebanon, and tied the Mountain to the global circulation and accumulation of capital, particularly to the French silk industry and banking. It was also a time of change from the classical dual structure of (mostly Druze and the Maronite Khazins) tax farmers (*multazims, muqāṭaʿjīs*) and peasants.[39] First, all tax farmers

---

an estimate of 70–80 percent of the cultivated area being dedicated to mulberry trees in 1912, when production had declined.

38. For more on the tithe and older taxes, see Faroqhi (1997, 531–35).

39. Since the sixteenth century, the Mountain had been a semiautonomous emirate governed by a governor from among the local prominent families who was responsible for delivering taxes to Istanbul. The governor then distributed various tax assignments to other prominent families. Most of the tax farmers were Druze (Jumblat, ʿImad, Abu Nakad, Talhuq, ʿAbd al-Malik) except for the Khazins in the northern district of Kisrawan and the Hubayshs in Jubayl, while most peasants were Christian in both places. For a description of the old order and what led to the sectarian balance, see Traboulsi (2007, 1–23).

had their privileges and tax-collection duties stripped away due to a combination of local circumstances and reforms emanating from Istanbul, starting with the 1839 Gülhane Rescript, which promised the abolition of tax farming and the institution of direct collection by salaried functionaries. The Maronite tax farmers lost their influence and control over land and peasants through a combination of the rise of influence of the Maronite Church, a commoners' revolt, and the increasing numbers of tax-farmers' family members, hence the need to support them and divide the riches. The Druze started losing their privileges as the main tax farmers of the Mountain during the reign of Bashir II (1789–1840). Indeed, in the 1820s, after he eliminated his main competitor, the rich Druze Bashir Jumblat, Bashir Shihab II, who had newly become a Maronite, dispossessed the Druze tax farmers of their "fiefs and a number of them went into exile in the Hawran. Of the twelve seigneurial domains in the Southern districts, only two remained in the hands of the Druze landlords. The rest were taken by Bashir and distributed between his relatives" (Traboulsi 2007, 11). After a brief Egyptian occupation, supported by the Shihabs, all factions united in revolt against the Egyptians' heavy taxation, forced labor, and military conscription. "Returning from exile, the Druze sheikhs tried to regain their domains and power over their Christian subjects and faced the hostility of the new prince [Bashir III] as well as the resistance of the Christians. Conflicts over landed property broke out everywhere" (Traboulsi 2007, 13). The Ottomans supported the Druze's "property rights" and abolished the semiautonomy of Mount Lebanon, creating a dual administrative unit (*qāʾimmaqāmiyyatayn*) in 1842 under an Ottoman ruler. The period after 1842 was full of contestations between Druze notables and mostly Christian commoners as the former tried to regain control over their lands, as well as between Christian commoners and Christian notables in the northern district. There was a commoners' revolt in the North, which led to the establishment of a short-lived "republic" ruled by the commoners demanding the abolishment of tax farming and land taxes and even a redistribution of land. Fearing a spread of that revolt to the South, the Druze notables initiated a preemptive strike. The situation exploded in the violence of 1860, where thousands lost their lives.[40] With the intervention of foreign powers, the Ottomans proceeded to punish the culprits, which was a complicated task (see Makdisi 2000, 146–65). For our purposes here, the Druze notables were stripped of their lands and required to pay reparations (Traboulsi 2007, 24–40).

In parallel to the loss of wealth suffered by the Druze and Christian tax farmers, the development of the silk industry allowed the rise of a richer class of peasants as well as a new elite of merchants (Buheiry 1984, 293; Chevallier 1971, 148–49). Silk production benefited small peasants because of the particular contracts under which they cultivated the mulberry trees. Indeed, large landowners entered into sharecropping agreements known as *mughārasa*, whereby peasants received half (Saba 1976, 4) or a quarter (Khater 2001, 199–200n25) of the land and the trees they planted after the trees reached maturity and started producing leaves (Buheiry

40. For a detailed description of the violence of 1860, see Makdisi (2000).

1984, 294).[41] In addition, these small growers also profited from the increased prices of cocoons in the 1860s and 1870s (Saba 1976, 14). Some of these small peasants then invested these sums in buying land (Traboulsi 2007, 19). Others engaged in trade, buying surpluses from other peasants and selling them to merchants in centers (Saba 1976, 4), eventually becoming merchants in their own right.

This new structure altered the debt regime in the Mountain. No longer a fixture of the cycle of production and reproduction between peasants and notables, debt was now owed to a new class of people. With the need for cash for the purchase of eggs and the production of silk cocoons,[42] the role of moneylenders sharply increased and much of the literature even frames the discussion in terms of usury (for example, Traboulsi 2007, 19; Saba 1976, 1, 7 passim; Chevallier 1971, 203). With the loss of their sources of income and their increasing family sizes (Saba 1976, 8), the old tax-farming families had to borrow, particularly from the traders and merchants who sold their silk to Lyon's spinning industries. "Speaking of feudal ruling families in the middle of the nineteenth century, a Lebanese merchant contemporary estimated that the sum of their debt, with interest, amounted to fifty per cent of their revenues" (Saba 1976, 10).[43] Chevallier (1971, 202) mentions that the most notable families were indebted, including the Shihabs, Abillamaʿs, and Khazins.[44] Traboulsi adds that "the Abu Nakad [the Druze tax farmers of Dayr al-Qamar] . . . were heavily indebted and sold many of their properties to their Christian creditors" (2007, 20). With their tax-farming privileges under threat, and during their many rebellions in the middle of the nineteenth century, the Druze notables would take the borrowed money with them when they left the Mountain seeking refuge in the Syrian Hawran (Chevallier 1971, 237).

Peasants were also indebted to the merchants and to their overlords, despite or even through the latter's own indebtedness. In irrigated areas of the Mountain, with more regular harvests, peasant debt was mostly related to big expenditures (such as weddings and funerals). However, in irregular harvest areas with precarious growing conditions, peasants needed to borrow even to subsist, and therefore they were much more indebted; and their debt, as a riskier one, carried higher interest rates, making it a longer term debt. Interest there could be between 10 and 15 percent but reached even 20 or 30 percent, making it impossible to reimburse upon harvest. Given the gains that could be made from moneylending, small traders in the interior "were prepared to sell their merchandise at loss or to

41. Chevallier (1971, 138) and Buheiry (1984, 294) point out that the *mughārasa* in the Kisrawan did not involve the transfer of property rights for immovables, which Buheiry sees as one of the reasons that led to the peasants' revolt in the Kisrawan in 1858.

42. Local eggs could not meet the increased demand for silk, so producers had to import eggs, thus needing cash to buy them from merchants.

43. Unfortunately, Saba (1976) does not mention his source.

44. Saba (1976) confirms this with the names of the merchant-creditors: Amir Bashir Shihab, Shaykh Qansuh al-Khazin, Shaykh Said Jumblat, Amir Ahmad Abillamaʿ, and Amir Amin Arslan.

borrow from French merchants at six percent interest in order to have the cash to lend money to the small peasants at twenty percent or more, in exchange of future silk harvest" (Chevallier 1971, 233). These local small merchants had then a sizeable portion of the silk produced and accumulated wealth from the difference in the price at which they bought the cocoons (when making cash advances to the peasants and the notables) and the price at harvest, but also from the increase in the price of silk on the global market in the 1850s and 1860s (Chevallier 1971, 230).[45] Owen estimates that, after a fall related to the financial crisis in 1857 in Europe, by "1863 the value of loans granted to peasant cultivators by Lebanese silk merchants was already four times as high as in 1858 or 1861" (1993, 163).

Unlike peasants and even tax farmers, for whom debt was part and parcel of the yearly life cycle, merchants dealing mostly with cash exchange came to see debt "as tinged with criminality" (Graeber 2011, 329). For the merchants involved in the global cash economy, the recovery of these debts took on a new importance, so they started calling on the state for mechanisms to enforce their rights. As early as 1853, some Beiruti merchants signed a petition along with French merchants of the city asking that lawsuits between them and people from Mount Lebanon be tried in the Commercial Tribunal of Beirut (est. 1850)[46] rather than the courts of the Mountain (Chevallier 1971, 207). With the Levant starting to feel the effect of the European financial crisis of 1857, "the result was a general increase in bad debts [debts that could not be repaid] and a rash of bankruptcies which made the foreign merchants more anxious than ever to find ways of bringing their debtors to court" (Owen 1993, 163). When the jurisdiction of the Commercial Tribunal of Beirut over all commercial transactions was extended to the Mountain in 1861 (Akarlı 1993, 132–33) under the new regime of the *mutaṣarrifiyya*,[47] European bankers and merchants of Beirut were thrilled because the Mountain had hitherto provided a refuge to the indebted individual who "could only be forced to return if his creditor could persuade one of the *muqatajis* [tax farmers] there to arrest him. This the *muqatajis*, many of whom were themselves in debt to foreign merchants, were often unwilling to do" (Owen 1993, 163). Given this structure of generalized indebtedness to merchants, it may be unsurprising that debtors tried to use waqf to escape the long reach of the merchants. It may also be unsurprising that mer-

45. Chevallier (1971, 233–37) explains in great detail the way the merchants tapped into the existing debt regime in the area, where peasants borrowed against their future harvests. Because they needed the advances, peasants agreed to sell their future cocoon harvests at much lower prices than expected. At the time of the harvest, the merchants would then receive the cocoons and sell them at much higher prices, making extra profit. This led to many rebellions by peasants, especially when the harvests were bad and they could not even pay their debts, leading to the Ottoman Porte intervening to fix interest rates.

46. Date from Chevallier (1971, 236).

47. As mentioned in footnote 1, the *mutaṣarrifiyya* is a special Ottoman governorate created after the violence of 1860, which granted Mount Lebanon limited autonomy, guaranteed by European powers, which had supported various factions in the strife. For more details on the development and operation of the *mutaṣarrifiyya*, see Akarlı (1992).

chants complained to the governor about recovering their debts. And indeed, the governor mentions one of these complaints in his inquiry to the Porte about the validity of waqfs with the intent to escape foreclosure. Let me now turn to the answer that the office of the şeyhülislâm provided after having received and examined the forty-six waqf deeds, in order to show how the grammar of intent in these documents had changed from the late Ḥanafī canon.

Waqf and Foreclosure: Scrutinizable Interiority

In his answer, the şeyhülislâm, represented by his secretary, the *amīn al-fatwā*,[48] starts by analyzing the waqf deeds at hand and the validity of the waqfs, rather than by addressing the question of debt and intent. The şeyhülislâm states: "According to the opinion of Imam Abu Yusuf, in the same way that the validity of a waqf does not require its registration nor its handing over to the administrator, its validity does not necessitate the naming of an eternal beneficiary." This move allows him to use the divergent opinions in the Ḥanafī tradition to confirm the validity of these waqfs, despite what would be errors and omissions according to the dominant opinions in the school. For instance, some of the waqf deeds do not specify an inextinguishable beneficiary like the poor (BOA. ŞD.MLK 2271.66/3/3A/3.444, 23 M 1285 [1868]); others do not name an administrator (BOA.ŞD.MLK 2271.66/4/3A/23.2531, 21 M 1293 [1876]). The şeyhülislâm seems intent on treating these waqf deeds as valid, even though some of them appear to be simply using the waqf as a form of inalienable property without consideration of the procedure, form, and technicalities of a waqf foundation. That is, the şeyhülislâm could have easily pointed out that all of the waqfs miss some key elements in their foundation deeds, making them invalid, without having to delve into the question of the intent to escape foreclosure.[49] However, his attempt to move away from the question of the proper form and procedure for waqf founding hints to the importance of addressing the question of intent and debt and alludes to matter's significance.

Since the founding fathers of the school do not discuss the question of intent and ultimate motive, the şeyhülislâm turns to "reputable fiqh books" (*muʿtabarât-i kutub-i fiqhiye*) of the late Ottoman Ḥanafī library. This terminology, as Guy Burak demonstrates, is not fortuitous: it refers to the Ottoman Ḥanafī canon and contains particular books to be taught in a specific order (2015, 130–35), indicating the authoritativeness of the opinions to be discussed. The fatwa continues: "reputable *fiqh* books state that if an indebted person who is sound of mind and body and not

48. Over the course of the sixteenth century, due to the enormous number of questions posed to the mufti, the office of the şeyhülislām became more bureaucratized, and a special office for the issuance of fatwas was established under the direction of the *fetvâ emînî*, the secretary of the fatwa. For more on that office and its functioning, see Heyd (1969, 46–49).

49. An attempt to question the validity of these waqf foundations based on procedural mistakes would have actually been very much in line with late-nineteenth-century Ottoman practice, in what Rubin calls "the age of procedure" (2011, 83–111).

interdicted [who is free to dispose of his possessions] makes all of his movables and immovables into a *waqf* for a pious purpose his *waqf* is valid and allowable."[50] Indeed, as we discussed, these books actually separate debt from legal capacity (*ahliyya*), including that of waqf making, because legal capacity is defined in terms of elements of the capacity to contract: freedom, sanity, adulthood, and the absence of interdiction. If you recall, al-Tarabulusi considers the waqf of an insolvent debtor valid.

It is here that the şeyhülislâm turns to the foundational figure in Ottoman fiqh, the jurist responsible for justifying many of the Ottoman legal preferences through the Islamic tradition, Ebüssuʿûd Efendi. The summary that the fatwa presents is based on an opinion of Ebüssuʿûd from his *Maʿrûzât*, which appears at first glance like a fatwa with a question by a subject and an answer by the jurist.[51] The question was "Zayd [the Muslim equivalent of John Doe] is healthy and indebted, and in order to escape from his creditors, he made all of his properties into a waqf for his children. Is the waqf valid?" Ebüssuʿûd's answer was clear and simple. "The waqf is neither valid nor irrevocable. Judges are forbidden from confirming and registering the part of the waqf equivalent to debt" (Ebüssuʿûd 2013, 114). It is important to note that even though Ebüssuʿûd's opinion is framed as a fatwa, Ebüssuʿûd's *Maʿrûzât* constitute questions written by the jurist himself then presented (Ar: *ʿarḍ*; Tr: *arz*)—hence the name *Maʿrûzât*—to the sultan for the latter's answer, although Ebüssuʿûd "often suggest[ed] the course of action to be followed as well" (Repp 1986, 282). Ebüssuʿûd's opinion was then not just the opinion of a learned scholar of the empire, an opinion that would have remained ultimately unenforceable. His opinion acquired force of law, because the sultan issued this opinion as a decree that was binding on judges (Repp 1986, 280, 282).

Ebüssuʿûd's attempt at legislating about indebted waqf makers attempting to escape from their creditors shows that debt and its recovery must have been an important enough issue at the time of his tenure (1545–1574) to warrant consideration. Unfortunately, we do not have studies that analyze his *Maʿrûzât* based on the social and economic conditions of the time, and a good amount of research would be needed to determine the reasons behind his attempt to legislate around such issues. One can perhaps assume that the monetization of the Ottoman Empire and the price revolution of the sixteenth century that wreaked havoc in the Ottoman Empire at the time might have made the question of foreclosure crucial. In these circumstances, Ebüssuʿûd's *arz* could be interpreted as an early modern formulation of the problem we encounter three hundred years later.

In his *Maʿrûzât*, Ebüssuʿûd used his own independent reasoning (*raʾy*), rather than following the dominant opinions of the Ḥanafī school, while still remaining

50. BOA.ŞD.MLK 2271.66/6.

51. The *Maʿrûzât* are presented as very short answers that do not display juridical justification.

within its bound (Repp 1986, 282). His opinion in this case constitutes a transformation of the grammar of intent in the Islamic legal tradition. Ebüssu'ûd's opinion actually draws on a common fatwa, here formulated by a Mamluk jurist known as the Reader of the *Hidāya*, which is also reproduced in the other work cited by the şeyhülislâm in the 1879 fatwa to support his opinion, the ultimate compendium of Ḥanafī fiqh by the illustrious late Ottoman Syrian jurist Ibn 'Abidin (d. 1842). The question in the older Mamluk fatwa concerns a man who owns movables and immovables and who is in prison because of a legal debt he owes to someone. This man then proceeds to dispose of his possessions, gifting, founding waqfs, selling, and spending in order to become poor and deprive his creditor of what he owes him. What is the ruling on his dissipation of wealth? Can the judge interdict him? The answer is yes, and the judge can even force him to sell property to pay back his debt (Qari' al-Hidaya 1999, 42–43). The question here is one of the legality of interdicting the debtor (rather than the validity of the waqf), which, as mentioned above, was a matter of debate in the tradition. Nonetheless, the effect of the interdiction is that the judge can act on behalf of the debtor to annul the waqf and previous contracts.

However, there is a crucial, albeit small, difference between this fatwa and the one by Ebüssu'ûd. Here the subject is imprisoned for refusing to pay his debt, a detail that Ebüssu'ûd does not mention. However, this small disparity makes a crucial legal difference. Imprisonment is the evidence that allows the jurist to establish that the man is trying to escape debt payment. Here, intent is not in and of itself open to scrutiny. It is again deduced from its expressions and signs, which act as evidence. Without these exterior signs, any man could be unjustly accused of trying to escape debt. In addition, forced sale, as seen in this fatwa—echoing our discussion of debt in Islamic law—was very much tied to questions of financial hardship or affluence. Indeed, the reason forced sale is allowed in this case is the affluence of the debtor. Had the endowed land been his only sustenance, something he could not do without, forced sale would not have been on the table. These small changes, then, are in fact crucial. They reverse the predominant ruling that even bankrupts can make a waqf, as long as they are not in prison for nonpayment of debt, unless they are trying to make a rahn into a waqf. They also open the door to legislation based on this suspicion, prioritizing the rights of creditors over good faith in debtors. Crucially, they signal a change in the grammar of intent, which becomes divorced from exterior signs, open to suspicion, and the basis of rulings independent of external expressions.

While Ebüssu'ûd had no qualms taking into account the possible intent of debtors to escape debt and harm their creditors, Ibn 'Abidin seems more reluctant to paper over the radical change that Ebüssu'ûd's opinion constitutes in the preponderant view of the Ḥanafī tradition. Ibn 'Abidin notes that Ebüssu'ûd's opinion contradicts the dominant opinion ("mukhālif li-ṣarīḥ al-manqūl") but then proceeds to justify his ruling following Ebüssu'ûd's opinion based on the argument used in another compendium, *al-Fatāwā al-Ismā ʿīliyya*, which utilizes procedural issues related to the judge's appointment (Ayoub 2014, 206–8). Ibn ʿAbidin quotes this collection's justification that the judge is a deputy of the sultan and is supposed therefore to follow the latter's directives. Since the sultan has prohibited judges from registering the waqfs of indebted founders, any judgment that contradicts this directive is considered invalid. Ibn ʿAbidin reports that Shaykh Ismaʿil al-Haʾik, author of *al-Fatāwā al-Ismā ʿīliyya* and student of al-Haskafi in Damascus, also explains that the sultan had prohibited his appointee (the judge) to register such waqfs in order to safeguard people's property ("ṣiyānatan li-amwāl al-nās"). Such an argument presents Ebüssuʿûd's fatwa as the sultan's legislation based on public benefit (*maṣlaḥa*) and thus as falling within the domain of *siyāsa*.[52] The sultan is going against the preponderant opinion in order to uphold one of the main purposes of the shariʿa, the preservation of property.[53]

An important question remains about how Ebüssuʿûd himself justifies his opinion within the *madhhab*, or whether he even justifies it at all through an argument other than the above-mentioned *maṣlaḥa*. Still, for the purpose of my argument here, the most notable element of Ebüssuʿûd's opinion is that he acts upon the suspicion about the intent of founders, instead of dismissing such concerns with ulterior motives and returning to the formalism of the school. The adoption of his ruling, no matter how he justifies that ruling, introduces suspicion towards the intent of waqf founders *and* legislation based on this suspicion into the Ḥanafī tradition.[54] However, the new grammar that he introduces remained a minor tradition, and it was only in the nineteenth century, under the particular material and legal conditions that I described, that this opinion started to be enforced systematically; it was in fact promulgated as a sultanic decree in 1879 (Hariz 1994, 35).

52. Ibn ʿAbidin is putting the sultan's law in the idiom of *siyāsā sharʿiyya*, whereby rulers are conceived as rendering justice "in the name of Sharia in contrast to the formal rules of the fiqh" (Rapoport, quoted in Fadel 2014, 100).

53. The justification to follow Ebüssuʿûd's opinion contrary to the preponderant opinion of the *madhhab* opens a window onto a vigorous debate in Ottoman and Islamic studies: the response of local scholars to the Ottoman state's attempt at "canonizing" the Ḥanafī *madhhab*. The relation and negotiations between the Ottoman state legislation and local Damascene scholars in matters of waqf forms an important aspect in Richard van Leeuwen's book (1999). Van Leeuwen argues that the qadi had acquired a "more and more prominent role," both through the state's efforts but also through an "increasingly institutionalized body of scholars" (1999, 116). According to him, the institution of waqf became, by the end of the sixteenth century, "an instrument of state policies" (1999, 117). Some reviewers of van Leeuwen's monograph (e.g., Ghazzal 2001) disagree with him about the extent of state control of the *madhhab*.

54. Such an effect, as Hussein Ali Agrama shows (2012, 130–59), is usually characteristic of the modern rule of law and is tied to modern law's aim of maintaining public order because loopholes create the possibility of descent into chaos, with mushrooming legislation further entrenching state sovereignty. One could argue that, given Ebüssuʿûd's ties to dynastic law, similar aims of public order animate his fatwa.

This new grammar of intent differs quite dramatically from the one I described in the first section, which takes exteriors for their apparent meaning rather than seeking subjective intent or ulterior motive. This does not mean that sincerity and the harmony between inside and outside of a believer were not essential virtues of the believer. While sincerity is an ideal between the believer and God, in society, questions of sincerity in the domain of adjudication are discouraged because of the mediated access to intent that I described. In addition, as Saba Mahmood (2005) has argued, in Aristotelian models of ethical pedagogy, external performative acts are understood to create corresponding inward dispositions. While in this model the subject still seeks to eliminate the dissonance between inside and outside, that dissonance is not read as hypocrisy or lying, but is usually understood as natural in the path of ethical self-discipline. There were very clear limits to human questioning of sincerity, of the kind done by the governor. The new grammar of intent, which gives direct access to the interiority of subjects, "splits open the heart of the believer to find out whether he declared the profession of faith [out of belief in it] or not," as a famous tradition of the Prophet has it (Muslim 2005, 1:140–41).[55]

It is the late nineteenth-century conception of the subject that was legally used to question the validity of certain waqfs as charitable acts.[56] In the governor's question, the opening of the heart to scrutiny actually served to tie the subject to a different moral economy, where rights of creditors are absolute and repayment of debt is a moral duty outside any consideration of hardship. The attempt to close the gap between the intentions and the actions of the waqf founders entrenched the new debt regime and restricted the use of waqf as a way to contain its reach. The requirements of capital accumulation contributed not only to the reshuffling of the control of the means of production and of social relations but also left a mark on the conception of the person and the grammar of intent in the Islamic tradition.

55. The tradition tells the story of a Muslim who kills an unbeliever during a battle, even after the latter had uttered the profession of faith. After hearing the story, the Prophet asked the Muslim if he tore "open the heart of the believer to see if it uttered the profession of faith." The questioning is taken as an injunction for Muslims to leave "real intent" to God and simply follow external signs (*al-ẓāhir)*.

56. I would like to point out that the intent of founders in the particular case raised by the governor of Mount Lebanon (and in Ebüssuʿûd's *arz*) is deemed suspicious because they are founding waqfs dedicated to their children. In the earlier fatwas and even in Ibn ʿAbidin's example, waqf *tout court*, whether dedicated to families or to the poor, in addition to other transactions that aimed to escape debt, was problematic. This particular targeting of family waqf prefigures and is essential to a debate arising a few decades later in Syria and Lebanon on the very validity of the family waqf. Thus, the questioning of the "real intent" of family waqf founders initiates the beginning of the questioning of the family as a legitimate recipient of charity and the transformation of family waqfs into simple economic transactions, which were not part of "religion." In this question, we see the separation of the economic from the religious and the restriction of the religious to worship (see chapter 4).

FRENCH MANDATE FORECLOSURE AS A REAL RIGHT AND GENERALIZED SUSPICION

The Ottoman nineteenth-century reforms liberalized foreclosure of property subject to rahn and bay' bi'l-wafā', making foreclosure possible, first on freehold and eventually on *miri* and waqf, without the consent of the debtor and during his or her lifetime. This new debt regime rendered waqf activity suspicious and "opened the hearts" of waqf founders to scrutiny. Ottoman legislators had nonetheless kept some restraints, preserving the livelihoods of people, especially peasants, and had limited foreclosure to assets that had been used as securities, except when the debt was owed to the Treasury. Did French Mandate legislation on debt and foreclosure take the Ottoman reforms to their natural conclusion and completely liberate foreclosures? What effect did this legislation have on the way the intent of the legal subject was conceptualized and scrutinized?

The French archive brims with contention and confusion about the various credit contracts and their effects, particularly forced expropriation (*naz' al-milkiyya al-jabrī*). Citizens addressed questions and complaints to the high commissioner or to his real-estate-matters delegate, Philippe Gennardi, about creditors who initiated forced expropriation but did not come to the auction and simply disappeared, about debtors trying to negotiate paper money equivalent to debts contracted in gold, about the righteous recipient of the compensation for the expropriation of certain waqfs, and about taxes on mortgages and forced expropriations (e.g., MAE251/2/Real Estate/23). These queries triggered correspondence among various French officials and between them and Lebanese/Syrian officials, indicating that the confusion partly stemmed from multiple legislation (the new Real Estate Property Code 3339/1930, the Code of Obligations and Contracts/1932, and the Code of Civil Procedure/1932) as well as French-Ottoman-Arabic translations. Let us examine the way this legislation tackled debt and foreclosure and its effects on intent.

The 1930 Real Estate Property Code follows existing contracts from the Ottoman period but redefines them as real rights of mortgage (*ruhūnāt*; sing. *rahn*) (Article 10): the right of rahn (Articles 101 to 116) and the right of sale with right of redemption (bay' bi'l-wafā') (Articles 91 to 100). Only valid against a legally proven debt, the rahn contract puts an immovable in the hands of a creditor or a third party and gives the creditor the right to confine (*ḥabs*) the immovable until the payment of the debt (Article 101). This article restricts the rahn contract to immovables, whereas the Ottoman Mecelle (Article 701) allowed any property (*māl*) that could be the subject of a sale to also be the subject of a rahn. Rights acquired on the immovable before the rahn, such as a lease, remain valid (Article 109). In rahn contracts, the same asset can act as a surety for more than one debt, contrary to bay' bi'l-wafā' contracts. The debtor and the creditor cannot agree that the creditor will become the proprietor of the collateral if the debtor fails to pay (Article 107). These clauses and rights about rahn are very much in continuity with

Ottoman practices. However, French regulations tightened the range of uses that the parties of the mortgage can engage in with mutual consent. For instance, contrary to Article 749 of the Mecelle, which allows the creditor to lend the collateral back to the debtor, the debtor cannot request the use (*al-tamattu*ʿ) of his immovable (Article 106). The creditor cannot make use of the mortgaged immovable freely and any revenues from the immovable go towards the payment of the debt (except repair costs) (Articles 111 and 112).[57] The latter allowance changes the Ottoman rahn contract, which did not give the creditor any rights to the usufruct or use of the immovable, but only to its *res* (see Ali Haydar's commentary on Article 747 [2010 2:157]).

Some continuity with Ottoman practice exists with bayʿ bi'l-wafāʾ contracts as well. Here, the seller sells an immovable (*ʿaqār*) with the option to repurchase it at any time or at the end of a specified time and with the buyer able to request the price with the return of the immovable (Article 91). Like Ottoman practice, and as stated in Article 3 of the Mecelle, the bayʿ bi'l-wafāʾ appears to follow the same rules as the rahn (*ḥukmuh ḥukm al-rahn*): it does not make the buyer the owner, but simply confines the object. This can be seen in Article 100, whereby if the seller does not return his debt, the buyer can request the sale of the immovable; he does not become the de facto owner. As a citizen attempting to clarify the differences between these contracts argued, the bayʿ bi'l-wafaʾ is a collateral, even if it involves transfer of property, because the buyer does not become the full and final owner of the immovable (MAE251/2/Real Estate/23). Neither buyer nor seller can sell, rent, or exercise any other real right on the immovable for the duration of the bayʿ bi'l-wafāʾ without the express consent of the other party (Article 93). The seller can remain an occupant of the immovable as a tenant (the contract will be then known as *bayʿ bi'l-istighlāl*) (Article 92). The contract can include a clause to allow the buyer to freely enjoy the immovable and part of its revenues (Article 94). The buyer is responsible for the care of the immovable if he or she receives it and for any damages to it that ensue, and any returns from the immovable are deducted from the debt owed (after the buyer takes for himself or herself the amount they agreed on and the amounts for maintenance and upkeep).

The continuities with Ottoman practice with regard to bayʿ bi'l-wafāʾ become less obvious when examining the articles discussing that contract in the Code of Obligations and Contracts of 9 March 1932 (Book I of Section III, Articles 473–486) because they contradict the Real Estate Code's discussion of the effects

57. The question of costs of repairs and maintenance is the subject of long discussions by the Mecelle's commentators because it revolves around the responsibility and liability of each of the parties. The general rule there is that the creditor is liable for the expenses necessary for the preservation (*al-muḥāfaẓa*) of the collateral (Article 723) or, as the commentator explains, for the intact return of the immovable (if he needs to rent a shed to keep some sheep used as collateral). The debtor is responsible for the expenses of repairs and upkeep (the feed for the sheep, for example) (Article 724). The creditor is not liable for damages incurred while he or she is in possession of the immovable, if he or she acted responsibly.

of the contract. In the Code of Obligations and Contracts, the sale is considered executed and the creditor has the right to sell, rent, or exercise other real rights on the immovable, without the permission of the debtor (Article 476). In addition, this code limits the timeframe of repossession to three years, a limit that even the judge cannot extend. These contradictions created confusion in the execution of contracts. We get a glimpse of the reason behind these contradictions in a note from the ubiquitous Gennardi to the high commissioner, where he explains that the Code of Obligations and Contracts in fact introduced a new contract, "unknown to Oriental legislations," the *vente à réméré* (a sale and repurchase agreement) (MAE251/2/Real Estate/31). Therefore, the Code of Obligations and Contracts called the *vente à réméré* "bay' bi'l-wafā'," a confusion, Gennardi notes, perpetuated earlier by Orientalists in the translation of the Mecelle. Gennardi proposes to rename the contract in the Code of Obligations and Contracts as *bay' bi'l-istirdād* instead of *bay' bi'l-wafā'*.

The introduction of such a contract, however, made debtors become more critical of the Ottoman bay' bi'l-wafā' because of its open-endedness. Thus, for instance, Princess Asma Samyé, granddaughter of Emir Abdelkader (al-Jaza'iri, the famous Algerian anti-colonial leader whose exile ended in Damascus) addressed a request to the high commissioner asking for a limit to the window of buyback of bay' bi'l-wafā' contracts (MAE251/2/Real Estate/23), arguing that creditors were pursuing reimbursement of the debt many years after the contract, when the immovable had lost much of its value, and were still demanding the original sum owed. "Even if one admits that this principle arises from the dispositions of the Mecelle," she writes, "it cannot be absolute and applied in all circumstances without consideration of the particularities of each case." Creditors seem to be exercising their right to demand their money back at any time as allowed by the Mecelle (Article 716), instead of exercising their right to demand a forced foreclosure, since the latter would not fulfill the debt given the change in value of the immovable. With the absence of the forbearance injunctions that existed in the late Ḥanafī Ottoman canon, this right to demand payment of the debt at any time appears like an arbitrary power given to creditors, privileging their absolute rights.

With regard to forced sales, the French Mandate Real Estate Property Code 3339 of 1930 continued with the broad foreclosures instituted by the Ottoman Code of Commerce, the Mecelle, and the various laws on *miri* and waqf land. This is no surprise since the Ottoman reforms had been the result of European pressures for capital accumulation and circulation as much as they were part of a global moment of modernization and codification (Rubin 2011, 25–26). Code 3339 instated the right of forced expropriation (Article 158) as a real right termed *ta'mīn* (security) that guarantees the performance of a duty (usually the payment of a debt) (Article 120). Forced foreclosure then was separated from contracts of rahn and bay' bi'l-wafā' and enshrined as a right on its own, which does not need to be tied to the transfer of an object. Nonetheless, Code 3339 notes that the rahn gives the creditor the right to request the forced expropriation through legal means if the debtor does not pay back (Article 101). These rights created an automatic process of foreclosure that bypasses the debtor and can be immediately executed by the creditor—through the courts. Articles 159–170 outline the process for forced expropriation: the creditor goes to the real estate judge to execute his right, the judge sends a note to the debtor warning him of the imminent foreclosure and requesting that he pays back within eight days (or show proof that he has paid); if he does not pay back, the judge can proceed to sell the immovable. The eight-day period allows the debtor to pay back without selling the property in question, as Ottoman practice (pre- and post-Mecelle) allowed.

A couple of years after the publication of Code 3339, however, forced foreclosures on rahn and bay' bi'l-wafā' contracts appear to have reverted to stricter pre-Mecelle requirements for foreclosure. Indeed, Article 158 was revised in 1932, with an added clause that requires an irrevocable right of attorney given to the creditor for forced expropriation in rahn and bay' bi'l-wafā' contracts.[58] Based on a communication between Gennardi and the inspector of real estate services, Amine Mouchawar, the revision of the law does not seem to have been brought by complaints against the earlier extension of foreclosure. After the revision of Article 158, Mouchawar asked Gennardi about its implications on rahn and bay' bi'l-wafā' contracts drafted before the revision (MAE251/2/Real Estate/13), many of which did not include such a power of attorney. Mouchawar wondered whether forced sales on these contracts should be allowed, given that at the time of their drafting, the power of attorney was not required and forced sales were allowed without such a power. Gennardi explained that the revised laws did not add any new requirements; they only made explicit old provisions of Ottoman law. Gennardi continued by clearly stating that for both these contracts, forced sale is possible only if the debtor gave the creditor the right to execute such a sale. Gennardi presented Ottoman practice as the basis of the law, implying that the absence of a requirement of a power of attorney in the 1930 code was just an oversight because it was taken for granted. Gennardi implied that the right of attorney was necessary before the French Mandate, when in fact the Mecelle did not require it, which is confirmed by Mouchawar's observation that many rahn and bay' bi'l-wafā' contracts did not include such a clause. Was Gennardi not aware of the new requirements of the Mecelle? Why was he trying to present the reinstatement of the power of attorney requirement for foreclosure in rahn and bay' bi'l-wafā' as a restoration? My data does not allow me to answer;[59] however, the revisions of the law and the questions

58. This clause remains in effect today. However, in practice, it is not enforced. There must be some other legislation that annuls it, but I have not been able to determine what it is.

59. An examination of foreclosures at the civil court archive of Beirut, of noteworthy court decisions about foreclosure in legal journals, and of newspaper articles about speculation and foreclosure in the Mandate press would definitely yield some results, but that is unfortunately beyond the scope of this book.

addressed to the French Mandatory government by citizens point to continued contestation around foreclosures.

That the questions of indebtedness and foreclosure, which we encountered in the late nineteenth century, continued unabated in the decades of the French Mandate reflects the disastrous economic situation of Lebanon and Syria after World War I. Lebanon was ravaged by the 1915–1918 famine and the war effort that conscripted able-bodied men. As Elizabeth Thompson notes, "Stories were told of peasants selling their homes and fields for a simple loaf of bread, and of speculators expropriating entire districts" (2000, 28). These were not simply rumors, and indeed, the French "decreed a law to dispossess Lebanese war profiteers who had amassed vast amounts of land" (2000, 29). Given these large-scale dispossessions, and considering these events in light of Ottoman questions around debt and foreclosure, we might wonder whether intent takes importance in the Mandate period as well. To do that, let us examine the way intent plays out in some of French Mandate legislation on debt and foreclosure.

French Mandate legislation enshrined some of the concerns with meaning and intentions stated in Article 3 of the Mecelle, as the civil law tradition allows investigations of intent in contract law. Indeed, a valid contract in the French Civil Code requires a "lawful cause" (Philippe 2004, 364). This requirement was present in the Lebanese Code of Obligations and Contracts (Article 177). The causes of contracts are standard: the cause of the obligation of the seller is the conveyance of the price and the cause of the obligation of the buyer is the conveyance of the merchandise. Motives are not relevant to the law, *except in as much they fit with "the conception of public policy or morality*" (2004, 382, italics mine). Thus Article 198 of the Code of Obligations states that an illicit cause is one that contravenes "public order, morals, and the obligatory rules of the law." In this framework, subjective intent is not scrutinized, but ulterior motive is. The "illegal or immoral intention of one of the parties must be known to, if not actually agreed [*convenu*] by the other" (Markesinis 1978, 70). Thus leasing a house to open a brothel was considered invalid if the owner knew of the intentions of the tenant.[60] Such a concern with ulterior motives echoes the concerns of the Mount Lebanon governor, for whom the family waqfs were questionable because of their ulterior motive of escaping foreclosure and the law.

Concern with the intent of debtors rears its head in French Mandate regulation of foreclosure. The Civil Procedure Code, promulgated in 1932, overrode the articles of the Real Estate Property Code dealing with foreclosure. The Civil Procedure Code regulated expropriation (*naz' al-milkiyya*) more broadly, including the impounding of money, movables, and immovables. Article 725 in the section

60. Arabi discusses the introduction of the notion of *cause* (*sabab*), which he renders as the "subjective determining motive" or "ulterior motive," in the Egyptian Civil Code of 1949 by the Egyptian "master-jurist" Sanhuri (1997, 201–2). French Mandate legislation seems to have introduced this notion in Lebanon and Syria earlier.

on immovables addresses the intent of debtors after an executive order for seizing real estate property: "Starting with the date of registration [of the seizing order?], the seized upon debtor [*al-maḥjūz ʿalayh*] cannot rent the immovable [*al-ʿaqār*] slated for seizure, nor can he promise future rents, with the purpose of harming the interests of the creditor seeking seizure [*iḍrāran bimaṣlaḥat al-ḥājiz*]." The article is very clear that it is the illegal intent behind these actions that makes them prohibited. Protection of creditors against stalling debtors also appears in the very strict procedure for bidding at public auction: Articles 785–793 punish winning bidders who fail to pay, charging them with the costs of the new auction and any difference in price were the new auction fail to reach the amount they bid for. Thus, such legislation seems to discourage "fake" bidding, most likely with the assumption that such bidding is used to give the debtor some time to pay off.

The question of intent behind the actions of debtors also arises in queries, as in the case of family waqfs done to escape foreclosure, and here too it is tied to the suspicion of giving to the family. One such query (MAE251/2/Real Estate/14) in 1933 from the same general inspector of the real estate office, Amine Mouchawar, to Gennardi utilizes the modern grammar of intent, and although the contract in question is a rental and not a waqf, the case highlights the deep suspicion of contracts that benefit the family. Mouchawar asks Gennardi about lease contracts on a foreclosed immovable, without specifying any particulars. He explains that, because they are less than three years old and not registered in the real estate registry (*livre foncier*), these contracts were contracted either during the auction of the forced sale or during the mortgage (*hypothèque*, or what the Real Estate Code calls *taʾmīn* [security]). Should the executive bureau delay seizure (*mise en possession*) or should he consider such contracts, which "evidently have no other *aim* than to hurt the interests of the third-party buyer [*tiers acquéreur*]," null and void, independently of their end date or their beneficiaries? asks Mouchawar.

Mouchawar appears quite concerned with the intent of the debtor and finds proof of the debtor's bad faith in the attempt to benefit the family. Indeed, after having explained the case in all its legally relevant details, Mouchawar ends his letter by pointing out that "by the way" (*en passant*), some of these contracts are between the debtor and his wife. The "by the way" introduces a piece of information that is supposed to be unnecessary to the case, but that nonetheless vindicates Mouchawar's interpretation of these leases as dishonest stratagems, implying that the two contracting parties conspired in an illicit cause. From Mouchawar's description, we do not get any of the details that were essential to the Ottoman late Ḥanafī canon. What was the financial condition of the debtor? Was he trying to shield his family from homelessness? Can the attempt to hurt the new debtor be interpreted as a moral critique of a person willing to make profit from the financial difficulties of a fellow citizen, and, more broadly of unrestrained foreclosures? We will not know, but, for Mouchawar, the debtor was simply attempting to forestall and cause injury to the new owner. During these precarious and transformative times, with the changes in the property regime and new distributions of the economy of legal knowledge, suspicion abounds.

Gennardi ignores Mouchawar's inquiries into the ulterior motive of debtors and replies with technical clarifications: a mortgage (*hypothèque*) leaves the debtor with the right to dispose of his immovable. Contracts done before the due date of the loan are valid. However, if at the end of the mortgage contract, the debtor has received notification of a forced expropriation, and the leases were contracted after that, they are null and void. The new owner (the winning bidder) can expel the tenants. Gennardi thus does not engage in the new grammar of intent and its scrutiny of ulterior motive in contracts. It is difficult to gauge why Gennardi does not follow Mouchawar's lead, questioning the legality of the cause of these contracts. As we discussed, Gennardi himself questioned the very institution of the family waqf and its charitable intent, and not only in relation to its use by indebted founders to escape foreclosure. The French expert on waqf can be seen applying an argument using the notion of "illicit cause" of escaping Islamic inheritance laws within a tradition (the Ḥanafī) that did not take such intent into consideration. With regard to debt, however, he seems to have stuck with the formalism of Ḥanafī law, and I wonder if that might be caused by his reading of the economic situation.

In sum, French Mandate regulations formalized the possibility to peer into the ulterior motives of contracting subjects, while continuing with the liberalization of foreclosure through the introduction of security (*ta'mīn*) as a real right. This eventually became the most used instrument to guarantee a debt, because it left the property in the hands of the debtor and did not involve the complexity of negotiations of use and usufruct under rahn and bay' bi'l-wafā' contracts. Nonetheless, because waqf foundation still fell under the jurisdiction of shari'a courts, it was still subject to the formalism of Ḥanafī law. Let me turn now to the contemporary moment to see how these different grammars of intent intersect in discussions I have had with waqf practitioners.

POSTCOLONIAL SUSPICION AND THE PERSISTENCE OF AN ETHIC OF ABSTINENCE

It had been quite difficult to get a hold of Salim Harb. Even though his name was mentioned on the waqf deed of the Karama Foundation, and even though I had already interviewed the lawyer of the organization and had gotten Harb's number from that lawyer, my attempts at scheduling a meeting kept failing. When he finally agreed to meet me, he remained suspicious. I drove to the suburb where he lived and parked on what looked like a very quiet street, with barely any pedestrians or activity. We were in a residential neighborhood. We met in a large office, furnished sparsely with a desk and its chair, facing two chairs. I sat across from him, but he averted his gaze. I started with some broad questions about his life history and encounter with waqf.

This was one of my early interviews and I was trying to understand the importance of the *qurba* intent from a legal perspective: "How does the Karama waqf fulfill the legal requirement of getting close to God?" From the expression of disbelief on his face to his long pause, I felt that Harb was saying, "Did you come all the way to the suburbs of Beirut to ask such a futile question? Are you taking up my time for that?" The answer came a few seconds later, ending the conversation and sealing my failure as an ethnographer: "You see us and what we are doing." It certainly is true that, although the Karama Foundation does not share the more common charitable purposes of waqfs of the day (supporting a mosque or an Islamic center), it could count among waqfs that immediately serve a charitable purpose. Indeed, the waqf mostly helped Islamists detained because of their views rather than because of any misdemeanor, vindicating "Islam" in the face of opponents. But I was asking about "subjective intent," which, as I detailed in the discussion on intent in the Ottoman Ḥanafī fiqh canon, belongs to the conscience of the believer and his or her relation to God. In the same way that praying is an act of worship in and of itself and that endowing a mosque was a *qurba* in and of itself, a waqf that "defended" Islam and Muslims was a *qurba*. Whether one is praying to show off to others or building a mosque to acquire fame and political clout, these are subjective intents between a Muslim and God, which will be accounted for on the Day of Judgment. Who was I to delve into Harb's "real" motives?

My question about the *qurba* intent of the waqf was triggered by my interview with the Karama waqf lawyer, who had explained, as detailed in chapter 1, that making Karama a waqf served legal purposes because it afforded this foreign NGO a legal personality and the possibility of operating in Lebanon without clearance, long delays, and supervision from the Ministry of Interior. My question stemmed from an assumption that the presence of external goods (here, practical advantages of the waqf) cast a shadow on the internal goods and the pious purpose of the waqf. It presumed that a charitable donation was to be completely disinterested, an ideology whose rise Jonathan Parry traces in parallel to the emergence of the "ideology of a purely interested exchange"—that is, commodity exchange in a capitalist market (1986, 458). However, here, the internal goods of the practice were not jeopardized by its legal advantages.

I surmise that Harb's incredulity, however, did not stem from my questioning of his "real motives." In our discussion, he had hinted a bit earlier to his life history: he had been the victim of arbitrary detention and enforced disappearance for being a Muslim engaged in charitable giving. Given that context, his disbelief might have stemmed from what he saw as my questioning his commitment to Islam when he has been so clearly associated with Islam, identified as an Islamist. On the one hand, he was being accused of being too Muslim, and here I was asking him whether he was a sincere Muslim.

Although my own questioning of Harb's intent might suggest that suspicion of intent had become naturalized to some, especially given the new property regime's deep entrenchment, other conversations brought up the question of intent in a different grammar. In an interview with a regional mufti, I asked about cash waqfs and their validity. The mufti explained how, in the 2000s, there had been a sudden burst in waqf foundation, where the object endowed was not land and immovable property, but movables and cash. "Ten personal computers from here, $100 from there," he explained. While I was listening intently, he noted that some of the founders had good intentions and the means to found waqfs. Others, he continued, had good intentions but no means. And finally, "Some others . . ." and then he paused, as if stopping himself from making a hasty accusation. "We can't tell because this is in the realm of the *ḍamāʾir* [sing. *ḍamīr*]." He was referring to a person's inner life and thought, the *forum internum* (Johansen 1999). As a scholar versed in the tradition, the mufti, in his refusal to attribute bad intentions to founders seems to follow the grammar of intent in the Ḥanafī fiqh. Intent cannot be known or directly accessed; all that judges have available are external actions that can be assessed for their legality based on following the requirements of a waqf foundation deed. And it is to such external signs that the mufti turned. He noted that the sudden abundance of waqfs is dubious (*tuthīr al-tasāʾul*), especially given the kinds of objects endowed for an everlasting endowment: ten personal computers are outdated in a very short while, so why are they made into a waqf, he asked. In these questions, he did not attribute dubious intent to the founders, but simply noted the "consumability" of the endowed objects and the questions it raised.

While the mufti refrained from passing judgment on the intent of these founders, the *question* of intent and ulterior motive arose unsolicited. Suspicion permeates the realm of waqf making, even when it follows the Ḥanafī fiqh in the shariʿa courts. This generalized suspicion that accompanies waqf foundations and practice echoes what Hussein Ali Agrama has proposed as an important particularity of the modern rule of law (beyond state monopoly over violence and bureaucratic legal rationality): an "overall disposition," an affect of "organized suspicion that continues to suffuse social life" (2012, 130). Furthermore, Agrama argues that when it operates under modern rule of law, shariʿa becomes subject to the same modality of suspicion. The suspicion of the mufti towards the founders seems to confirm Agrama's analysis. Furthermore, Abu Samah of al-Irshad wa al-Islah explained to me that it was the grand mufti's suspicion about cash waqfs and their misuse by some to collect donations and then disappear that prompted the mufti to issue a memo requiring his approval of all waqfs. Such generalized suspicion, as Agrama observed in Egypt, leads to the exercise of sovereign power to control manipulations of waqf foundation.[61]

61. In Egypt, for Agrama (2012), who is interested in thinking about secularism, the intervention of sovereign power produces questions about religion and politics and is therefore very closely tied to questions of secularism. In the case of the waqfs, the question of secularism does not arise in this

The generalized suspicion about waqfs and their manipulation by ill-intentioned founders and even by the DGIW is so prevalent that suspicion was itself the subject of commentary during the waqf exchanges in the reconstruction of downtown Beirut at the end of the Lebanese Civil War (1975–1990), which I will discuss further in chapter 5. Some members of parliament associated with the Jamaʿa Islamiyya criticized the plan to exchange waqfs for shares in the company in charge of the reconstruction of the city center (Sawalha 2010, 38). An article in *Annahar* reports that these MPs noted the "obscurity and vagueness surrounding the fate of the waqf parcels in downtown Beirut is the reason behind the turmoil around them, regarding the good intent, vigilance, or the 'aim in Jacob's desire' [*al-ghāya fī nafs yaʿqūb*]" (14 January 1994, 6). The expression "al-ghāya fī nafs yaʿqūb" is a variation on the Qurʾanic "ḥāja fī nafs yaʿqūb" (12:68), an expression explaining why Prophet Jacob directed his sons to enter Egypt from different gates. This advice, this verse states, could not avert what God had written for them, but it satisfied a desire in "Jacob's heart." Qurʾanic commentators generally agree that Jacob's desire was to protect his sons from the evil eye. The expression mentions a desire that is "in Jacob's heart," his *nafs*, that locus of interiority and intent, which is usually inaccessible. The article thus reflects the suspicion over the DGIW's intent in handling the waqfs, while also putting the blame on the DGIW's own actions for this suspicion.

It is important to note here that such accusations are not done in the context of the judiciary where, in the Ḥanafī tradition, intent alone is not the object of scrutiny. Nonetheless, many traditions enjoin Muslims in their daily lives, even more than in the judicial context, not to impute bad intent to others. Revelation clearly advices Muslims to "avoid most guesswork [about one another], for behold, some of [such] guesswork is [in itself] a sin" (Qurʾan 49:12). As Muhammad Asad explains, guesswork, *ẓann*, in this context "may lead to unfounded suspicion of another person's motives" (2003, 904n14).[62] Such injunctions, along with

particular context of suspicion towards intent, although it does arise in the circulation of waqf revenues and people between the state and foundations as I mention in chapter 2 and further elaborate in the conclusion.

62. Another important series of verses on accusation and guesswork appears in chapter 22, Al-Nur (The Light), especially verses 11–20, which commentators take as a response to accusations of adultery against the wife of the Prophet, ʿAʾisha, in what is known in Islamic history as the "Account of the Lie." She was accompanying the Prophet to a battle, and as the troops decamped returning to Medina, she was inadvertently left behind. She was found and brought back by one of the Companions, and so gossip about her spread, causing much distress to the Prophet, with some Companions even suggesting that the Prophet should divorce her, since the Prophet's wives' moral probity should be above any doubt. Revelation cleared her of these accusations and promised her slanderers suffering. The greatest suffering was promised to the person "who takes it upon himself to enhance this [sin]" (Qurʾan 24:11). Muhammad Asad argues that such people are those who stress "in a legally and morally inadmissible manner, certain 'circumstantial' details or aspects of the case in order to make the slanderous, unfounded allegation more believable" (2003, 596n14).

substantial traditions discouraging presumptions about others and related issues, like gossip, encourage an ethic and disposition of abstinence and avoidance of discussing others' intents and their actions (as we saw in the above discussed hadith about "splitting believer's hearts"). Even more, as Islamic legal historian Ahmed El Shamsy shows, "Subjecting the faults of others [with respect to the rights of God] to public view" was strongly condemned in various traditions as it infringes upon the right to privacy of the individual, who was encouraged to hide sins and repent and work on developing the right dispositions through practice (2015, 243). These condemnations and dispositions, along with attempts to avoid gossip and rumor, necessitated some finesse during my interviews discussing the actions of and rumors surrounding founders, the DGIW, and the grand mufti, with pious subjects—and sometimes to no avail. This abstinence was compounded by my being a researcher affiliated with an American university, whose political affiliations were not very clear, especially since I come from a very small family with diverse political views. Interlocutors would dodge my questions about the accusations the grand mufti's corruption or answer in some very elusive language.

CONCLUSION

In this chapter, I have shown how, starting in the mid-nineteenth century, new debt and property regimes in Mount Lebanon and Beirut were associated with increased scrutiny of intent in some transactions like waqf. Until then, waqf operated under a different debt and property regime, where formalism dominated transactions: intent was judged though actions, leaving subjective intent to God in the hereafter. Furthermore, debt was socially productive and coupled with injunctions of forgiveness. The new debt regime instated by the Ottomans in the nineteenth century sought to guarantee the rights of creditors, who in Mount Lebanon were mostly merchants tied to global capital. It allowed foreclosure for debt on private property and allowed the mortgaging of lands considered up to then inalienable (*miri* and waqf). This new debt regime brought up a heightened scrutiny of intent, particularly the intent to escape debt, because the old debt regime allowed an escape from the new, more systematic foreclosures.

The development of a new debt and property regime was an important crucible for the development of ideas that ulterior motive and inner intent reflect the "true" self. This modern idea that the true self is the inner one, which awaits to be discovered and which is the only way to achieve certain capacities, has usually been explored throughout religious and philosophical texts. For instance, Charles Taylor (1992) discusses the way philosophers and social and political theorists (from Plato to Descartes, Locke and Kant, Augustine and Montaigne) have approached the self. He traces, in their theorizations of the self, the rise of these new inner depths. In the history of waqf in Lebanon, we see the development of this novel form of subjectivity in response to material conditions. By animating suspicion over the intent of founders, this new form of subjectivity allowed the curtailing of waqfs and became crucial to the reproduction of new debt and property regimes.

This new suspicion towards the intent of founders and waqf administrators permeates contemporary debates on waqf foundations, academic studies of the waqf, and even my own sensibilities. Yet, despite this suspicion, the older grammar of intent, which tied it to expressions in the here and now and left it to God in the hereafter, with its ethic of abstinence from guesswork, continues to inform practitioners' discussions of waqf founders' intent and of intent more broadly. Suspicion towards founders' intent dovetails with the demands that charitable giving should be selfless, a conception that arises with the conceptualization of the free market as a sphere of pure self-interest. In this bifurcated world, waqfs that serve the founder and their family, in addition to protecting from foreclosure, came to be seen as not charitable. We turn in the next chapter to the project of distinguishing between truly charitable (for collective benefit) as opposed to self-interested (for private benefit) family waqfs. This distinction was crucially enabled by the new conception of the self and its "real" intent discussed in this chapter.

4

Charity and the Family

It was a hot day in Ramadan of 2009, and I had just finished interviewing a prominent member of the Supreme Islamic Legal Council (SILC). We had chatted about the difference between a waqf and an NGO, Decree 18/1955,[1] the building of a new mosque, the largest in downtown Beirut, and had broached the relation of the head of the Sunni shariʿa courts to the grand mufti. It had been a good and illuminating interview, and I was getting ready to leave when the secretary brought the lawyer a fax that had just arrived. He turned to me and said, "So you were asking about the grand mufti. Here you go!"

The fax was an angry letter from a certain Muhammad Rashid Qarduhi, who was refusing to attend any Ramadan *ifṭār* (break-of-fast meal) where the grand mufti would be present because the grand mufti "had signed some documents for his [own] son." Qarduhi also derided the way the mufti referred to his own son as "shaykh" Raghib, since the son does not have religious scholarly credentials. To punctuate his derision, Qarduhi appended a satirical parenthetical "God bless . . ." to the mufti's son's name. Qarduhi also sent ten documents to "prove the embezzlement of Islamic waqf funds." The first document showed the mufti's son's connection to a company that goes by the name G(5) Trade and Consultants. The rest of the documents were contracts with G(5) from Dar al-Fatwa for restoration work of waqf buildings, for a total of around $300,000. "These documents prove how the father signs for his son (God bless . . .)," the cover letter ended.

1. The decree that organizes the Muslim "sect" and its organizations (Dar al-Fatwa and the waqf directorates).

The scandal of the grand mufti's nepotism reverberated far and wide and was exacerbated by the mufti's silence on the topic. It occupied newspapers, the web, and various members of the Sunni community. It elicited an open letter from the former prime minister Salim al-Hoss, urging the grand mufti to either sue the author of the tracts for defamation or step down. An auditor was solicited to examine the accounting of the transactions. The grand mufti dealt with the crisis through a silence that infuriated the community. "You have to respond to these hideous [*shanīʿa*] accusations . . . and if you do not provide a potent retort [*al-radd al-mufḥim*], then people will rightly see that the silence about these accusations for all this time is proof of their accuracy and truth," wrote al-Hoss (*al-Akhbar*, 2 February 2010, 2). The scandal is not "just" about nepotism; it is one incident in a long-time friendship turned antagonistic between the grand mufti and the author of the tract (and various opponents of the mufti). However, the fact that one of Qarduhi's most effective attacks, which eventually cost the grand mufti his position, came to be couched in such terms shows the potency of this discourse.

Yet, what might seem heinous today was a well-established ethics of care for one's family in the past. As my archive showed, the transmission of waqf revenues from father to son was until the early twentieth century the main avenue of transmission of such revenues, even in waqfs dedicated to mosques, schools, and other "public" facilities, as I show in detail below. Furthermore, as we saw in chapter 1 with the waqf of Mustafa Agha Qabbani, which was dedicated to his daughter ʿAʾisha and her descendants before reaching the poor upon the extinction of this lineage, it was acceptable for founders to dedicate a waqf's revenues to their family as a pious deed; even more, such an act was one of the *most* pious deeds. Indeed, in nineteenth-century Beiruti waqf practices, sites of beneficence were not confined to "public" goals, be they poverty relief, mosques, madrasas, or fountains. Of the 135 waqfs founded between 1843 and 1912, 56 percent named family beneficiaries (Adada 2009, 141) before the waqf reached its perpetual beneficiaries (usually the poor),[2] as did the waqf of Mustafa Agha Qabbani in 1854. The sensibility reflected in the scandal over the mufti's nepotism, thoroughly chronicled in my notebook, which divorced giving to family from piety especially when it involved public resources, found echoes in an event in my archive of the Qabbani waqf. There, court decisions document the descendants of Mustafa Agha fighting over the waqf in the mid-1920s in order to revert it back to their own private property. To these descendants too, a waqf dedicated to family was no longer a pious deed that brought rewards to their ancestor; it had become just a piece of land, its pious aims irrelevant.

How did giving to family as an act of piety become an impossibility, or even more, nepotism? I ask this question not "in praise of nepotism" (Bellow 2003), nor to legitimize the mufti's actions, nor with a nostalgia for previous modes of

2. Percentage based on Adada's (2006) tables 26 and 27.

giving and care.[3] I follow this line of inquiry to historicize the particular framing of corruption and nepotism in a facile opposition to merit, which gives the illusion that once corruption, nepotism, and, more broadly in Lebanon, clientelism and sectarianism are eliminated, democracy, the rule of law, and a more just society will ensue. I take my cue from anthropologies of corruption that have argued that "corruption" is not a result of so-called weak states, but that it is endemic to modern bureaucratic states (Haller and Shore 2005, 11) or the rule of law. Historicizing the notion of corruption in the Ottoman Empire, Cengiz Kırlı (2015) notes that corruption in its financial meaning was "invented" during the Tanzimat with the creation of the state official whose only compensation was from a salary. Before that, there had been no clear distinction between the personal pockets of the officials and the state's coffers, so gifts to the officials that had been considered part of their salary became recast as bribes.

Questioning corruption is a politically fraught endeavor everywhere and especially in Lebanon, where state resources are so often squandered through clientelistic networks without even providing reliable basic services (such as electricity, internet, schools) (e.g., Leenders 2012). Yet, for these same reasons, the question of corruption is also particularly relevant because it asks us to understand the effects of this ethic of care under very different political-economic conditions with a different understanding of the state and the social contract, where the (Ottoman) state did not provide for its citizens and where the principle of equality did not hold sway. If nepotism and clientelism are not pre-modern holdouts, but produced by the very structures that claim to provide equality to all, then eradicating them might not be a possibility; instead, the more interesting scholarly focus becomes the analysis of the work both accusations and practices of corruption do.

I propose that the answer to this question of the rising unease with giving to family, especially if giving involves resources now deemed public, hinges on changing conceptions of charity, religion, and economy based upon and reproducing novel understandings of the public and private spheres. Starting in the nineteenth century, a waqf's charitable purpose of supporting the founder's family was brought into question.[4] Despite their designation as "family waqfs," these waqfs benefited families only as intermediary beneficiaries before the extinction of these families and the waqfs' reversion to perpetual charitable purposes like helping the poor, which, given the life expectancy in the medieval and early modern periods,

3. Indeed, as anthropologists have shown, family is not simply about unconditional love, solidarity, and reciprocity. It is as much a site of power struggles and the reproduction of hierarchies (Abu-Lughod 1986; Joseph 1994), of heavy expectations and obligations, and of rivalries and latent hostilities (Peletz 2001). This appears in Doumani's work (2017) on the waqfs of Tripoli and Nablus, where lawsuits among kin are one of his main archives.

4. Because it reflects broader modern understandings of the private and the public, the questioning of the validity of family waqfs occurs across the world, even under very different forms of rule. See, for example, Kozlowski (1985) for British India; and Yahaya (2020) for British and Dutch Southeast Asia.

happened quite quickly (Hoexter 1998b, 479). These family waqfs also followed the same fiqh regulations as other waqfs that went directly to the poor.[5] Such "family waqfs" became constructed, in both scholarship and popular discourse, as a deviation from truly "charitable waqfs." This chapter first excavates this privileging of the family as an act of piety, and thus historicizes the assumption that giving to strangers is "altruistic"[6] and pious, whereas giving to one's family is "selfish" and thus not truly pious. It then traces the suppression and afterlives of an ethic of care of the family as piety against the hegemony of an ethic of merit and a new grammar of family that overlays family with the private sphere. This new grammar thus refigures the act of giving to one's family in the public into "nepotism." By subjecting charitable waqfs and family waqfs to different legislation, French Mandatory powers later produced in yet another way the private/public division essential to modern states and the rule of law. In this process, because the family waqf was considered to be part of the economy (as we discussed in chapter 2) arguments as to its economic effects came to be considered even by religious scholars, who in their debates over the validity of family waqf introduced statistical styles of reasoning into the Islamic tradition. My analysis, as in the previous chapters, develops in four moments, starting with the Ḥanafī tradition just before the nineteenth century reforms, followed by the Ottoman reforms, French Mandate debates, and postcolonial practices.

OTTOMAN LATE ḤANAFĪ CHARITY: THE PRIMACY OF THE FAMILY

Spending on Family as Piety

Like their Jewish and Christian counterparts, Islamic notions of charity in my medieval and early modern library differ from modern ones in their relation to the

5. Studies of waqf have noted this point from early on, like Anderson (1951, 296) and Cahen (1961, 47), and it has been confirmed by studies of early waqf manuals (e.g., Hennigan 2004, xivn5). Manuals discuss family beneficiaries along with expenditures on a particular mosque as examples of extinguishable beneficiaries and their effect on the perpetuity of the waqf (see, e.g., al-Khassaf 1999, 18, 112) rather than as examples of "selfish" giving to family as opposed to altruistic giving to strangers (Kozlowski 1985, 60). Even as historians acknowledge that legal texts do not make a distinction between these two kinds of waqfs, they maintain this distinction since these waqfs had very different "social and economic consequences," especially due to their scale (McChesney 1991, 9). Historians therefore usually take as their subject either charitable waqfs (e.g., McChesney 1991; Hoexter 1998a; van Leeuwen 1999) or family waqfs (e.g., Layish 1983; Powers 1989; Reiter 1995; Doumani 2017). In this chapter, I will linger on the significance of the lack of legal differences between family and charitable waqfs in order to examine assumptions about charity and the family and how they overlap with the private/public distinction.

6. These are salient debates in the anthropological literature on the gift, which I will engage below. On the question of selfishness versus altruism, see Parry (1986, 466–69); on the care of strangers versus kin, see Bornstein (2012, 145–70).

family.[7] Let us start with the Christian definition because its assumptions structure contemporary understandings of charity in the Anglophone world but also de-exceptionalize the medieval and early modern Islamic understanding. A first definition of *charity* in the Oxford English Dictionary is "Christian love, which implies both God's love of man, man's love of God and his neighbour, and especially to his fellow-men." In this view, such love was expressed though piety, whose meaning and expression underwent significant changes from its Greco-Roman incarnation. Indeed, piety in Greek, as Augustine notes, referred to the worship of God, dutifulness towards parents, and, in popular talk, works of charity (Garrison 1992, 12). While Augustine restricted "true" piety to the worship of God, the association of piety with duty towards the family continued during the medieval period (Garrison 1992, 12). The association of piety with family appears in the relation between church office and family, whereby popes favored their families and "nephews" in their appointments (Reinhard 2002, 1031). As historian Wolfgang Reinhard notes, the very term nepotism, "designating relatives of popes who enjoyed significant favoritism" (2002, 1030), arose only in the seventeenth century as the practice of care of the family through and in government was coming under attack.[8] Before that, as he details, care of the family was considered piety and an expression of charity (along with being the way government operated through the hereditary principle).

In a second, "secularized" definition of charity in the OED, God disappears since charity is "benevolence to one's neighbours, especially to the poor; the practical beneficences in which this manifests itself as a feeling or disposition or as action (almsgiving)." Yet, the connotation of charity as religious giving remains even today (Scherz 2014, 7).

In both the Christian and secularized English definitions of charity, and in Ḥanafī ones, sites of benevolence receive considerable mention. The poor are the recipients of charity par excellence in the definitions above. This is the case also of Islamic charity, *ṣadaqa*,[9] as Ibn ʿAbidin clearly states that "the place of charity [in principle/originally] is the poor" ("maḥall al-ṣadaqa [fī al-aṣl] al-fuqarāʾ"). That is why, he explains, when one says, "I made a ṣadaqa," there is no need to specify that it is for the poor and that the ṣadaqa goes to the poor (*Ḥāshiya*, 3:365–66).[10] Yet the grammar of ṣadaqa in the Islamic legal tradition differs because it is associated

7. Scholars of Islam have noted many continuities between the Muslim *ṣadaqa*, the Jewish *ṣedaḳa*, and Christian alms (s.v. "ṣadaka" in *EI2*). For an example of modern notions, the US Internal Revenue Service defines charitable organizations that are worthy of support and tax exemption as those excluding private interests and the family (https://www.irs.gov/charities-non-profits/charitable-organizations/inurement-private-benefit-charitable-organizations).

8. I owe this reference to Yazan Doughan (2018), whose work on *fasād* (corruption) and *wāsṭa* (the practice of using the mediation of a person to get something from another person/entity) examines in detail the logic of this practice and its entwinement with different regimes of care.

9. For an excellent introduction to the historical development of *ṣadaqa*, see *EI2*.

10. I discuss below the possibility of giving to the rich as ṣadaqa.

with voluntariness and *qurba* (the intent of bringing the benefactor closer to God), which surface in relation to other forms of spending and giving.[11]

Ṣadaqa's voluntariness is highlighted in its opposition to zakat (almsgiving) and *nafaqa* (support or maintenance). Zakat is often termed *ṣadaqa* and is required of every Muslim who can afford it and should be distributed to the Muslim poor. Over the years, however, *ṣadaqa* came to imply *voluntary* giving, as opposed to zakat, obligatory giving.[12] *Nafaqa* denotes spending in general terms, but in legal manuals, it usually follows divorce and refers to the rights of others on one's spending. *Nafaqa* consists of "food, shelter, and clothing" and is required for another person related through "three things: marriage, *qarāba* (nearness of kin),[13] and ownership" (Ibn ʿAbidin, *Ḥāshiya* 2:644). Hence *nafaqa* usually refers to the required maintenance of one's wife, one's near of kin, and one's slaves.[14] Beyond these requirements, spending on near of kin counts as an act of piety if performed with the right intent: in submission to God, seeking his rewards.

Besides its voluntariness, ṣadaqa is associated with qurba. The term itself comes from the verb root *ṣ-d-q*, which means "to be truthful." *Ṣadaqa* signifies then "the truthfulness of the slave [of God] in his worship" (al-ʿAyni, *Ramz* 1:85), and its mandatory component, the zakat, is an "integral part of religious ritual" (Hallaq 2009, 231).[15] This hints at the main characteristic of ṣadaqa, drawing its donor closer to God. Ṣadaqa is discussed with gifts (sing., *hiba*) in an attempt to distinguish them, because both involve the transfer of property without compensation. Ṣadaqa differs by its motive, "ibtighāʾ wajh allāh taʿālā" (al-ʿAyni, *Ramz* 2:186) ("to please God . . . in the hope of a reward in the hereafter. . . . It must, that is, constitute a *ḳurba*, an act performed as a means of coming closer to God" [*EI2*]). Ṣadaqa is then primarily distinguished from *zakat* and gifts and from its Christian and Jewish counterparts by its intentionality and the qurba intention behind it.

In my library, discussions in the waqf chapter of fiqh manuals do not always elaborate on the qurba purpose of waqf.[16] If the definitions of waqf according to

11. Hadith collections and the Islamic law manuals in my library do not address ṣadaqa in a separate chapter (*kitāb*). They usually tackle it within sections on zakat (alms), waqf, *nafaqa*, and gifts (*hiba*).

12. There is a disagreement on whether this is a modern understanding, as the Qurʾan and many fiqh manuals use *ṣadaqa* for *zakat* in many places (s.v. "ṣadaka" in *EI2*).

13. Based on Muhammad Asad's translation of "dhawī al-qurbā" in Qur'an 2:177 (2003, 46), I use "near of kin" instead of "next of kin" because the Arabic word implies proximity.

14. Here, one's near of kin are one's parents and one's children. For more detail on *zakat* and *nafaqa*, see Mattson (2003).

15. *Zakat* has a connotation of return, "of paying out of the growth of one's property with a view to purifying that property" (Hallaq 2009, 231). See also Bonner (2003).

16. While qurba is discussed as an essential element of the waqf in most Ḥanafī fiqh manuals, Ibn Nujaym, in his legal maxims classic, *al-Ashbāh wa al-Naẓāʾir*, considers the intent of qurba as a "bonus" rather than essential for the validity of waqfs (1999, 20). He notes that waqf-making does not need a statement of intent because it is not an act of worship, since it is valid if done by a non-Muslim. However, he continues, if the founder intends qurba, he receives rewards, and if he does not make

Abu Hanifa or his students do not include an explicit mention of qurba,[17] nonetheless qurba is implicit in the term *taṣadduq* which denotes an act whose aim is qurba, as discussed above. Ibn Nujaym and Ibn ʿAbidin, however, dwell on qurba in the meaning, reasons, and conditions of waqf making. Most prominently, Ibn Nujaym mentions, citing al-Sarakhsi, that "the reason behind waqf making is the will of the commendable soul to do good to his 'beloved' [*birr al-aḥbāb*] in this world, and to get nearer to the Almighty in the hereafter [*al-taqarrub ilā rabb al-arbāb*]" (Ibn Nujaym, *Baḥr*, 5:188). While waqf is not solely an act of worship ("lays mawḍūʿan li'l-taʿabbud bih"), like prayer and pilgrimage are—which, as we discussed in chapter 3, do not necessitate proper intent because they can be done only for worship—it incurs, with the right intent, the reward of closeness to God (Ibn ʿAbidin, *Ḥāshiya*, 3:358).[18]

Before turning to the question of family and ṣadaqa recipients, a remark on the use of the term *family* is necessary. Because the argument advanced in this chapter hinges on the inclusion or exclusion of family from charity, the question of what type of family it is that waqf and Islamic law privilege is irrelevant. Whether ṣadaqa injunctions and waqf practices favor the nuclear family, patrilineal descendants, or cognatic groups matters less than the sheer presence of any part of the family in the (worthy) recipients of ṣadaqa. Therefore, I will continue to use *family* to denote any of these groups.

Furthermore, rather than engaging in the debates on the relation between the nuclear family and capitalism (Engels and Leacock 1972; Smith and Wallerstein 1992) and the effect of waqf on the production of such families (a debate compellingly addressed by Doumani [2017]), I am interested in contributing to discussions on the supposed deleterious effects that family ties and identities have on building noncorrupt democratic states—a debate that is at the center of contemporary Lebanese politics, as I further discuss in the conclusion of this chapter.

Regardless of the form family takes, it appears in discussions of ṣadaqa in the Islamic tradition. Both the Qurʾan and hadith enjoin privileging family members as the primary recipients of charity. In the Qurʾan, for instance, a key verse describing the principles of piety places spending on one's family immediately after the basic beliefs in God, Judgment Day, the angels, revelation, and the prophets. "Truly

---

an express intent, he does not receive such rewards. Nonetheless, in his discussion of the waqf of the *dhimmī*, Ibn Nujaym (*Baḥr*, 5:188) specifies that the charitable purpose needs to be a qurba for "us and for them," implying that even for non-Muslims, waqf is a qurba in their tradition.

17. As might be recalled from chapter 1, for Abu Hanifa, waqf is "the confinement of a *ʿayn* [the corpus of a specific object, or the principal, to use endowment terminology] to the ownership of the waqf founder, and the gift of its *manfaʿa* (yield or usufruct) to some charitable purpose" (al-ʿAyni, *Ramz* 1:343). For his students it is "the confinement of the corpus [of a specific property] [*ʿayn*] to the ownership of God . . . and the gift of its yield or usufruct [*manfaʿa*] to some charitable purpose [*al-taṣadduq b-il-manfaʿa*]."

18. I elaborate later in this section on the necessity of this intent in discussions of the waqfs of non-Muslims.

pious [*al-birr*] is he who spends his substance upon his near of kin" (Qur'an 2:177). The family (*dhawī al-qurbā*) comes first in pious spending, followed only afterwards by orphans (*al-yatāmā*), the needy (*al-masākīn*), the traveler/wayfarer (*ibn al-sabīl*), and beggars (*al-sā'ilīn*). Many hadiths echo the Qur'an regarding the piety of spending on one's family: for instance, "when a Muslim spends on his family [*ahlih*] seeking reward for it from Allah, it counts for him as ṣadaqa" (Muslim 2005). Another hadith introduces an even more radical suggestion—that spending should start with oneself—after one has fulfilled one's obligations to family. "Start with your own self and spend it on yourself [*taṣaddaq 'alayhā*], and if anything is left, it should be spent on your family [*ahl*], and if anything is left [after meeting the needs of the family], it should be spent on relatives [*qarāba*], and if anything is left from the family, it should be spent like this, like this" (Muslim 2005). These are but a few examples of a central theme in the Qur'an and Islamic ethics: the care of the family, and especially parents. In these ethics, the dichotomy between care of family (as an extension of the self and thus as selfish) and care of strangers (as selfless and thus altruistic) does not appear.

These general injunctions of giving to family as acts of piety take a different form in the manuals of my fiqh library. It is surprising in its absence, either as an injunction or as admonition. The question of whether making one's family the beneficiary of a waqf counts as a valid ṣadaqa that will fulfill the goal of the waqf as a qurba is never discussed. Instead, in the late Ḥanafī canon, three categories of beneficiaries might threaten a waqf's validity: the self, the wealthy,[19] and non-Muslims. Jurists debate whether dedicating the usufruct to one of these three categories of beneficiaries counts as a ṣadaqa and hence provides for a valid waqf. This absence of family from noncharitable beneficiaries suggests that, in this period, naming family as waqf beneficiaries was not seen as suspicious or different from naming particular individuals.

The first category of possible noncharitable waqf beneficiaries involves the self. Al-'Ayni, for example, discusses the permissibility of making oneself the beneficiary of one's waqf during one's lifetime and among other beneficiaries (*Ramz*, 1:346). He reports two opinions: the dominant one, Abu Yusuf's, which allows the practice and has been adopted so as to encourage the making of waqfs; and al-Shaybani's, which declares that this stipulation makes the waqf invalid. The justification for this invalidation of the waqf is that such a stipulation prohibits qurba. Qurba, according to al-'Ayni, occurs through relinquishing ownership rights—the rights to sell, bequeath, pawn—and here the right to usufruct seems to be among those. Keeping the right of usufruct counters complete relinquishing and hence invalidates the waqf. Ibn Nujaym however disputes this opinion and

19. "The wealthy" (*al-aghniyā'*) refers to anyone who pays *zakat* because they have a certain amount of savings held for a year. However, this technical meaning of *wealthy* should not imply that these waqfs were dedicated to people who are well-off; rather just that they were dedicated to those who would not be eligible for *zakat*.

argues that in fact waqfing involves the "relinquishing of ownership to God to get close to him, so the founder's stipulation of some or all the revenues for himself consists of dedicating what now belongs to God to himself, rather than dedicating what belongs to himself for himself" (*Baḥr*, 5:368). Ibn Nujaym also quotes a prophetic tradition that disputes the noncharitableness of giving to oneself: "a man's spending on himself is a ṣadaqa" (*Baḥr*, 5:368).

The second category of possible noncharitable waqf beneficiaries is the wealthy. The wealthy could be any particular person and not necessarily kin. They surface very early in Ibn Nujaym's chapter on waqf, right after the second waqf definition that he quotes, that of Abu Hanifa's students: the confinement of a res as if it was the ownership of God. Ibn Nujaym then adds to that definition, quoting the elaboration of Ibn al-Humam (d. 1457 [861]), a leading Mamluk scholar writing prior to the Ottoman conquest: "and spending of the usufruct on whomever he wishes" ("ṣarf manfaʿatihā ʿalā man aḥabb").[20] Ibn al-Humam explains his liberal interpretation of waqf recipients with the fact that "gifting the usufruct to any wealthy person the founder chooses, without the intention of qurba, is valid, even if, for the waqf to be valid, its ultimate beneficiaries need to be a qurba as it is a condition for perpetuity, at which points the waqf [for a wealthy person] becomes equivalent to the waqf for the poor or a mosque. However, it remains a waqf even before extinction of the wealthy, *without it being an act of charity*" (quoted in Ibn Nujaym, *Baḥr*, 5:187; italics added).[21] Giving to a wealthy person, it would appear, is *not* charity.

However, Ibn Nujaym elaborates on this opinion and adduces another position: "One could say that the waqf benefiting the wealthy constitutes a ṣadaqa of the usufruct because the ṣadaqa is as valid for the rich as it is for the poor . . . and giving ṣadaqa to the rich is a kind of qurba that is different from the qurba of giving to the poor" (Ibn Nujaym, *Baḥr*, 5:187). Ibn Nujaym seems clear that giving to the rich is charity, albeit inferior to giving to the poor.[22] More debates ensue in the centuries and commentaries that follow. A commentator on a different text argues that "if the qurba from giving to the rich was a kind of qurba that was sufficient for a waqf, the waqf that benefits the rich would be valid without it needing to benefit

20. I have translated *ʿalā man aḥabb* as "on whomever he wishes" even though the same root, ḥ-b-b, appears above in the sense of "the beloved" in the discussion of the purpose of waqf-making to "do good to his 'beloved' [*aḥbāb*] in this world." The waqf-maker's beloved are not those whom he knows and loves, as a literal translation might imply. Ibn ʿAbidin explains that the *aḥbāb* are "those to whom he wishes to do good, from a near of kin or an unrelated poor person" (*Ḥāshiya* 3:358). Note that the near of kin are not problematized as a recipient of charity.

21. "Al-waqf yaṣuḥḥ li-man āhabb min al-aghniyāʾ bilā qaṣd al-qurba, wa huwa wa in kān lā budd fī ākhirih min al-qurba ka-sharṭ al-taʾbīd wa huwa bidhālik ka'l-fuqarāʾ wa maṣāliḥ al-masjid lakinnahu yakūn waqfan qabl inqirāḍ al-aghniyāʾ bilā taṣadduq."

22. This opinion echoes the statement in the *Encyclopedia of Islam* entry for *ṣadaqa* that, for Muslim jurists, it can be given to the wealthy. However, the statement there that the jurists are unanimous about this position seems exaggerated, as we can see in this discussion.

the poor as its endpoint" (Ibn ʿAbidin, *Ḥāshiya*, 3:357). However, this argument is picked up by Ibn ʿAbidin in his gloss and challenged.

> The correct answer is that the waqf is a ṣadaqa from beginning to end, as it is necessary to state clearly that it is a ṣadaqa in perpetuity or through what stands in place of that perpetuity [*lā budd min al-taṣrīḥ aw mā yaqūm maqāmah*], but if the founder makes its first beneficiaries specific [*muʿayyan*], he would be excluding these revenues from the poor . . . so it is a waqf from the beginning and spending its revenues on a specified beneficiary does not take away this charitable quality. (*Ḥāshiya*, 3:357–58)

Later in the text, Ibn ʿAbidin explains what he means by "what stands in the place of perpetuity":

> The stipulation to spend the revenues on a specified beneficiary [*muʿayyan*] is like [*bi-manzilat*] the exclusion of the spending [of the waqf revenue] on the poor, so the specified beneficiary stands in the place of the poor [*qāʾiman maqāmahum*], so the spending on the particular [wealthy] becomes in all significance a ṣadaqa [*fī maʿnā al-ṣadaqa*] because the particular takes the place of the poor. (*Ḥāshiya*, 3:417)

In other words, through a formalistic syllogistic move, Ibn ʿAbidin deemed giving to specified wealthy extinguishable beneficiaries as charity.

The wealthy also appear in the discussion of invalid classes of recipients like the blind, Qurʾanic reciters, poets, the inhabitants of Baghdad, Arabs, the Muslims, and "the people" (*al-nās*). Thus a waqf that benefits "the Muslims," for example, is invalid according to al-Khassaf, because they are innumerable and include the wealthy along with the poor, and so are eternal beneficiaries that would not allow the waqf to reach the poor (1999, 107, 232).[23] By contrast, a waqf for one's poor neighbors or for a named individual and his or her family is valid: for the first because of their poverty and for the second because they are numerable and extinguishable and the waqf would eventually reach the poor. Here again, then, wealth is not an issue for recipients so long as they are one stop before the endpoint of the waqf.

The last discussion of noncharitable waqf beneficiaries occurs around the waqfs of non-Muslims. If the founder is not a Muslim, what counts as a qurba for this founder? Ibn Nujaym advances that the waqf needs to be a qurba "for us and for them" (*Baḥr*, 5:189). For instance, the waqf of a Jew on a synagogue is considered invalid because it is not a qurba for "us," and the waqf of a Christian or a Jew to support the hajj is also considered invalid because it is not a qurba for "them." The

23. Note that this invalidity does not apply to waqfs dedicated to facilities that can be used *and are needed* by the rich and the poor, such as inns (*ribāṭ*), caravanserais (*khān*), cemeteries, canals, bridges, mosques, and mills. Thus, need (*ḥāja*) becomes an important criterion in determining whether the perpetual beneficiaries are valid, and later jurists start to argue that blindness stands in the way of gainful employment and so the blind should be assumed to be poor, making the waqf for the blind valid (Ibn ʿAbidin, *Ḥāshiya*, 3:430).

waqf of a Christian or a Jew for any poor, even if they are disbelievers (as long as they are not engaged in warfare against Muslims), is considered a qurba.

In these discussions of waqf beneficiaries who invalidate the qurba in waqf-making, the family is never raised as a topic of attention. The absence of the family in discussions of invalid and noncharitable beneficiaries points to its unproblematic status in the practice of waqf foundation. The injunctions of being charitable to one's near-of-kin coupled with the taken-for-granted charitableness of making waqfs benefiting one's family highlight a regime of care and giving that privileges both the near and the familiar. This regime of giving differs from now-dominant models of charitable giving, like humanitarianism, which, as Erica Bornstein concisely puts it, "assert radical and abstract notions of equality in which all humans are worthy of rights and the care of strangers is privileged to the care of kin" (2012, 146). Bornstein contrasts this model with what she terms "relational giving" in India, where giving to family is privileged, and giving to strangers requires a discursive, affective, and even behavioral transformation of strangers into kin. Giving to family is duty, sometimes perceived as a burden, but it is also "the social life that sustains and rewards" (2012, 149). Giving to kin, in the cases that Bornstein discusses, however, remains quite distinct from charitable giving like the *dan*, a form of free gift. Furthermore, Bornstein highlights how giving to strangers is transformed into the first kind of model and thus keeps the distinction between kin and others, even though it parochializes liberal humanitarian models of giving. In the case of the waqf, giving to family moves beyond duty (when it goes beyond the legally required) and can become charity. It thus further blurs the clear liberal distinction between giving to the family in the private sphere as duty and to anonymous strangers in the public as charity.

Family as the Logic of Charity

Family, then, was a legitimate and even privileged beneficiary of charity and waqf in the late Ḥanafi Ottoman tradition. This privileging of the family is epitomized in one Beiruti waqf that today is seen as an exemplary "charitable waqf": the ʿUmari Mosque, the main mosque of the city in the nineteenth century. This might appear like an argument that such "public" waqfs still had a "personal dimension," as Gregory Kozlowski wrote about Indian waqfs (1985, 25). However, we need instead to rethink the "public" and the "private" because the "personal" was no simple dimension and was not restricted to private persons. Family was the very logic of transmission of charity in these endowments.

Based on accounting documents sent from Beirut to Istanbul, the waqf's main expenditures appear to be repairs and salaries (see appendix 2). Repairs, as the jurists had called for, come as a first priority, as they guarantee the continuous existence of the revenue-bearing object and the waqf itself (al-Khassaf 1999, 92). In the case of al-ʿUmari, they were the biggest expense. Offices follow, and they consist of the various employed positions necessary for the the mosque's upkeep and operation. Offices constitute a considerable expense, usually at least a third of the waqf's regular expenditures. Finally, lanterns and their oil, rugs, pitchers for ablutions, and similar commodities and consumables necessary for the running of the mosque form another type of expenditure. To examine the role of the family in these expenditures, I analyze the variety of offices and the logic of their transmission from one officeholder to another. Such appointments were documented in the archive of the shariʿa court in Beirut and in the center in Istanbul. The logic of family could have also directed the distribution of charitable funds in the expenditures of repairs and mosque equipment, as many crafts were passed on from fathers to sons within a system of apprenticeships and guilds.

Following the transmission of offices from holder to holder reveals the channels along which charity is distributed across the limits of tenure and reveals that the primary route of transmission is from father to son,[24] with supplementary criteria (such as merit, experience, and character) also coming into play. I followed the transmission of these offices through documents held at the Ottoman state archives. Indeed, the Treasury held detailed waqf accounting ledgers (first as Hazine/Muhasebe Defterleri and after 1882 [1300] as Esas-i Cihat Defterleri) arranged by city, recording the details of the main waqfs, such as offices, names of officeholders, salaries, dates and types of appointments, and documents delivered to the officeholders for their appointments.[25] These "*muhasebe*" registers constituted a "base record" or summary/index of positions, but they also included pointers to the various documents that supplemented this base record.

For Beirut, the base record of the register dated 1786 originally listed six waqfs, including three mosques, a madrasa, and a Sufi lodge. Later on, at various dates, a few different hands added the waqfs of ten other mosques and Sufi lodges. In the first list, the câmii-i kebîr-i ʿUmarî listed the largest number of offices: a supervisor, a *khaṭīb*,[26] two imams (prayer leaders), a Ḥanafi professor, seven callers to prayer, a reader of the Qurʾanic chapter *yāsīn* after the noon prayer, a caretaker (*qayyim*), an imam for the afternoon prayer (*imâm-i ʿasr*), and two *türbedârs* (caretakers of the burial grounds—in this case, the "mausoleum" that supposedly entombs a few hairs of the Prophet). This totaled seventeen offices just for the ʿUmari Mosque. The 1786 and the 1882 base records detailed changes in six of the seventeen offices: a *khaṭīb*, two imams, two burial ground caretakers, and the Ḥanafi professor. The earliest "update" after the original positions listed in the 1786 register came in 1850 (28 S 1266 [12 January 1850]), the date when the mosque's administration was transferred to the Imperial Waqf Ministry, implying that

24. Most of these offices, like imams and *khaṭībs*, can be held only by men.

25. Exhaustive surveys of waqfs are also included in the land surveys, carried at the time of conquest and updated at the enthronement (*culûs*) of a new sultan. BOA.TT393 (1520 [926 AH]) is the earliest exhaustive record of the waqfs of Bilad al-Sham.

26. The person in charge of making the *khuṭba*, the sermon preceding the Friday prayer and other special prayers.

beforehand, the administration was occurring at the local level, without interference from the capital. It was only in 1870 that the Ottoman state issued new regulations for appointments to offices, so I assume that appointment letters before then continue in the late Ḥanafī tradition.

It appears from the 1786 and the 1882 base records for Beirut's ʿUmari Mosque that the logic of appointment to offices was articulated around the family. When an office became vacant, as upon the death of its holder, it was filled by his (usually eldest) son, after his competence was established. The appointments mentioned in the 1786 and the 1882 base records fall into two categories: those where the name of the new holder shows that he is the son of the older one,[27] and those where the names of new holders seem unrelated to the older one. Appointments of the second type might imply that offices did not necessarily stay within a family and that these appointments can be used to disprove the pervasiveness of family logic. However, the sultan-signed appointment letters (*berât-i ʿâlî*),[28] which described the details of the new appointments, explain that the new (unrelated) officeholder was appointed either in the absence of heirs of the original holder or in case of their incompetence, as I will elaborate below.[29] The family remains then the primary determinant, supplanted only in its absence or because of incompetence. That said, competence is a necessary condition for appointment in Beirut in this period, even though in larger cities, many of these positions were passed on to minors or traded (more below). The necessity of competence as a limit to family logic appears in Ibn ʿAbidin's criticism of the practice of appointment of children to positions as administrators, teachers, and personnel in charitable institutions. The illustrious jurist explicitly denounced the argument that "the bread of the father belongs to his son" as useless (*lā yafīd*) because it changes the rule of law (*ḥukm al-sharʿ*). Following such practice stems from "ignorance and following a customary practice that contradicts the explicit truth [*al-ʿāda al-mukhālifa li-ṣarīḥ al-ḥaqq*]," and the appointment of minors is unreasonable (*lā yuʿqal*), and the ruling of the Ḥanafī judge as to its validity is pure error (*khaṭaʾ maḥḍ*). In exasperation, Ibn ʿAbidin ends this section of his commentary with "There is no might nor power except in God!" (*Ḥāshiya*, 3:385).

27. The classical naming practice in these documents was "X, son of Y." In the case of Beirut, it seems that family names were commonly used, so many times the name mentioned would be "X, son of Y Surname," which makes tracing patrilineal family connections easier. Family connections through marriage are harder to get at without deep family histories of these families.

28. Why and how *berats* were issued is itself a topic worthy of investigation as a window onto legal authority. For instance, VGM 515.177 mentions that the *khaṭīb* had received a *berat* from the qadi of Beirut in 1712 [1124], while the new officeholder received a *berat* from the sultan. Why and when does an office claimant refer to the qadi or to Istanbul? These questions fall beyond the scope of this book. I owe this point to a discussion with Guy Burak.

29. Appointment letters do not describe how competence was determined and by whom. In the section "Nineteenth-Century Reforms," I discuss the institution of exams and the composition of examination committees.

It might appear at first glance that my documentation of the logic of the family and the way it operates even in "public offices" is yet another example of what Max Weber describes as patrimonialism, as documented, for instance, by Carter Findley (1989) in civil offices of the Ottoman Empire. In his description of the recruitment, training, and promotion of scribal officers at the Ottoman Porte before the Tanzimat, Findley details the way apprentices started at a very young age to be attached to a scribe, but given the highly specialized language of their work, they were expected to come from "from homes where needed skills were known and presumably taught to them" (1989, 55). When one did not come from such a family, one had to attach oneself to an expert and develop links of patronage that would then allow for placement. Findley recognizes that family and close personal relations were the main organizational principles in the Ottoman Empire (in addition to guilds and semiautonomous religious groups) and warns the reader that these were not necessarily less efficient than modern bureaucracy. However, he still sees this logic as problematic, often referring to it as "favoritism" and "nepotism" (1989, 49, 55, for example), because all civil servants were ultimately at the mercy of the absolute power of the sultan, leading to factionalism and intrigue.

Contrary to this view, as Pierre Bourdieu and many others show, families remain important spaces for the transmission of knowledge, especially embodied knowledge. Rather than seeing modern rationalized bureaucracy and patrimonialism as opposites, with the first representing equal opportunity based on merit, and the other reproducing inequality by distributing underserved favors to kin, I suggest that they are logics that serve different groups. Modern rational bureaucracies replace one type of relationality (families) with another (mostly based on networks related to class, gender, race, education, and so on) and are, thus, far from the "equal opportunity" myth. While modern bureaucracies might allow for more upward mobility, they are nonetheless on a continuum with patrimonialism. Furthermore, occupation requires not only knowledge of content but also bodily dispositions and sensibilities, which are very often inculcated in families through education from a young age (even if they can also be transformed through disciplines of the self).

While the principle of family right to office might lead to the assumption that most of these offices remained within one family, this was not the case (see table 2 in appendix 2). Within one office, and for all offices except the *türbedâr*, appointments move in and out of families. First, the different life spans and expectations in the pre-modern period and up to the end of the nineteenth century precluded the assurance of having surviving offspring.[30] In addition, and as will be discussed below, competence intersected with the familial right to office and was a necessary criterion for appointment. Therefore, the logic of transmission to

30. Miriam Hoexter notes that "many families eventually died out, and in the course of time, many properties . . . found their way to the ultimate charitable beneficiaries of originally family *awqāf*" (1995, 138).

family served as a guiding principle, not as an iron rule. Rather than a perpetuation of privilege, it provided security for the precarious lives of many of these officeholders.

The operation of the logic of family in office transmission in a small town like mid-nineteenth-century Beirut differs quite dramatically from that described by Ottoman historian Madeline Zilfi for the highest offices of the religious class (*ilmiye*) in pre-Tanzimat Istanbul. Through a study of the highest echelons of religious positions (şeyhülislâms and *kazasker*) in the eighteenth century, Zilfi shows that most officeholders had fathers who were also in such positions and who used their appointment privileges (of novices) to ease their sons into the religious hierarchy with "scant regard to the son's own merit or ineptitude" (1983, 358). While candidates trying to enter the religious hierarchy as novices were required to submit to interrogation by the şeyhülislâm to judge "their scholarly competence," sons of ʿulamaʾ were exempted from that questioning (1983, 340). Furthermore, to Zilfi, family connection (being the son of a *molla* [member of the legal-religious administration, in English rendered as *mullah*], i.e., being a Mollazade) guaranteed undue privilege to these scholarly families and allowed for the creation of an ʿulamaʾ "aristocracy" (1983, 358).

It is important to note, however, that this aristocracy did not acquire property rights in appointments to judgeships and other positions in the religious hierarchy. Such positions were yearly appointments, between which the *mollas* "languished" sometimes many years, even though they increasingly had access to grants against the supervision of lesser judgeship (1983, 353–54) that allowed them to live during these "out" times. In eighteenth-century Istanbul, the logic of the family ensured the creation of a class that had access to these positions (with some possibility for outsiders to get into that class, but with much difficulty). That is markedly different from the positions at the ʿUmari Mosque in the second half of the nineteenth century, which were for life and inheritable but nonetheless moved much more outside of one family.

Logic of Appointment: Family and Supplementary Reasoning

Examining the base records' supporting documents with their more detailed descriptions of appointments provides a deeper understanding of the logic of transmission of these rights and duties in the moment before modernizing reforms. Though it is true that family forms the overarching logic under which offices are transmitted, that logic is nonetheless entwined with other requirements. For example, when the transmission of office necessitates the fulfillment of duties like teaching or leading prayers, certain competencies and traits of character become necessary. The transmission of one office in particular—the Ḥanafī professorship—provides a good example of an interruption of the family-based logic, where the other criteria for eligibility and the choice of the new holder were explicitly mentioned in the appointment letters.

The Ḥanafī professorship was made a permanent office in 1856 [1273] in the ʿUmari Mosque, after a petition by various ʿulamaʾ and notables from Beirut. The petition names Shaykh Muhyi al-Din al-Yafi as a possible inaugural professor and presents the following credentials for his appointment in the position: his assiduous devotion in teaching at the mosque and his being among the most esteemed and magnificent ʿulamaʾ ("min ajall al-ʿulamāʾ").[31] The shaykh became the mufti of Beirut sometime between 1848 and 1858 [1265–1275] and was a member of the Sufi Khalwatiyya[32] before becoming its leader in Damascus, housed in a lodge named after him (Wali 1993, 250).[33]

In this case, the appointment letter specified supporting criteria outside family connection: competence, character, and duration of experience in the position. The last criterion, experience, represents an official sanctioning of an ongoing performance of a task and finds echo in various parts of the law. A legal maxim states that "the old order of things should be maintained" ("al-qadīm yutrak ʿalā qidamih").[34] For instance, the continuous cultivation of a piece of land endows one with rights to that land (Mundy and Smith 2007, 29). In the offices of the ʿUmari Mosque, Shaykh Muhyi al-Din al-Yafi was favored because he had been teaching for some time. While he had no qualified or suitable sons, the person appointed after him was the person who occupied the same position of mufti. Other appointment letters often refer to the length of service, officeholders having served "for a long time," in the case of the imam (VGM299.340, 1853 [1269]).

Following length of service, the second criterion mentioned in the appointment letters is a demonstration of the potential appointee's ethical behavior. These letters discuss the uprightness, righteousness, and integrity of the officeholder, and hence appraise his moral character. This concern constitutes a common theme in Islamic law that is dealt with extensively for witnesses[35] and is discussed for jurists

31. BOA.I.MVL 371/16311.

32. The memory of Sufi practices in Beirut seems to have been completely eradicated and made the exclusive realm of more "Islamic" cities like Tripoli and Damascus. The history of these practices, references to which abound in the Ottoman archive, and their eradication from practice and memory remains to be written. Fakhuri (2018) begins this project based on shariʿa court records.

33. Wali mentions that al-Yafi was mufti for a short period and moved in his later years to Damascus (1993, 250). If al-Yafi was indeed in Damascus at the time of his appointment, the question of offices becoming in practice mere rights to revenue without the performance of the duties associated with the position arises. Given the long petition for giving al-Yafi the position however, it seems unlikely that he would have been an "absentee" officeholder. After all, absenteeism could be a cause for dismissal from office in fiqh discussions (Ibn ʿAbidin, *Ḥāshiya*, 3:407), even if, in practice, it seems to be more widespread. At the same time, the transfer of the office to Fakhuri, and not the son of al-Yafi, might imply that actually Fakhuri had been holding the professorship.

34. I borrow the translation from Meier (2016, 23).

35. In Islamic law, testimony is the primary kind of evidence, an "embodiment of 'presence,' of the testifying human witness, [which] stood opposed to the dangerously open interpretability, and the human absence and alienation of the written text" (Messick 1993, 205).

and judges. "The human links involved in witnessing also are comparable to those in the transmission of hadiths, the traditions of the Prophet. Both represent crucial types of knowledge," whose trustworthiness depends on the "integrity of the transmission links, represented by the human relayers" (Messick 2002, 232). Even if a person had witnessed certain events, the acceptance of that person's testimony ultimately depended on that person's moral character; hence, the determination of that character is a crucial factor for the judges. In the case of jurists, their authority derives as much from the qualifications of their knowledge (epistemic authority) as their moral character (moral authority) (Hallaq 2009, 44–45). Knowledge of the law cannot be separated from the embodiment of the values it advocates; knowledge is tied to its carrier. *ʿAdāla* (rectitude or justness) and the importance of "instilling a deep sense of morality" emphasized a sense of knowledge as embodiment of the ethics of the law. "Piety itself [is] an integral part of this [legal] knowledge, for piety dictated behavior in keeping with the Qur'an and the good example of the predecessors' customs [*sunan*]" (Hallaq 2009, 44). The assessment of the rectitude and moral character of candidates reflects their responsibilities in transmitting and performing the knowledge they possess.

Finally, the most frequent criterion supporting appointments, mentioned in almost every appointment letter or summary, is competence (*al-ahliyya*). Shaykh ʿAbd al-Rahman al-Nahhas's "competence at *khaṭāba* [performing the *khuṭba*] was proven in an exam" in 1851 [1268].[36] It appears that determining competence does not rely on the holding of *ijāzāt* (diplomas),[37] but rather on the results of examination. A testing system appears in place as early as 1851, nearly two decades prior to the promulgation of the Appointment to Offices Regulations (Tevcîh-i Cihât Nizâmleri) (1870 [8 Za 1286]).

In both the library and the archive then, the family was not problematized as a recipient of charity. While some jurists considered rich family recipients to be a temporary phase of that waqf that did not fulfill the charitable purposes of the waqf, others considered care of the family beyond the legally required spending done with the intent to be close to God as an act of charity, whether the family was rich or not. Further, even in waqfs dedicated to mosques and other institutions that served a wider public, revenues were seen as rights of various recipients (imams, caretakers, etc.) who could transmit them to their children as long as the latter had the required aptitudes, from knowledge to character, and experience.

36. VGM 299.340.

37. On the *ijāza* system, especially under the Mamluks, see Makdisi (1981) and Berkey (1992) for two differing interpretations of the importance of the institution and that of the teacher in granting diplomas. The absence of the scholarly genealogy and the *ijāza* of the law professor echoes the observation of Guy Burak that the state appointment system seems to have competed with the traditional institution of the *ijāza*. Burak notes that biographical dictionaries of Ottoman scholars contain many fewer references to *ijāza*s than Mamluk ones (2015, 34–38).

NINETEENTH-CENTURY REFORM: SHIFTING PRIORITIES IN THE LOGIC OF APPOINTMENT

Increased state control of waqf revenues, the creation of the Waqf Ministry, and the ensuing accounting reforms brought about systematization in the realm of accounting as well as the appointment to offices. The latter came to be regulated by the above-mentioned law, the 1870 Appointment to Offices Regulations. At first the 1870 Regulations confirmed the logic of family supplemented by merit, while taking steps towards dislodging it, but a later revision of the Regulations shifted the priority in appointment to merit. The codified manuals, on the other hand, perpetuated the logic of the family.

The 1870 Appointment to Offices Regulations maintained the priority of family transmission of offices, with continuity and competence as supporting criteria. The first article states: "When the holder of an office pertaining to a seized or semi-autonomous waqf dies, his son whose competence and capacity are confirmed is appointed to this office." In the basic case of an officeholder dying and leaving a competent son, the rule of transmission documented in my archive—the competent son inherits his father's position—is enshrined in the Regulations. In the more complicated cases, the law unsettles the priority of the family in transmission. To whom is an office transmitted when the officeholder dies without sons? Or if he leaves only minor sons?[38] What if his sons are incompetent?

Article 10 of the Regulations, on office transmission in the absence of heirs, crystallizes the new priorities in the logic of transmission. Among eligible candidates, the most competent receives the office. If many candidates are equally competent, the law first gives priority to the "near of kin" of the deceased officeholder ("müteveffâya karâbetî olân"). In the absence of such near of kin, the law gives priority to candidates who do not hold any other office, and thirdly to candidates found to be poor ("fakr ḥâlî bulunân"). As a last resort, if none of the candidates is of kin, free of other offices, or poor, a drawing of lots breaks the tie. This article indicates the beginning of the change in the logic of appointments, from one based on family ties towards one based on an abstract meritocratic ethic of competence.

The 1870 Regulations also systematized the protocol for testing competence. Article 8 draws a distinction between scholarly offices (such as professors, imams, and *khaṭībs*) and manual offices (such as caretakers of the mosques). For the former, examination determines competence; for the latter, physical ability (*vucûdca iqtidâr*). Both types of offices require a declaration from those responsible for the waqf about the competence of the future holders, and this brings us back to the primacy of testimony as evidence in the fiqh. Examinations, like written evidence, can be falsified, while testimony of competence from the knowledgeable and the upright carries with it the moral and epistemic authority of the testifier.

38. Islamic law defines a minor (*ṣaghīr*) in terms of biological maturity, but distinguishes biological maturity from mental maturity (*rushd*).

The Appointment to Offices Regulations were subject to many revisions that altered the priority of family and competence in appointments. In its final version of August 1913 [2 N 1331], the priority previously accorded to family was superseded by the criterion of competence, as eligibility to take the examination was extended to whoever wished to compete for the office even when the officeholder left a competent son. The successful candidate was simply the most competent. Only in the case of a tie between two or more applicants of equal competence would the son of the former officeholder be given priority. Thus, while family remained an operative principle in determining appointments to office, its former centrality was supplanted by competence as the foundations of an ethics of meritocracy were being laid slowly but surely.[39]

Such a move that eliminates the hereditary right to office could be analyzed as part of the rationalization of the Ottoman state and the creation of a modern bureaucracy, as we saw above in Carter Findley's Weberian analysis (1989) where such a transition reflects a move from patrimonialism to rational modern bureaucracy. In the Weberian ideal of modern bureaucracy, offices are hierarchically organized, with distinct and specific functions, whereby officials are free and recruited based on qualifications, receive salaries, and have no proprietary rights in offices. While this discourse of rationalization is certainly hegemonic and adopted by reformers and states in modernization projects (through the creation of a hierarchy in cadres, strict rules about family connections in hires, etc.), as will be even clearer in our discussion of the French Mandate, I suggest it as a discourse that lacks analytic purchase. Indeed, an analysis based on "rationalization/bureaucratization" abstracts merit and knowledge outside their social world and embodiment and thus presents merit as an "objective" category. It assumes that the ethic of merit and that of family are opposed and that family is an interference in a world that could be based on merit alone. However, as the continuation and even proliferation of nepotism and corruption charges in the modern world show, family, patron-client, mentor-mentee, and a host of other social relations cannot be severed in the operation and assessment of merit.

The discussion of appointments to offices in the nineteenth-century codified waqf manuals of our late Ḥanafī library echoes its commentaries; the manuals include discussions of the stipulations of beneficiaries with a nineteenth-century twist. Both Ömer Hilmi and Qadri Pasha discuss stipends (*waẓā'if*) when elaborating on founder stipulations regarding administrators. Both administrators and stipend holders (*arbāb al-waẓā'if*) are often specified by stipulation and receive a certain portion of waqf revenues either against services or as entitlements. Therefore, administrators and stipend holders mostly appear in articles specifying who can appoint them and how they can transmit their entitlements. Most of

39. The Appointment to Offices Regulations in their multiple iterations apply only to offices held without a stipulation of the founder. The stipulations of the founder retained the same force of law they have in waqf doctrine in that domain, unlike in the stipulations for expenditures.

these articles emphasize the need for a judge's appointment, unless the recipient is clearly identified and uncontested (named person, one competent son in a named position) and can be seen as an attempt of the central state to control appointments or to rein in the sale of offices. That said, in both Ömer Ḥilmi's and Qadri Pasha's manuals, the logic of the family appears in appointments of administrators upon the death of the current one. Even in the absence of a stipulation from the founder as to the administrator, the judge is to prioritize competent and deserving kin ("ahl ve mustaḥiqq evlâdı ve ahl-i beytinden") over any "stranger" (*ecnebî*), that is a non-family member (Ömer Hilmi, Article 296) (echoed in Qadri Pasha's Article 161).

Regarding the appointment of stipend holders, the two manuals diverge. Qadri Pasha does not discuss how the administrator or the qadi is to assess and appoint stipend holders. Ömer Hilmi includes a discussion of appointments to offices and echoes very much the position of the first iteration of the Appointments to Offices Regulations. He dedicates two sections totaling eleven articles to offices (*jihāt*). These sections follow a section on stipends (*waẓā'if*), which are defined by Ömer Hilmi as payments stipulated by the founder to certain persons from the revenues of a waqf in return for services rendered ("khidmet muqâbilesinde olân") or without work required (Article 359). The presence of a section on stipends, distinct from offices, might be surprising at first, since stipends should include offices as the latter are also a right to revenue. Ömer Hilmi specifies that offices are a particular kind of stipend for services in "charitable foundations [*müessesât-i hayriyye*] such as those of imams, *khaṭībs*, professors" (Article 375), which require specialized knowledge. The distinction he creates enshrines a distinction between these offices and other stipends and may reflect the beginning of their differentiation and mapping onto different regulations. As with the Appointments to Offices Regulations, Ömer Hilmi affirms merit as an essential condition for appointment. Article 376 states that "it is illegal to appoint to an office someone who does not have the competency for the position." Nonetheless, a few articles later, Ömer Hilmi reinscribes the logic of the family. Article 378 plainly states that if an officeholder dies leaving a competent adult descendent, that descendent should be the recipient of the office. Ömer Hilmi seems then to remain much closer to the prioritization of the family, even though his emphasis on merit (as a first article in appointments) signals the rise in importance of an ethic of merit.

While the ethic of merit started to take precedence over the ethic of care of the family, particularly in these offices that were now under the administration of the Waqf Ministry as seen in the Appointments to Offices Regulations, none of the manuals openly questioned or defended the charity of dedicating waqfs to family members, be they particular individuals or the founder's family. However, the appearance of the family in discussions of beneficiaries that could invalidate the waqf—while affirming the charitable character of these family waqfs—points to possible debates around that question.

For Qadri Pasha, the fixing of the family as a charitable beneficiary occurs in discussions of stipulations of founders for beneficiaries. While late Ḥanafī Ottoman commentaries discussed the self, the rich, and the non-Muslim only as potentially uncharitable beneficiaries before arriving at the conclusion that these did not invalidate waqfs, here the family is included in these questionable charitable purposes that need to be specified. Therefore, Qadri Pasha opens his first article of the section on stipulations of beneficiaries (Article 103) by stating that stipulating some or all of the waqf's revenue to the founder *and his family* is valid. As discussed above, earlier manuals restrict this discussion of stipulating waqf revenues to the founder, with a section discussing the validity of the "waqf for the founder himself" ("al-waqf ʿalā nafs al-wāqif") (Ibn ʿAbidin, *Ḥāshiya*, 3:387), while the sections on the children or the poor of his near of kin are discussions about who falls under such a category of beneficiaries, without needing to affirm its validity. In addition, sometimes but not systematically, Qadri Pasha refers to these waqfs as family waqfs. For instance, Article 108 begins with this hypothetical statement: "If the founder establishes his waqf as a family waqf" ("idhā anshaʾ al-wāqif waqfan ahliyyan"). The article, however, considers the validity of different ways of distributing revenues among sons and daughters, a common issue in fiqh manuals. Despite containing some traces of the rise of an ethic of merit, these codified waqf manuals continue to reaffirm the value and validity of the ethic of care of the family in charitable endeavors.

The rise of a new ethic of merit in appointment helped produce a distinction between public and private as the waqfs that were under state supervision came under the Appointment to Offices Regulations, whereas those that had stipulated beneficiaries and administrators continued in the older logic of transmission. As discussed in chapter 2, the Ottoman center subjected different kinds of waqfs to different regulations and introduced the new Waqf Ministry as an actor with jurisdiction over seized and semiautonomous waqfs, taking away from the jurisdiction of judges and legally differentiating between waqfs. However, in these seized waqfs, the criterion for state seizing was not articulated around kinds of beneficiaries but around the corrupt practices of their administrators and the absence of such caretakers.

These regulations created confusion among administrators and judges as to jurisdiction. In a study of these reforms in Damascus, Astrid Meier (2002) uncovers a response by a waqf director classifying waqfs to determine which fell under these new state regulations: waqfs endowed for the common good and pious purposes with the remainder going to descendants, waqfs for descendents with stipulations for other people and purposes, and waqfs going only to descendents. The waqf director argued that these last two categories are "waqf only in name, not in essence." They are like "absolute property [*milk*]" with restrictions as to the sale of the assets (Meier 2002, 216). As Meier notes, waqfs were no longer treated as one legal category, and a "new dividing line ran clearly along the private/public dichotomy" (2002, 216). Yet, the classification of the director did not resemble any of the waqf categories discussed in the fiqh. The waqf director differentiated between these waqfs benefiting particulars based on whether the intermediary beneficiaries (before the waqf reaches the poor as an ultimate recipient after the extinction of these intermediary recipients) were purely familial, familial and particulars, or mostly charitable with some familial. Such distinctions did not exist in the shariʿa, where discussions of beneficiaries were centered on their perpetuity and extinction. In this way, the director began to distinguish "true" waqfs from waqfs that are closer to *milk* and thus unfit to be termed waqf, indicating the possibility of their exclusion from waqf rules. Yet, the director's categorization does not match waqf categorization in regulations, either. While it does not present proof of the operationalization of a legal distinction between family versus charitable waqf, the director's categorization can signal the beginning of the questioning of the validity of waqfs dedicated to family, a questioning underway in French Algeria and that would bloom under the French Mandate in Lebanon.

FRENCH MANDATE DEBATES: FAMILY WAQF AS ECONOMY NOT CHARITY

The privileging of on an ethic of merit over the logic of family in the now public (i.e., state-administered) offices of charitable works seems to come from the same place as the arguments for "good administration" that the Ottoman Waqf Ministry used to seize many of these waqfs.[40] The differentiation of examination and its minute regulation certainly reflected and embodied the claim of good administration. Be that as it may, the Ottoman state never questioned the legitimacy of family waqfs. The French Mandatory powers that succeeded it in Beirut had had a different experience with waqf (chapter 1) and had an explicit program of "modernization" of waqfs and other institutions, which included restricting family waqfs. Indeed, as the French High Commissioner reported to the League of Nations, a legislative organ of the state (the Supreme Waqf Council)[41] had carried out some studies "with the aim to modernize as much as possible, and to adapt to needs, the very special law of waqf." These studies aimed, among others, to "make disappear certain institutions like the family waqfs" (Ministère français 1926, 106). In its "needs" to govern, and to govern waqf in particular, the colonial state, as I will illustrate in this section, subjected waqf to new understandings of religion and economy, which constructed family waqfs as self-interested and thus uncharitable.

However, was waqf an area that the French colonial power could claim to modernize? As I discussed in chapter 2, the charter of the Mandate distinguished

40. For an expanded version of this section, see Moumtaz (2018).

41. The archives of the heir of the Supreme Waqf Council, the Supreme Legal Islamic Council, would be a great source to elaborate on this debate further. Unfortunately, I have not had access to them.

between two realms: "personal status" (marriage, divorce, inheritance), the realm of religion where the various religious traditions had legal sovereignty, and "real status," the realm of the economy regulated by state law. To be modernized, then, to be subjected to the laws of economy, waqfs—at least some of them—had to be stripped of the "religious element" (Anderson 1951) that also appeared in the description of these waqfs as "religious property" by Decree 753. Therefore, the project of modernizing waqfs involved two interrelated processes: on the one hand, there was the categorization of waqfs dedicated to mosques, Sufi lodges, and education (so-called charitable waqfs) as "religious," while on the other, there was the categorization of waqfs dedicated to families (the so-called family waqfs) as nonreligious, and therefore abolishable as waqfs. The French High Commissioner's reports to the League of Nations articulated an argument paralleling this approach. The legality of the abolition of family waqfs, he claimed, can be decided only by Muslim jurists, among whom, he was pleased to report, there is a group supporting this position from within the Islamic tradition. That would be no small feat, as these reforms would "bring into the domain of civil law, and with the approval of the highest religious council under the Mandate, rules considered up to this day as intangible and forming an integral part of Muslim religious law" (Ministère français 1926, 109).

A proposal calling for the abolition of the institution, forwarded to the Syrian parliament in December 1937 (see Mudiriyyat al-Awqaf al-ʿAmma 1938), spearheaded a public debate on the family waqf in French Mandate Syria and Lebanon.[42] The author of the proposal was the then-director of Islamic waqfs, Hasan al-Hakim.[43] A staunch anti-colonialist who participated in the anti-French Syrian Revolt of 1925–27, he was accused of sedition by the French and fled to Egypt and Palestine. After the general amnesty, he returned to Damascus in 1937 and occupied several posts in the government before becoming prime minister (Al-Jundi 1960, 183). It would not be unreasonable to suggest that his presence in Egypt in the 1920s, at the very time when debates about the abolition of family waqfs were occurring (Baer 1958), had an influence on his proposal.

The bill elicited strong reactions and divided the ʿulamaʾ; even the so-called reformist ones were clearly divided. The main voice of opponents of the bill, who wanted to preserve family waqfs and whom I will term waqf conservationists, was that of the Scholars' Association in Damascus (Jamʿiyyat al-ʿUlamaʾ bi-Dimashq),

42. The year 1937 is certainly not the first time the abolition of the family waqf was brought up in French Mandate Lebanon and Syria, as can be inferred from the 1926 report of the high commissioner referred to at the beginning of this section, which mentions the aim to "make disappear certain institutions like the family waqfs" (Ministère français 1926, 106). However, the Supreme Council seems to have tabled the study for reasons relating to jurisdiction, as we learn in the 1928 report (Ministère français 1928, 77). This earlier study must have not reached the public.

43. Al-Hakim was born in Damascus 1886. He participated in the Arab government of King Faysal (Al-Jundi 1960, 183).

led by Muhammad Kamil al-Qassab. One of the most vocal supporters of the bill, or waqf abolitionists, was shaykh Ramiz al-Malak, an Azharite scholar from Tripoli. In epistles, newspaper articles, and fatwas,[44] these scholars fleshed out their arguments and scrutinized those of their opponents, explicitly referencing and borrowing from arguments developed in Egypt.[45] Let us examine their arguments.

Extracting Family Waqf from Religion

The first move of the waqf abolitionist attack on family waqfs involved the extraction of waqfs from the sphere of religion. Certain Muslim reformers argued that waqfs, like that of Mustafa Agha, which were dedicated to the families of founders, did not belong to the sphere of religion and thus did not need to follow "religious law." To support the claim that the family waqf was not a *religious* institution, waqf abolitionists presented arguments that both reflected and advanced an understanding of religion, *dīn*, as a discrete sphere of social life. They favored a literalist reading of the Qur'anic text, which would require the word *waqf* itself to appear in the Qur'an and to be condoned in order for the practice to be considered Islamic.[46] In a section entitled "Are the Proofs for Waqf Based in Religion?" ("Asl al-Waqf Hal Huwa min al-Din"), a waqf abolitionist from Syria quotes former Egyptian waqf minister Mohamed Aly Allouba, also a waqf abolitionist, as saying that the "current waqf regime, a national catastrophe,"[47] is "far from religion" (Allouba in Alwani n.d., 4). To illustrate his point, the former waqf minister notes the absence of any Qur'anic injunctions on waqf, which, in his view, means that waqf is not a religious concept or institution, but a civil one.

For waqf conservationists, the literalism of waqf abolitionists, as in their assertion that there was no mention of waqf in the Qur'an, was "bizarre" (*gharīb*) coming from those who "claim to understand the Qur'an and how to derive rules from it"[48] (Bakhit 1928, 5). They reminded waqf abolitionists of the limited number of

44. The Institut français du Proche Orient (IFPO) in Damascus holds a bound collection of many articles and pamphlets that served as the main object of my analysis. I learned of the debate and the collection from Randi Deguilhem-Schoem (1986) and from her presentation at the IFPO in Beirut in 2009, entitled "Réveil de l'opinion publique en Syrie Mandataire: Des pamphlets de la Jam'iyyat al-'Ulamā' comme outil de résistance politique."

45. The late nineteenth and early twentieth centuries were a period of great movement of people because of political volatility (and porous borders), in addition to the usual travel for studying under particular teachers and in institutions like al-Azhar. See, for example, Skovgaard-Petersen (1997, 119); Commins (1990); and Zaman (2012).

46. Robert Gleave (2012) argues that all classical Islamic legal theory is literalist in the sense that it accepts the notion that a word or a sentence has an inherent meaning, a position one might call "weak literalism." However, jurists disagree as to whether this literal meaning should be privileged and preclude any search for intent, a position one might call "strong literalism." I use *literalism* here in the strong sense.

47. This is a paraphrase of Mohamed Aly Allouba's formulation.

48. In this quote Bakhit is talking about his opponent, Allouba (and not about waqf abolitionists in general). However, such arguments are repeated by other waqf conservationists, as seen in the following paragraphs.

legal verses (*āyāt al-aḥkām*) and the finitude of the Qur'an, which cannot include the infinity of occurrences (*ḥawādith*). Instead, the Qur'an provides universal principles (*qawā'id kulliyya*) used to derive rules for particular occurrences.

This countermove reaffirmed the waqf conservationists' epistemic authority, as deriving law was not open to anyone but rather required proper training and knowledge of Islamic legal theory and the Islamic sciences. Taking up this epistemic challenge, most waqf abolitionists, rather than reject classical legal methodology and styles of reasoning outright, acknowledged that the validity of family waqfs should be based on the Qur'an, the Sunna, consensus, and analogy. A Damascene administrator of a family waqf, Hamdi al-Samman, for example, opened a pamphlet with the following statement: "Islamic legal rulings are derived from the book of God, the Sunnah of his Prophet (peace be upon him), the consensus of the scholars (may they be blessed and forgiven), and analogy" (n.d.a, 1). However, what we witness from waqf abolitionists is a transformation in the way these methods are put to practice.

Waqf abolitionists sometimes dismissed the school's consensus, claiming that waqf conservationists based their arguments on the "opinions of Frick or Frack or a hadith transmitted by John Doe" ("lā 'alā ra'y fulān wa 'illatān[49] aw ḥadīth Hayyān bin Bayyān") (Samman n.d.b). Scholarly arguments were thus reduced to "opinions,"[50] and the scholars who made them were stripped of their authority and identity. Most commonly, we find waqf abolitionists selecting opinions from the various *madhhab*s, taking certain arguments out of their original contexts, where they were often rebutted immediately following the quotes used. After establishing that waqf was a contested issue (*mas'ala khilāfiyya*), Tripolitan Azharite and waqf abolitionist Ramiz Malak assessed various proofs for the validity of family waqf according to different *madhhab*s, referencing and quoting their jurists. Malak here uses the tradition as a resource, accepting the multiplicity of truths on unsettled matters, and he picks and chooses whatever arguments fit his position that family waqfs are invalid.

While drawing on the *madhhab*s in their arguments, waqf abolitionists accorded primacy to a literalist understanding of the Qur'an and hadith. In this reimagined legal edifice, the Qur'anic inheritance injunctions gained a new import. It was not sufficient that some hadiths support waqf; now, the institution needed to not contradict the Qur'anic law of inheritance. Indeed, waqf abolitionists argued, since the institution of family waqf contradicts the laws of inheritance as clearly expounded in the Qur'an, it is a sin and a heretical innovation[51] that should be

49. "*Fulān wa 'illatān*" is an expression that denotes "this person or that person" in the Levantine dialect.

50. As will be explicit in the rebuttal of the waqf conservationists, "*ra'y*" is used pejoratively to describe falling prey to one's desires (*ahwā'*) because *madhhab*s rejected *ra'y* as a method of deriving law.

51. The argument that waqf is a *bid'a*, an innovation, was cited by two waqf abolitionists as one of the grounds for the abolition of the family waqf. For example, Tripolitan scholar Muhammad Rahim

abolished; "changing God's law and His religion and using tricks to hide that [sin] behind a veneer of good deeds are among the gravest sins" (Muhammad b. ʿAbd al-Wahhab, in Nasif 1928). It did not matter to them that inheritance laws apply only after one's death (Bakhit 1928, 7) or during a death-sickness,[52] and that these laws can be circumvented by gifts or sales before a death-sickness (Bakhit 1928, 13).

Waqf abolitionist arguments for restricting what counts as "religious" to injunctions explicitly stated in the Qurʾan and hadith did not go unchallenged. Waqf conservationists counterattacked, challenging the attempt to limit the shariʿa to a particular sphere of religion and emphasizing a very different understanding of *dīn*, as discussed in chapter 2. Waqf conservationists argued that even if waqf were a civil institution and not a religious one, it would still need to follow the shariʿa because the shariʿa encompasses all of a Muslim's life. Even "transactions among men, which are common to the nation, from sales to purchases, to leases, commissions, donations, wills, and charitable acts . . . are still among the acts of a legally responsible Muslim and cannot be changed except based on rules of the shariʿa" (Makhluf 1932, 16–17). In this way, waqf conservationists opposed the "proposition to consider waqf as a civil institution" (Bakhit in Sekaly 1929, 432), showing that "the family waqf is not a pure civil system" (Makhluf 1932, 16). The argument here resists the attempt by waqf abolitionists to limit the shariʿa to a particular sphere and presents the Islamic tradition as a guide to the totality of a Muslim's life.

Assessing Waqf According to the Laws of the Economy

Unconvinced by waqf conservationist arguments, waqf abolitionists proposed, in a second move, that since waqf is not a religious institution, it should follow economic law. Waqf abolitionists invoked economic expertise and reasoning to argue that waqf is harmful to the country's economy, using terms that evoke an image of the nation as possessing an economy governed by economic laws and measurable through statistics. Expressions such as "the country's economy" (*iqtiṣādiyyāt al-bilād*)[53] (Samman n.d.b) or a decrease in "the country's credit"[54] (Allouba in Bakhit 1928, 33) point to conceptions of the economy and credit as separate

presents the *bidʿa* argument as the second reason for why the family waqf should be abolished (Rahim in Bakhit 1926, 3). However, this is a minor argument (dismissed by waqf conservationists based on hadiths that show that some family waqfs were founded at the time of the Prophet). The main debate in this first move was about whether the family waqf is a "civil institution," as I demonstrate here.

52. I use "death-sickness," a translation of *maraḍ al-mawt*, to denote a legally defined illness that has particular legal effects. On the concept, see further Yanagihashi (1998). The rules of inheritance limit how one can dispose of one's estate during a death-sickness.

53. Note that the term I am translating as "economy" is not the common *iqtiṣād* but *iqtiṣādiyyāt* (it would be worthwhile, but beyond the scope of this book, to investigate when the term was first used in the sense we use it today). Be that as it may, Hans Wehr (1960) renders *iqtiṣādiyyāt* (or economics) as "the economy."

54. "The country's credit" is the translation of *al-thiqa al-māliyya* by Cassi Bey in *L'Égypte Contemporaine* (Allouba 1927) and is contemporaneous with the debate analyzed in this section on the French Mandate debates. I therefore use it instead of the literal translation "financial trustworthiness."

attributes of the nation. Waqf abolitionists posited the effects of waqf on the economy as natural consequences of the economy's laws. (If more land is transformed into waqf, Egypt will lose its credit, argues Allouba [cited in Sekaly (1929, 407)].) They argued that waqf was contrary to the "principles of political economy" (Rida 1903, 731), supporting arguments of harm to the economy by "official statistics" (Allouba 1927, 392, 395, 397) and tables with data, because "nothing is more eloquent than official statistics" (Allouba 1927, 397). Elsewhere, Allouba laments that the "government has not compiled any official statistics (pertaining to certain waqfs). In my opinion, they reach 400,000 feddans. . . . We also know that the area of arable land in Egypt is 5,200,000 feddan" (1927, 392). Waqfs thus constitute 8 percent of all arable land in the country. We see here the transformation of waqfs into "data," analyzed in terms of one variable, their area, compared to a composite, the total area of arable land, in order to assess the effect of waqf on Egypt's prime economic resource. It is through such statistics, analyzed with reference to economic laws, that waqf abolitionists came to assess harm to the economy.

Waqf abolitionists argued that, because of their inalienability, waqfs "stand in the way of freedom of transaction" (Samman n.d.a, 3). Since they cannot be sold except under exceptional circumstances, they are "immobilized." By contrast, "free property is active, alive, fertile; it changes hands; it can easily find its most suitable owner, the one who will know best how to exploit it [*la faire valoir*]" (Saad 1928, 76). According to this understanding of property and of the market, free circulation of assets is the basis of economic progress; it is only through circulation that land will find its most appropriate owner, the one who can exploit it best. These arguments assume that humans have a moral duty to exploit the land, that one should perform labor, a particular kind of labor that increases the fruits of the earth. They are the same arguments that labor is what creates value, which John Locke advanced to justify the dispossession of the indigenous people of the Americas, since they did not till the land and make it valuable (1989, 298).

The argument for freedom of circulation and for alienability thus has moral and evolutionary undertones. Restoring the freedom to dispose of patrimony, waqf abolitionists argued, will push beneficiaries "who have been used to idleness and indolence into labor and responsibility, and they will strive to improve their lot of waqf lands and to increase their revenues. . . . This will turn these beneficiaries into active, productive, and useful organs in the body of their nation after having been paralyzed and decayed" (Samman n.d., 2–3). This concern for continuous improvement and accumulation runs very much counter to the logic of waqf exchange and administration in the late Ottoman Ḥanafī tradition, as I will describe in chapter 5 with the Ottoman opposition to the exchange of waqfs just for improvement.

The other main economic critique of waqf was made by waqf abolitionists on the basis of property rights. The institution of waqf is built on the separation of the right of use, the right of usufruct, and the right of alienation. For instance, in Mustafa Agha's case, as discussed in chapter 1, on one piece of land, there were two different waqfs: the land, originally Mustafa Agha's, whose rent went to Aisha and her descendants; and the houses built on that land, whose revenues supported her husband's family.[55] This led to a high degree of complexity in property rights, rather than their concentration in the hands of one person. The multiplicity of right holders on one piece of land contradicted an essential assumption in modern understandings of private property as the "sole and despotic dominion which *one man* claims and exercises over the external things of the world," to use Blackstone's often quoted definition of property (1766, 2:2). In addition, beneficiaries had only usufruct rights and could not, for example, borrow money using the waqf as collateral (waqfs cannot be mortgaged).[56] Waqf abolitionists argued that this prohibition decreased the total "credit" of the country.

In the same way that claims of expertise and authority by waqf conservationists compelled waqf abolitionists to argue on the grounds of tradition and to use opinions from the *madhhab*s, the appeal to economic expertise by waqf abolitionists drew waqf conservationists toward economic reasoning. Thus, despite the claims of some waqf conservationists that the "real authority [*marja*ʿ] in such an affair is the esteemed scholars" (Jamʿiyyat al-ʿUlamaʾ bi-Dimashq 1938b, 4), we find them using economic reasoning in addition to invoking other shariʿa-based values and benefits of family waqf. Indeed, the Scholars' Association in Damascus argued that one of the advantages of waqfs is that their revenues allow for the "creation of commercial enterprises . . . and exploitation [of the waqf] in the most developed ways that modern civilization and working nations have prescribed" (Jamʿiyyat al-ʿUlamaʾ bi-Dimashq 1938a, 34). In addition, Bakhit argues that putting all these waqfs on the market will "create a decline in the value [of real estate] and decrease the value of public wealth, and this will create a real estate crisis and a more general one, which we don't need" (1928, 37).

Reforming the Shariʿa Based on the Laws of the Economy

We have thus far covered the first two arguments used by waqf abolitionists: that family waqf is not part of the sphere of religion, and thus is not to be assessed by religious law, and that it brings economic harm. The continued existence of family waqf and the legislation that would manage it were now called into question.

State law, without shariʿa justification, might abolish or restrict waqf, as had happened in Algeria in 1858[57] (and would eventually happen for family waqfs in Egypt in 1946 and in Syria in 1949 [s.v. "wakf," *EI2*]). However, because these scholars were arguing from within the tradition, they were concerned with reforming the

55. Waqf deeds from the private collection of the Qabbani family.

56. While a waqf may not be mortgaged, beneficiaries did use their entitlements to shares in waqf revenue as collateral.

57. As I discuss in chapter 1, page 50, in Algeria, based on French ordinances, waqfs became alienable in 1844 in transactions between Muslims and Europeans and in 1858 in transactions between and among Muslims (Janssens 1951, 16).

shari'a itself and with providing shari'a justifications for reforms to be enacted as state law. Their argument attempted to bring parts of the shari'a into the realm of the economy by assessing shari'a rules and legal determinations based on the laws of the economy, as discussed above. However, claims for the necessity of reforming the shari'a were based on arguments from the Islamic tradition. To accomplish this reform of the shari'a, waqf abolitionists like Samman proposed that the shari'a itself requires the avoidance of harm.

In a third move, invoking legal maxims such as "do not inflict harm or repay one injury with another" ("lā ḍarar wa lā ḍirār") and "bring about benefits and repel harms" ("jalb al-maṣāliḥ wa dar' al-mafāsid"), waqf abolitionists argued that the harm created by the waqf institution should be averted and benefits accrued through the abolition of family waqf. Such maxims about harm and benefit have been a staple in modern reform movements (see, for example, Hourani 1962; and Hallaq 1997), and they exemplify the use of the concept of benefit, *maṣlaḥa*, to justify reforms of the shari'a. For instance, in his fatwa, Muhammad Rahim's last argument for allowing the sale of family waqf is that "even if family waqf is not a heretical innovation [*bid'a*] and even if all the jurists [*aṣḥāb*] of the *madhhab* have discussed it and the opinions on its validity and its invalidity are of equal strength, its contemporary consequences—namely, enmity and rancor, the severing of family ties [*qaṭī'at al-raḥm*], and embezzlement by administrators—are sufficient to make preponderant [*tarjīḥ*] the opinion of those who claim the family waqf's invalidity [*buṭlānih*]" (Rahim, in Bakhit 1926, 7). Based on the *current* harms that the waqf is producing, Rahim argues that family waqf should be invalidated.

Does this use of the concept of benefit, *maṣlaḥa*, by waqf abolitionists constitute a rearticulation or an extension of practices of the Ottoman Ḥanafī legal tradition? In the hypothetical example above, Rahim is exercising *tarjīḥ*, the weighing of different opinions on a single matter to determine the soundest one (Hallaq 2001, 127). The legal reasoning used in this exercise, as Hallaq explains, might marshal textual evidence, experience and expertise, customary practices, necessity and social need, or, simply, numbers (2001, 139–44). Rahim argues for the invalidity of family waqf on the grounds of necessity or social need, so, in this case at least, he invokes benefit and necessity to assess valid opinions within a *madhhab*, all of which are based on sound sources and hence are valid. It is noteworthy that Rahim does *not* say, "Even if the opinion on the invalidity of family waqf is weak, family waqfs should be invalidated because of the harm [they cause]," for such a claim would actually cause benefit to transcend textual evidence or analogy (*qiyās*).[58] In Rahim's example, then, benefit and necessity still operate as secondary principles under the main sources of the law and are not independent legal norms. We do not

58. In order to make a weak opinion preponderant, a jurist must reassess and reinterpret the evidence (Hallaq 2001, 139). Alternatively, the state can implement as state law a weak opinion; see, for example, the use of the *şeyhülislâm* by the Ottomans to render a weak opinion on the validity of cash waqfs the dominant opinion in Ottoman lands (Mandaville 1979).

observe here the use, by waqf abolitionist scholars, of benefit as an independent measure for the assessment of harm, or what Wael Hallaq calls "religious utilitarianism," which "amplified the concept of public interest to such an extent that it would stand on its own as a legal theory and philosophy" (1997, 214).

This is not to say, however, that waqf conservationists did not criticize the waqf abolitionists' assessment of harm and benefit. To the contrary, scholars such as Bakhit highlighted the complex and contested nature of *maṣlaḥa* in legal theory, pointing out, first, that the fact that waqf causes harm does not justify changing its legal norm from recommended to prohibited or reprehensible, because jurists do not consider harm to be absolutely unacceptable. Acts deemed obligatory or recommended may include harm, but their benefit exceeds their harm. Waqf abolitionists, however, were aware of the complexity of the assessment of harm and benefit. As Samman argues:

> Each action has both advantages and disadvantages, causes benefits and harms, and it is agreed that actions whose benefits are greater than their harms are considered beneficial and must be performed and executed. It has also been proven by experience [*bi'l-tajriba*] that the harms and disadvantages [*sayyi'āt*] of maintaining family waqfs are beyond measure, and its benefits minimal. (n.d.a, 3)

In this argument, the question returns to the assessment of the balance of harm and benefit, as discussed above, but in fact, this was not the waqf conservationists' main line of argument. Rather, more prevalent among these scholars was the assertion that the harms attributed to waqf are inessential and accidental (*min al-ʿawāriḍ*) (Makhluf 1932, 40),[59] and they have no effect on the nature of waqf and its legality. The problem with family waqfs does not stem from the institution itself, but from the individuals who administer them. For instance, to show the absurdity of the argument that the misuse and negative consequences of waqf are reason for its abolition, Bakhit compares waqf to marriage. Despite the possibility of "husbands acting unjustly towards their wives, or wives violating their marital duties" (Bakhit 1926, 30), he analogizes that marriage is a recommended act, and nobody would question its validity despite these possible harms, which are much more widespread than those of the family waqf.

Most importantly, waqf conservationists reminded their opponents of the superiority of divine revelation over human reason and hence reaffirmed traditional legal methodology, particularly the role of benefit in it. They argued that

59. Makhluf admonishes the "reprehensible intent" behind founding waqfs: "pride, showing off, causing harm, prohibiting those who have priority" (1932, 40), and he compares the founders of such waqfs to Muslims who take up learning without practicing what they preach and to Muslims who pray and fast in order to obtain worldly advantages (by being recognized as a Muslim) rather than with the intent to submit to God's law and seek the good as He defines it. "These goals [*aghrāḍ*] do not change the original legislation on waqf [*lā tukhrij al-waqf ʿan aṣl waḍʿih*]. One should teach people God's rules, and stop them from these prohibited purposes, through restraints [ordered] by the Sultan [*bi-wāziʿ al-sulṭān*], and if that does not exist, through a group of Muslims, and if that does not exist, then through advice and guidance [*al-nuṣḥ wa'l-irshād*]" (1932, 40).

humans should trust God the Legislator who knows best what brings benefit to humans, thereby suggesting that humans are unable to assess harms and benefits *against revelation*. In a passage exemplary of this argument, a grand mufti of Egypt, Muhammad Hasanayn Makhluf, writes: "Whatever benefits or harms are the basis of the rules of the shariʿa cannot be determined solely by human reason" ("mā yunāṭ bih al-aḥkām al-sharʿiyya min al-maṣāliḥ wa al-mafāsid lā tastaqill bih ʿuqūl al-bashar") (1932, 20). This position suggests a clear hierarchy in the derivation of law: revealed rules should be obeyed even if they bring harm, because there may be benefits that humans cannot comprehend. "There is no doubt that the Legislator's intent behind waqf is the will to do good, and the fact that one fears ill from those who administer it does not necessitate the prohibition of the founding of waqfs" (Bakhit 1926, 31).

Here, we see clearly that waqf conservationists were *not* arguing that human reason cannot assess harm and benefit but rather reasserting the supremacy of revelation over arguments based on benefit. This reassertion exposes the threat that waqf abolitionists posed to the principles of Islamic jurisprudence (*uṣūl al-fiqh*), despite their affirmation of these principles. Yet, as we saw in Rahim's use of benefit, waqf abolitionist scholars most often used benefit in line with classical legal theory.

By contrast, the argument that legislation should be based on benefit as an independent legal norm was put forward by waqf abolitionists who were state agents. In explaining the need for family law legislation, the parliamentary committee argued that "the legislator is responsible for realizing benefit [*taḥqīq al-maṣlaḥa*]" (Mudiriyyat al-Awqaf al-ʿAmma 1938, 2). Under the modern state and with the rise of economic reasoning and its authority, as we will see further in the next chapter, *maṣlaḥa*, or benefit, became centered around progress and the nation-state's economy (the welfare of the population). The waqf conservationists' rejection of this use of benefit constitutes a rejection of the modern state's prioritization of "public benefit" as (economic) progress and a cleaving to a definition of *maṣlaḥa* that is much more expansive. Thus, while waqf conservationists' use of economic reasoning manifested their acknowledgement that economics occupies a domain of truth outside of the shariʿa, these scholars nonetheless maintained a hierarchy whereby the truth of revelation trumps that of economic reasoning.

While the threefold argument ended with waqf conservationists reasserting their authority in defining the proper use of *maṣlaḥa*, it was waqf abolitionists who found themselves in the position to legislate on waqf in the postcolonial Lebanese state. Their views formed the basis of colonial and postcolonial legislation on family waqf,[60] most importantly the 1947 Family Waqf Law. However, the waqf

60. In his book on family waqf legislation in Lebanon and its sources, eminent Lebanese legal scholar and judge Zuhdi Yakan includes the report of the Legal Commission explaining the grounds of its proposed family waqf reform: "The current waqf regime does not agree very much with the contemporary system, which is distinct from previous eras because of the liberation of parcels from various shackles that hinder their development, productivity, and use" (1964, 15). These are very much the economic arguments used by waqf abolitionists, as discussed above.

abolitionists' views were adopted not only on epistemological grounds but also by marshalling the powers of the modern state and its legal sovereignty. Waqf abolitionists "won" because the state adopted legislation based on their arguments, and it was this legislation that opened space for the heirs of Mustafa Agha to attempt to revert his waqf to private property, irrespective of its original pious purpose.

Arguments about what practices are part of "religion" or about the place of statistical reasoning and economic proof in Islamic law paved the way for legislation that assigned religion to one sphere while carving out another sphere for the economy and its laws. The adoption of the waqf abolitionist position and its enactment as state law may have silenced this debate, but it did not eradicate the different logics embodied by waqfs and the ethic of the family that I describe above. Let us turn to the postcolonial moment to examine in detail the conditions set by the 1947 Family Waqf Law and how the ethic of the family continues to survive in discourses on family care, in embodied carriers, and in family waqfs that have survived mostly through disputes and lawsuits, like the waqf of Mustafa Agha.

POSTCOLONIAL RUPTURES AND CONTINUITIES: AN ENSHRINED ETHIC OF MERIT

Legislating the End of Family Waqf

Conceptually, the 1947 Family Waqf Law solidified the modern grammar of family waqf and charitable waqf through the superposition of these two categories onto different legislations. The law did not only affect future family waqf foundation, but it also applied to existing family waqfs. Concerning new family waqfs founded after its promulgation, the law's main innovation was to restrict the perpetuity of family waqfs, their irrevocability, and the percentage of possessions that a founder could actually make into a family waqf. The foundation of family waqfs that benefited families up to their extinction before reverting to the poor became invalid. Family waqfs could be founded only for two generations (Article 8), after which the family waqf reverted to the ownership of the founder's heirs (Article 10).[61] This "temporary waqf" was contrary to the late Hanafi canon's most dominant opinion that required waqfs to be perpetual and dedicated the revenues of waqfs whose family beneficiaries became extinct to the poor. Regarding existing waqfs, the 1947 law allowed their consensual subdivision (*qisma*) among beneficiaries (Article 17), dictated the exchange (*istibdāl jabrī*) of some family waqfs (Article 22), and permitted the liquidation (*taṣfiya*) of ruined family waqfs. The message was

61. For those familiar with US and UK trust law, such a provision is similar to the Rule Against Perpetuities, which sought to prohibit founders' "rule beyond the grave" and to help keep property in circulation; see, for example, Gray (2003). The prohibition against perpetual dynastic trusts plays an important role in taxing wealth transmission.

clear: these family waqfs were not truly charitable or religious; they were therefore not inalienable and should revert back to private property.

Consensual subdivision, forced subdivision, and liquidation of family waqfs introduced by the law entail different jurisdictions and end products in terms of "ownership." In the case of a consensual subdivision of a family waqf, the waqf does not cease to exist; instead of having beneficiaries divide the fruits of the waqfed object (say, the rental revenues of a building), these beneficiaries subdivide that object according to their shares. This way, there would be no need for an administrator to manage and fructify the waqf, and each beneficiary would be the administrator of his or her own share. As for the forced exchange and liquidation of family waqfs, the waqfs cease to exist and revert to the private property of the beneficiaries in exchange for a lump sum paid for the ownership of the right of alienation (*raqaba*) (Article 20). In terms of jurisdiction, consensual subdivision and forced exchange would, and still do, fall under the auspices of the DGIW. The process of liquidation of family waqfs is carried out by civil courts. The Qabbani waqf dispute over its reversion to private property, which I mention in the introduction of this chapter, revolved exactly around jurisdiction.

Understood as such, the 1947 law was effective in "modernizing" family waqf or, to be more accurate, in almost eradicating the foundation of any new family waqfs. By eliminating the perpetuity of family waqf and allowing its subdivision and revocation, the particularity of waqf as practiced in Beirut (and the Ottoman Empire at large) was completely obliterated. Compared to the waqf's purpose of creating rewards in eternity for the founder, the reinvented family waqf, which could be dismantled after two generations, was unrecognizable; it was an altogether different concept. It was now closer to a bequest, except that it was executable the moment it was drafted rather than upon the death of the founder. Indeed, the 1947 Family Waqf Law introduced one of the legal determinations governing bequests (that a bequest cannot exceed a third of one's possessions) into the law of waqf, even if it left the founder free to choose beneficiaries for this third (contra the rule of bequests that there is "no bequest for an heir—except with the approval of all heirs"). "An owner can make into a waqf no more than a third of his possessions, whether to the benefit of his heirs, other people, or a charitable purpose" (Article 37). For anything that exceeds the third, the following article specifies, the offspring of the founder, his wife, and his parents need to receive shares from the waqf in accordance with inheritance law.

From the day that the law was promulgated and up until the late 2000s, the archive of the shari'a court shows no new family waqfs being founded. But then suddenly, three new family waqfs appear on record, one in June 2006, the other two in 2009. These are too few to form a trend and to be read as the fruition of the efforts of some Muslim organizations to revive waqf as a practice, especially since these efforts were not targeted at family waqf to start with. However, my conversations with founders and in the court, and my observations at court, recorded in my notebook, suggest that such family waqfs constitute continuities of the ethic of care of the family by individuals for whom the practice of family waqf remained alive for a variety of reasons. While these might be numerically insignificant, and do not at all represent a "revival" of family waqfs, they do provide nonetheless a lens to examine the actualization of the 1947 Family Waqf Law as well as the discourse on the ethic of care of the family.

Judges between State Law and Fiqh Regulations

The 1947 law attempted to foreclose certain possibilities, such as the foundation of family waqfs that could last for longer than two generations. While most family beneficiaries usually extinguished in a relatively short period of time, a few such waqfs in Beirut have survived many generations.[62] The text of the law points to the debates around such a decision and the possibility of contestation of such a law. Article 6 specifies: "Shariʿa judges are prohibited from hearing a deposition for the creation of a new family waqf that would be contrary to the provisions of this law." The existence of an article prohibiting shariʿa judges from founding waqfs against this state law, based on the late Ḥanafī position that waqfs, including those dedicated at first to families, should be perpetual, actually acknowledges its contested and contestable nature.

How did shariʿa judges relate to the state-issued 1947 Family Waqf Law? How did they negotiate their location in the state and the authority it afforded to them—as well as its requirement of loyalty and submission to certain of its rules that contradict the fiqh and their training and authority as religious scholars? Clarke (2012) argues that these two diverging roles of the judge make him a tragic hero and discusses different strategies for negotiating these two opposite roles. Judges usually choose one role or the other through, for example, temporal distinctions (Clarke 2012, 112). Two of the new family waqfs from the archive, supplemented with observations and discussions from my notebook, present a good illustration of this negotiation, in addition to providing some insights on the tensions and anxieties around the logic of family.

The first new family waqf consists of three apartments on the fifth, sixth, and seventh floors of a building in one of the most expensive stretches in Beirut, featuring unobstructed sea views in proximity to the American University of Beirut.[63] The founder of the waqf preserved for himself the right of usufruct of all apartments during his lifetime, then transferred that of the fifth-floor apartment to one of his sons and one of his daughters, that of the sixth floor to two other sons, and the seventh floor to another daughter. Subsequently, their respective heirs would inherit that right of usufruct. The deed then specifies that after ninety-nine years from the date of foundation, the waqf would revert to the Directorate General of

62. As we saw in the transmission of offices at the ʿUmari mosque and as Hoexter shows in her study of the Haramayn waqf (see note 30 above).

63. MBSS.S2006/1027.

Islamic Waqfs. The deed therefore abides by the two-generation limit set forth by the 1947 Family Waqf Law (Article 7), but instead of reverting the ownership of the waqf to the founder and his heirs after that period, as the law suggests, the deed turns the first post-1947-law family waqf into a perpetual charitable waqf under the administration of the DGIW.

The waqf deed bore the signature of Judge Muhammad ʿAssaf, who, as the main judge having jurisdiction over waqf at the time,[64] drafted the waqf deed. Judge ʿAssaf, as he was commonly called, had been my main entry point into the court, especially because he wrote his thesis on waqf exchanges after his studies at the Beirut Shariʿa College. He also taught at the college about the Personal Status Code that formed the basis of most deeds and judgments in the court. Being a waqf expert, Judge ʿAssaf had strong opinions about waqf-related legislation and processes, and I listened carefully to his views on all things waqf.

Instead of the two-generation waqf reverting to the ownership of the founder and his heirs, Judge ʿAssaf reconciled the demands of state law for a non-perpetual family waqf and the shariʿa's requirement for a perpetual waqf and pious purpose. Instead of allowing the reversion to private property, which would be against the dominant late-Ottoman Ḥanafī view, Judge ʿAssaf fit the desire of the founder to found a family waqf into a common *sharʿī* practice: the waqf that had specific beneficiaries before reverting to the general charitable purpose. He therefore reconciled the demands of the state-issued Family Waqf Law with the shariʿa's. One should note, however, that Judge ʿAssaf's work-around might not appeal to everyone, as it actually also worked for the benefit of the DGIW, a gesture that other judges or founders might not be very keen on.[65] His way around state-issued legislation points to the continuing importance of debates about orthodoxy and the proper and most authoritative views on waqf founding, exchange, administration, and more general practices.

Like Judge ʿAssaf, other judges in the court engaged with the Family Waqf Law. But, while ʿAssaf avoided the state-issued rule against perpetuity by making the waqf a charitable one at the end of two generations, the other judges adopted more ambiguous stances.

The second post-1947-law family waqf only specified the first generation of beneficiaries.[66] Jurists considered such a waqf valid when some expression in the deed explicitly indicates perpetuity (such as "I made this into a waqf in perpetuity") or directed the waqf after the death of the beneficiary to the poor, but it was nonetheless surprising to see the deed not mention any eternal charitable beneficiary (setting it apart from all waqf deeds that I had encountered in the court).

64. Judges have specialized jurisdictions: some do inheritances, other marriages, and so on. For a lively description of the court, see Clarke (2018, 111–15).

65. One should remember the competition between Dar al-Fatwa/the DGIW and the courts, discussed in chapter 2.

66. MBSS.S2009/268.

It was an unusual waqf in many other ways. First, the waqf deed did not include a specific object, like a certain lot or an amount of money; what was waqfed was the "contents of the Fransabank account" of the founder. And, additionally, it did not elaborate on the ways the money should be fructified or even include a clause stipulating that only profits accrued could be spent, in order to ensure the perpetuity of the waqf. On a less unusual note, it was framed as a will (*waṣiyya*).[67] Indeed, in addition to the performative utterances that make waqf and the most common verbs used in waqf deeds "I waqfed, confined, and perpetuated" (*waqaftu, ḥabbastu, abbadtu*), this waqf deed started with "I willed" (*awṣaytu*). Although conditioning the waqf on the fulfillment of a future condition (*ta ʿlīq*)—for instance, if I have a boy, I will found a waqf—or specifying a future time when the waqf will become effective invalidates the waqf (see, for example, Article 8 of Qadri Pasha's manual), founding a waqf as part of one's will is the only case where the fiqh allows such a conditioning. However, in this case, the waqf is considered part of the bequest, and follows the stipulations of wills.

The Furtive Persistence of an Ethic of the Family

The founder of this second family waqf established in 2009 was a faculty member of the Shariʿa College in Beirut. I had met the professor-founder early in my research because I had asked for his help seeking permission to enroll in some of the classes at the college. I had discussed my project with him in order to explain why I wanted to audit these classes. But when, in the course of my research in the court archive, I encountered the waqf that he had founded, I was surprised. He had not mentioned that he had founded such a waqf. I set up a meeting with him. Although he was gracious and answered my questions, he was not keen on discussing the waqf.

Our meeting was short. When he founded the waqf, he explained, he had been thinking about his sister after the death of his brother—"In our society, a woman suffers if she does not have money or property"—and he decided to dedicate a waqf to her, so she could live "in dignity." Although the founder of this family waqf couched the reasons behind his waqf in a social analysis about the place of women in society, the responsibility that he expressed towards his sister embodies the injunctions discussed earlier in the chapter of an ethic of care of the family—after all, he did not found a waqf to support aging women in general.

Furthermore, while the founder elaborated his foundation in terms of care for his sister, he brought up, unsolicited, the issue of bequests, inheritance, and

67. Even though I use "wills" as a translation of *waṣiyya* for expediency, the translation obscures the many differences between wills in the United States and Europe and the particularities of the *waṣiyya* in Islamic law, such as the facts that it is restricted to one third of one's possessions and that it cannot be done for an heir.

waqf; anxieties about the charitable character of such a waqf (and questions about its contradicting the law of inheritance) surfaced. After answering my question about the particular form (*ṣīgha*) of the waqf deed, he explained the socioeconomic and moral basis behind his urge to care for his sister, but then went on to what seemed to me, back then, as proof of his familiarity with the law of waqf. "Anyone who is sane of mind can make all of his possessions into waqf," he interjected. While this statement does indeed show the founder's familiarity with the law of waqf, the way he volunteered it points to the contested nature of his foundation under the current legal regime of waqf. He was not only challenging the restriction of the 1947 law on the amount of possessions that could be made into waqf but also justifying the validity of his endeavor. The running arguments about the contradictions between founding a family waqf and the laws of inheritance yielded anxieties about family waqf foundation as a charitable endeavor.

These anxieties over one's charitableness and the way they push subjects to reassert their charitable intent was made even more apparent in a non sequitur. The founder brought up a piece of land that he owned in an upscale "modern" neighborhood and said that he was thinking of making it into a mosque. The suspicion around the charitableness of family waqf incited the founder to assert his willingness to give of what is dear to him, to show his piety, echoing the Qur'anic injunction "Never shall you attain true piety unless you spend on others out of what you cherish yourselves" (3:92). Not only was the professor-founder giving a very valuable piece of land, but he was also considering giving it to what today represents religious piety par excellence, a mosque, as we saw in chapter 1.

The ethic of the family and the anxieties around it, as exemplified by this founder of a new family waqf, do not only surface among subjects familiar with the practice of family waqf. They also appear in mundane conversations, as I recorded in my notebook during my work at the shari'a court's archive, which was manned single-handedly by Abu Ali, the court's archivist.

Abu Ali has occupied this position for some twenty-five years. He remembers when the court was in a different location, as well as the various makeovers at the current location. Abu Ali ranted regularly about a particular aspect of the last renovation that Saudi Prince al-Walid bin Talal sponsored in 2007: it had robbed him of his metal shelving system and replaced it with cheap particleboard shelves that were like cardboard and broke easily and harbored insects and roaches. During a visit in the summer of 2011, Abu Ali's pleas had been answered and new metal-frame shelves filled the three-by-four-meter room. This was *his* archive, these were *his* registers. He knew the archive inside out, and he was a combination of help desk, gossip central, and memory of the court.

Abu Ali told me he was going to retire soon and was expecting his son to take over his office. Ali, the son in question, was a handsome, gym-going nineteen-year-old attending college. He harbored dreams of going to Australia, where a friend's family could help him enroll at a university or make a living. In front of me, Abu Ali always sang his son's praises: how fast he had learned about the archive, how good a son he was. However, when I was working in the back, I could catch glimpses of Abu Ali gently rebuking his son, as he seemed unable to stay put: a cigarette break here, going to buy stamps there, or hanging out with some of the court functionaries everywhere.

One day, as I was close to the door making some copies, I witnessed a conversation between Abu Ali and a lawyer. She stood up straight at the side of the doorway as she engaged in small talk with Abu Ali, asking the standard questions about his health and family. She wore makeup, with the court-mandated scarf nonchalantly thrown over her head, half covering her fresh coiffure. When Abu Ali started explaining that he was about to retire, but that his son was most likely going to be taking over his position, she exclaimed, "What's wrong with that?" ("eh, shū fiya?").

But nobody had said that there was anything wrong with that. The lawyer's defensive outburst indexed the association of nepotism with the logic of family in public office. The lawyer then told Abu Ali how her father had passed away as she had been completing her compulsory training before the bar examination. He was a famous lawyer who had important clients. After he passed away, many of his clients trusted her and tried working with her despite her young age and lack of experience. She worked very hard, she explained, and was able to prove her skills and retain all the clients. The lawyer drew a parallel between herself and Ali, without distinguishing between the public nature of his office and her private law practice. While her father had helped her, she could not have been a successful lawyer without her competence. In her argument, we see enacted the very logic of family that was at work in the transmission of offices: that family privilege had to be accompanied and confirmed by merit.

Such moments, the "so what" moments, however, remain fleeting in a legally enshrined association of corruption with the privileging of family in public office. This is not to say that preferential treatment/favoritism (*muḥābā*) was an acceptable practice for late Ottoman jurists: it is a complex legal issue in sales, inheritance, and divorce with varying legal effects. However, the distinction lies in the conceptualization of the positions of waqf administrator or mosque caretaker or archivist as inheritable rights and their not being articulated along the same private/public distinction (favoritism was as much an issue for jurists in "private law", such as in inheritance). The passing of such positions to family did not count as favoritism. Conversely, Abu Ali's attempt to place his son is considered today evidence of corruption rather than an ethic of care of one's family. The discourse of corruption reverberated and became more pronounced the higher up the socioeconomic ladder the people in question were. As we saw in the opening scene of this chapter, even the mufti of the republic was not spared. Indeed, the accusations of corruption leveled at the mufti led to the filing of lawsuits by Qarduhi and other religious scholars, the arrest of the business partner of the mufti's son, a petition calling for the mufti to resign, and eventually the election of a new grand mufti. The corruption charges were used in a much larger political fallout and disagreement between the grand mufti and the Sunni Future movement, which had originally championed the mufti. One can read the nepotism accusations as cards played in a political game, but the effectiveness of these accusations shows the entrenchment of the modern grammar of family.

CONCLUSION

In this chapter, I started by describing late Ottoman understandings and practices of charity that privileged the family and were anchored in the Islamic tradition. This approach to charity favored the family as the primary recipient of charity, as appears in the prevalence of waqf foundations for the family. Even more, this family-centered charity, I showed, was pervasive even in those waqfs that had "public" beneficiaries, like mosques, as their personnel and administrators held offices transmitted through families. However, I argued that this logic of the family did not stand in contradiction to the logic of abstract merit; rather it was conditional on merit, character, and experience. It enacted, therefore, ideals of knowledge as transmitted within families and of social relations as centered around it, rather than just a "blind" favoring of the family in a patrimonial state. I then traced the beginning of the transformation of this approach to charity through the legislative efforts of the modernizing Ottoman state. The primacy of the family over merit started to be reversed with state legislation on appointments to offices. With a new education system in place, exams and tests became primary for the assessment of candidates—the family only factoring in to distinguish equal candidates.

I then followed the devaluing of the family as a legitimate recipient of charity, through debates between Muslim reformers of various trends and new legislation. The debate happened during the French Mandate and centered on whether family waqfs were really part of religion, when compared to the true charitable waqfs dedicated to mosques and other charitable works. I showed how this debate introduced a statistical style of reasoning with the tradition, whereby jurists accepted the authority of economic sciences to assess harm to the economy. When the newly created Lebanese state took over the legislation on family waqfs as part of its claim to sovereignty, family waqfs were deemed to be not "really charitable" through an understanding of charity that privileged "public," rather than family, recipients. New family waqfs were limited to two generations, and old ones could be divided among beneficiaries as private property. In that way, most waqfs were relegated to the sphere of the economy, and only "truly charitable endowments" that privileged public good were deemed to belong to the sphere of religion. This division of waqfs into "religious" and "economic" subsumed waqfs to the new architecture of the modern state, with its constant attempts to separate the spheres of religion and economy. It helped uproot an institution that perpetuated ties that bound people as families and with God and the dead, allowing for the family to be governmentalized and for new forms of belonging, new desires, and new commitments. However, the tension between these two approaches to the family persists today. Drawing on narratives of contemporary family waqf founders and the discourse around the support of one's family read against the recent scandal of the nepotism of the Lebanese Sunni grand mufti, the last section showed how the discourse of the "care of the family" and the ethic of merit are rearticulated in the postcolonial moment. The ethic of care of the family came to be limited to the "private," even if disrupted fleetingly.

The logics of family and merit I described here still constitute the idiom of political discussion and academic analysis on state formation in Lebanon and the Middle East. Reflecting assumptions of modernization theory, some social scientists and the media often present "family and sectarian identities" hand in hand and in opposition to modern ideals of democracy and meritocracy. Of late, scholarship has started to interrogate the assumptions of these claims and the work they do (Joseph 1997; Makdisi 2000; Obeid 2011). In an article describing municipal elections in a border village in Lebanon, anthropologist Michelle Obeid questions the argument that family connections stand in the way of democratization. She shows how "the idiom of *'ā'ila* [family] is malleable and shaped and reshaped by the sociopolitical environment in which it is embedded, allowing it to be unifying, divisive, or a principal idiom of democracy" (2011, 254). By discussing the workings of the logic of family, this chapter stands in such a lineage of research, outlining the various articulations of family and merit, rather than assuming a progressive move from family to merit. It has historicized the association of giving to the family with nepotism and reminded us that an abstract logic of merit obscures the social relations necessary in the making of merit. After this chapter that showed how waqf was subjected to and helped produce these new understandings of family and divisions between the public and the private, the last chapter will dwell on the way these new divisions rearticulated the notion of public benefit and, with it, the waqf's benefit.

5

The "Waqf's Benefit" and Public Benefit

In the 1990s, after the end of a fifteen-year war, Beirut's newspapers were replete with articles discussing the reconstruction of the city center.[1] When the proposal for charging a private real estate holding company with rebuilding passed the legislature in 1991,[2] the debate continued and intensified; the urban plan put forward met with criticism from rights holders (*aṣḥāb al-ḥuqūq*), architects, and planners.[3] The rights holders' grievances concerned the decision to expropriate their holdings for reasons of public benefit and to compensate them with shares in stock of the company later known as Solidere.[4] This was a massive operation of dispossession

1. The literature on the reconstruction of the city center is considerable. Some of the classics include Kabbani (1992); Khalaf and Khoury (1993); Beyhum (1995); Tabit (1996); Makdisi (1997); Rowe and Sarkis (1998); Becherer (2005); Hourani (2005); and Sawalha (2010). Addressing postwar state building more broadly, Leenders (2012) provides excellent data on the reconstruction.

2. The company was a private one, but it entered into a public-private partnership with the Lebanese government for the process of reconstruction.

3. One of the first plans treated the whole area as a tabula rasa and was built on a modernist plan with very clear-cut zoning based on function. Planners and architects called for a more democratic approach to the design, including public debate (which happened de facto because of the ire of all, but opinions of rights holders were not actively sought nor included in the process), and advocated a more sensitive approach to the fabric. For more on this debate, see especially Hourani (2005) and Makdisi (1997) in the literature cited in note 1.

4. Expropriation is the equivalent of the American eminent domain. Solidere is the acronym of the French name of the company: Société libanaise pour le développement et la reconstruction. For discussions of whether the compensation for Solidere shares constitutes expropriation see Mango (2004) and Sharp (2018, 192–94).

that threatened to take away their ownership of land, shops, and apartments, whether in whole or in part. Most importantly, the new law would rob them of the possibilities the city center held for their future. However, despite the campaigns and lawsuits filed against it, the company proceeded with the expropriations, using political and legal maneuvering, and even force, with backing from the government led by Prime Minister Rafiq Hariri, who was—not coincidentally—a major stakeholder in Solidere.

The waqfs that existed in the city center seemed to me, at first, to have succumbed to that expropriation. My mention of waqfs and Solidere to various interlocutors in my research often elicited disapproving head shakes and accusations. "They sold the Muslims' waqfs," said Tante In'am, a matriarch of the Qabbanis contesting the Directorate General of Islamic Waqfs' (DGIW) control of the family's waqf. With her short, dark-blonde dyed hair, her below-the-knee straight skirt, and her Beiruti accent, Tante In'am represented the disappointment of many Sunni Muslims I had talked to about how the DGIW handled the waqfs in Beirut's city center in the face of Solidere. The DGIW had sold what was supposed to be inalienable, these interlocutors lamented.

Yet, I discovered in the course of archival research that the DGIW was one of the very few rights holders able to escape this dispossession and to retain some physical assets (buildings and lands) instead of company shares.[5] A newspaper headline in 1994 announced, "All the Parcels of the DGIW [*'aqārāt al-awqāf al-islāmiyya*][6] Will Be Returned" (*Annahar*, 15 January 1994, 6). In a nation-state where *public* benefit (Ar: *maṣlaḥa 'āmma*; Fr: *intérêt général*) forms the highest reason and the only constitutional limit to the right of property, how was the DGIW able to negotiate such an exception in the name of the waqf's benefit,[7] and Muslim benefit more broadly? I contend that one can begin to understand this contradiction by examining the genealogy of "public benefit" and "the waqf's benefit" and their

5. The waqfs of the various Christian denominations had this privilege also; see the section "Explaining Waqf Exchange" below. I tackle the reasons for the failure of organization based on individual rights and the success of those marshaling religious benefit in another work. However, the reader should not assume that waqfs successfully escaped expropriation because they played on alliances between Sunni religious and political elites due to consociationalism. Indeed, the religious leaders had been to a large degree co-opted in the original plan, as I show in the section "Marshaling the Waqf's Benefit," and it was a more popular mobilization, even if by a religious community, around waqf inalienability, that opposed the Sunni religious-political elite alliance in power.

6. An alternative translation of the Arabic title ("Kull 'Aqārāt al-Awaqāf al-Islāmiyya Satustaradd") is "all the Islamic waqf parcels," but I opt for "all the parcels of the DGIW" because the statement was issued by the Supreme Islamic Legal Council and describes some of the agreements reached between the DGIW and Solidere regarding the waqfs of the DGIW.

7. I translate *maṣlaḥat al-waqf* as "the waqf's benefit" rather than "waqf benefit" because "the waqf" conveys better what I will demonstrate in this chapter: that benefit was singular, particular, and individualized, in each case.

articulations in the context of Beirut, under the architectures of state, law, and religious community I described earlier. Therefore, in this chapter, I will turn to focus on the relations between the state and individual endeavors of waqf and the ideals of life sustained by each. What happens to the waqf's benefit when the public benefit that the state preserves ceases to be limited by the shariʿa and to include care for the afterlives of citizens, and becomes defined as the well-being of citizens and economy, with the state having ultimate jurisdiction in deciding what counts as such public benefit?

Excavating the grammar of the waqf's benefit in the library of the late Ottoman Ḥanafī tradition, I show that jurists used the concept in the administration of waqf in conjunction with the concepts of the founder's stipulations and necessity, but never as the principle guiding administration. In that grammar, caring for the waqf's benefit did not mean seeking more profit but rather perpetuating the waqf as its founder had stipulated. The properties of a waqf could be exchanged for more prosperous ones in the late Ottoman Ḥanafī tradition only in cases of necessity. The perpetuation of these waqfs as individual endeavors defined in the shariʿa, in both their worldly and otherworldly effects, was part of the public benefits that the (Islamic) state promoted. With the rise of modern governmentality—the focus of the state on the well-being of its population in this world, on growth and progress—public benefit became wedded to such notions of progress and the here and now, and the waqf's inalienability became a hurdle to public benefit. The confrontation between the Ottoman state's preservation of public benefit as an Islamic state and as a modern state created contradictory demands, which the state resolved through procedure rather than by making a choice between these two sometimes contradictory notions of benefit. The French Mandate officials used the waqf's benefit as a principle of administration, divorced from founder stipulations and necessity, to argue for the liberalization of exchanges. At the same time, with the articulation of a Muslim community separate from the civil state, the waqf's benefit was tied to the Muslim community's and to a "religious" benefit rather than a public benefit. And it was a benefit that the state guaranteed. This introduction of a "religious" (collective) benefit distinct from the public benefit of the national state and from the public (Islamic) benefit of the Ottomans is what allowed for the mobilization of the Sunni Muslim community against the expropriation of the waqfs in the city center. In the Ottoman state, such a mobilization for the "religious benefit" of the Muslim community would have been impossible, given that the Ottoman state was an Islamic state preserving the benefit of Muslims. In contemporary Lebanon, the state's commitment to preserving "religious benefit" in addition to public benefit, and with the contention surrounding the expropriation of all rights holders by a private company in the name of public benefit, made possible a preservation of these waqfs against public benefit.

OTTOMAN LATE ḤANAFĪ BENEFIT: SHARIʿA-DEFINED AND STATE-PRESERVED WAQF BENEFIT

Benefit (Maṣlaḥa) between the Purpose of the Law and a Principle of Action

Before delving into a snapshot of the grammar governing the waqf's benefit on the eve of the Ottoman reforms of the nineteenth century, I would like to unpack the term *benefit—maṣlaḥa* (pl. *maṣāliḥ*) in the late Ottoman Ḥanafī library—since it stands at the core of both the waqf's benefit and public benefit. Jurists use *maṣlaḥa* in two meanings: a technical concept of Islamic legal theory and a common use of what is good.

Maṣlaḥa became a technical concept in Islamic legal theory in the eleventh century with the Shāfiʿī scholar al-Ghazali (d. 1111) (Opwis 2005, 188).[8] Ghazali distinguished this technical legal concept from more pedestrian understandings of *benefit* as "bringing utility [*manfaʿa*] and fending off harm" (Ghazali 1997, 416). In this distinction between *maṣlaḥa* and *manfaʿa*, Ghazali might be drawing on the linguistic roots of the two words *ṣ-l-ḥ*, "the good," more broadly, and *n-f-ʿ*, "what is useful." The good that is about utility and avoidance of harm in the here and now is a distinctly human, self-centered, and limited understanding of the good. For Ghazali, this human assessment alone does not suffice to determine the good.[9] Instead Ghazali proposes an understanding of maṣlaḥa, the good, as exceeding what is useful (*manfaʿa*) and human understanding. Maṣlaḥa is "the embodiment of the purpose of the law" (Opwis 2005, 183), which Ghazali specified in "tangible terms" (Opwis 2010, 7) as maintaining the five necessities of humans: religion, life, mind, progeny, and property. Ghazali deduces these five purposes of the law inductively from a multiplicity of legal determinations explicit in the Qurʾan (Opwis 2010, 74).[10] This "good" is what God chooses for humans accounting for the hereafter. Maṣlaḥa as a legal concept is not a lesser source of law; for Ghazali,[11] it applies only exceptionally and supplants all four other sources in cases such as necessities (*ḍarūrāt*), but only if the necessity is certain (or beyond any reasonable doubt) (*qaṭʿiyya*) and universal (involving the totality of Muslims) (*kulliyya*) (Opwis 2010, 73).[12] Therefore, maṣlaḥa as a technical legal

8. Ghazali is not just any scholar; he is one of the most important philosophers, theologians, jurists, and sufis of Sunni Islam.

9. This position reflects the Ashʿarī theology that Ghazali espoused and helped make dominant. Other Muslim theologies accepted the capacity of humans to figure out the good on their own.

10. For instance, the presence of a punishment for unlawful intercourse shows that the preservation of lineage is a benefit that the shariʿa seeks to preserve (Opwis 2010, 68).

11. By the time Ghazali was writing, the sources of Islamic law had crystallized as the Qurʾan, sunna, consensus, and analogy.

12. Maṣlaḥa's place in the derivation of laws differs among scholars. See Opwis (2010) for a discussion of this variety of positions. Ghazali's example of a valid use of maṣlaḥa in the derivation of law is the following: it is permissible to kill a Muslim that the enemy is using as a shield, if the enemy's winning could reasonably lead to the enemy's victory and the death of all Muslims (Opwis 2010, 73).

concept goes beyond a state's or an individual's assessment of harm and benefit and takes the form of the purposes of the shari'a as jurists derived them from scripture.[13]

Maṣlaḥa, however, also appears in the library in the more general sense of "bringing benefits and averting harms" ("jalb al-maṣāliḥ wa dar' al-mafāsid"), which Ghazali had dismissed as not what he means by the Islamic legal concept of maṣlaḥa. This use of *maṣlaḥa* appears, for instance, in the legal maxim that the actions of the ruler towards his subjects are contingent on benefit.[14] The use of *benefit* here concerns the ways the ruler governs and exercises the powers delegated to him, what I will call a principle of action. This is not about necessary and universal circumstances. The examples jurists use to illustrate this maxim are about how the ruler distributes the spoils of truce, what he orders the inhabitants of a city to build, and the like. Ibn Nujaym's discussion of the maxim extends this rule to the actions of qadis entrusted with the property of orphans, the deceased, and waqfs (1999, 207). *Maṣlaḥa* here is open to interpretation as long as it does not contradict the shari'a.

The "Waqf's Benefit"

In light of this discussion of maṣlaḥa in Islamic legal theory, let us turn to the discussion of the waqf's maṣlaḥa in the fiqh books of the library, to see whether the term is used in the technical legal sense or as a principle of action. The discussion of the waqf's benefit arises mostly in relation to exchanges/substitutions (*istibdāl*) and rents (*ijāra*), but it is most common in the lengthy discussions of exchanges. *Exchange* is here a technical term referring to a specialized transaction of waqf property: selling a waqf's principal (*'ayn*), or part thereof, either for cash (*badal*) or, most commonly, for cash that is immediately used to buy another principal that takes the place of the old one in terms of the stipulations of the founder. It is termed *exchange* (the most common term used in waqf studies) because the original principal is exchanged for another while the waqf's conditions continue as they were. This is an exceptional procedure as it contradicts the inalienability and perpetuity of the waqfs.[15]

However, those on a sinking or an abandoned ship cannot dispose of or eat one of their fellows to save the rest of them, because this is not a necessity that affects all Muslims (Opwis 2010, 74).

13. Any other interest that is not explicit in scriptures is known as *maṣlaḥa mursala* and for Ghazali is not an acceptable source for legal determinations (1997, 420).

14. "Taṣarruf al-imām 'alā al-ra'iyya manūṭ bi'l-maṣlaḥa" (Ibn Nujaym, *Ashbāh*, 104).

15. Even the earliest waqf compendia, al-Khassaf's and Hilal al-Basri's—both written in the ninth century—discuss waqf exchange, but the criteria of exchange, or the various parameters used to assess the exchanged waqf and its substitute, had not yet crystallized into the generic "waqf's benefit" that would become dominant in later manuals. On one hand, al-Khassaf's discussion does not even formulate the waqf as an entity having interests. For him, the substituted waqf was to be more productive and more advantageous for the beneficiaries (*ahl al-waqf*), and not for the abstract legal entity "the waqf" (1999, 21). Hilal al-Basri, on the other hand, does speak of the waqf as such an entity when he is surprised that his interlocutor forbids exchanges not explicitly allowed by the founder in his stipulations, even

When jurists argued that exchange of a waqf in case of necessity would be permissible *because it is for the waqf's benefit*, is *maṣlaḥa* used in the technical sense I explained above? Are the jurists making a legal determination based on maṣlaḥa, *maṣlaḥa* being the purpose of the shariʿa that applies in exceptional circumstances, or in the more pedestrian understanding of *maṣlaḥa* as "the good" as a principle of action? The coupling of "*ḍarūra*" (necessity) with the argument for exchange based on maṣlaḥa might suggest that the latter is used in the technical legal sense. In that case, the maṣlaḥa of the waqf needs to be an indispensable one (part of the five necessities that the shariʿa preserves), universal, and certain. One could argue that the preservation of the waqf helps in preserving property and religion. However, would the disrepair of waqf lead to "severe harm" for property and religion for all Muslims? Given the extent of the use of waqf for mosques and madrasas, one might argue that this is indeed so. However, given that the disrepair of *one* waqf would not lead to such drastic consequences, the exchange of waqf does not serve the universal preservation of religion. In these discussions, then, *maṣlaḥa* seems to be used in a much more casual sense of the "good," as a principle of action instead of the technical meaning of preserving the aims of the shariʿa.

Some other examples confirm the use of benefit as a principle of action. Towards the end of the eighteenth century, the Damascene scholar Ibn ʿAbidin argues for the validity of exchange in the case of a waqf generating some revenue that does not suffice for its repairs: "if the qadi allows it and he sees benefit in it"[16] (*Ḥāshiya*, 3:387). Here the argument closely parallels the principle of the actions of the qadi being bound by benefit; if the exchange is "better" for the waqf, then it is allowed. Another use of *maṣlaḥa* associates it with the "benefits of the beneficiaries," as when Ibn ʿAbidin explains why a stipulation that prohibits the qadi from exchange is invalid "because it is a stipulation that involves forgoing benefit [*maṣlaḥa*] for the beneficiaries and ruining the waqf. It is therefore a stipulation that has no utility [*fāʾida*] nor benefit [*maṣlaḥa*] for the waqf, making it unacceptable" (*Ḥāshiya*, 3:388). The juxtaposition of *maṣlaḥa* with synonyms like *fāʾida* pushes one to think that in this case *maṣlaḥa* is being used as a principle guiding the action of fiduciaries and determining their legality rather than

---

when it is "good for the waqf" (*wa huwa khayr l-il-waqf*) (1936, 95). Still, in this case, the exchange itself is beneficial and good for the waqf; it does not serve an independent good called "the waqf's benefit." The various criteria that enter into assessing the worth of the substitute-to-be and comparing it with the existing waqfed asset (size, revenue, etc., as discussed below in the section "Calculable Economic Benefit") had not yet formed a compound, all-encompassing term, *benefit* (*maṣlaḥa*), which concurrently would become a much more elusive concept. Coincidentally or not, however, the second characteristic of the substitute mentioned in al-Khassaf, that it be "more advantageous" (*aṣlaḥ*), has the same root as the principle of the benefit (*maṣlaḥa*) of the waqf. Both *ṣāliḥ* (*aṣlaḥ* being the comparative form of the adjective) and *maṣlaḥa* are derived from the same root, *ṣ-l-ḥ*, which is the opposite of degeneration and decay (*fasād*). This is not to say that it presages the later crystallization of all criteria under maṣlaḥa, but that the *ṣalāḥ* and *khayr* of the waqf—its good—have always been something to care for.

16. "Idhā kān bi-idhn al-qāḍī wa raʾyuh al-maṣlaḥa fīh."

as an exceptional source of legislation. It is important to note that it is the qadi who decides what is for the benefit of each waqf and that he should base his decision on criteria elaborated by scholars (as described below), while taking into account the various regulations issued by the sultan/imam to preserve benefit, as long as these regulations do not contradict the shariʿa.

"Waqf Is No Business" versus the Waqf's Benefit: Exchange as Individualized Exception

While caring for the waqf and preserving its benefit are arguments presented in discussions of exchange, it is important to understand the place of an argument on the benefit of the waqf within questions of its administration. I will show how the dominant logic of exchange (*istibdāl*) (as well as administration in general) preserves the waqf as its founder created and imagined it, thereby making the "waqf's benefit" the criterion for assessing an exchange rather than the logic that drives it—even if there is a drive towards making it the logic of administration. The logic of preservation seeks to keep exchange as exceptional as possible through a literal reading of stipulations and through constrictive conditions of necessity for exchange, making waqf, in this logic, unconducive to increased accumulation.

Discussions of waqf exchange usually occur under the main heading of stipulations of founders. The titles of the sections in waqf manuals—"The Stipulation of Sale and Exchange is Valid for Abu Hanifa" (al-Khassaf 1999, 21), "A Man Waqfs a Land of His on the Condition That He Can Sell It" (al-Basri 1936, 91), "On the Stipulation of Exchange" (al-Tarabulusi 2005, 31)—already point to the intimate connection between exchange and its stipulation. Discussions of the validity of unstipulated exchanges for "the benefit of the waqf" occur in these same sections. These are, however, in dialectical tension with the stipulated ones and are not discussed under the duties of the administrator and the manner of administration. According to Abu Yusuf, the dominant opinion allows for the founder's stipulation of exchange,[17] so that the founder, the administrator, or any other person named in the founding document can carry it out.[18] Without such a stipulation, only the qadi can proceed with the exchange and there must be grounds for it; there must be a necessity (*ḍarūra*) for exchange (more below in the section "Defining Necessity").[19] For the waqf administrator, therefore, the waqf's benefit would not be the principle guiding the administrator's actions and opening possibilities for

17. This is the most authoritative position. However, an opinion attributed to al-Shaybani makes the stipulation invalid without invalidating the waqf itself (al-Tarabulusi 2005, 31). On the other hand, for Abu Hanifa, the stipulation of exchange or even sale is not controversial because for him a waqf is not perpetual, and therefore a sale or an exchange can be made even without a stipulation.

18. In the section "Constricting Founders' Stipulations of Exchange," I discuss the restrictions on the person who can carry out the exchange as a way to restrict it.

19. That is the dominant opinion in Ottoman Beirut. I will discuss other opinions below in this section.

exchange to fulfill that benefit. As discussed in chapter 2, the highest principle of administration is following the stipulations of the founder, as long as they do not contradict the *shar*ʿ.

The waqf's benefit is simply the principle that guides the choice of exchanged objects, not the principle that determines the possibility of exchange.[20] To illustrate this principle, one can imagine the order of questions concerning the possibility of exchange: First, did the founder stipulate the exchange? If he or she did, then exchange can proceed. If the founder did not stipulate it, the second question and option that could allow the exchange becomes, Is the waqf in a state of complete disrepair—that is, is there a necessity for exchange? It is after answering yes to this question that the waqf's benefit comes into play when comparing the old waqfed object to the new one. Prioritizing and making the waqf's benefit the highest principle of administration would shift the order of the questions, bringing to the forefront the question, Is it for the waqf's benefit? Even more than a different priority, such an ordering would change the grammar of the concept of waqf benefit: it would disentangle the principle of the waqf's benefit from the web of stipulations and necessity, rendering the latter two concepts irrelevant. If the administrator administered solely on the basis of benefit, the founder would not need to leave any stipulations.

The logic of exchange and the place of the waqf's benefit in it come into relief in discussions of the thorny question of the unstipulated exchange of a prosperous waqf (what I will term the unstipulated unnecessary exchange): Can one exchange a *prosperous* waqf for a different object that is for the "benefit" of the waqf if the founder has not allowed exchanges in the stipulations? This is a complex question, with different answers by different jurists. As described above, according to jurists, two main reasons can lead to exchange: stipulation and necessity.[21] If the founder had stipulated exchange, a prosperous waqf could have been exchanged. Given that stipulation of exchange is absent in this question and given that the waqf is prosperous, there is no necessity and so there should be no exchange. Allowing such an exchange would make the benefit of the waqf an operating logic of administration, where *mutawallī*s would manage waqfs as commercial endeavors seeking and planning for profit.

20. Note that Ibn ʿAbidin's abovementioned opinion (that the stipulation that prohibits the qadi's exchange is invalid because it is contrary to the waqf's benefit) considers the harm and possibility of extinction of this waqf after need. Indeed, qadi exchange happens only in case of necessity. Therefore, a stipulation that prohibits administrators from an exchange or the absence of stipulations allowing exchange would be valid.

21. Historians have found that many exchanges happened when there was no necessity and only because some founder, many times a powerful notable, wanted to make his or her waqf on properties that were already endowed—for instance, in an attempt to delegitimize a previous founder (e.g. Crecelius 1991). Although the exchanges in the court records state necessity as the cause of exchange, historians point to the existence of tenancy contracts for the supposedly destitute exchanged waqf.

Even if many of the profits accrued are redistributed to beneficiaries rather than being accumulated, making the benefit of the waqf the logic of administration is explicitly denounced in one of the earliest waqf treatises: "Waqf is done neither for business nor for making profit" (al-Basri 1936, 95).[22] Hilal al-Basri continues to reject the unstipulated unnecessary exchange: "If it was valid to sell the waqf without a stipulation specified in the foundation document, he could sell (again) the object he exchanged the waqf for. This way, the waqf could be sold every day, and that is not how waqf works [*wa laysa hākadhā al-waqf*]" (1936, 95). The way waqf works is to follow the founder's stipulations. In their rejection of unstipulated unnecessary exchange, jurists articulated this principle explicitly: "It was called waqf because it remains [*tabqā*] and is not sold" (al-Basri 1936, 95). "Duty is keeping the waqf as is without any additions [*al-ziyāda*]" (Ibn Nujaym, *Nahr*, 3:320). Increase, profit, or growth are not imperative.[23]

Against this logic of perpetuation, jurists continued to debate whether "the waqf's benefit" alone can govern unstipulated unnecessary exchange. In Mamluk Egypt, al-Tarabulusi mentions that an unstipulated unnecessary exchange is allowed, but as a prerogative of a qadi (and not the mutawallī) and only if he sees benefit in it (2005, 32). This is also the opinion of the jurist known as Qari' al-Hidaya, based on Abu Yusuf's opinion, who allows the unstipulated exchange of a prosperous waqf that has revenues if there is a "person who wishes to exchange it and give instead a replacement [*badal*] that is more productive and in a better location" (reported in Ibn 'Abidin, *Ḥāshiya*, 3:389). Qari' al-Hidaya reports that the permissibility of this exchange is the preponderant opinion. And indeed, both historians of the Mamluk period (Fernandes 2000; Petry 1998) and Mamluk jurists like Siraj al-Din Ibn Nujaym (the less known brother of Zayn al-Din) had also noted that exchanges were very numerous and unscrupulously done (*Nahr*, 3:320). While this is a much more liberal approach to exchanges, the waqf's benefit, even as it displaces necessity, does not become the highest principle of *administration* (as practiced by mutawallīs) because unstipulated unnecessary exchanges hinging on benefit belong solely to qadis and cannot be practiced by mutawallīs.[24]

Nonetheless, the opinion of Qari' al-Hidaya about the permissibility of an unstipulated unnecessary exchange was challenged by many of his fellow jurists even in the Mamluk period. Given the risk of annulling waqfs that a more

22. "Al-waqf lā tuṭlab bih al-tijāra wa lā tuṭlab bih al-arbāḥ."

23. Although not brought up by jurists, the theme of keeping continuity and perpetuating the waqf as its founder created it echoes the legal maxim to keep old usage as is ("al-qadīm yutrak 'alā qidamih"), as discussed in chapter 2.

24. The highest principle of administration remains the following of the founders' stipulations. In this opinion, a non-stipulated exchange hinges solely on interest and not on necessity, but it does remain framed in relation to stipulation and its absence, making it an exceptional instance in administration.

liberal exchange allows, jurists attempted to put conditions on unstipulated unnecessary exchanges. Al-Tarabulusi (2005, 32; also cited in *Nahr* 3:320), for example, requires the qadi to be known for his uprightness, whereas Zayn al-Din Ibn Nujaym (cited in *Nahr*, 3:320) requires the exchange to be for an immovable and not cash, in addition to reintroducing the stipulation of necessity.

Between these two extremes of impermissibility and permissibility of the unstipulated unnecessary exchange, other jurists advocate principles of caution over the waqf's benefit. Al-Tarabulusi himself warns that such exchanges can be "attempts at revoking the Muslims' waqfs, as is common in our time" (2005, 32). Rereading these lines after my research was done was uncanny, as they echoed almost word for word some of my observations in my notebooks, like the exclamation of Tante Inʿam, "They sold the Muslims' waqfs." The argument of the fear of annulment of waqfs constitutes one of the most enduring rhetorical fields around waqf. To this day, it is used to both justify certain opinions and put into question the moral rectitude of qadis and waqf administrators. Statements by Mamluk jurists, such as "We have observed immeasurable corruption as unjust qadis have used it as a subterfuge to annul the waqfs of Muslims, and they did what they did" (Ibn Nujaym, *Nahr*, 3:320), sound as familiar and incendiary today as they did ten centuries ago. According to these jurists, the risk of exchange leading to a loss for the waqf is not worth the benefit that might accrue to the waqf. Ibn ʿAbidin breaks out in unusual emotional praise for Siraj al-Din Ibn Nujaym's refusal to allow unstipulated unnecessary exchanges: "By my life, this opinion is more precious than a philosopher's stone!"[25] (*Ḥāshiya*, 3:389). He then explains that it is more appropriate to prohibit such exchanges out of fear of transgressing the law and to prohibit exchanges for cash as "a measure of precaution"[26] (*Ḥāshiya*, 3:389).

The Ottomans leaned towards such a view, as a 1544 [951] sultanic edict based on Ebüssuʿûd's opinion required the permission not only of a qadi but also that of the sultan (Ibn ʿAbidin, *Ḥāshiya*, 3:390).[27] Such a measure confirms and extends the exceptionality of exchanges, which is enhanced in the fiqh through constrictive readings and requirements of the two conditions allowing exchanges: founder stipulations and necessity, as I will now describe.

25. "Wa la-ʿumrī an hādhā aʿazz min al-kibrīt al-aḥmar." It continues: "fa'l-aḥrā fīh al-sadd khawfan min mujāwazat al-ḥadd" (it is thus preferable to block the means [a reference to the juristic principle of preventing an evil before it happens] for fear of and to avoid a major sin).

26. "La shakk ann hādhā huwā al-iḥtiyāṭ."

27. For an erudite discussion of an exchange in Damascus, which elaborates further on the local Syrian reception of the sultanic order, see Meier (2015). Meier argues that it took a while to impose this measure and to create a uniform procedure for exchange (2015, 102). In Beirut, exchanges are few and far between; Meier mentions that in Damascus they were neither prevalent nor completely absent (personal communication, 2019).

Constricting Founders' Stipulations of Exchange. This favoring of perpetuating rather than increasing in administration appears in the precise ways of formulating stipulations of exchange and in restrictive readings of founder stipulations. The most "explicit" stipulation would be "On the condition that I can sell it and buy in its place an object that would be waqfed in eternity, like this object" (al-Basri 1936, 91). Eliminating the phrase "that would be waqfed" is permissible only based on *istiḥsān* (juristic preference), but not on strict analogy (al-Basri 1936, 92). However, dropping "and buy in its place" would invalidate the stipulation and the waqf because a stipulation of sale goes against the definition of the waqf (al-Basri 1936, 91).[28] However, in its "ideal" formulation, jurists read this stipulation literally: to them, this stipulation allows an exchange once. For more than one exchange, the stipulation needs to indicate that (Ibn ʿAbidin, *Ḥāshiya*, 3:388).

The question of who can carry out the exchange elicits even more restrictions. A stipulation that the founder can carry out an exchange does not transfer that right to the administrator after the death of the founder. One could argue that this stipulation belongs to the founder as administrator and could then be transmitted to future waqf administrators. However, jurists explain the basis of this right (and the restriction in this case) through the concept of agency, saying that if the founder names a particular person, this person is the founder's agent in that transaction, and this right cannot be transferred. Restrictions also extend to whether named persons can keep this right after the death of the founder (al-Basri 1936, 98). Such a named person cannot exchange the waqf after the death of the founder, unless the founder mentions that this right extends beyond his or her own death, because "they are like agents, and agency ends with death" (Ibn Nujaym, *Baḥr*, 5:223).[29] We can see here how exchanges are not only subject to stipulations, but that the stipulations themselves are then read restrictively and eventually result in the limiting of exchanges.

Defining Necessity. Jurists also restricted exchanges in the other case where such exchanges are allowed: necessity. As discussed above, in the case of necessity, the dominant opinion is that only the qadi can complete a waqf exchange. Furthermore, as mentioned above, al-Tarabulusi specifies that not any qadi can exchange a waqf—only the "qadi of heaven,"[30] known for his knowledge and uprightness

28. This same reasoning is repeated in Ibn ʿAbidin's nineteenth-century supercommentary (*Ḥāshiya*, 3:387)

29. This is the opinion of Abu Yusuf. Muhammad al-Shaybani considers the named person an agent of the poor (recall the discussion on chapter 2 on the qadi as representing the poor) and therefore the named person's agency does not end with the death of the founder (Ibn Nujaym, *Baḥr*, 5:222).

30. Being at the service of worldly powers seeking to legitimize themselves and their rule, qadis had a reputation of power-mongering and self-interest, and a Prophetic tradition sought to curb the eagerness of scholars to a judgeship career: "Of every three qadis, two are in hell." The third is the "qadi of heaven" that al-Tarabulusi was alluding to.

(*al-ʿilm wa al-ʿamal*), has this right (2005, 32). Such conditions on the person carrying out the exchange are mostly rhetorical, because establishing who is an upright qadi is far from obvious, yet these conditions signal the care with which such exchanges should be carried out and establish them as rather out-of-the-ordinary transactions.

The definition of *necessity* (*ḍarūra*) posed a challenge for jurists. As many modern scholars have pointed out, the answer to the question, What is necessity? is far from obvious (Illich 1992). After all, for most of the modern world, electricity is a necessity, or even a right that citizens demand of their governments, but this was not so for our medieval ancestors. Needs and necessities are products of social, economic, and technological conditions. Therefore, in the nineteenth century, when there might have been a necessity to exchange a waqf that became a swamp, modern technology might now allow for its drainage and subsequent use. Jurists addressed this relativism through the use of two temporal frames in the assessment of necessity: the present and the future. In the present, the waqf needs to be in a state that is completely unusable ("yakhruj ʿan al-intifāʿ biʾl-kulliyya") (Ibn Nujaym, *Baḥr*, 5:223). However, this is not enough to warrant exchange. It should also be impossible to repair the waqf, meaning that its future usability is also not guaranteed (Ibn Nujaym, *Baḥr*, 5:223). It is when the waqf is unusable in both the present and the future that necessity for exchange arises.

This condition (of complete unusability) then produces the need to define *use*, or *intifāʿ*, and its end, the limit beyond which an argument for the necessity of exchange arises. The reader will recall that the one of the most common definitions of *waqf* includes the gifting of an object's *manfaʿa* (yield or usufruct) to some charitable purpose. There must then be such yields for the waqf to achieve the goals of its founder. Jurists attempted to distinguish when necessity for exchange arises for different types of waqfed objects (Ibn Nujaym, cited in Ibn ʿAbidin, *Ḥāshiya*, 3:387). Land ceases to have usufruct when it cannot be cultivated or rented, or when its maintenance exceeds its revenue so that there are no yields that could benefit the waqf. The usability of a house comes into question when it is falling apart and becoming rubble, and nobody wishes to rent it. These criteria appear to be unambiguous cutting points, but their clarity can be questioned. Is the waqf considered usable if there remain only a few *para*s after repairs, a few *akçe*s, or a few *guruş*? For how many years should the administrator have attempted to rent the waqf's asset without success before concluding that it cannot be rented?[31] Jurists did not specify these details, but entrusted them to qadis, leaving some leeway in the assessment of necessity.

31. These discussions bring out the way natural disasters like plagues, earthquakes, and floods challenge the perpetuity of the res and the revenue of the waqf. However, given that many waqfs and institutions today have existed for hundreds of year, waqfs have been notably resilient.

Calculable Economic Benefit: Revenue, Size, Location, and Value

Although jurists left to qadis some appraisal of necessity, they provided very detailed instructions about how to appraise equivalence between exchanged properties and benefit for the waqf: "economic" factors determine the choice of the exchanged object. In his very short discussion of exchange, al-Khassaf brings in the example of a waqfed palm tree orchard whose trees had been uprooted and which had become a wasteland. In this case, he says, it is valid for the qadi to exchange it for another piece of land that is "more productive [*aʿwad*] and more advantageous [*aṣlaḥ*] for the beneficiaries" even if smaller (1999, 21). Economic rationality based on this calculation privileges yield as the highest principle, rather than size or value, for instance. Abstract calculation detaches the purpose of waqf from the particular object made into waqf. In such a formulation, the other "functions," such as purpose and the actual role of waqf in the urban fabric and the community, do not figure in the weighing of the various options for exchange. For instance, a soup kitchen provides for the poor of a certain neighborhood, so its transfer to a different area could be detrimental to the well-being of that neighborhood. However, such considerations do not enter into the assessment of an exchange.

Hilal al-Basri's discussion of exchange is much more expansive and brings up other criteria for comparing the waqfed land to be exchanged and its substitute. As discussed in the introduction, his discussion forms the backbone of al-Tarabulusi's waqf compendium, written six hundred years later, and together, these two manuals inform all subsequent sections on waqf exchanges in the fiqh. These discussions center on the *legal* validity of the content of the stipulation, the criteria of exchange. According to Hilal al-Basri, a founder who stipulates exchanging for a piece of land cannot exchange for a house. If she specifies that she is to exchange for a land in Basra, she cannot exchange it for a piece a land in any other place. Lest it be thought that these elaborations are actually about entrenching founders and their stipulations, one should note that al-Tarabulusi explains the reason behind the non-interchangeability of lands of two villages—and it is not that "because the founder stipulated so." It is because "the lands of villages vary in their provisioning and productivity" (al-Tarabulusi 2005, 32). Location matters also because of long-term calculations of economic benefit, "even if the new piece[32] is larger, more valuable, and because of the possibility of its [the waqf's] ruin in the worse-off of the two locations and its undesirability" (Ibn Nujaym, *Baḥr*, 5:223). Al-Tarabulusi adds yet another case to illustrate that the original and exchanged waqfed lands do not have to have the same tax status, arguing that there is no land without tax. Therefore, by this logic, type and location, but not tax status, are the criteria for assessing the validity of exchange. Location trumps both value

32. The word used is *al-mamlūka*, referring to the status of the land as freehold and not waqfed yet.

and revenue, which trumps size (and tax status) in assessing the exchanged parcels.[33] Ottoman jurists like Qınalızade generalize a rule that the exchanged objects have to be of the same kind (land for land, building for building) (Ibn ʿAbidin, *Ḥāshiya*, 3:388).

In these criteria of exchange, one can notice an attempt to remain as close as possible to the letter of the waqf deed and its original object. Waqf exchanges did not treat waqf principals as contingent and temporary assets that are used to generate maximum revenue by investing them in the most revenue-producing project possible. Such is the rhythm of the preindustrial world, not conscripted yet by the notion of progress and ever-increasing accumulation.

POST-TANZIMAT OTTOMAN BENEFIT: UPHOLDING PUBLIC UTILITY AND THE "WAQF'S BENEFIT"

The nineteenth century saw a reconfiguration of the concept of the waqf's benefit, not only because of changes within the shariʿa itself and its relationship to the state, but especially because of competing benefits introduced with the redefinition of the state and its role. Among these new competing benefits, a law of "expropriation," dated 11 March 1856 [4 B 1272], introduced the notion of a public utility (*manâfiʿ-i ʿumûmiyye*). I use scare quotes around the word *expropriation* because the law was not called the Expropriation Law (İstimlâk Niẓâmnâmesî) but had a much longer title: "Regulations about Lands to be Bought from their Owners against Proper Compensation in the Necessity [*lüzûm*] of the Sultanate's Planning of Matters Including Public Utility [*manâfiʿ-i ʿumûmiyye*]." It appears that the term *istimlâk*, or "expropriation," had not yet crystallized as a concept. Indeed, while Şemseddîn Sâmî's 1890 *Turkish Dictionary* includes the word and defines it in exactly the same terms as the title of the law (the state's voluntary or forced buying of a property for public utility), he actually notes that "even though it is correct language [*güzel bir lügat*], it is not Arabic." The concept, with its assumption of the state ("the Sultanate") being responsible for and carrying out works for public utility, seems then to have taken on this meaning in the nineteenth century. A new role of the modern state, the planning of cities that makes populations and spaces legible and governable, crystallizes with the solidification and creation of the term *istimlâk*.[34]

It is important to note that this does not mean that Islamic law did not conceive of such possibilities of expropriation.[35] In legal maxims manuals, a famous exam-

33. It seems that the real estate motto "Location, location, location" has been in vogue for longer than we realize.

34. See the work of James Scott (1998) on this project of the modern state to make people and spaces legible, and its failures.

35. I am thus compelled by Susan Reynolds's argument (2010) that the idea of taking individual property for the common good for compensation was widespread, contrary to the claim that it arose only with modern liberal democracy because under "feudalism" and "Oriental despotism" the feudal

ple of the principle that "private/particular harm should be borne to avert public/general harm" is that of a privately owned (*mamlūk*) wall that has tipped onto the collectivity's road (*ṭarīq al-ʿāmma*) and therefore presents a threat or blocks the road and should be demolished and removed at the expense of the owner to avoid general harm (*ḍarar ʿāmm*) (Ibn Nujaym, *Ashbāh*, 75). Similarly, a private individual can be forced to sell part of his or her land to make space for the widening of mosque (al-ʿAyni, *Ramz*, 1:348). These maxims and examples do not make clear which agency or person is in charge of ensuring the enlarging of these utilities or the safety of the streets. While jurists make the imam responsible for the rights of God and the collectivity and public benefit, rule before the nineteenth century was not governmentalized and such processes of expropriation were not a sole prerogative of the state.[36] Indeed, when there were no municipalities nor central planning authorities, many public utilities at the level of the neighborhood were provided by guilds, charitable foundations, and various individuals and communities, while the state provided the institutional framework of courts and the like.[37] Thus collectivities could themselves exercise powers of expropriation. In contrast, eminent domain and expropriations are now prerogatives of the state and used in the state's new purpose of "the welfare of the population, the improvement of its conditions, the increase of its longevity, health" through governing that relies in the particular dispositions of people and things (Foucault 1991, 100). The state now provides for the public, which necessitates sacrifices in the name of this very public utility, a facet of public benefit.

It might be worthwhile to probe a little further the meaning of *public* in public utility and public benefit. The term here summons the meaning "what is collective, or affects the interests of a collectivity of individuals" (Weintraub 1997, 5), rather than what is open and not hidden.[38] In that sense, the *public* in "public utility" seems to echo the meaning of collectivity summoned in the shariʿa concepts of "public benefit" (*maṣlaḥa ʿāmma*) and "public harm" (*ḍarar ʿāmm*) discussed

lord or ruler had absolute ownership and could take land at will, at any time and without reason or compensation. Yet, as I discuss in this section, there were some radical transformations of the way expropriation worked in the modern state, especially in the role the state has in these expropriations.

36. See Miriam Hoexter (1995) for an argument that the care of public benefit has always been conceptualized by Islamic political theorists as the responsibility of the imam/state. Note also that one of the main areas of contention with Solidere was whether the state delegated its power of expropriation to a private company, showing that in a neoliberal era, even such powers of the state are renegotiated and privatized.

37. See, for example, Marcus (1989, ch. 8).

38. The relation of these two meanings is far from clear, and so is their distinction. One might wonder if the notion of openness and visibility was derived from the notion of collectivity. In his genealogy of the use of the term *private*, Raymond Williams (1976) first traces it to religious orders that have withdrawn from public life (*deprived*). He notes that the "sense of secret and concealed both in politics and in the sexual sense of private parts" was later acquired (1976, 242). Its opposition to *public* only came later. I would like to keep this note in mind, because I will show later that the notion of public can evoke visibility and transparency.

above. However, there is another dimension to the notion of public utility: its relation to the state. The French legal tradition equivalent of public benefit, from which the Ottoman and Lebanese codes are derived, is *intérêt général*. In their genealogy of the term in French political and social theory, Pierre Crétois and Stéphanie Roza (2017) argue that the concept has been polysemic since its inception, without a stable social or juridical meaning, yet has served to mark a position or a political-philosophical thesis. The concept is thus used by liberal, republican, and egalitarian thinkers alike as a ground for critique or for an argument. An important use of the "intérêt général" was in relation to the state, demanding that it serve not only reasons of state or the interests of princes, but the interest of the people. The intérêt général became the "the conceptual knot that is the very object of the modern state and its law, its new horizon, and its new legitimacy" (Crétois and Roza 2017, 4). For Crétois and Roza, intérêt général is concerned with "overarching considerations based on the rationalization of social phenomena," whether enforced by the state or an agency. It is distinct from both the common interest, the intersecting interests of various individuals, and the "*intérêt public*," the interest of the state itself. These distinctions highlight two senses of *public* meshed together in English: the connection to the state and the collectivity. Yet, because the intérêt général has become the guiding principle of the state, it is adjudicated by the state. That is why, as may be recalled from chapter 2, under the Mandate, the *state* classifies certain amenities as *public utilities* (public needs that should be satisfied for the public good, not for profit) that are important to be fulfilled (and therefore not left to individual initiatives/effort/enterprise) and are best served if administered independently (Yakan 1963, 128). Therefore, a public utility in the modern sense is one that the state defines, for the benefit of the collective.

Waqf and Public Utility

After this detour that only begins to shed some light on the many complexities and specifics of "expropriation," "utilities," and the "public," it is time to analyze the effect that the introduction of a notion such as public utility, with the particular role of the state that it assumes, had on the notion of the waqf's benefit. Let us return, then, to our late Ottoman "law of expropriation."

The first article of this 1856 law already defines what counts as public utility: "the creation of hygiene and health establishments, the foundation of public schools whether by the Imperial government or by populations, the building of barracks, hospitals, water tanks for fires, fountains, sidewalks, rails, docks, harbors, canals to prevent the floods of rivers for navigation, the establishment of water pipes, the creation of promenades, public gardens, the construction and the widening of quays, markets, squares, and streets" (Young 1905, 127). Note that mosques and other prayer halls do not fall within this definition. We notice already the secularization of the role of the state and its withdrawal from the care for the afterlives of its subjects. In Beirut, expropriation law was heavily relied on when Ottomans set out to make the cities of the empire conform to the model of European cities, especially as Beirut was to become a showcase of Ottoman cities during the reign of Abdülhamid II (1876–1909) (Hanssen 1998, 44). For that reason, "urban renewal" became necessary: building new government offices, a municipality, and the opening and widening of new roads. The construction of such a project allows us to examine how the notion of public utility intersected with that of the waqf's benefit.

On Tuesday, 5 June 1894 [1 Z 1314], the municipality of Beirut destroyed a series of shops and buildings in order to widen the road leading from Bab Idris, the western gate of the city, to the government seat at the eastern "Saray" gate.[39] Among those, four shops were waqfs. The revenues of two of these shops supported the ʿUmari Mosque, located off the road that was widened. The rents of the two other shops supported the families of their founders. The expropriation law of 1879 [1296] required that owners be paid in full before proceeding to their eviction. From the court records, this seems to have been the case: the two administrators of the "family" waqfs came to court and bought assets for the waqf in exchange for the destroyed shops within a few months of the expropriation. This does not seem to be the case, however, for the ʿUmari's waqfs, which were administered by the Waqf Ministry in Istanbul through the waqf director of Beirut. The case of these two shops seems to have caused a great deal of tension between the local administrative council of Beirut and the Waqf Ministry, eliciting long and multiple communications involving not only the council and the Waqf Ministry but also the Ministry of Interior, the State Council, and the grand vizier.

At the crux of the dispute was the amount of compensation that the municipal council should pay the Waqf Ministry. The original shops were assessed to be worth a total of 70,000 piasters. This would have been a simple exchange, with the Waqf Ministry receiving the 70,000 piasters and then proceeding to buy another property in exchange. Trouble started when the ministry turned out to be the administrator of a bakery, a waqf for a different mosque, on the side of the widened street, that would therefore benefit from the widening. Beirut's administrative council proceeded to assess and impose on the bakery, that is, on the Waqf Ministry, some fees—as it did to all properties on either side of the road (to be attached to that bakery). These included an improvement tax (*şerefiye*), the price of the remainder of the parcel in front of it, as well as some fees for the execution of the road widening, totaling 11,441 piasters.[40] The Waqf Ministry, whose opinion the Ministry of Interior endorsed, argued that the leveling and paving of the street did not benefit the waqf (the bakery, that is) but actually harmed it. The

39. The information for this exchange is culled from documents included in BOA.ŞD 2289.36 and from the court records of waqf exchanges due to this expropriation, MBSS.S33/63.147 and 102.96. For more on the larger urban project, see Hanssen (2005, ch. 8; the street alignment project leading to this exchange is discussed on 216–21).

40. BOA.ŞD 2289/36/2.2.

Waqf Ministry was probably referring to the decrease in the exchange price of the waqf that the payment of the tax would cause (some 15 percent of the assessed value of the bakery), rather than any harm produced by the widening and paving of a street.

Yet, here again it is the arguments in the dispute that allow us to understand the changes in the grammar of benefit. Both ministries challenged the improvement tax and the widening of the road. Pitted against each other are "the waqf's benefit" and "public utility" (and thus, by extension, public benefit). The State Council avoided a direct assessment of the two benefits and instead argued based on a procedural issue: since all shops on the widened street paid these fees, the waqf could not be exempt. It therefore avoided making an explicit pronouncement on what mattered in the last instance, or on the relation of the waqf's benefit to public benefit. The State Council's decision did not explicitly appeal to any general rule or principle behind the equal treatment of all; however, one could maybe venture to argue that its position is based on the principle of the equality of all before the law, an important proclamation of the Tanzimat Edict.

MANDATE ARTICULATIONS: SUBORDINATING THE WAQF'S BENEFIT TO PUBLIC UTILITY

While Ottoman legislation and practice preserved the role of the state as a guarantor of both the benefits of the waqf and those of the "public," the French Mandatory power, which replaced the Ottoman state in Lebanon after World War I, presented itself, as discussed in chapter 2, as the necessary guarantor of the benefits of the various sects, but reserved for itself the right to intervene in waqf affairs for "reasons of public benefit." In the introduction to Decision 753 of 1921 on the administration of Islamic waqfs, the word *maṣlaḥa* is used six times in a two-page fourteen-point preamble.

Decision 753 introduced a benefit of a higher order than the waqf's benefit, now parochialized as part of "religious benefit" of a particular community within the nation. This ordering of rights does not mean that the "waqf's benefit" disappeared from legal reasoning. Even more, a memo on waqf leases which is part of the civil law of the State of Greater Lebanon, issued by the general secretary, the French officer Pierre Carlier, presents arguments using the concept of the "waqf's benefit" to justify the imposition of a fair rent (*ijārat al-mithl*)[41] on all waqf properties (Al-Mudiriyya al-ʿAmma li'l-Awqaf al-Islamiyya n.d., 43–44). The memo starts

41. As I mentioned at the beginning of this chapter, the concept of the waqf's interest appears also in rent discussions. I use here the French law on fair rent because it illustrates more starkly the way the waqf's interest continues to be used and in which grammar. Most commentaries in my library stipulate that waqfs should be rented at market value and for a maximum of three years to avoid a devaluing of their leases. Longer leases, like exchanges, were exceptional and to be decided by the qadis in individual cases. These, however, became very common (see, for example, Hoexter 1997). For a discussion of *ijārat al-mithl* in the Mamluk period, see Johansen (1988).

with a grand claim: the "scholars of Islam" have agreed that contracts with rents lower than the fair rent are void, because they harm the waqf. It buttresses this claim by citing an opinion by Ibn ʿAbidin, whose commentaries and fatwas were authoritative in the courts, as the reader may recall. The memo notes that Ibn ʿAbidin settled a dispute between an administrator and a qadi as to the legality of paying a rent lower than the fair rent by arguing that a contract below the fair rent was invalid. Finally, the memo advances "a general principle" from Islamic law, accepted in Islamic courts: the rent amount had to be for the "benefit of the waqf" and was thus obligatorily constrained by the fair rent. Hence, Carlier presents French Mandatory authorities as restoring the integrity of the Islamic legal tradition.[42] However, examining the logic of Carlier's argument attests to changes in the grammar of the "waqf's benefit." Although Muslim jurists reached similar conclusions requiring a fair rent for the benefit of the waqf, their discussion always addressed the stipulations of the founder (whether he or she had conditions about the rent); in Carlier's memo, the stipulations of founders are nowhere to be found, signalling the detachment of the waqf's benefit from its associated concepts of stipulations and necessity and its operation as a general principle.

This approach to waqf's benefit as a general principle reflects the different property regime and understandings of property and waqf that the French Mandate solidified. Reports of the French high commissioner to the League of Nations explicitly refer to waqfs as patrimony, as the totality of possessions of a community, thought of as real estate wealth that could be made to grow, if managed well: "Studies aimed to ensure the free circulation of waqf immovables, whose inalienability constituted an obstacle to the economic development of the country. They also aimed at improving the possibilities of the management and exploitation of the communities' patrimony" (Ministère français 1926, 106). Discussing some of the waqf legislation issued, the high commissioner highlights that it will allow "the rational development of land and provide better conditions for the management of the real estate capital that waqf immovables represent" (Ministère français 1926, 108). Here again, what is marshaled to explain these reforms and justify the intervention in waqf affairs is public benefit. Indeed, the French perceived these waqfs as "prominently harmful for public benefit, collective or individual" (Ministère français 1926, 106). The value of the individual endeavor of the founder, of bringing good deeds to its founder, along with the shariʿa purposes it embodies of preserving family and religion, for example, seem very far behind. This is an era of developing national economies and increasing real estate wealth.

French Mandate waqf legislation inverted what had been the dominant Ottoman paradigm throughout the four hundred years of Ottoman rule in the Arab provinces: the exceptionalism of exchanges, which required the approval of the sultan himself. Between 1921 and 1930, waqf legislation under the French Mandate

42. This is also the case in the introduction to Decree 753/1921.

centered on the exchange of waqf, encouraging and even forcing the exchange of waqfs for money in various cases. Decision 80/1926 forced the exchange of all waqfs having rights of usufruct that were inheritable (Article 4). The decision specified how these moneys were to be then reinvested, since these were exchanges. For the waqfs of the DGIW, it did not couple the exchange with the stipulations of the founders and allowed the use of the money for any purpose the Supreme Waqf Council approved. For "exempt" waqfs, those left to the administrators stipulated by founders, however, the stipulations of the founder would then reapply to the new waqf. However, Decision 3/1930 allowed any rights holder or beneficiary to exchange any waqf, except for "religious institutes" (Article 3), without further delimiting the use of the funds according to any stipulations. With Decision 3, after an "exchange," the waqf could simply end. Exchanges ceased to be exceptions bound by stipulations of founders and necessity, and, as importantly, eliminated the defining feature of Ottoman waqf—perpetuity.

POSTWAR RECONSTRUCTION: MARSHALING THE WAQF'S BENEFIT AGAINST PUBLIC BENEFIT

Despite all the legislation and practice that subsumed the waqf's benefit to new conceptions of property and to public benefit, the waqf's benefit remained a powerful reason that, even if used in its modern grammar (unhinged from stipulations and necessity), could challenge the very public benefit to which it is to be subsumed. I return now to the contradiction I described in the opening of this chapter, the exemption of some waqfs from expropriation in the reconstruction of downtown Beirut. This political, economic, and moral struggle centered on the concepts of "public benefit" and "waqf's benefit" and prevented the systematic dispossession of the DGIW from the city center. Such an exceptional episode does not deny the truth, extent, and violence of the dispossession that in reality did take place, but it does illustrate the incompleteness and contradictions that exist in the reasoning of modern states. This religious mobilization, with various members of the Muslim community speaking about the waqfs of the Muslim community, does not reflect any "weakness" of the state in Lebanon or its failure to create citizens more loyal to the state than to their sect. Nor does it reflect a religious resistance that adopts the sectarian logic of the state. Rather, by providing reasons that can win over "public benefit," reasons steeped in other benefits (the waqf's), this mobilization underscores both the constant battles that modern states wage to uphold the ideals they present and the tenacity of other traditions in interpellating citizens.

Explaining Waqf Exchange

The process of waqf exchange in the reconstruction of downtown Beirut since the early 1990s remains a quasi-mystery. The negotiations that occurred around waqf possessions in the reconstruction of Beirut's city center are almost absent in the numerous articles, books, dissertations, and research that the reconstruction triggered.[43] In the most detailed study of the waqfs in the process of reconstruction, Heiko Schmid (1997, 2002) places waqf exchanges within his analysis of how Solidere and Hariri managed to defeat the various opponents and visions for the city center: through force, bribery, compromise, political influence, and economic power.[44] He portrays the reconstruction process as a battle among actors mobilizing strategies and resources: the DGIW, churches, refugees, old tenants and owners, academics, architects, and planners. While the resistance of these various actors did have an effect on the original reconstruction and its plan—from modifications of the master plan to slowing the process, to various actors retaining some of their possessions—the story that Schmid tells is the story of dispossession, of Solidere proceeding with its plans. Instead, I think it is important to highlight the process that allowed the DGIW to keep real estate assets instead of shares. This episode may be thought of as insignificant if one approaches history from its end, if one of thinks simply of winners and losers, but it might help us question the narrative of the inevitability of neoliberal dispossession.

In Schmid's narrative, the story of waqfs in downtown Beirut is that of the triumph of neoliberalism, where their administrators initially refused expropriation but were then co-opted by different means. He distinguishes between Muslim and Christian reasons behind the refusals of expropriations in order to explain the different strategies Solidere and Hariri used to reach agreements with the two communities. The DGIW based its argument against expropriations on "religious reasons" (Schmid 2002, 238), while the Christian foundations echoed the opposition to the reconstruction as voiced by Christian lay leaders. Therefore, Schmid suggests, it was easier to curb the resistance of the Christian foundations through economic and symbolic retribution. Using big Christian families as contractors in the reconstruction "embedded" them in the reconstruction process. They then had "a strong influence on the religious decision-makers of their denominations and were able to break up the resistance" (2002, 239). Financial lures were also effective to tame the DGIW. "Far better compensation was unofficially granted to the religious foundations than to normal owners, anyway. Simultaneously, the areas around the places of worship were generously restored, in order to emphasize symbolically the role of the foundations in the city centre" (2002, 239). In addition, in both cases, Hariri "recruited supporters among the respective religious foundations" (2002, 239). Schmid does not explain how Hariri managed to do so or why these individuals supported the project, but given Hariri's wealth and his political power, one can imagine personal profit played a role. In Schmid's narrative, the DGIW originally resisted expropriation but the Sunni political and religious elites

43. See also the literature cited in note 1 of this chapter.

44. Leenders (2012, 58–64) also provides much detail about these processes even though his concern is not about the waqfs in particular but the process of expropriation.

eventually struck a deal that benefited them at the expense of the waqfs of the community's nonreligious patrimony.

Schmid's study is based on "action-oriented political geographical analysis that particularly tries to re- and deconstruct the different perspectives of the protagonists" (2002, 232). Because the author places emphasis on actors, history appears to be made by main characters, willful and woeful; "Hariri proved to be a clever strategist and superior tactician, understanding how to use his resources and power to resolve the conflict in his way" (2002, 238). Schmid also emphasizes the intent of actors, making assumptions about their desires and interests. The "main interest of the Christian and Muslim foundations," he argues, "was to maintain a symbolic representation of their religion in the city center of Beirut, in addition to mosques and church buildings" (2002, 236). The DGIW and the various churches appear as uniform bodies with clear motives. Because the actors are concerned with outcomes, Schmid's analysis treats arguments as *instruments* that various actors mobilize in a power struggle. The DGIW, for instance, "declined the expropriation for religious reasons," whereas their real motive and desire was to keep a symbolic presence. I raise these issues not to say that Schmid's analysis is incorrect; to the contrary, he actually forwards many of the issues at stake and the strategies at play. However, it is also important to acknowledge structural limitations and possibilities beyond the motives of actors and direct causes. Most importantly, however, we must recognize that religious reasons are more than just excuses; they stir feelings, galvanize subjects, and produce public debates. Here, therefore, I will not take these arguments to be epiphenomenal means, mere instruments to an end, but will approach them as logics embedded in traditions and representing ideals of life.

Marshaling the Waqf's Benefit

In trying to get a better sense of the negotiations and mobilizations surrounding waqf expropriations in the city center, I delved into the archives of the DGIW and of the newspapers of the period. The story turned out to be more complicated than the one told by Schmid. The co-optation of the DGIW by Solidere after its initial resistance to expropriation did not go unnoticed. A popular mobilization, aligning political opponents of the grand mufti, religious scholars, and Sunni Beirutis, drew on the old grammar of the waqf and engrained notions of waqf inalienability. In the name of the waqf's benefit and religious benefit, the mobilization stopped the arrangement between the Sunni political and religious elite to expropriate all the DGIW's waqfs (save religious buildings) for Solidere shares, ultimately allowing the DGIW to retain valuable real estate in the city center.

At the beginning of 1994, a short news brief buried in the local pages informed readers that the members of parliament of the Jamaʿa Islamiyya[45] had issued a

45. The Islamic Group, discussed in chapter 2.

statement saying that the "obscurity and vagueness that surround the fate of the waqf parcels in downtown Beirut are the reason behind the turmoil around them, regarding the good intent, vigilance/jealousy, or even unstated intentions" (*Annahar*, 14 January 1994, 6). The brief refers to the many questions and the commotion surrounding the waqfs of the DGIW in downtown Beirut (see, for example, *Annahar*, 30 April 1992, 4; 25 May 1992, 6; 15 December 1992, 7; 31 December 1992, 13). However, instead of blaming a certain party or gesturing to the often-used *corruption*, the Jama'a brought up not an action or a decision but an attitude and a characteristic of the process of decision-making about waqfs and their exchange: the disclosure of information. In this, we can note the association of "public" with visibility. They refrain from pointing fingers, but their declaration is an invitation to a more "open" and transparent waqf administration.

These accusations of lack of transparency echoed many observations in my notebook, which had, at that time, led me to write: "The DGIW operates through opacity." Indeed, the DGIW does not publish annual (or other types of) reports, nor does it distribute them.[46] Security guards strictly regulate access to its offices because they are part of Dar al-Fatwa, where the mufti holds office. In addition, although the land registry is public and one can request a list of all parcels any person owns, I was denied the request for such a list for the DGIW because the "approval of the DGIW is required." I encountered that opacity in action as I was trying to do research at the DGIW. I was allowed access only to the Ottoman record of waqf deeds, which seemed harmless, far from contemporary debates on the exchanges with Solidere or any claims of "corruption."[47] Therefore, when I asked to see the file of one of the family waqfs involving a lawsuit with the DGIW, I was shown the file in one of the cupboards in the director's office: the issue is so sensitive that the file remains under the protection of the director and is inaccessible even to DGIW employees. That was also the fate of minutes of meetings of waqf committees: they were sitting in a cupboard. The hidden geography of the DGIW also included an archive in the basement, locked and inaccessible. The opacity that the DGIW sustains reflects its uneasy position between the state and the Muslim community, bound as it is to both public benefit and the community's benefit, as we shall see.[48]

The conflicting position of the Lebanese religious leadership, including the mufti, between state and community is one that the leaders themselves

46. I was able to get hold of a single report of the activity of the DGIW in the form of a booklet published during the civil war (Al-Mudiriyya al-'Amma li'l-Awqaf al-Islamiyya 1982).

47. Because of a myopic vision of history echoing nationalist histories that place the Ottoman past in the prehistory of Lebanon as a nation-state, Ottoman records are thought to bear no connection to the present. Indeed, with the radical changes the French introduced, crucially the new land survey, mapping nineteenth-century waqf is a complicated (but not impossible) task (see for e.g. Rustom 2012).

48. As the brief published by the Jama'a Islamiyya suggests, the opacity also raises suspicion of corruption and mismanagement of these vast resources controlled by the DGIW.

acknowledge. The grand mufti, the "religious head" of the Muslims (a 1967 revision of his title of the "religious head of the Sunni Muslim community," as Decree 18/1955 had defined him), along with the religious representatives of the various communities to the state, explicitly defined public benefit and the benefits of their communities as separate.[49] On an August night in 1991, the acting grand mufti, Muhammad Rashid Qabbani; the Metropolitan of the Greek Orthodox Church in Beirut, Bishop Elias Audi; and the Maronite Archbishop of Beirut, Bishop Khalil Abi Nadir attended a dinner hosted by Tammam Salam, a prominent Beiruti leader.[50] They discussed the reconstruction of downtown Beirut and said they "sought public benefit, in addition to preserving the existence of the waqfs that belong to their communities and institutions" (*Annahar*, 17 August 1992). We have here two benefits against each other: the "public" benefit and the benefit of the (religious) community. Herein lies the conundrum for these men: they stand in a position where they need to preserve both. As heads of their communities, they are accountable to preserve the benefits of their community and its waqfs. As state agents, they are supposed to uphold the public benefit. While the Lebanese constitution protects the various religious communities and their benefits, it also places public order above religious interest (Article 9).[51] The position of these leaders within the state and their commitment to uphold public benefit subjects them to the suspicion of both state and community.

As discussed in chapter 2, the waqfs of the DGIW fall between public utilities and collective private goods of the Muslim community. Because the DGIW is part of the state apparatus, waqfs can be constructed as part of public funds (*māl ʿāmm*). However, because Decree 753 defines them as the patrimony of the Muslim community, they belong to the "private" affairs of the community. Whether one considers them to be public goods or the property of the Muslim community, waqfs were the object of an act of "commoning" (Harvey 2012, 73).[52] David

49. The Shiʿi official representative was not present because there are no Shiʿi waqfs in the city center, reflecting the small number of the Shiʿa in Beirut in the nineteenth century. See Fawaz (1983) for the religious composition of the city. This did not stop a symbolic battle over whether an uncovered religious shrine was Sunni or Shiʿi. See al-Harithy (2008).

50. Salam became an MP in 1992 and 1996, and he was then the director of the Islamic Charitable Association (al-Maqasid), one of the oldest Muslim associations in Beirut. The association built a network of modern Muslim schools in Beirut, starting in the late nineteenth century, and it is responsible for the Muslim cemeteries in Beirut. On the rise of the Salams, see Johnson (1986). On the Maqasid, see Schatkowski (1969) and Shibaru (2000).

51. The text of the Article states: "Freedom of conscience is absolute. In assuming the obligations of glorifying God, the Most High, the State respects all religions and creeds and safeguards the freedom of exercising the religious rites under its protection, without disturbing the public order. It also guarantees the respect of the system of personal status and religious interests of the people, regardless of their different creeds."

52. As I mention in footnote 5 above, while this opposition mobilized Muslims as Muslims, the question of whether this mobilization reproduced subjects as members of a sect rather than as citizens

Harvey distinguishes between public spaces and public goods on the one hand and commons on the other. While public goods and utilities are provided by the state and are open, commons can be privately owned and exclusive. What renders them commons is their summoning the energies of their users into their creation, shaping, and perpetuation. Whether Muslim waqfs belong to the state-connected "public" goods might be a matter of contestation; however, they are undoubtedly commons. It is important to note that waqfs are not necessarily exclusive—in fact, shops and rooms waqfed for the benefit of various Islamic charitable purposes were rented on the real estate market to Christians and Muslims alike. Furthermore, the revenues of these waqfs founded by Muslims and dedicated to the poor of Beirut were distributed to people in need regardless of religion. As the fiery debates within the Sunni Muslim community show, the waqfs of the DGIW in downtown Beirut were a common not as in "a particular kind of thing, asset or even social process, but as an unstable social relation between a particular self-defined social group and those aspects of its actually existing or yet-to-be-created social and/or physical environment deemed crucial for its life and livelihood" (Harvey 2012, 73). The waqfs represented the symbolic existence of the community as such, and their expropriation provoked a heated debate between various groups of Sunni Muslims, each marshaling the waqf's benefit within a different grammar.

The opposition to the possibility of expropriation marshaled the concept of the waqf's benefit as described in the first section: in conjunction with the stipulations of the founder and as an exception to the logic of preservation of waqfs. Opening the debate on the last day of the year in 1992, the Association of the Azhar Graduates in Lebanon called for the "preservation of waqfs in downtown Beirut . . . and their development according to applicable regulations, while respecting the founder's stipulations" (*Annahar*, 31 December 1992). A few months later, the Association for the Preservation of the Qur'an also made a statement that it would "work to preserve the Islamic waqf properties in Beirut totally, in terms of their limits and location, without any change or exchange. It will not accept any attempts at harming, decreasing, or changing the waqfs or their locations" (*Annahar*, 28 July 2007). We see here arguments echoing the logic of preserving waqfs as per the wills of the founders, rather than seeing in the expropriations a possibility to incur *further* benefit for the waqf; as al-Basri stated, "Waqf is no business" (1936, 95). Coinciding with the height of the revival, this is a return to the old grammar, which had been abandoned in the French legislation that liberated the benefit of the waqf from stipulation and necessity. Indeed, based on the French-era regulations discussed above, the DGIW could actually exchange these waqfs for cash.

is the subject of another work. My preliminary answer, as might be apparent from my use of a framework of commoning, is that it is not, given that it involved a grassroots mobilization against the Sunni elites in the state and used arguments from the tradition, which the state had marginalized.

The DGIW responded using the same rhetoric, but it marshaled the waqf's benefit within the grammar of the modern state, a logic that the Ottomans had introduced and the French enshrined. In a published article, the DGIW used the waqf's benefit as an abstract principle: "The responsibility for the Islamic waqfs in Lebanon falls on the Supreme Islamic Legal Council,[53] which has previously taken decisions with regard to waqfs in Beirut's central district so as to fulfill *Islamic benefit* and to preserve the waqf parcels" (*Annahar*, 13 January 1994; italics added). The council then asserted its independence and autonomy. It is true that it is part of the state, but its allegiance also cleaves to the shariʿa. The Supreme Islamic Legal Council "takes its decisions after examining the waqf issue from all its angles and adopting a sound position that fulfills *the waqf's benefit* . . . and accords with the shariʿa rules and the highest *Islamic benefit*" (*Annahar*, 13 January 1994, 6; italics added). We see here the waqf's benefit detached from the legal edifice that produced it, the stipulations of founders, and necessity; and the rise of the notion of an "Islamic benefit" that is distinct from the public benefit preserved by the state.

These statements echo the justification of the preservation of the waqfs from within state law and with the new place of the waqfs under the secular architecture. In 1977, Mufti Qabbani, who was then the DGIW director, argued when the Public Works Ministry attempted to take over war-damaged waqfs: "The waqf parcels are not the private property of a single individual, but they are the property of the whole community [*ṭāʾifa*]. Consequently, they have the character of public utility [*lahā ṣifat al-manfaʿa al-ʿāmma*], and therefore cannot be sold" (quoted in *Al-Akhbar*, 2 February 2010, 3). He then cited the article from the Real Estate Code that affirms the inalienability of waqf before concluding, "This is the rule of the *sharʿ* and the law." Contrary to Schmid's argument, the mufti justifies the inalienability of waqfs through an argument of public utility and not by reverting to the legal determinations of the shariʿa; he does not bring anything outside of state law to make his argument for the inalienability of waqfs.

Furthermore, while the critiques of the DGIW and the waqf expropriations used the waqf's interest in the grammar of late Ottoman Ḥanafī tradition, the grand mufti was speaking a different language, appealing to the waqf's interest in a grammar made possible by the architecture of state, law, and religious community instated with the Mandate. The secular configuration opens a different grammar for mobilizing against an expropriation done in the name of public benefit. Because the constitution guarantees the sects and their benefits, and Decree 753 "religious benefit," the grand mufti called on this "religious benefit" and equated it with "public benefit." Rather than an individual endeavor confronting the collective good promoted by the Ottoman state, waqfs now served the "religious benefit"

53. After the DGIW's administrative committee (*majlis idārī*) approves the exchanges, this is the organ within Dar al-Fatwa that gives the final approval of exchanges. Yet, in the case of the Solidere waqfs, it is not clear that this procedure was followed.

of that community, a benefit that the state is supposed to guarantee. The grand mufti, like the Supreme Islamic Legal Council, introduced the notion of a religious benefit that is distinct from the waqf's benefit and public benefit. However, the situation is more complicated than the mufti's argument suggests because Decree 753 distinguishes between the waqfs as the property of the community and a higher public benefit and its associated public domain. The mufti's jump from the community to the public is not obvious. In addition, even immovables belonging to the public domain can be sold. Crucially, other state-issued regulations allow the exchange and alienability of waqfs, when, as we described in the first section, the *sharʿ* itself allows for exchanges based on stipulations and necessity. The grand mufti thus spoke in a grammar that tied the waqf's benefit to *religious* benefit (that of the Sunni Muslim community), playing on these dual commitments of the state to the sects and the larger national public good.

The New Logic of Exchange

Beyond these discourses about benefit, what did in fact happen to the DGIW waqfs in the city center? The opacity surrounding the exchanges and deals between the DGIW and Solidere fueled intense speculations and accusations, which continue up to this day. From "The Corrupt: The Grave Seller" (al-Nusuli 2010) to "Dar al-Fatwa: The Required Corruption and Reprehensible Squander" (*Al-Akhbar*, 2 February 2010), newspaper articles and online posts continue to point fingers to the DGIW, Dar al-Fatwa, and the mufti. The press used the mufti's own statements about the inalienability of waqf in 1977 to discredit the course of action on waqfs in the 1990s reconstruction of the city center. In one of the many articles on Solidere that Al-Akhbar periodically releases in line with its political opposition to Hariri, titled "Dar al-Fatwa committed a monumental real estate massacre" (*Al-Akhbar*, 2 February 2010) turns to the Sunni religious establishment. Among its crimes, the article declares, Dar al-Fatwa merged and apportioned waqfed parcels, relinquished most of the fifty-six waqfed parcels it owned in downtown Beirut, subdivided and sold waqfed parcels, including a cemetery,[54] and sold the air rights (*amtār hawāʾ*) above the newly built al-Amin Mosque.[55]

Comparing the list of waqfed parcels in downtown Beirut that were under the supervision of the DGIW in 1989 and today shows much less of a massacre. The

54. The Suntiyya cemetery has been the center of a controversy of its own (see *Annahar*, 4, 7, 9, and 12 July 2006). Like all of Beirut's cemeteries, it is under the supervision of the Maqasid rather than the DGIW.

55. *Air rights* refers to the square footage that urban regulations allow for a certain parcel based on factors of exploitation. As a mosque, al-Amin did not use up all the legally allowed square footage, and so it "sold" these rights to build a certain volume (air rights) to be transferred to another parcel. This practice is not allowed in Lebanese urban and building regulations and would have been possible only because the whole downtown was considered a single parcel for the purpose of calculating total square footage, which Solidere then distributed according to a master plan.

number of parcels quoted in the newspaper reflects the number of entries in the 1993 DGIW-produced "Table of Waqf Parcels [ʿ*aqārāt*] in the City Center." Yet, more than a third of these (twenty-two, if one is conservative) are shops in the old suqs and khans (where they constituted less than 5 percent of the value of these parcels), and two more were buildings slated for demolition (and were not even open for recuperation) in Solidere's master plan.[56] A further thirteen were religious buildings that were originally or eventually excluded from the expropriation scheme. The DGIW then "owned" around nineteen parcels and parts thereof in downtown Beirut that could be subject to exchange.[57] The "presence" of Islamic waqfs was not in fact as prominent as portrayed by detractors of the then Hariri-aligned DGIW and imagined by Sunni Beirutis nostalgic for a Sunni Beirut past. However, it is worth mentioning that back then, like today, even if these parcels were not numerous, they had high resale value and generated considerable rents for the DGIW. A list of current waqfs shows that all the religious buildings remain, and seven of the nineteen immovables are still in the hands of the DGIW. How did the exchange happen, and was it in the benefit of the waqf?

After the grassroots mobilization against the expropriation, between 1995 and 1997, the DGIW struck deals with Solidere to recuperate some of its waqfs. The parcels recuperated were the ones where the DGIW was the biggest or sole owner and that held most potential for redevelopment: buildings where war damages were minimal and unbuilt parcels of land, which under Solidere's bylaws could not be recuperated. The dollar value of these seven parcels, appraised by committees of judges, was twice the dollar value of the remaining thirty-four parcels (since there were thirteen religious buildings that were eventually excluded from exchange). These remaining parcels were given up as a lump sum, rather than through individualized exchanges, as we shall see.

While exchanges in downtown Beirut resembled earlier exchanges in the importance given to the value of the parcels and in the use of a monetized assessment, they were not done on a one-to-one basis. In earlier expropriations, as we have described, administrators, with the approval of qadis, compensated for, then exchanged, each waqfed asset for another asset that was for the "benefit of the waqf." In the case of Solidere, exchanges took the form of a monetized debt swap. Monetization was always a necessary stage in every waqf exchange, since waqfs were assessed a monetary value during exchanges. The Ottoman reforms started a different process that made waqf revenues fungible (mutually identical and interchangeable): the waqf revenues of the seized waqfs were centralized into one fund at the Waqf Ministry and spent irrespective of the stipulations of each waqf's founder. In the nineteenth-century exchange I described above, despite this revenue fungibility, waqf exchanges were individualized: done by a qadi on

56. For a study of the replacement of these old suqs by new malls, see Hourani (2012).

57. There were however other waqfs, mostly family waqfs under the administration of the founders' families, which the DGIW was not in charge of.

a one-to-one basis and registered as such in the shariʿa court registers. In the 1990s, the fungibility of waqfs reached a different level as even individualized waqf exchanges became superfluous.

Indeed, a former DGIW director explained that he hired an accounting firm to settle the question of the city center waqfs and Solidere. The accounting firm compiled tables of credit and debit. The "credit" tables include the monetized assessment of what the DGIW owns—for instance, shares of parcels, waqfed shops, and apartments. The "debit" tables include the monetized assessment of what the DGIW owes: the amounts due to recuperate some of these expropriated waqfs, the rights of others to the assets of the DGIW (servitudes and shares) that Solidere paid for, dues to Solidere for infrastructural works (10 percent of the value of the parcel), and any cost Solidere expends on the assets of the DGIW (for restoration, for instance). Therefore, a waqf that the DGIW owned (say, two hundred shares out the 2,400 that make up parcel Marfaʾ 89/11) was not exchanged for an object of equivalent value. Instead, the accounting company added the amounts Solidere owed to the DGIW for expropriating all its waqfs and subtracted from them the amounts the DGIW owed to Solidere according to the debit tables. Adding up the various amounts due from and owed to the DGIW made the parcels fungible, where all that mattered was the balance. The two hundred shares went toward a lump sum that the DGIW virtually received in exchange for expropriating that waqf, which the DGIW then used towards the total amount it owed Solidere. Fungibility expanded to obliterate one-on-one exchanges, even exchanges for cash, as allowed by the Mandate-era legislation. The exchange therefore embodied the modern understanding of waqf as real estate wealth geared towards growth rather than preservation as per the will of the founder. While the DGIW did not preserve the benefit of each and every waqf, one can construct its preservation of the most valuable parcels as a preservation of a collective Islamic benefit now operating disjointed from the shariʿa defined concepts of founders stipulations and necessity but joined with state and DGIW- mandated general requirements and understandings of necessity.

CONCLUSION

As we saw in this chapter, between Tante Inʿam's reproach "They sold the Muslims' waqfs" and the DGIW's announcement that "all the DGIW waqfs will be returned" lies a much more complex reality. Tante Inʿam and the opponents to the 1990s deal struck between the DGIW and Solidere to expropriate the DGIW waqfs in the city center were drawing on notions of the inalienability of waqf that required their preservation as per the stipulations of their founders and allowed for their exchange in exceptional circumstances of dire necessity. Such notions continue to exist in the discourses of scholars trained in the tradition and embodied in older generations familiar with waqfs as inalienable eternal endeavors. Yet, this was not the grammar dominant in the law since the French Mandate and not the grammar that the DGIW used to challenge these expropriations, which were legally permissible according to modern state law, if not the shariʿa. Instead the mufti and the DGIW marshaled a notion of the "Islamic interest," which the modern Lebanese state is bound to preserve in its constitution. Despite the subordination of this religious benefit to a larger public benefit, the grassroots mobilization and the challenges that Solidere faced to its claim of working for the public benefit allowed the DGIW to preserve some of its waqfs—even through the new grammar of waqf benefit, abstracted from stipulations and necessity.

The modern state subordinated individual waqfs to the logic of improvement, even while the subordination of the waqf's benefit to public utility continues to be a subject of contention and struggle. In early nineteenth-century Ottoman Beirut, the waqf's benefit was a concept used in conjunction with the stipulations of the founders to assess whether exchanges based on necessity were fair for the waqf. Each waqf exchange was assessed and effected individually, and each was an exception that the sultan had to approve. The Ottoman state's introduction of the concept of public utility, coupled with the state's duty to preserve these individual acts done according to the shariʿa, created deadlocks that resulted in endless lawsuits.

The colonial state resolved these conflicts and subordinated the waqf's benefit to a public benefit that was the state's duty to maintain. When waqfs became constructed as real estate wealth, the waqf's benefit became an individual goal guiding the administration of waqfs. Instead of seeking the preservation of each waqf as its founder created it, legislation encouraged exchanges for the waqf's benefit. The waqf's benefit was decoupled from founders' stipulations and necessity, and made to be what guides the logic of exchange. While the Mandate legislation subsumed the concept of the "waqf's benefit" to the grammar of the secular architecture, tied to both religious and public benefit, one should not conclude that the new grammar now determines the terms of the debates on waqf and that Muslim scholars simply adopted the new grammar. This became particularly apparent in 1991, when Solidere expropriated owners in exchange for shares in the company, to the owners' great dissatisfaction. After an outcry about the role of the DGIW to preserve waqf and religious benefit, the DGIW was able to marshal the concept of the "waqf's benefit" in these particular exchanges to refuse the exchange of parcels instead of shares and therefore to escape expropriation. Some of these older grammars continue to exist and reappear, to great effect.

Conclusion

"Tax the Waqfs" (*ḍarība ʿalā al-awqāf*). This was one of the slogans spray-painted in Beirut's city center during one of the largest uprisings—if not the largest—in the history of the Lebanese nation. On 17 October 2019, demonstrations erupted in Beirut, protestors burning tires and expressing anger at yet another tax imposed on the general population in an attempt to reduce the budget deficit. Such a tax fell in line with the general fiscal strategy of the government; it avoided measures that would target the rich and members of the political class or the widespread shady deals that divert state funds into private pockets. Within days, the uprising had reached over 1.2 million people of the 5 million estimated inhabitants and the majority of the Lebanese territory. The chants, signs, and graffiti have led commentators (e.g., Majed and Salman 2019) to term this a class uprising, or more specifically, an uprising against the neoliberal model that has led to one of the highest rates of inequality in the world, exacerbated by the government's fiscal policies (Salti and Chaaban 2010; Salti 2015; Assouad 2018).

Shared struggles with poverty and precarity had brought together a notably fragmented society, and the protest in its early days was remarkable in its "color": the red, white, and green of the Lebanese flag.[1] Absent were the yellows, oranges, blues, and greens of the various parties. A major discourse of the protestors in the first month of the demonstrations was that of the unified Lebanese, who are now beyond "sectarianism." "You are sectarianism and we are coexistence" (*antum*

1. I say "early days" because around the third day, Hizbullah encouraged its supporters to withdraw from the protests.

al-ṭāʾifiyya wa naḥnu al-ʿaysh al-mushtarak)[2] read one banner, while another described the uprising as a "revolution against sectarianism." Protestors addressed politicians by telling them that the Lebanese have woken up and will not be dragged into the sectarian logic that divides them against their (class) interest and reproduces the wealth of political and religious leaders. This discourse portrays the Lebanese before the revolution as identifying first and foremost with their sect, since sect was the main axis for access to resources and jobs, especially with public offices and civil servant positions apportioned via sectarian proportional representation in the consociational political model.

Amidst these very broad unifying statements framed in two of the most widespread idioms of critique in Lebanon, inequality and sectarianism, it might be puzzling to see such a specific call to tax a little known institution like the waqf. Yet, I suggest that this call echoes these concerns of the protestors, illustrating also many of the arguments that this books has put forward. As a plea for taxation, the graffiti first denounces the inequality produced by the fiscal privileges afforded to waqfs. But as a demand to tax *religious* nonprofits or property, it also points to the support of religion by the state, and can be read as a critique of the breach of (or an invitation to reconsider) the secular principle of separation of religion and state. Finally, it unravels popular conceptions of waqf as imbricated with and perpetuating sectarianism. Let me elaborate.

"Tax the Waqfs" echoes the many calls to "Tax the Rich" in the worldwide revolts against rising inequality. The graffiti can appear as a critique of the neoliberal model that leaves the provision of education, poverty relief, and other social services to "civil society" and "nonprofits" and as a call for a welfare state that provides these services to its citizens. By revoking tax exemptions, which also indirectly subsidize many of the services these religious institutions provide (like schooling), the state would be filling its coffers and itself providing these necessities. In Lebanon, such a call might be surprising given the lack of trust in "the state," the corruption accusations charged at the government, the scandals of ministers approving unnecessary or unsound projects for a cut of the profits, and the appointment of employees in state agencies as a way to reward supporters. Yet, combined with the revolutionary demand of changing the whole political class (*kellon yaʿne kellon*), one can read the call as part of an agenda for a welfare state.

However, the graffiti does specify: "Tax the *Waqfs*," and it was sprayed on both the al-Amin Mosque, the largest congregational mosque in the city, built in the 2000s during the reconstruction of the city center and the adjacent Maronite

2. The expression *coexistence* comes from the Lebanese Constitution's preamble, which declares, "There is no legitimacy to any authority contradicting the charter of coexistence." The question of coexistence forms a major trope of political discourse in Lebanon, especially after the end of the war of 1975–1990, when the new national pact that ended the war was termed "mīthāq al-ʿaysh al-mushtarak" (the pact of coexistence).

cathedral, the Saint-George, dating back to the nineteenth century.[3] It targets the waqfs as part of "religion." But it also leaves it open whether the waqfs should be taxed as religious property (like other private property), whose owner ("the religious community" or sect) should pay taxes; or whether waqfs should be taxed as moral persons (like nonprofits) that are not considered to provide a public good worthy of exemption (because religion is a private good); or finally whether waqfs stand here as religious institutions, like the DGIW or the Maronite Church, which are autonomous from the state. Despite that ambiguity, in all these readings, religious property or the provision of religious space and service appear as private (individual or group) endeavors that should not be assisted by the state (through exemptions)—suggesting perhaps that tax exemptions stand in the way of a secular government because they constitute state support of religion.

Yet, as this book has argued, the very definition of waqf as the religious property of a religious community and its cordoning off as part of the personal-status law of each community is itself part of the secular configuration in Lebanon (the architecture of state, law, and religious community). It is a reminder that, contrary to the ideal of separation common in popular discourse, secular states constantly interfere in defining and regulating religion. This is further confirmed in the tax exemptions afforded to religious organizations in states taken as secular, like France and the United States. There, depending on the place of religion in the state, they are at times framed as exceptions to the secular principle or an extension of it. In France, for example, churches that are recognized by the state as private religious associations benefit from tax exemptions, can receive assistance from municipal governments to build houses of worship, and are allowed to use public space for worship (Bowen 2008, 19).[4] According to a 1987 law, gifts made to religious associations receive tax exemptions, as these associations provide "a general public service" (Asad 2006, 506). In the United States, religious organizations are often considered charitable foundations, profiting from the general presumption of public benefit that accrues to trusts for religious purposes.[5] In US tax

3. For excellent studies of the politics of the construction of the mosque and its relation to the church, see Rustom (2011); Mermier (2015); Vloeberghs (2016).

4. I use France as an example since it is an important referent for Lebanon because of the French Mandate. Not all religious associations are given legal recognition by the French state: Jehovah's Witnesses, for example, were not recognized for a long time because they do not conform to the (Catholic) model of what counts as religion for the French republic ("a liturgy, performed inside a familiar sacred place once a week, with teachings intended to guide private life") (Bowen 2008, 18–20).

5. For religious trusts to count as charitable foundations that are tax-exempt, they have to benefit the public. Thus, famously, a trust that benefited cloistered nuns was not considered charitable by British courts, because the public could not benefit from their prayers by attending mass, and prayers were not considered to be a tangible benefit. On that example, see Lundwall (1994, 1359–60). However, generally, the presumption is that religious organizations benefit the public, unless flagged otherwise, although in certain places like Australia religious organizations now have the burden to prove that they benefit the public (see Harding 2008).

law, for example, rental income of religious institutions, which is mostly how waqf income is generated, is not taxable.[6] In addition, for policy-makers and lawyers who take separation at face value, exemption from taxation creates more entanglement as exemption only requires the state to define religion, whereas taxation would require a much more involved valuation.

But the graffiti, in criticizing exemption as state support for religion, is not only an exhortation for the state not to support religion, but is also a plea to tax *religious* property or organizations. In the realm of taxation and economy, the call for the privatization of religion does not appear as a demand of separation of religious and public funds, but rather of flows of funds from religious institutions to state coffers through taxation. In the graffiti, there seems to be less concern with separating religion and state, and even a call for state interference in religion.

Besides its call for circulation of funds from religion to state, "Tax the Waqfs" can also be read in another sense—as a critique of political consociationalism because state provision of services would decrease the reliance of citizens on the services provided by the religious-political elites of the consociational regime. Taxing the waqfs would cut into the financial power of the religious institutions in charge of these waqfs, the assumption here being that these religious institutions are imbricated with the political class.

However, as we saw earlier in the book and above, these fiscal privileges are not inherently the product of political consociationalism. They are carryovers from the Ottoman state's nineteenth-century reforms, which created the Waqf Ministry and seized much of the income of many waqfs. At the time, the tax exemption of these waqfs was an effect of their transformation into public assets, especially as their incomes were captured by the Ministry of Finance and used for various state expenses. The French Mandatory power moved the Waqf Ministry to the margins of the state, transforming it into a public authority named the Directorate General of Islamic Waqf (DGIW), which had its financial independence but was attached to the Prime Minister. The tax exemptions were carried over from the Waqf Ministry to the DGIW. However, now the incomes of the waqfs did not go into state coffers but to the DGIW and, by extension, to the "Muslim community." Other state apparatuses and other religious communities, which did not receive the same exemptions, challenged these tax exemptions under the civil state time and again. In the 1950s and 1960s, they argued that the financial independence of religious communities from the state makes these waqf directorates not part of the state, and they should thus not benefit from the exemptions that accrue to "public" entities. However, in the 1990s, the argument against these Ottoman carry-over

6. One can contrast the American model of secularism with the French model of secularism as to the role of religion in the public sphere. The French model does not consider religion a public good and requires keeping religion outside the public sphere. Any state funding or tax exemptions granted to religious institutions are construed as exceptions to the absolute neutrality of the state (Asad 2006, 504–8).

exemptions based on the privatization of religious communities was dropped. Instead, using arguments about equality and justice among religious communities, similar exemptions were extended to the waqfs of all religious communities. Therefore, it was again the secular principle of equality that served as the reason for these tax exemptions, with the assumption that these waqfs were deserving of exemptions because they served the public or because religion is a public good.

REMAKING THE WAQF IN LEBANON AND BEYOND

Despite the fact that the tax exemptions of the waqf are not a result of political consociationalism, the graffiti's targeting of waqfs and their tax exemption as a symptom of sectarian ills confirms an argument of this book: that the waqfs in Lebanon have followed the state's architecture of religion, state, and law; they have been, in many ways, "sectarianized." In public discourse (like the graffiti) and in institutional settings, waqfs are today associated with the various "sects" (*ṭāʾifa*s) defined in the constitution.[7] As we saw in the example of the Sunni Muslim community, they have come to stand, as a whole, for the community's patrimony that helps fund education and ritual and reproduce the community. Waqfs today are not simply individual Muslims' endeavors that serve the founders' worldly interests and bring them rewards in their afterlife, as they had been in late Ottoman Beirut. Since the birth of the French Mandatory Lebanese republic, the Muslim community came to be characterized as one "community" among others that make up the national body politic and that are defined by the civil state. Muslims were no longer simply represented by the Ottoman state as part of the umma that represents true religion and could include all humanity. Defined in law collectively as the religious property of the Muslim (Sunni) "sect," waqfs reproduce Muslims as a community and serve its "religious" benefit, which is now separate from the national interest and could even be opposed to it.

To understand how novel this conceptualization of waqfs as the property of the community (*ṭāʾifa*) is, one should recall that medieval and early modern Muslim jurists considered a waqf whose revenues were dedicated to "Muslims"

7. As I noted in chapter 2, footnote 61, one might think that because Christians and Jews in the Ottoman Empire were recognized as religious communities (*millet*) that had jurisdiction over some of the affairs of their communities, their waqfs were already thought of as the waqfs of their communities. Such an assumption follows a common argument in both scholarship on and public discourse in Lebanon that takes the sectarian regime in Lebanon as a legacy of the Ottoman *millet* system. However, as Abillama (2018, 151) notes, sectarianism, which he suggests is the Lebanese form of secularism, rests on entirely different assumptions about the state: it is based on legal recognition rather than being a privilege bestowed by the ruler, and it is based on the assumed equality of all communities. We can see the difference between waqf practices of Christians and Jews in the Ottoman Empire and current ones when we realize that Ottoman religious minorities founded waqfs in the shariʿa court as individual endeavors that were not necessarily managed by the archbishops but were left to families and each parish (see Mohasseb Saliba 2008).

invalid.[8] Jurists asserted that such a waqf would benefit the rich (along with the poor) in perpetuity,[9] and thus foreclosed the necessary perpetual charitable end of the waqf, in the form of benefiting the poor alone. While jurists did speak of the "Muslims' waqfs," these were the aggregate of individual endeavors, rather than of the Muslim community, the *umma*. Furthermore, because many of these waqfs were rented on the real-estate market, and it was their income that served to support charitable causes, the religious affiliation of the tenant was not the main criterion for selection but rather the price offered. Waqf properties whose rents supported a mosque (like al-ʿUmari) were routinely leased to non-Muslim tenants. Finally, many waqfs served the poor at large, of Beirut for example, without consideration of religion.

This sectarianization, this book has also argued, was a facet of the "secularization" of the waqf, which entails a refiguration of religion. There is first a secularization in the sense of an immanent frame because the private property regime instituted by the French Mandate did not recognize God as an owner of the waqf, as was dominant in the late Ḥanafī tradition. When God ceased to be the owner, the "owner" of each individual parcel became the waqf itself, now endowed with a legal personality. No more simply an object in property relations, the waqf also acquired a life of its own and could become a subject, owning lands and buildings. This transformation opened the door to novel uses of the waqf, like the waqf as nonprofit.

The subjection of waqfs to a different legal and property regime also secularized the waqf in another sense: the project and the constant question of the structural differentiation of the sphere of religion from other spheres, especially the economy. With new distinctions between real law and personal law (each under the legal sovereignty of different bodies), between civil state and religious community, between persons and things, between private and public, waqfs posed a problem of categorization: were they religion or economy? On the one hand, French Mandatory officials considered waqfs like mosques and shrines, and the parcels and buildings and lands that supported them, as religion following religious law, and thus sacred and inalienable. These waqfs thus became "religious" property. On the other hand, waqfs that benefited families came to be considered neither truly charitable nor religious and thus belonging to the real economy. Laws and regulations aimed to "liberate" these waqfs and bring them back to private property.

8. While this book took as its subject the transformation of the waqfs established by Sunnis into the waqfs of the Muslim Sunni community, I surmise that a similar process happened to the other communities like the Shiʿa, Maronite, Orthodox, and Druze.

9. As we saw in chapter 4, a waqf that benefited the rich for a limited period of time before reverting to the poor or another perpetual charitable purpose was valid. The problem arises when the rich are a perpetual recipient, blocking the ultimate charitable recipients.

These transformations of the waqf, its sectarianization and its secularization, may appear particular to Lebanon. However, this book has suggested that many of these changes are intrinsic to the modern state and its conceptualization of economy and progress and the private property regime. Many of these transformations stem from modern conceptions of charity, property, and economy and the private/public distinction essential to the operation of modern states. Most Muslim-majority countries implemented similar reforms that secularized waqfs. Reflecting and reproducing new sensibilities (e.g., that charity should be altruistic) and newly operative distinctions between the religious and the economic, each subject to a different regime of governance, most nation-states in the Middle East and North Africa have limited family waqfs to two generations, allowed their revocation, or abolished them.[10] Furthermore, the categorization of certain waqfs as religious property has had similar effects, related to modern conceptions of religion as worship: when making waqfs, most founders across the Muslim world privilege mosques and, to a lesser degree, educational facilities, without waqfing rent-yielding assets to sustain these charitable institutions (see, for example, Ridwan and Santi 2018, 55, for Indonesia). Waqf as a form of financing charity seems to have receded as a practice, almost forgotten outside embodied practitioners and objects.

These common understandings of charity, religion, and economy exist under different architectures of state, law, and religion, affecting the relation of waqf to religious community. The "sectarianization" of waqf—that is, its association with a religious sect—is therefore not universal to the Muslim world writ large. Whether these nations are Muslim-majority nations with minority religious groups or whether they are "multi-religious," the notion of the equality of all recognized religious communities guaranteed by the constitution is shared. In Syria, Egypt, Iraq, Turkey, Morocco, Tunisia, and Algeria, where there was a clear Muslim majority that the state represented, Muslim waqfs became part of the public domain of the state, administered by a waqf ministry.[11] In places where they are unmarked, where the Waqf Ministry effectively means the Islamic Waqf Ministry, claims about the waqf imbricate the state more broadly, rather than a religious community and its leaders.

10. Turkey abolished them in 1927, Syria in 1949, Libya in 1973, and the UAE in 1980. Egypt limited them in 1946, then abolished them in 1952.

11. In Iraq, this situation prevailed until the 2003 US invasion and the change in regime, when the national (unmarked Muslim) Waqf Ministry became two separate offices, one for Shiʿa waqfs and the other for Sunni waqfs. This is closer to the Lebanese situation, and indeed Hasan (2019) describes it as the confessionalization of waqf. In Turkey, waqfs were abolished in 1926 and many of their properties (especially schools) were transferred to the Ministry of Education or reverted to private property (through tenants buying out the right of alienation or through auctions). In Egypt, waqfs were nationalized and redistributed in 1952 as part of the agrarian reforms and land distribution to peasants.

RETHINKING CHARITY, PROPERTY, AND THE MODERN STATE THROUGH THE WAQF

Beyond the particularities of waqf transformations in Lebanon, this book has traced intricacies of the waqf to understand the deeper contours of our modern present. The transformation of the Ottoman property regime into a private property regime with its attendant secularization has had profound implications beyond political economy, proving once again the insight that political-economic change involves changes in subjectivity, kinship, and community. The new regimes of debt that replaced forgiveness with foreclosure and that tied debt to particular objects rendered the creation of waqf suspicious. "Are indebted founders trying to avoid foreclosure?" asked Ottoman officials. An emphasis on the sincerity of founders and suspicion towards people and their "real intent" started to occupy judges, officials, and individuals. As such, the intent of founders became newly open to scrutiny, rather than being derived from their actions. A new grammar of intent arose that separated intent from action and emphasized the inner self as the locus of the true self that was accessible in the here and now rather than only to God. Philosophers like Charles Taylor (1992) have explored the rise of inwardness in connection with processes of self-reflection and self-exploration, which, he suggests, secularized the inward turn to find God within the self as Augustine had done. This book has highlighted the development and reproduction of this subjectivity in the crucible of property relations and lawsuits, and its importance for the reproduction of this new property regime and its associated debt regime.

The quest for truly charitable waqfs was pursued around a new articulation of the private/public distinction that associated family with the private and economy with the public. Starting with the French Mandate, waqfs that were deemed truly charitable were those that served "public benefit." Waqfs that benefited family were then cast by officials and even some scholars as "really" aiming to perpetuate the wealth of families and immobilize capital, rather than allowing it to freely circulate in the market.

Yet, waqfs in the late Ottoman period embodied an understanding of charity that prioritized an ethics of care of the family and that was structured not along a private/private distinction but rather along a perpetual/nonperpetual distinction. Thus, in Ottoman Beirut, waqfs that are today classified as charitable (public) institutions, like mosques, benefited beneficiaries along family lines. Such an ethic of care of the family even in charity decenters contemporary understandings of charity that overlay it with the public (as reflected in tax legislation, in Lebanon but also in places such as the United States and France, which exempt charities that are of public benefit).[12] It also reminds us that the notion of "giving to family in the

12. In British legislation, for example, trusts for education where beneficiaries are determined through personal connection such as kinship or employment in a particular company are not considered charitable. See Atiyah (1958, 148).

public" as a form of nepotism arises from a particular configuration of the private and the public, which was produced and reproduced through the remaking of institutions and practices that followed different logics.

Late Ottoman waqfs, as a form of charity that provided both services and the financial tools to support them in perpetuity, invite us to rethink the assumption that charity, before the dominance of the call for sustainability and long-term poverty-alleviation efforts, was directed to immediate relief in the here and now and was subject to the whims and fortunes of donors. Institutions like waqfs, whose legal validity required perpetuity, provided revenues to sustain endeavors like schools, bridges, soup kitchens, hospices, hospitals, or poor relief. Yet, the horizon of such endeavors was not yet conscripted by notions of progress, and thus delinked sustainability from progress. Indeed, these projects did not seek to eliminate poverty. The poor were the paramount beneficiary of charity because they were assumed to always be there.

Such assumptions behind charitable giving, which do not seek to solve the problem of poverty but just to alleviate it, present in both contemporary charitable giving and waqf, grate very much against ideals of social justice and the fight against inequality and poverty. The critiques are numerous. These practices of giving appear insufficient, a "Band-Aid," because they do not address the root problem of poverty nor do they attempt to eradicate it. Charity, by focusing on individual giving and relief, diverts from the structural causes of need and poverty, thus disabling forms of resistance to such structural inequality and reproducing poverty and need. The contemporary waqf revival can also appear to undermine the view that citizens have rights and entitlements from their governments and to render citizens in need (of food, shelter, income, education) dependent on the goodwill of others. This goodwill is based on the compassion of donors, an affect that mobilizes racialized and gendered tropes of those deserving of charity and compassion.[13] Furthermore, charity has been increasingly used as a biopolitical technology for disciplining poor and homeless people, as donations are often tied to specific requirements from recipients.[14] Finally, the delegation of the provision of services to individual benefactors is based on these benefactors' priorities and visions rather than on the needs and desires of communities, and they are not accountable when their actions have unintended effects that harm the communities they aim to help.[15]

However, there are important lessons from these approaches to charity which otherwise grate against dominant understandings of social justice as equalizing wealth. In the waqf practices examined here, social justice was not equated with

13. See Ticktin (2006, 43) for the differentiation of migrants that fit the model of victims needing to be saved.

14. See, for example, O'Neill (2013) on the disciplining of child recipients of Christian charity in Guatemala; and Murphy (2009) for the disciplining of homeless people in San Francisco.

15. See McGoey's excellent study (2015) of these issues in the work of the Gates Foundation.

economic equality but rather with mutual rights and duties, the duty of the rich to the poor and the right of the poor to the wealth of the rich. Sustaining family relations and having parents' blessing (*riḍā*) were more valuable than wealth, because without them there was no possibility of redemption in the hereafter. Furthermore, as Amira Mittermaier incisively puts it in the context of contemporary Egypt, "Placing God in the foreground, and the suffering Other in the background, disrupts both the liberal conceit of compassion *and* the neoliberal imperative of self-help" (2019, 4). Such forms of charity refuse to locate justice in the future, in the linear time of development and social justice, and thus work for justice right now—even if the givers were not working towards better presents and futures but rather just for the sake of God and reward in the afterlife.

Many of these transformations of waqf conceptions and practices, I have intimated, arise with the consolidation of the modern state. Yet, the story I have told is not simply a story of a shift from the premodern to the modern, because—as the structure of the chapters, always articulated around different moments, suggests—the modern state is a project that takes different forms under different conditions. Although there are certainly particularities to that state, like the fact that it takes the progress of the newly created object, "the nation's economy," as its target, the way this project is implemented differs considerably at various conjunctures, articulations, and re-articulations of state-society relations. We saw the common threads of this project in the transmission of knowledge across various contexts, as with French colonial knowledge about the waqf and its management developed in French North Africa and with debates on the family waqf in Egypt. I also highlighted them above in the widespread transformation of waqfs into "religious" holdings and the delegitimization of family waqfs. Yet, even these transformations are ongoing rather than accomplished once and for all.

These transformations are also continuous because other lifeworlds, traditions, and grammars continue to exist in practitioners and objects, in memories and legal texts. Some of these remnants are fragments: it is not that a practitioner or a building is simply a reflection of an older grammar. There are usually different and contradictory layers. The same man who remembered the importance of waqf was calling for its agility. The same woman who criticized the transforming of all waqfs into "religion" was questioning the intent of new waqf founders and calling for greater scrutiny of them. The same waqf buildings that provided revenues and reflected the economic function of the waqf were also being outfitted with "properly" religious functions. The same Islamic legal texts dismissed in legal reforms were being used by scholars and the public to question the legal expropriation of waqfs.

The changes I trace in the grammar of concepts as well as the continuities in the older grammar became visible through the methodological trinity of archive/library/notebook. Indeed, without my encounter with waqf in the archive and the library, I would not have realized the novelty of many of the waqf practices in

Beirut today. These encounters helped me to historicize and depict the changes in understandings and practices of Islamic waqf over the last two hundred years. Through the library and the archive, I unearthed different ways of doing waqf, showing that the "sectarianization" of waqf was the product of historical conjunctures and opening space for re-appropriating this archive. Waqfs are part of our modern world and they have been partly remade in its image. This historicization of contemporary waqf also avoids presenting contemporary Islamic waqf practices as an essential "other" to Western practices of charity. At the same time, the notebook, by documenting the dynamism of the contemporary waqf practices and the lingering of older sensibilities, forecloses the temptation to see that earlier moment as the "true" waqf practice. Thus, this methodological trinity averts constructing contemporary waqf as outside time and place and highlights the contingency of every one of its iterations.

Indeed, a revival of waqf practices under a modern state and global capitalism is not simply a revival of older practices. It is a re-figuration of the tradition under these new conditions, conditions not conducive to older ways of doing and being, of supporting family as charity, of trusting in and leaving intent to God. And it is a revival that occurs under a legal regime very much designed to end many of these earlier waqf practices. This revival has produced new ways of doing Islamic waqfs, aligned with the modern public and private dichotomy and with the distinctions between religion and economy: waqf-NGOs, a plenitude of Islamic centers and mosques. Yet, as the unearthed continuities of older logics demonstrate, it is not simply a submission of this tradition to these new logics. Nevertheless, it is a revival that showcases the constant acts of interpreting and reinterpreting the tradition that keep it alive.

APPENDIX A

Main Ottoman *Mutūn*, Commentaries, and Glosses of the Beirut Court

These *mutūn* are not those known as the "four *mutūn*" in the Ottoman legal tradition (which are Ibn al-Sa'ati's *Majma' al-Baḥrayn wa Multaqā al-Nahrayn*, al-Mawsili's *al-Mukhtār*, al-Mahbubi's *Wiqāyat al-Riwāya*, also known as *al-Wiqāya li-Riwāyat Masā'il al-Hidāya*, in addition to the below cited *Kanz*). Instead, these are the *mutūn* that appear through their commentaries and glosses in the court cases in Beirut and in the waqf chapter of Ibn 'Abidin's expansive *Ḥāshiya*, which in the nineteenth century was considered the most authoritative account of the various legal opinions. Thus, this is not a comprehensive list of these texts' commentaries or glosses. Bracketed text indicates a book that exists only in manuscript form.

Matn: al-Nasafi, Abu al-Barakat (d. 710/1310), *Kanz al-Daqā'iq*
Commentaries:

1. al-'Ayni, Badr al-Din (d. 855/1451), *Ramz al-Ḥaqā'iq**
2. Ibn Nujaym, Zayn al-Din ibn Ibrahim (d. 970/1563), *Al-Baḥr al-Rā'iq**
   Gloss:
   Ibn 'Abidin, Muhammad Amin (d. 1252/1836), *Minḥat al-Khāliq 'alā al-Baḥr al-Rā'iq**
3. Ibn Nujaym, Siraj al-Din 'Umar ibn Ibrahim (d.1005/1596), *Al-Nahr al-Fā'iq**

Matn: Al-Halabi, Ibrahim b. Muhammad (d. 956/1549), *Multaqā al-Abḥur*
Commentaries:

1. Shaykhizade Damad (d. 1078/1667), *Majma' al-Anhur**
2. Haskafi, 'Ala' al-Din (d. 1088/1677), *Al-Durr al-Muntaqā fī Sharḥ al-Multaqā**

Matn: Timurtashi, Muhammad b. ʿAbd Allah (d. 1006/1598), *Tanwīr al-Abṣār*
Commentary:

1. Haskafi, ʿAla' al-Din (d. 1088/1677), *Al-Durr al-Mukhtār*
   Glosses:
   1. [Al-Halabi, Ibrahim b. Mustafa (d. ?), *Tuḥfat al-Akhyār*]
   2. Al-Tahtawi, Ahmad b. Muhammad (d. 1231/1816), *Ḥāshiya ʿalā al-Durr al-Mukhtār*
   3. Ibn ʿAbidin, Muhammad Amin (d. 1252/1836), *Radd al-Muḥtār ʿalā al-Durr al-Mukhtār* (known as Ibn ʿAbidin's *Ḥāshiya*)*

* Manual that I consulted.

APPENDIX B

ʿUmari Mosque Expenditures and Appointments

TABLE 1 Expenditures of the ʿUmari waqf, in qurush (paras were dropped)

Year	Regular expenditures (*mu ʿtâdât*)		Total regular expenditures	Share of offices in regular expenditures	Extraordinary expenditures (repairs, etc.) (*zuhûrât*)	Total expenditures	Share of offices in total expenditures
	Offices	Equipment for the mosque					
1841	3,815	5,385	9,200	41%	20,099	29,299	13%
1842	4,042	6,960	11,002	37%	14,606	25,608	16%
1843	5,012	9,926	14,938	34%	17,697	32,635	15%
1874	38,580	3,172	41,752	92%	8,072	49,824	77%
1876	38,580	—	—	—	33,428	72,008	54%
1882	35,760	5,188	40,948	87%	31,276	72,224	48%

SOURCE: Based on accounting documents sent from Beirut waqf administrators to the central state in Istanbul during the nineteenth century (BOA. EV11192, EV23231, EV23127, EV25507).

There is a gap in the record between 1843 and 1874. In 1874, quarterly accounts replaced the yearly ones. Because the record is spotty, if I did not have a full year's expenditures, I multiplied a trimester's report by four (given that amounts of various semesters were equivalent).

As is the case for many Ottoman accounting documents with spotty records, it is difficult to explain the jump in amounts from the 1840s to the 1870s, even though the increase also overlaps with the huge rise in the population of the city and a booming economy.

TABLE 2 ʿUmari Mosque officeholder chronology

Khaṭīb	First imam, afternoon prayer (*ʿaṣr*)	Second imam, noon prayer (*ẓuhr*)	First *türbedâr*	Second *türbedâr*	Ḥanafi professor
Shaykh Barzanji (1712/1124)	Shaykh Muhammad				
No historical record					
Al-Sayyid al-Shaykh ʿAbd al-Rahman al-Nahhas (1851/1268)	*[Shaykh ʿAli Fakhuri]*	Muhammad Hammud (1853/1269)	*Sayyid ʿAbd Allah son of ʿAbd al-Sattar Bikdash (1873/1290)*	Shaykh Muhammad Khatib	Shaykh Muhyi al-Din (1856/1273)
	Sayyid ʿAbd al-Basit efendi son of shaykh ʿAli Fakhuri (1864/1281)	Shaykhs ʿAbd al-Rahman and Muhammad sons of Muhammad (1860/1277)	*ʿAbd al-Rahman son of sayyid ʿAbd Allah (1898/1316)*	*ʿAbd al-Ghani bin ʿAbd al-Rahman al-Bindaq (1890/1308)*	*ʿAbd al-Basit [Fakhuri] (1889/1307)*
ʿAbd al-Qadir son of ʿAbd al-Rahman (1908/1326)		*Shaykh Muhammad Tawfiq Khalid (1915/1334)*	*Hassan brother of ʿAbd al-Rahman (1911/1330)*		Shaykh Hamid (1908/1326)

SOURCE: Based on base-records VGM515, VGM162.5, and VGM161.300 and the documents they point to, and the waqf accounting records in the series BOA.EV.

Dates in parenthesis indicate the appointment date. The Ḥanafi professorship was established in 1856.

In the column for each office, a change in italicization indicates a change in the family of the officeholders. Note that here I take family as restricted to patrilineal descent because I take a common surname and the mention of "son of" as evidence of family. Offices could have gone to a son-in-law or the son of a sister, but these require evidence not readily available.[1]

1. Oral histories of families and family trees would be helpful here, but unfortunately I have not been able to pursue them.

GLOSSARY

The definitions reflect the main usage in this book.

ʿaqār	immovable property
ʿayn	corpus of a specific object, substance; res in Roman law; the principal in endowment terminology
al-Azhar	one of the leading madrasas of the Muslim world, located in Cairo
Azharite	graduate of al-Azhar
bayʿ biʾl-wafāʾ	contract of sale with the right of redemption if the seller (debtor) pays back the price
berat	official appointment letter
daʿwā	lawsuit
daʿwa	invitation to an Islamic way of life
ḍarūra	necessity
DGIW	Directorate General of Islamic Waqfs
dīn	religion
dhimma	legal personality; when used in the expression *lah(ā) fi dhimmatih(ā)*, denotes debt owed to a person
fatwā	nonbinding legal opinion
firmân	decree
fiqh	Islamic law
hadith	Prophetic tradition, transmitted as a report about what the Prophet did, said, or approved and disapproved

ḥukm	ruling; qualification of an action in the legal-moral scale: obligatory, recommended, permissible, reprehensible, prohibited
ḥüsn-i idâre	good management
ʿibādāt	worship, transactions between God and humans (classification of legal actions)
ilmiye	Ottoman religious institution/ class
istibdāl	exchange or substitution; procedure whereby a waqf's principal is exchanged for cash or another principal and all the stipulations of the old waqf deed apply to the new principal
istimlāk	expropriation; buying out property for the "public good"
jamʿiyya	association; also nongovernmental organization (NGO) in Lebanon and nonprofit in the United States
jiha	in a waqf institution like a school, an office whose holder is entitled to a stipend from the revenues of the waqf
kazasker	chief judge in the Ottoman Empire
khaṭīb	the person in charge of making the *khuṭba*, the sermon preceding the Friday prayer and other special prayers
lāzim	binding
māl	property
manfaʿa	in property law, usufruct or yield; more broadly, interest or benefit, sometimes used as an equivalent to *maṣlaḥa*
maṣlaḥa	well-being; benefit
matn	core text; legal manual (pl., *mutūn*)
Mecelle	short name for *Mecelle-i Aḥkâm-i ʿAdliyye*, compendium of codified Islamic law produced by the Ottoman Empire starting in the 1860s
milk	type of property, freehold, also used to talk about ownership and property more broadly
mîrî	type of property, whose rights of alienation belong to the state but whose rights of use and usufruct belong to subjects and can be transmitted
muʿāmalāt	pecuniary transactions; transactions between humans (classification of legal actions)
mufti	scholar who dispenses fatwas, legal and other opinions
mutawallī	(waqf) administrator
mutūn	plural of *matn*, see above
nāẓir	supervisor
Nezâret-i Evkâf-i Hümâyûn	Ottoman Imperial Waqf Ministry
niyya	intent

Nizamiye	new courts instated in the Ottoman Empire after the Tanzimat
qadi	judge, who also served as public notary and had other functions
qāḍī al-quḍāt	chief justice
qawāʿid	legal maxims; genre of legal literature
qaṣd	intent, purpose
qayyim	caretaker; also, administrator of a waqf
qiyās	analogy, a method for deriving legal rulings on matters not in the sources of the Qurʾan and Sunna (the normative legacy of the Prophet, whose unit is the hadith)
qurba	closeness to God
raqaba	right of alienation
rahn	contract that acts as a surety on a debt by putting an immovable in the hands of a creditor or third party and giving the creditor the right to confine (*ḥabs*) the immovable until payment of the debt
rukn	essential element (for a legal transaction)
ṣadaqa	charity
ṣaḥīḥ	valid
sharʿ	shariʿa/law
sharʿī	legal
sharḥ	commentary (pl., *shurūḥ*)
sharṭ	necessary condition for a legal transaction; stipulation for waqf, usually from the founder and recorded in the waqf deed (*sharṭ al-wāqif*)
şeyhülislâm	the mufti of Istanbul, the highest Islamic scholarly hierarchy in the Ottoman Empire
sijill	register
siyāsa/siyāsa sharʿiyya	positive law of the state, devised by the ruler in the name of shariʿa, in contrast to the formal rules of the *fiqh*
Sufi	pertaining to the spiritual dimension of the Islamic tradition; Muslim mystic
sura	Qurʾanic chapter
ṭāʾifa	religious community; sect
Tanzimat	program of reforms initiated in the Ottoman Empire in 1839
tarjīḥ	weighing of different legal opinions on a single matter to determine the soundest one
umma	Muslim community

ʿulamaʾ	jurist-scholars/learned community
uṣūl al-fiqh	principles of Islamic jurisprudence; genre of legal literature concerned with the methods of deriving and the sources of legal rulings
wāqif(a)	founder of a waqf (masc., *wāqif*; fem., *wāqifa*)
waqfiyya	waqf deed
waṣiyy	custodian, guardian
wakīl	agent
zakat	obligatory alms
zāwiya	Sufi lodge
zabt	seizing (Turkish for Arabic *ḍabṭ*)

BIBLIOGRAPHY

ARCHIVAL SOURCES

1. Başbakanlık Osmanlı Arşivi (BOA)—Prime Ministry Archives, Istanbul

a. Evkaf Defterleri (EV): Waqf registers, particularly waqf accounting documents sent to the Waqf Ministry

b. İradeler (I): Imperial decrees, and in particular those of the Meclis-i Vala (MVL), the High Council

c. Şura-i Develet (ŞD): Documents from the Council of State

BOA documents are identified in the following manner: Archive. Collection. Subcollection. Box number/document number/page number

2. Vakıflar Genel Müdürlüğü (VGM)—Directorate General of Waqfs, Ankara

a. Muhasebe Defterleri: Accounting records

b. Muhasebe Tafsilleri: Registers containing detailed accounting records

c. Hulasalar: Registers containing summaries, usually of appointment letters

d. Esas Defterleri: Base registers

VGM registers and documents have serial numbers, so they are identified in the following manner: Archive/register number/page number/case number

3. Al-Mahkama al-Shar'iyya al-Sunniyya fi Bayrut (MSSB)—Beirut Sunni Shari'a Court Records

a. Ottoman Sijillat al-Mahadir, al-Hujaj wa al-Da'awa (S): Ottoman registers of summary records, deeds, and lawsuits

b. Ottoman Jara'id al-Dabt (D): Ottoman registers of minutes

c. Contemporary Sijillat al-Hujaj (H): Contemporary registers of deeds

MSB documents are identified in this way: Archive. Collection Register number/page/case number (if the cases are numbered). In the contemporary registers, the page number is omitted because the archive is organized serially by case number (*asās*).

4. **Ministère des Affaires Étrangères, Nantes, Fonds Syrie/Liban, 1er versement (MAE)**
   a. Papiers Gennardi
   b. Cabinet Politique
   c. Petits Fonds Politiques ou Administratifs

5. **Private collection of the Qabbani family**

PUBLISHED PRIMARY SOURCES

1. *Islamic Law*

Abu al-Su'ud, Muhammad ibn Muhammad. 1990. *Tafsīr Abī al-Su'ūd: al-Musamma Irshād al-'Aql al-Salīm ilā Mazāyā al-Qur'ān al-Karīm*. Bayrut: Dar Ihya' al-Turath al-'Arabi.
al-'Ayni, Badr al-Din Mahmud ibn Ahmad. 1285 [1868 or 69]. *Ramz al-Ḥaqa'iq fī Sharḥ Kanz al-Daqā'iq*. 2 vols. Bulaq: Dar al-Tiba'a al-'Amira. (Abbreviated as *Ramz*)
al-Basri, Hilal ibn Yahya al-Ra'y. 1936. *Kitāb Aḥkām al-Waqf*. Haydarabad: Matba'at Majlis Da'irat al-Ma'arif al-'Uthmaniyya.
Ali, Efendi. 1995. *Şeyhülislâm Fetvâları*, ed. İbrahim Ural. Istanbul: Fey Vakfı.
Ebüssu'ûd, Muhammad ibn Muhammad. 2013. *Ma'rûzât Şeyhülislâm Ebussuûd Efendi*. Edited by Pehlül Düzenli. Istanbul: Klasik.
al-Ghazali, Abu Hamid. 1997. *Al-Mustaṣfā min 'Ilm al-Uṣūl*. Bayrut: Mu'assasat al-Risala.
Haydar, Ali. 1340 [1922]. *Tertîbü'ş-Şunûf fi Ahkâmi'l-Vukûf*. İstanbul: Şirket-i Mürettibiye Matba'ası.
———. 2010. *Durar al-Ḥukkām Sharḥ Majallat al-Aḥkām*. Translated by Fahmi al-Husayni. 4 vols. Bayrut: Dar al-Kutub al-'Ilmiyya.
Hilmi, Ömer. 1909. *İtḥâfü'l-Akhlâf fi Mushkilâti'l-Evkâf*. Translated by Muhammad al-Ghazzi al-Halabi. Halab: Matba'at al-Baha'.
Ibn 'Abidin, Muhammad Amin ibn 'Umar. 1300 [1882]. *Al-'Uqūd al-Durriyya fī Tanqīḥ al-Fatāwā al-Ḥāmidiyya*. Bulaq: Al-Matba'a al-'Amira al-Miriyya. (Abbreviated as *Tanqīḥ*)
———. 1272 [1855]. *Ḥāshiyat Radd al-Muḥtār 'alā al-Durr al-Mukhtār*. Bulaq, Misr: s.n. (Abbreviated as *Ḥāshiya*)
Ibn Nujaym, 'Umar ibn Ibrahim. 2002. *Al-Nahr al-Fā'iq: Sharḥ Kanz al-Daqā'iq*, 3 vols. Bayrut: Dar al-Kutub al-'Ilmiyya. (Abbreviated as *Nahr*)
Ibn Nujaym, Zayn al-Din ibn Ibrahim. 1334 [1916]. *Al-Baḥr al-Rā'iq, Sharḥ Kanz al-Daqā'iq*. Misr: Dar al-Kutub al-Gharbiyya al-Kubra. (Abbreviated as *Baḥr*)
———. 1999. *Al-Ashbāh wa al-Naẓā'ir fī Qawā'id wa Furū' Fiqh al-Ḥanafiyya*. Bayrut: Dar al-Kutub al-'Ilmiyya. (Abbreviated as *Ashbāh*)
al-Khassaf, Aḥmad ibn 'Amr al-Shaybani. 1999. *Kitāb Aḥkām al-Awqāf*. Bayrut: Dar al-Kutub al-'Ilmiyya.
Muslim, Abu al-Husayn ibn al-Hajjaj al-Qushayri. 1972. *Ṣaḥīḥ Muslim*. Dimashq: al-Maktab al-Islami; Bayrut: Dar al-'Arabiyya.
———. 2005. *Ṣaḥīḥ Muslim: The Authentic Hadiths of Muslim with Full Arabic Text*. Translated by Muhammad Mahdi Sharif. Bayrut: Dar al-Kutub al-'Ilmiyya.

Nasafi, ʿAbd Allah ibn Ahmad. 2005. *Kanz al-Daqāʾiq*. Sayda: Al-Maktaba al-ʿAsriyya. (Abbreviated as *Kanz*)

Qadri, Muhammad. 2006 [1893]. *Qānūn al-ʿAdl wa al-Inṣāf fī al-Qaḍāʾ ʿalā Mushkilāt al-Awqāf*. Edited by ʿAli Jumʿa and Muhammad Ahmad Siraj. Al-Qahira: Dar al-Salam.

Qariʾ al-Hidaya. 1999. *Kitāb Fatāwā Qāriʾ al-Hidāya*. Edited by ʿUmar ibn ʿAli, Muhammad al-Ruhayyil Gharayiba, and Muhammad ʿAli Zughul. ʿAmman: Dar al-Furqan.

al-Ramli, Khayr al-Din. 1300 [1882]. *Al-Fatāwā al-Khayriyya*. Bulaq, Misr: s.n.

al-Shaykh Nizam wa Jamaʿa min ʿUlamaʾ al-Hind. 1310 [1893]. *Al-Fatāwā al-Hindiyya fī Madhhab al-Imām Abī Ḥanīfa al-Nuʿmān*. Bulaq, Misr: Al-Matbaʿa al-Kubra al-Amiriyya. (Abbreviated as *al-Fatāwā al-Hindiyya*, without an author because it is a collective work)

Tabari, Muhammad ibn Jarir. 2003. *Tafsīr al-Ṭabarī: Jāmiʿ al-Bayān ʿan Taʾwīl Āyāt al-Qurʾān*. Edited by ʿAbd Allah ibn ʿAbd al-Muhsin Turki. al-Riyad: Dar ʿAlam al-Kutub.

al-Tarabulusi, Burhan al-Din. 2005. *Kitāb al-Isʿāf fī Aḥkām al-Awqāf*. Al-Qahira: Al-Maktaba al-Azhariyya li'l-Turath.

Turkey. 1289 [1873]. *Düstur*. 1. Tertip. İstanbul: Matbaa-yi Amire. https://catalog.hathitrust.org/Record/100344733/Home.

Turkey. 1872. *Düstur*. Vol. 2. Ankara: Başbkanlık basımevi. https://catalog.hathitrust.org/Record/007908603.

Yazır, Muhammed Hamdi. 1995. *Elmalılı M. Hamdi Yazır Gözüyle Vakıflar: İrşâd'ül-Akhlâf Fi Ahkâm'ül-Avkâf*. Edited by Nazif Öztürk. Ankara: Türkiye Diyanet Vakfı.

2. Collection of Tracts and Pamphlets on Family Waqf, Institut Français du Proche-Orient, Damascus

ʿAdili, Muhammad Kamil. n.d. *Qaḍiyyat al-Awqāf al-Dhurriyya*. Halab: Matbaʿat al-Maʿarif Najib Kunaydir.

ʿAlwani, Muhammad Dhaki. n.d. *Al-Aqwāl al-Ḥaqīqiyya fī Luzūm Izālat al-Awqāf al-Dhurriyya*. Hamah: Matbaʿat al-Islah.

al-Samman, Hamid. n.d.a. *Nidāʾ li-Nuwwābinā al-Kirām bi-Shaʾn al-Tashrīʿ bi-Mashrūʿ Ilghāʾ al-Awqāf al-Dhurriyya*.

———. n.d.b. *Bayān Ḥaqīqat Mashrūʿ Ilghāʾ al-Awqāf al-Dhurriyya wa Ḍarūriyyatih li'l-Bilād*.

Jamʿiyyat al-ʿUlamaʾ bi-Dimashq. 1938a. *Naqd li-Bayān Mudīriyyat al-Awqāf Ḥawl Bayʿ al-Waqf al-Dhurrī*. Dimashq: Matbaʿat al-Taraqqi.

———. 1938b. *Risāla fī Ibṭāl Risālat al-Ustādh al-Shaykh Rāmiz al-Malak fī Jawāz Ḥall Awqāf al-Dhurriyya*. Dimashq: Matbaʿat al-Taraqqi.

———. 1938c. *Taʾyīd Shaykh al-Islām, Shaykh al-Jāmiʿ al-Azhar li-Mashrūʿiyyat al-Waqf al-Dhurrī wa Taḥrim Bayʿih*. Dimashq: Matbaʿat al-Taraqqi.

Malak, Ramiz. 1938. *Risāla Ḥawl Irjāʿ al-Awqāf al-Dhurriyya Milkan*. Tarabulus: Matbaʿat al-Liwaʾ.

———. 1939a. *Naẓra fī-mā Jāʾ fī Naqḍ Jamʿiyyat al-ʿUlamāʾ bi-Dimashq bi-Bayān Mudīriyyat al-Awqāf Ḥawl Bayʿ al-Waqf al-Dhurrī*. Tarabulus: Matbaʿat al-Liwaʾ.

———. 1939b. *Raʾy Faḍīlat Shaykh al-Azhar fī al-Awqāf al-Dhurriyya*. Tarabulus: Matbaʿat al-Liwaʾ.

3. French Diplomatic Documents

Haut Commissariat de la République française en Syrie et au Liban. 1921. *Rapport général sur les études foncières effectuées en Syrie et au Liban*. Beyrouth: Les services fonciers.

———. 1924. *La Syrie et le Liban sous l'occupation et le mandat français 1919–1927*. Nancy: Berger-Levrault.

Haut Commissariat en Syrie et au Liban. 1922. *La Syrie et le Liban en 1922*. http://catalog.hathitrust.org/api/volumes/oclc/22564818.html.

Ministère des Affaires Étrangères. 1867. *Documents diplomatiques*. Paris: Imprimerie Impériale.

Ministère français des Affaires Étrangères. 1922. *Rapport à la Société des Nations sur la situation de la Syrie et du Liban*. Paris: Imprimerie Nationale. (Abbreviated as *Rapport*)

———. 1924. *Rapport à la Société des Nations sur la situation de la Syrie et du Liban*. Paris: Imprimerie Nationale. (Abbreviated as *Rapport*)

———. 1926. *Rapport à la Société des Nations sur la situation de la Syrie et du Liban*. Paris: Imprimerie Nationale. (Abbreviated as *Rapport*)

———. 1928. *Rapport à la Société des Nations sur la situation de la Syrie et du Liban*. Paris: Imprimerie Nationale. (Abbreviated as *Rapport*)

PERIODICALS

Annahar

Al-Akhbar

Revue Algérienne et Tunisienne de Législation et de Jurisprudence

Salname-i Beirut

REFERENCE WORKS

al-Zabidi, Murtada. 1965. *Tāj al-ʿArūs min Jawāhir al-Qāmūs*. Al-Kuwayt: Matbaʿat Hukumat al-Kuwayt.

Bearman, P., Th. Bianquis, C. E. Bosworth, E. van Donzel and W. P. Heinrichs, eds. 2012. *Encyclopaedia of Islam*. 2nd ed. Leiden: Brill. https://referenceworks.brillonline.com/browse/encyclopaedia-of-islam-2. (Abbreviated as *EI2*)

Firuzabadi, Muhammad ibn Yaʿqub. 1280 [1863]. *Al-Qāmūs al-Muḥīṭ*, 4 vols. Al-Qahira: al-Matbaʿa al-Kustaliyya. (Abbreviated as *al-Qāmūs al-Muḥīṭ*)

İslâm Ansiklopedisi. 1988–. Üsküdar, İstanbul: Türkiye Diyanet Vakfı. https://islamansiklopedisi.org.tr/.

Sami, Şemseddiin. 1317 [1900]. *Kamus-u Türkî*. Dar-i Saadet: İkdam Matbaası.

Wehr, Hans. 1960. *Arabic-English Dictionary*. Wiesbaden: Harrassowitz.

OTHER PUBLISHED TEXTS

Abbasi, Rushain. 2020. "Did Premodern Muslims Distinguish the Religious and Secular? The *Dīn–Dunyā* Binary in Medieval Islamic Thought." *Journal of Islamic Studies* 31 (2): 185–225.

Abdallah, Tarak. 2018. "Naḥwa Mawja Thāniya li-Iḥyāʾ al-Waqf fī al-ʿĀlam al-Islāmī." *Journal of King Abdulaziz University: Islamic Economics* 31 (3). https://papers.ssrn.com/abstract=3469098.

Abillama, Raja. 2018. "Contesting Secularism: Civil Marriage and Those Who Do Not Belong to a Religious Community in Lebanon." *PoLAR: Political and Legal Anthropology Review* 41 (S1): 148–62.

Abou El-Haj, Rifaat Ali. 1984. *The 1703 Rebellion and the Structure of Ottoman Politics*. Leiden: Nederlands Historisch-Archaeologisch Instituut te Istanbul.

Abou-Hodeib, Toufoul. 2017. *A Taste for Home: The Modern Middle Class in Ottoman Beirut*. Stanford, CA: Stanford University Press.

Abu-Lughod, Lila. 1986. *Veiled Sentiments: Honor and Poetry in a Bedouin Society*. Berkeley: University of California Press.

Abu-Manneh, Butrus. 1994. "The Islamic Roots of the Gülhane Rescript." *Die Welt des Islams* 34 (2): 173–203.

Abu-Odeh, Lama. 2004. "Modernizing Muslim Family Law: The Case of Egypt." *Vanderbilt Journal of Transnational Law* 37 (4): 1043–146.

Abu Zahra, Muḥammad. 2005. *Muḥāḍarāt fī al-Waqf*. Al-Qahira: Dar al-Fikr al-ʿArabi.

Adada, Aurore. 2009. "Réseaux socioculturels et économiques à Beyrouth Ottoman (1843–1909) à travers les waqfs." PhD diss., Université de Provence.

ʿAfifi, Muhammad. 1991. *Al-Awqāf wa al-Ḥayāt al-Iqtiṣādiyya fī Miṣr fī al-ʿAṣr al-ʿUthmānī*. Al-Qahira: Al-Hayʾa al-Misriyya al-ʿAmma li'l-Kitab.

Agrama, Hussein Ali. 2010. "Ethics, Tradition, Authority: Toward an Anthropology of the Fatwa." *American Ethnologist* 37 (1): 2–18.

———. 2012. *Questioning Secularism: Islam, Sovereignty, and the Rule of Law in Modern Egypt*. Chicago: University of Chicago Press.

Akarlı, Engin Deniz. 1993. *The Long Peace: Ottoman Lebanon, 1861–1920*. Berkeley: University of California Press.

Akgündüz, Ahmet. 1988. *İslâm Hukukunda ve Osmanlı Tatbikatında Vakıf Müessesesi*. Ankara: Türk Tarih Kurumu Basımevi.

Akiba, Jun. 2004. "From Kadi to Naib: Reorganization of the Ottoman Sharia Judiciary in the Tanzimat Period." In *Frontiers of Ottoman Studies*, edited by Colin Imber and Keiko Kiyotaki. London: I. B. Tauris.

Alley, Kelly D. 2019. "River Goddesses, Personhood and Rights of Nature: Implications for Spiritual Ecology." *Religions* 10 (9): 502.

Allouba, Mohamed Aly Pacha. 1927. "Le wakf est-il une institution religieuse?" *L'Égypte Contemporaine* 18: 385–402.

Amin, Muhammad Muhammad. 1980. *Al-Awqāf wa al-Ḥayāt al-Ijtimāʿiyya fī Miṣr, 648–923 A.H./1250–1517 A.D.: Dirāsa Tārīkhiyya Wathāʾiqiyya*. Al-Qahira: Dar al-Nahda al-ʿArabiyya.

Anderson, J. N. D. 1951. "The Religious Element in Waqf Endowments." *Journal of the Royal Central Asian Society* 38 (4): 292–99.

ʿAqiqi, Viviane. 2017. "Al-Ṭawāʾif Muʿfāt min al-Ḍarāʾib . . . wa al-Raʿāyā Muthqalūn bihā." *Al-Akhbar*, July 20, 2017. https://al-akhbar.com/Community/235138.

Arabi, Oussama. 1997. "Intention and Method in Sanhūrī's Fiqh: Cause as Ulterior Motive." *Islamic Law and Society* 4 (2): 200–23. https://doi.org/10.1163/1568519972599824.

———. 1998. "Contract Stipulations (*Shurūṭ*) in Islamic Law: The Ottoman Majalla and Ibn Taymiyya." *International Journal of Middle East Studies* 30 (1): 29–50.

Arendt, Hannah. 1998. *The Human Condition*. 2nd ed. Chicago: University of Chicago Press.

Asad, Muhammad. 2003 [1980]. *The Message of the Qur'ān*. Bristol, UK: The Book Foundation.

Asad, Talal. 1986. *The Idea of an Anthropology of Islam*. Washington, DC: Center for Contemporary Arab Studies, Georgetown University.

———. 1992. "Conscripts of Western Civilization." In *Dialectical Anthropology: Essays in Honor of Stanley Diamond*, edited by Christine W. Gailey, 333–51. Tallahassee: University of Florida Press.

———. 1993. *Genealogies of Religion: Discipline and Reasons of Power in Christianity and Islam*. Baltimore: Johns Hopkins University Press.

———. 2003. *Formations of the Secular: Christianity, Islam, Modernity*. Stanford, CA: Stanford University Press.

———. 2006. "Trying to Understand French Secularism." In *Political Theologies: Public Religions in a Post-Secular World*, edited by Hent de Vries and Lawrence Eugene Sullivan, 494–526. New York: Fordham University Press.

———. 2007. "Explaining the Global Religious Revival: The Egyptian Case." In *Religion and Society: An Agenda for the 21st Century*, edited by Gerrie ter Haar and Yoshio Tsuruoka, 83–103. Leiden: Brill.

Ashtiyya, Muhammad Salim. 2001. *Iqtiṣādiyyāt al-Waqf al-Islāmī fī Arāḍī al-Sulṭa al-Waṭaniyya al-Filasṭīniyya: Dirāsa Taḥlīliyya*. Al-Quds: Da'irat al-Siyasat al-Iqtisadiyya.

ʿAshur, Saʿid ʿAbd al-Fattah. 1966. *Al-Sayyid Ahmad al-Badawi, Shaykh wa-Ṭariqa*. Al-Qahira: Al-Dar al-Misriyya li'l-Ta'lif wa al-Tarjama.

ʿAssaf, Muhammad Ahmad. 2005. "Al-Waqf Inshā'uh wa Istibdāluh: Dirāsa Muqārana." Ph.D. diss., Jamiʿat Bayrut al-Islamiyya.

Assouad, Lydia. 2018. *Rethinking the Lebanese Economic Miracle: The Extreme Concentration of Income and Wealth in Lebanon*. World Inequality Database, WID.world Working Paper no. 2017/13, 19 September 2018. https://wid.world/news-article/new-paper-inequality-lebanon/.

Atia, Mona. 2013. *Building a House in Heaven: Pious Neoliberalism and Islamic Charity in Egypt*. Minneapolis: University of Minnesota Press.

Atiyah, Patrick Selim. 1958. "Public Benefit in Charities." *Modern Law Review* 21 (2): 138–54. https://doi.org/10.1111/j.1468-2230.1958.tb00465.x.

Austin, John Langshaw. 1962. *How to Do Things with Words*. 1955. Oxford: Clarendon Press.

Awad, Abed, and Robert E. Michael. 2010. "Iflas and Chapter 11: Classical Islamic Law and Modern Bankruptcy." *International Lawyer*, 975–1000.

Aydın, Mehmet Âkif. 2003. "Mecelle-i Ahkâm-ı Adliyye." In *İslam Ansiklopedisi* 28: 231–35. Üsküdar: Türkiye Diyanet Vakfı

Ayoub, Samy. 2014. "We're Not in Kufa Anymore: The Construction of Late Hanafism in the Early Modern Ottoman Empire, 16th-19th Centuries CE." PhD diss., University of Arizona.

———. 2016. "The Mecelle, Sharia, and the Ottoman State: Fashioning and Refashioning of Islamic Law in the Nineteenth and Twentieth Centuries." In *Law and Legality in the Ottoman Empire and Republic of Turkey*, edited by Kent F. Schull, M. Safa Saracoglu, and Robert W. Zens, 129–55. Bloomington: Indiana University Press.

Aytekin, E. Attila. 2008. "Cultivators, Creditors and the State: Rural Indebtedness in the Nineteenth Century Ottoman Empire." *Journal of Peasant Studies* 35 (2): 292–313. https://doi.org/10.1080/03066150802151041.

Badr, ʿAdnan Ahmad. 1992. *Al-Iftāʾ wa-al-Awqāf al-Islāmiyya fī Lubnān: Māḍiyan wa Ḥāḍiran wa-Mustaqbalan*. Bayrut: al-Muʾassasa al-Jamiʿiyya li'l-Dirasat wa al-Nashr wa al-Tawziʿ.

Baer, Gabriel. 1958. "Waqf Reform in Egypt." *Middle Eastern Affairs* 1: 61–76.

———. 1979. "Dismemberment of *Awqāf* in 19th-Century Jerusalem." *Asian and African Studies* 13 (3): 220–41.

Bakhit, Muhammad. 1926. *Al-Murhafāt al-Yamāniyya fī ʿUnq Man Qāl bi-Buṭlān al-Waqf ʿalā al-Dhurriyya*. Al-Qahira: al-Matbaʿa al-Salafiyya.

———. 1928. *Fī Niẓām al-Waqf*. Al-Qahira: al-Matbaʿa al-Salafiyya.

Barkey, Karen. 2008. *Empire of Difference: The Ottomans in Comparative Perspective*. Cambridge: Cambridge University Press.

Barnes, John Robert. 1986. *An Introduction to Religious Foundations in the Ottoman Empire*. Leiden: Brill.

Bashkow, Ira. 2014. "Afterword: What Kind of a Person Is the Corporation?" *PoLAR: Political and Legal Anthropology Review* 37 (2): 296–307.

Becherer, Richard. 2005. "A Matter of Life and Debt: The Untold Costs of Rafiq Hariri's New Beirut." *Journal of Architecture* 10 (1): 1–42.

Behrens-Abouseif, Doris. 1994. *Egypt's Adjustment to Ottoman Rule: Institutions, Waqf and Architecture in Cairo, 16th and 17th Centuries*. Leiden: Brill.

———. 2009. "The Waqf: A Legal Personality?" In *Eigentum für Alle Zeiten? Islamische Stiftungen von den Anfängen bis zur Gegenwart*, edited by Astrid Meier et al. Berlin: Akademie-Verlag.

———. 2012. "Waḳf. In the Arab Lands." In *Encyclopaedia of Islam*, 2nd ed., edited by P. J. Bearman et al. Leiden: Brill.

Belin, M. 1853. "Extrait d'un mémoire sur l'origine et la constitution des biens de mainmorte en pays musulman." *Journal Asiatique*, November-December: 377–427.

Bellow, Adam. 2003. *In Praise of Nepotism: A Natural History*. New York: Anchor Books.

Benson, Peter, and Stuart Kirsch, eds. 2014. "Imagining Corporate Personhood." Symposium, *PoLAR: Political and Legal Anthropology Review* 37 (2): 207–307.

Benton, Lauren A. 2002. *Law and Colonial Cultures: Legal Regimes in World History, 1400–1900*. Cambridge: Cambridge University Press.

Berkes, Niyazi. 1998. *The Development of Secularism in Turkey*. Montreal: McGill University Press.

Berkey, Jonathan Porter. 1992. *The Transmission of Knowledge in Medieval Cairo: A Social History of Islamic Education*. Princeton, NJ: Princeton University Press.

Beyhum, Nabil. 1995. *Al-Iʿmār wa al-Maṣlaḥa al-ʿĀmma fī al-Ijtimāʿ wa al-Thaqāfa: Maʿnā al-Madīna Sukkānuhā*. Bayrut: Dar al-Jadid.

Bidair, A. Shoukry. 1924. "L'institution des biens dits 'habous' ou 'wakf' dans le droit de l'Islam." PhD diss., Université de Paris.

Birla, Ritu. 2009. *Stages of Capital: Law, Culture, and Market Governance in Late Colonial India*. Durham, NC: Duke University Press.

Bishara, Fahad Ahmad. 2017. *A Sea of Debt: Law and Economic Life in the Western Indian Ocean, 1780–1950*. Cambridge: Cambridge University Press.

Blackstone, William. 1766. *Commentaries on the Laws of England: Book the First*. 2nd ed. Vol. 2. 2 vols. Oxford: Clarendon Press.

Bleuchot, Hervé. 1999. "Habous." In *Encyclopédie Berbère*. Vol. 21, 3265–72. Aix-en-Provence, France: EDISUD.

Bonner, Michael David. 2003. "Poverty and Charity in the Rise of Islam." In *Poverty and Charity in Middle Eastern Contexts*, edited by Michael David Bonner, Mine Ener, and Amy Singer, 13–30. Albany: SUNY Press.

Bornstein, Erica. 2012. *Disquieting Gifts: Humanitarianism in New Delhi*. Stanford, CA: Stanford University Press.

Bou Akar, Hiba. 2018. *For the War Yet to Come: Planning Beirut's Frontiers*. Stanford, CA: Stanford University Press.

Bowen, John R. 2008. *Why the French Don't Like Headscarves: Islam, the State, and Public Space*. Princeton, NJ: Princeton University Press.

———. 1993. *Muslims through Discourse: Religion and Ritual in Gayo Society*. Princeton, NJ: Princeton University Press.

Braude, Benjamin. 1982. "Foundation Myths of the Millet System." In *Christians and Jews in the Ottoman Empire: The Functioning of a Plural Society*, by Benjamin Braude and Bernard Lewis, 1:69–88. New York: Holmes & Meier.

Brown, Nathan J. 1995. "Retrospective: Law and Imperialism: Egypt in Comparative Perspective." *Law and Society Review*, 103–25.

Brown, Peter. 2012. *Through the Eye of a Needle: Wealth, the Fall of Rome, and the Making of Christianity in the West, 350–550 AD*. Princeton, NJ: Princeton University Press.

Buheiry, Marwan. 1984. "The Peasant Revolt of 1858 in Mount Lebanon: Rising Expectations, Economic Malaise and the Incentive to Arm." In *Land Tenure and Social Transformation in the Middle East*, edited by Tarif Khalidi, 291–301. Beirut: American University of Beirut.

Burak, Guy. 2013. "Faith, Law and Empire in the Ottoman 'Age of Confessionalization' (Fifteenth–Seventeenth Centuries): The Case of 'Renewal of Faith.'" *Mediterranean Historical Review* 28 (1): 1–23. https://doi.org/10.1080/09518967.2013.782670.

———. 2015. *The Second Formation of Islamic Law: The Hanafi School in the Early Modern Ottoman Empire*. New York: Cambridge University Press.

———. 2017. "Codification, Legal Borrowing and the Localization of 'Islamic Law.'" In *Routledge Handbook of Islamic Law*, edited by Khaled Abou El-Fadl, Hossein Moderrissi, and Ahmad Atif Ahmad. Abingdon, Oxon: Routledge.

Burckhardt, Jacob. 1921. *The Civilisation of the Renaissance in Italy*. London: Allen & Unwin.

Burke, Edmund, III. 1973. "A Comparative View of French Native Policy in Morocco and Syria, 1912–1925." *Middle Eastern Studies* 9 (2): 175–86. https://doi.org/10.1080/00263207308700238.

Cahen, Claude. 1961. "Réflexions sur le waqf ancien." *Studia Islamica*, no. 14: 37–56. https://doi.org/10.2307/1595184.

Campos, Michelle U. 2011. *Ottoman Brothers: Muslims, Christians, and Jews in Early Twentieth-Century Palestine*. Stanford, CA: Stanford University Press.

Cannon, Byron D. 1982. "The Beylical Habus Council and Suburban Development: Tunis, 1881–1914." *Maghreb Review* 7 (1–2): 32–40.

———. 1985. "Entrepreneurial Management of Tunisia's Private Habous Patrimony, 1902–1914." *Maghreb Review* 10 (2–3): 41–50.

Casanova, José. 1994. *Public Religions in the Modern World*. Chicago: University of Chicago Press.

Casey, James. 2019. "Sacred Surveillance: Indian Muslims, Waqf, and the Evolution of State Power in French Mandate Syria." In *British and French Colonialism in Africa, Asia and the Middle East*, edited by James R. Fichter, 89–110. Cham, Switz.: Springer.

Çelik, Kurşat. 2010. "Osmanlı Hâkimiyetinde Beyrut (1839–1918)." PhD diss., Fırat Üniversitesi, Elaziğ, Turkey.

Chehata, Chafik. 2012. "Dhimma." In *Encyclopaedia of Islam*, 2nd ed., edited by P. Bearman et al. Leiden: Brill.

Chevallier, Dominique. 1971. *La société du Mont Liban à l'époque de la révolution industrielle en Europe*. Paris: Geuthner.

Çilingir, Hamdi. 2015. "Elmalılı Muhammed Hamdi Yazır'ın Gözüyle Osmanlı Son Dönemi Vakıf Meseleleri." *İnsan & Toplum* 5 (9): 33–54.

Çizakça, Murat. 1995. "Cash Waqfs of Bursa, 1555–1823." *Journal of the Economic and Social History of the Orient* 38 (3): 313–54.

———. 2000. *A History of Philanthropic Foundations: The Islamic World from the Seventh Century to the Present*. İstanbul: Boğaziçi University Press.

Clarke, Morgan. 2012. "The Judge as Tragic Hero: Judicial Ethics in Lebanon's Shariʿa Courts." *American Ethnologist* 39 (1): 106–21. https://doi.org/10.1111/j.1548-1425.2011.01352.x.

———. 2018. *Islam and Law in Lebanon: Sharia within and without the State*. Cambridge: Cambridge University Press.

Commins, David Dean. 1990. *Islamic Reform: Politics and Social Change in Late Ottoman Syria*. New York: Oxford University Press.

Cotta, A. 1926. "Le régime du wakf en Égypte." PhD diss., Université de Paris, Faculté de droit.

Crecelius, Daniel. 1991. "The Waqf of Muhammad Bey Abu Al-Dhahab in Historical Perspective." *International Journal of Middle East Studies* 23 (1): 57–81.

Crétois, Pierre, and Stéphanie Roza. 2017. "De l'intérêt général: introduction." *Astérion: Philosophie, histoire des idées, pensée politique* 17 (novembre). http://journals.openedition.org/asterion/2996.

Cuno, Kenneth M. 1995. "Was the Land of Ottoman Syria *Miri* or *Milk?* An Examination of Juridical Differences within the Hanafi School." *Studia Islamica* 81: 121–52.

———. 1999. "Ideology and Juridical Discourse in Ottoman Egypt: The Uses of the Concept of *Irṣād*." *Islamic Law and Society* 6 (2): 136–63.

Darling, Linda T. 2013. *A History of Social Justice and Political Power in the Middle East: The Circle of Justice from Mesopotamia to Globalization*. New York: Routledge.

Das, Veena, and Deborah Poole, eds. 2004. *Anthropology in the Margins of the State*. Santa Fe, NM: School of American Research Press.

Davison, Roderic H. 1963. *Reform in the Ottoman Empire, 1856–1876*. Princeton, NJ: Princeton University Press.

Debasa, Ana María Carballeira. 2017. "The Use of Charity as a Means of Political Legitimation in Umayyad Al-Andalus." *Journal of the Economic and Social History of the Orient* 60 (3): 233–62. https://doi.org/10.1163/15685209-12341425.

Debs, Richard A. 2010. *Islamic Law and Civil Code: The Law of Property in Egypt*. New York: Columbia University Press.

Deeb, Lara. 2006. *An Enchanted Modern: Gender and Public Piety in Shi'i Lebanon*. Princeton, NJ: Princeton University Press.

Deguilhem, Randi. 2004. "On the Nature of Waqf: Pious Foundations in Contemporary Syria: A Break in the Tradition." In *Les fondations pieuses (waqf) en Méditerranée :*

enjeux de société, enjeux de pouvoir, edited by Randi Deguilhem and Abdelhamid Hénia, 395–430. Koweït: Fondation Publique des Awqaf du Koweït.

Deguilhem, Randi, and Abdelhamid Hénia, eds. 2004. *Les fondations pieuses (waqf) en Méditerranée: enjeux de société, enjeux de pouvoir*. Koweït: Fondation Publique des Awqaf du Koweït.

Deguilhem-Schoem, Randi Carolyn. 1986. "History of Waqf and Case Studies from Damascus in Late Ottoman and French Mandatory Times (Islam)." PhD diss., New York University.

Delavor, Youssef Mohamed. 1926. *Le wakf et l'utilité économique de son maintien en Egypte*. Paris: Marcel Vigné.

Donzelot, Jacques. 1979. *The Policing of Families*. New York: Pantheon Books.

Doughan, Yazan. 2018. "Corruption, Authority and the Discursive Production of Reform and Revolution in Jordan." PhD diss., University of Chicago.

Doumani, Beshara. 2017. *Family Life in the Ottoman Mediterranean: A Social History*. Cambridge: Cambridge University Press.

Dumper, Michael. 1994. *Islam and Israel: Muslim Religious Endowments and the Jewish State*. Washington, DC: Institute for Palestine Studies.

Eddé, Carla. 2009. *Beyrouth, naissance d'une capitale: 1918–1924*. Paris: Sindbad; Arles: Actes Sud.

El Shamsy, Ahmed. 2015. "Shame, Sin, and Virtue: Islamic Notions of Privacy." In *Public and Private in Ancient Mediterranean Law and Religion*, edited by Clifford Ando and Jörg Rüpke, 237–49. London: De Gruyter.

Eickelman, Dale F. 1992. "Mass Higher Education and the Religious Imagination in Contemporary Arab Societies." *American Ethnologist* 19 (4): 643–55.

Emrence, Cem. 2007. "Three Waves of Late Ottoman Historiography, 1950–2007." *Middle East Studies Association Bulletin* 41 (2): 137–51.

Ener, Mine. 2003. *Managing Egypt's Poor and the Politics of Benevolence, 1800–1952*. Princeton, NJ: Princeton University Press.

Engels, Friedrich, with introduction and notes by Eleanor Burke Leacock. 1972. *The Origin of the Family, Private Property, and the State, in the Light of the Researchs of Lewis H. Morgan*. New York: International Publishers.

Erie, Matthew S. 2016. "Sharia, Charity, and Minjian Autonomy in Muslim China: Gift Giving in a Plural World." *American Ethnologist* 43 (2): 311–24. https://doi.org/10.1111/amet.12307.

ESCWA. 2013. *Arab Forum: "Towards a New Welfare Mix: Rethinking the Roles of the State, Market and Civil Society in the Provision of Basic Social Services."* Beirut: Economic and Social Commission for Western Asia. https://www.unescwa.org/events/arab-forum-towards-new-welfare-mix-rethinking-roles-state-market-and-civil-society-provision.

Esmeir, Samera. 2012. *Juridical Humanity: A Colonial History*. Stanford, CA: Stanford University Press.

Eychenne, Mathie. 2018. "La gestion de la Mosquée des Omeyyades et de son *Waqf*." In *Le Waqf de la Mosquée des Omeyyades de Damas: Le manuscrit Ottoman d'un inventaire Mamelouk établi en 816/1413*, edited by Mathieu Eychenne, Astrid Meier, and Elodie Vigouroux, 311–26. Beyrouth: Institut français du Proche-Orient.

Fadel, Mohammad. 2007. "Riba, Efficiency, and Prudential Regulation: Preliminary Thoughts." *Wisconsin International Law Journal* 25 (4): 655–702.

———. 2014. "State and Sharia." In *The Ashgate Research Companion to Islamic Law*, edited by Rudolph Peters and P. J. Bearman, 93–107. Farnham: Ashgate.

———. 2017. "Islamic Law Reform: Between Reinterpretation and Democracy." *Yearbook of Islamic and Middle Eastern Law* 18 (2013–2015): 44–90.
Fakhuri, ʿAbd al-Latif. 2018. *Zawāyā Bayrūt*. Tanja: Dar al-Hadith al-Kattaniyya.
Faroqhi, Suraiya. 1997. "Part II: Crisis and Change, 1590–1699." In *An Economic and Social History of the Ottoman Empire*. Vol. 2, *1600–1914*, edited by Bruce McGowan, Donald Quataert, Sevket Pamuk, Halil Inalcik, and Suraiya Faroqhi, 411–636. Cambridge: Cambridge University Press.
Fawaz, Leila Tarazi. 1983. *Merchants and Migrants in Nineteenth-Century Beirut*. Cambridge, MA: Harvard University Press.
Fernandes, Leonor. 2000. "*Istibdal*: The Game of Exchange and Its Impact on the Urbanization of Mamluk Cairo." In *The Cairo Heritage: Essays in Honor of Laila Ali Ibrahim*, edited by Doris Behrens-Abouseif, 203–22. Cairo: American University in Cairo Press.
Fierro, Maribel. 2014. "Codifying the Law: The Case of the Medieval Islamic West." In *Diverging Paths?: The Shapes of Power and Institutions in Medieval Christendom and Islam*, edited by John Hudson and Ana Rodríguez, 98–118. Leiden: Brill.
Findley, Carter V. 1980. *Bureaucratic Reform in the Ottoman Empire: The Sublime Porte, 1789–1922*. Princeton, NJ: Princeton University Press.
———. 1989. *Ottoman Civil Officialdom: A Social History*. Princeton, NJ: Princeton University Press.
———. 1999. "A Quixotic Author and His Great Taxonomy: Mouradgea d'Ohsson and His *Tableau Général de l'Empire Othoman*." Paper presented at the 19th International Congress of Historical Sciences, Oslo.
Firro, Kais. 1990. "Silk and Agrarian Changes in Lebanon, 1860–1914." *International Journal of Middle East Studies* 22 (2): 151–69.
Fleischacker, Samuel. 2004. *A Short History of Distributive Justice*. Cambridge, MA: Harvard University Press.
Forster, Michael N. 2004. *Wittgenstein on the Arbitrariness of Grammar*. Princeton, NJ: Princeton University Press.
Foucault, Michel. 1991. "Governmentality." In *The Foucault Effect: Studies in Governmentality, with Two Lectures by and an Interview with Michel Foucault*, edited by Graham Burchell, Colin Gordon, and Peter Miller, 87–104. Chicago: University of Chicago Press.
———. 2008. *The Birth of Biopolitics: Lectures at the Collège de France, 1978–1979*, edited by Michel Senellart. Translated by Graham Burchell. New York: Palgrave Macmillan.
Gardet, L. 2012. "Dīn." In *Encyclopaedia of Islam*, 2nd ed., edited by P. J. Bearman et al. Leiden: Brill. https://referenceworks.brillonline.com/entries/encyclopaedia-of-islam-2/din-COM_0168.
Garrison, James D. 1992. *Pietas from Vergil to Dryden*. University Park: Pennsylvania State University Press.
Gaspard, Toufic K. 2004. *A Political Economy of Lebanon, 1948–2002: The Limits of Laissez-Faire*. Leiden: Brill.
Gatteschi, D. 1884. *Real Property, Mortgage and Wakf according to Ottoman Law*. London: Wyman & Sons.
Gaudiosi, Monica M. 1988. "The Influence of the Islamic Law of Waqf on the Development of the Trust in England: The Case of Merton College." *University of Pennsylvania Law Review* 136 (4): 1231–61.

Gebhardt, Hans, and Jens Hanssen, eds. 2005. *History, Space and Social Conflict in Beirut: The Quarter of Zokak El-Blat*. Beirut: Orient-Institut; Würzburg: Ergon Verlag in Kommission.

Gerber, Haim. 1985. *Ottoman Rule in Jerusalem: 1890–1914*. Berlin: K. Schwarz.

———. 1987. *The Social Origins of the Modern Middle East*. Boulder, CO: L. Rienner; London: Mansell.

———. 2002. "The Public Sphere and Civil Society in the Ottoman Empire." In *The Public Sphere in Muslim Societies*, edited by Miriam Hoexter, S. N. Eisenstadt, and Nehemia Levtzion, 65–82. Albany: State University of New York Press.

Gesink, Indira Falk. 2009. *Islamic Reform and Conservatism: Al-Azhar and the Evolution of Modern Sunni Islam*. London: I. B.Tauris.

Ghazzal, Zouhair. 2001. Review of "Richard van Leeuwen. 1999. *Waqfs and Urban Structures: The Case of Ottoman Damascus*. Leiden: Brill." *International Journal of Middle East Studies* 33 (4): 618–20.

———. 2007. *The Grammars of Adjudication: The Economics of Judicial Decision Making in Fin-de-Siècle Ottoman Beirut and Damascus*. Beyrouth: Institut Français du Proche-Orient.

al-Ghazzi al-Halabi, Muhammad. 1909. "Muqaddima." In Ömer Hilmi, *İtḥâf*. Halab: Matbaʿat al-Bahaʾ.

Gleave, R. 2012. *Islam and Literalism: Literal Meaning and Interpretation in Islamic Legal Theory*. Edinburgh: Edinburgh University Press.

Graeber, David. 2011. *Debt: The First 5,000 Years*. Brooklyn, NY: Melville House.

Gray, John Chipman. 1886. *The Rule Against Perpetuities*. Boston: Little, Brown.

Güçlü, Eda. 2009. "Transformation of Waqf Property in the Nineteenth-Century Ottoman Empire." MA thesis, Sabancı University, Istanbul.

Gunn, J. A. W. 1969. *Politics and the Public Interest in the Seventeenth Century*. London: Routledge & Paul; Toronto: University of Toronto Press.

Güran, Tevfik. 2006. *Ekonomik ve Malî Yönleriyle Vakıflar: Süleymaniye ve Şehzade Süleyman Paşa Vakıfları*. İstanbul: Kitabevi.

Haddad, George ʿAzar al-. 2015. "Al-Ṭāʾifiyya al-Māliyya wa al-Ḍarībiyya fī Lubnān." *Legal Agenda* 31: 14-15. https://www.legal-agenda.com/article.php?id=1221.

Haddad, Yvonne Yazbeck, and John L. Esposito. 1997. *The Islamic Revival since 1988: A Critical Survey and Bibliography*. Westport, CT: Greenwood Press.

Haj, Samira. 2011. *Reconfiguring Islamic Tradition: Reform, Rationality, and Modernity*. Stanford, CA: Stanford University Press.

Halley, Janet, and Kerry Rittich. 2010. "Critical Directions in Comparative Family Law: Genealogies and Contemporary Studies of Family Law Exceptionalism." *American Journal of Comparative Law* 58: 753–76.

Hallaq, Hassan. 1985. *Awqāf al-Muslimīn fī Bayrūt fī al-ʿAhd al-ʿUthmānī: Sijillāt al-Maḥkama al-Sharʿiyya fī Bayrūt*. Bayrut: Al-Markaz al-Islamī li'l-Iʿlam wa al-Inmaʾ.

Hallaq, Wael B. 1984. "Was the Gate of Ijtihad Closed?" *International Journal of Middle East Studies* 16 (1): 3–41.

———. 1997. *A History of Islamic Legal Theories: An Introduction to Sunnī* Uṣūl al-Fiqh. Cambridge: Cambridge University Press.

———. 1998. "The '*Qāḍī's Dīwān* (*Sijill*)' before the Ottomans." *Bulletin of the School of Oriental and African Studies* 61 (3): 415–36.

———. 2001. *Authority, Continuity and Change in Islamic Law*. Cambridge: Cambridge University Press.

———. 2005. "What Is Shariʿa?" *Yearbook of Islamic and Middle Eastern Law, 2005–2006* 12: 151–80.

———. 2009. *Sharīʿa: Theory, Practice, Transformations*. Cambridge: Cambridge University Press.

———. 2013. *The Impossible State: Islam, Politics, and Modernity's Moral Predicament*. New York: Columbia University Press.

Haller, Dieter, and Cris Shore. 2005. "Introduction." In *Corruption: Anthropological Perspectives*, edited by Dieter Haller and Cris Shore, 1–26. London and Ann Arbor, MI: Pluto.

Hamdy, Sherine. 2012. *Our Bodies Belong to God: Organ Transplants, Islam, and the Struggle for Human Dignity in Egypt*. Berkeley: University of California Press.

Hanioğlu, M. Şükrü. 2008. *A Brief History of the Late Ottoman Empire*. Princeton, NJ: Princeton University Press.

Hann, Chris M. 1998. "Introduction: The Embeddedness of Property." In *Property Relations: Renewing the Anthropological Tradition*, edited by Chris M. Hann. 1-47. Cambridge: Cambridge University Press.

Hanssen, Jens. 1998. "'Your Beirut Is on My Desk:' Ottomanizing Beirut under Sultan Abdulhamid II." In *Projecting Beirut: Episodes in the Construction and Reconstruction of a Modern City*, edited by Peter G. Rowe and Hashim Sarkis, 41–67. Munich: Prestel.

———. 2002. "Practices of Integration: Center-Periphery Relations in the Ottoman Empire." In *The Empire in the City: Arab Provincial Capitals in the Late Ottoman Empire*, edited by Jens Hanssen, Thomas Philipp, and Stefan Weber, 49–74. Würzburg: Ergon in Kommission.

———. 2005. *Fin de Siècle Beirut: The Making of an Ottoman Provincial Capital*. Oxford: Clarendon Press; New York: Oxford University Press.

Hanssen, Jens, Thomas Philipp, and Stefan Weber. 2002. "Introduction: Towards a New Urban Paradigm." In *The Empire in the City: Arab Provincial Capitals in the Late Ottoman Empire*, edited by Jens Hanssen, Thomas Philipp, and Stefan Weber, 1–25. Würzburg: Ergon in Kommission.

Harding, Matthew. 2008. "Trusts for Religious Purposes and the Question of Public Benefit." *Modern Law Review* 71 (2): 159–82.

al-Harithy, Howayda. 2008. "Weaving Historical Narratives: Beirut's Last Mamluk Monument." *Muqarnas* 25: 215–30.

Hariz, Salim. 1994. *Al-Waqf: Dirāsāt wa Abḥāth*. Edited by Fadi Salim Hariz. Bayrut: Manshurat al-Jamiʿa al-Lubnaniyya.

Harvey, David. 2006. *The Limits to Capital*. London: Verso. Originally published in 1982.

———. 2012. *Rebel Cities: From the Right to the City to the Urban Revolution*. New York: Verso.

Hasan, Harith. 2019. "Religious Authority and the Politics of Islamic Endowments in Iraq." Carnegie Middle East Center, 29 March. https://carnegie-mec.org/2019/03/29/religious-authority-and-politics-of-islamic-endowments-in-iraq-pub-78726.

Hénia, Abdelhamid. 2004. "La Gestion des waqf khayri en Tunisie à l'époque coloniale: Du monopole privé au monopole public." In *Les Fondations pieuses (waqf) en Méditerranée:*

Enjeux de société, enjeux de pouvoir, edited by Randi Deguilhem and Abdelhamid Hénia, 285–321. Koweït: Fondation Publique des Awqaf du Koweït.

Henley, Alexander. 2013. "Politics of Religious Leadership in Modern Lebanon." PhD diss., University of Manchester.

Hennigan, Peter C. 2004. *The Birth of a Legal Institution: The Formation of the Waqf in Third-Century AH Ḥanafī Legal Discourse*. Leiden: Brill.

Heyd, Uriel. 1969. "Some Aspects of the Ottoman Fetvā." *Bulletin of the School of Oriental and African Studies* 32 (1): 35–56.

Heyworth-Dunne, J. 1939. "Rifāʿah Badawī Rāfiʿ aṭ-Ṭahṭāwī: The Egyptian Revivalist." *Bulletin of the School of Oriental Studies, University of London* 9 (4): 961–67.

Hirschman, Albert O. 1977. *The Passions and the Interests: Political Arguments for Capitalism before Its Triumph*. Princeton, NJ: Princeton University Press.

Hodgson, Marshall G. S. 1974. *The Venture of Islam: Conscience and History in a World Civilization*. 3 vols. Chicago: University of Chicago Press.

Hoexter, Miriam. 1984. "Le Contrat de quasi-aliénation des awqāf à Alger à la fin de la domination turque: Étude de deux documents d'ʾ*Anā*ʾ." *Bulletin of the School of Oriental and African Studies* 47 (2): 243–59.

———. 1995. "*Ḥuqūq Allāh* and *Ḥuqūq al-ʿIbād* as Reflected in the *Waqf* Institution." *Jerusalem Studies in Arabic and Islam* 19: 133–56.

———. 1997. "Adaptation to Changing Circumstances: Perpetual Leases and Exchange Transactions in Waqf Property in Ottoman Algiers." *Islamic Law and Society* 4 (3): 319–33.

———. 1998a. *Endowments, Rulers, and Community: Waqf Al-Haramayn in Ottoman Algiers*. Leiden: Brill.

———. 1998b. "Waqf Studies in the Twentieth Century: The State of the Art." *Journal of the Economic and Social History of the Orient* 41 (4): 474–95.

Hoexter, Miriam, S. N. Eisenstadt, and Nehemia Levtzion, eds. 2002. *The Public Sphere in Muslim Societies*. Albany: State University of New York Press.

Hourani, Albert. 1962. *Arabic Thought in the Liberal Age 1798–1939*. Cambridge: Cambridge University Press.

Hourani, Najib. 2005. "Capitalists in Conflict: A Political Economy of the Life, Death and Rebirth of Beirut." PhD diss., New York University.

———. 2012. "From National Utopia to Elite Enclave: The Selling of the Beirut Souqs." In *Global Downtowns*, edited by Gary McDonogh and Marina Peterson. Philadelphia: University of Pennsylvania Press.

Hovden, Eirik. 2019. *Waqf in Zaydi Yemen: Legal Theory, Codification, and Local Practice*. Leiden: Brill.

Humphrey, Caroline, and Katherine Verdery. 2004. "Introduction: Raising Questions about Property." In *Property in Question: Value Transformation in the Global Economy*, edited by Katherine Verdery and Caroline Humphrey, 1–25. Oxford: Berg.

Huri, Tawfiq. n.d. *Al-Muʾassasāt al-Waqfiyya . . . Min Minẓār Ḥadīth-Qadīm*. Beirut: s.n.

———. 1989. *Al-Awqāf al-khayriyya dhāt manfaʿa ʿāmma*. Beirut: s.n.

Hut, ʿAbd al-Rahman al-. 1984. *Al-Awqāf al-Islāmiyya fī Lubnān*. Beirut: ʿAbd al-Rahman al-Hut.

Ibnülemin Inal, Mahmud Kemal, and Hüseyin Hüsâmeddîn Yasar. 1917. *Evḳâf-i Hümâyûn Neẓâretinin Târîhçe Teşkîlâti*. Darül-Hilafet ül-ʿAliyye: Evkaf-i Islamiyye Matbaʿasi.

Ibrahim, Ahmed Fekry. 2015. "The Codification Episteme in Islamic Juristic Discourse between Inertia and Change." *Islamic Law and Society* 22 (3): 157–220.

Igarashi, Daisuke. 2019. "The Waqf-Endowment Strategy of a Mamluk Military Man: The Contexts, Motives, and Purposes of the Endowments of Qijmās al-Isḥāqī (d. 1487)." *Bulletin of the School of Oriental and African Studies* 82 (1): 25–53. https://doi.org/10.1017/S0041977X18001519.

Illich, Ivan. 1992. "Needs." In *The Development Dictionary: A Guide to Knowledge as Power*, edited by Wolfgang Sachs, 130–45. London: Zed Books.

İnalcık, Halil. 2012. "Imtiyāzāt. In the Ottoman Empire." In *Encyclopaedia of Islam*, 2nd ed., edited by P. Bearman et al. Leiden: Brill.

Iqtidar, Humeira. 2011. *Secularizing Islamists?: Jamaʿat-e-Islami and Jamaʿat-ud-Daʿwa in Urban Pakistan*. Chicago: University of Chicago Press.

Isin, Engin, and Ebru Üstündağ. 2008. "Wills, Deeds, Acts: Women's Civic Gift-Giving in Ottoman Istanbul." *Gender, Place and Culture* 15 (5): 519–32.

İslamoğlu-İnan, Huri, ed. 1988. *The Ottoman Empire and the World-Economy*. Cambridge: Cambridge University Press; Paris: Éditions de la Maison des Sciences de l'Homme.

İslamoğlu, Huri. 2000. "Property as a Contested Domain: A Reevaluation of the Ottoman Land Code of 1858." In *New Perspectives on Property and Land in the Middle East*, edited by Roger Owen, 3–62. Cambridge, MA: Harvard Center for Middle Eastern Studies.

Jakobsen, Janet R., and Ann Pellegrini, eds. 2008. *Secularisms*. Durham, NC: Duke University Press.

Janssens, Gérard Busson de. 1951. "Les Wakfs dans l'Islam Contemporain." *Revue des Études Islamiques* 19: 5–72.

Johansen, Baber. 1988. *The Islamic Law on Land Tax and Rent: The Peasants' Loss of Property Rights under the Hanafite Doctrine*. London: Croom Helm.

———. 1999. *Contingency in a Sacred Law: Legal and Ethical Norms in the Muslim Fiqh*. Leiden: Brill.

Johnson, Michael. 1986. *Class & Client in Beirut: The Sunni Muslim Community and the Lebanese State, 1840–1985*. London: Ithaca Press.

Joseph, Sabrina. 2014. "*Waqf* in Historical Perspective: Online *Fatāwā* and Contemporary Discourses by Muslim Scholars." *Journal of Muslim Minority Affairs* 34 (4): 425–37.

Joseph, Suad. 1994. "Brother/Sister Relationships: Connectivity, Love, and Power in the Reproduction of Patriarchy in Lebanon." *American Ethnologist* 21 (1): 50–73. https://doi.org/10.1525/ae.1994.21.1.02a00030.

———. 1997. "The Public/Private: The Imagined Boundary in the Imagined Nation/State/Community: The Lebanese Case." *Feminist Review*, no. 57: 73–92.

al-Jundi, Adham. 1960. *Tārīkh al-Thawrāt al-Sūriyya fī ʿAhd al-Intidāb al-Faransī*. Dimashq: Matbaʿat al-Ittihad.

Kabbani, Oussama. 1992. *The Reconstruction of Beirut*. Oxford: Centre for Lebanese Studies.

Kahf, Monzer. 2004. "Al-Dawr al-Iqtiṣādī li'l-Waqf fī al-Taṣawwur al-Islāmī". http://monzer.kahf.com/papers/arabic/adawr_al-iqtisadi_lilwaqf.pdf.

Karamustafa, Ahmet T. 2017. "Islamic *Dīn* as an Alternative to Western Models of 'Religion.'" In *Religion, Theory, Critique: Classic and Contemporary Approaches and Methodologies*, edited by Richard King, 163–71. New York: Columbia University Press.

Karataş, Hasan. 2011. "The Cash Waqfs Debate of 1545–1548: Anatomy of a Legal Debate at the Age of Süleyman the Lawgiver." *İnsan ve Toplum* 1 (1): 45–66.

Keeler, Annabel. 2017. "The Concept of Adab in Early Sufism with Particular Reference to the Teachings of Sahl b. ʿAbdallāh al-Tustarī (d. 283/896)." In *Ethics and Spirituality in Islam: Sufi Adab*, edited by Francesco Chiabotti, Ève Feuillebois, Catherine Mayeur-Jaouen, and Luca Patrizi, 63–101. Leiden: Brill.

Keyder, Çağlar, and Faruk Tabak, eds. 1991. *Landholding and Commercial Agriculture in the Middle East*. Albany: State University of New York Press.

Khalaf, Samir, and Philip S. Khoury, eds. 1993. *Recovering Beirut: Urban Design and Post-War Reconstruction*. Leiden: Brill.

Khater, Akram Fouad. 2001. *Inventing Home: Emigration, Gender, and the Middle Class in Lebanon, 1870–1920*. Berkeley: University of California Press.

Khayat, Habeeb Albert. 1962. "Waqfs in Palestine and Israel from the Ottoman Reforms to the Present." PhD diss., American University, Washington, DC.

Khoury, Philip S. 1987. *Syria and the French Mandate: The Politics of Arab Nationalism, 1920–1945*. Princeton, NJ: Princeton University Press.

Kilborn, Jason J. 2011. "Foundations of Forgiveness in Islamic Bankruptcy Law: Sources, Methodology, Diversity." *American Bankruptcy Law Journal* 85: 323–62.

Kırlı, Cengiz. 2015. *Yolsuzluğun icadı: 1840 ceza kanunu, iktidar, ve bürokrasi*. İstanbul: Verita.

Kirsch, Stuart. 2014. "Imagining Corporate Personhood." *PoLAR: Political and Legal Anthropology Review* 37 (2): 207–17. https://anthrosource.onlinelibrary.wiley.com/doi/abs/10.1111/plar.12070.

Klassen, Pamela. 2014. "Mentality, Fundamentality, and the Colonial Secular; or How Real Is Real Estate?" In *Transformations of Religion and the Public Sphere*, edited by Rosi Braidotti, Bolette Blaagaard, Tobijn de Graauw, and Eva Midden, 175–94. London: Palgrave Macmillan.

Klat, P. J. 1961. "Waqf, or Mortmain, Property in Lebanon." *Middle East Economic Papers*, 34–44.

Knost, Stefan. 2010. "The Impact of the 1822 Earthquake on the Administration of *Waqf* in Aleppo." In *Syria and Bilad Al-Sham under Ottoman Rule: Essays in Honour of Abdul Karim Rafeq*, edited by Peter Sluglett and Stefan Weber, 293–305. Leiden: Brill.

Kogelmann, Franz. 2005. "Legal Regulation of Moroccan Habous under French Rule: Local Practice vs. Islamic Law?" In *Shattering Tradition: Custom, Law and the Individual in the Muslim Mediterranean*, edited by Walter Dostal and Wolfgang Kraus, 208–32. London: I. B. Tauris.

Kosmatopoulos, Nikolas. 2011. "Toward an Anthropology of 'State Failure': Lebanon's Leviathan and Peace Expertise." *Social Analysis* 55 (3): 115–42.

Kozlowski, Gregory C. 1985. *Muslim Endowments and Society in British India*. New York: Cambridge University Press.

Kupferschmidt, Uri. 2008. "The Illusion of British and French Waqf Control: Some Comparisons between the Mandates for Palestine and Syria-Lebanon." Paper presented to the 2nd Waqf Conference: Modern State Control and Nationalization, Islamic Legal Studies Program, Harvard University, Cambridge, MA, 16–18 May 2008.

Kuran, Timur. 2005. "The Absence of the Corporation in Islamic Law: Origins and Persistence." *American Journal of Comparative Law* 53 (4): 785–834.

Lajnat Huquq al-Insan al-Niyabiyya and UNDP. 2008. *Ḥurriyyat al-Jamʿiyyāt*. Bayrut: Majlis al-Nuwwab, al-Jumhuriyya al-Lubnaniyya. https://www.lp.gov.lb/ViewPublications.aspx?id=11.

Latron, André. 1936. *La Vie rurale en Syrie et au Liban: Étude d'économie sociale*. Beyrouth: Imprimerie Catholique.

Layish, Aharon. 1983. "The Mālikī Family *Waqf* according to Wills and *Waqfiyyāt*." *Bulletin of the School of Oriental and African Studies* 46 (1): 1–32.

Leenders, Reinoud. 2012. *Spoils of Truce: Corruption and State-Building in Postwar Lebanon*. Ithaca, NY: Cornell University Press.

Lemons, Katherine. 2019. *Divorcing Traditions: Islamic Marriage Law and the Making of Indian Secularism*. Ithaca, NY: Cornell University Press.

Locke, John. 2005. *Two Treaties of Government*. Edited by Peter Laslett. Cambridge: Cambridge University Press.

Longrigg, Stephen Hemsley. 1958. *Syria and Lebanon under French Mandate*. London: Oxford University Press.

Luccioni, Joseph. 1982. *Les Fondations pieuses "habous" au Maroc: Depuis les origines jusquà 1956*. Rabat: Imprimerie Royale.

Lundwall, Mary Kay. 1994. "Inconsistency and Uncertainty in the Charitable Purposes Doctrine." *Wayne Law Review* 41: 1341–84.

MacIntyre, Alasdair. 1984. *After Virtue: A Study in Moral Theory*, 2nd ed. South Bend, IN: University of Notre Dame Press.

Madelung, W. 2012. "Imāma." In *Encyclopaedia of Islam*, 2nd ed., edited by P. J. Bearman et al. Leiden: Brill. https://referenceworks.brillonline.com/entries/encyclopaedia-of-islam-2/imama-COM_0369.

Mahmood, Saba. 2005. *Politics of Piety: The Islamic Revival and the Feminist Subject*. Princeton, NJ: Princeton University Press.

Maʿoz, Moshe. 1968. *Ottoman Reform in Syria and Palestine, 1840–1861: The Impact of the Tanzimat on Politics and Society*. Oxford: Clarendon.

Maitland, F. W. 2003. *Maitland: State, Trust and Corporation*. Edited by David Runciman and Magnus Ryan. New York: Cambridge University Press.

Majed, Rima, and Lana Salman. 2019. "Lebanon's Thawra | MERIP." *Middle East Report* 292 (3). https://merip.org/2019/12/lebanons-thawra/.

Makdisi, George. 1981. *The Rise of Colleges: Institutions of Learning in Islam and the West*. Edinburgh: Edinburgh University Press.

Makdisi, Saree. 1997. "Laying Claim to Beirut: Urban Narrative and Spatial Identity in the Age of Solidere." *Critical Inquiry* 23 (3): 661–705. https://doi.org/10.1086/448848.

Makdisi, Ussama Samir. 2000. *Culture of Sectarianism: Community, History, and Violence in Nineteenth-Century Ottoman Lebanon*. Berkeley: University of California Press.

Makhluf, Muhammad Hasanayn al-ʿAdwI al-Maliki. 1932. *Manhaj al-Yaqīn fī Bayān anna al-Waqf al-Ahlī min al-Dīn*. Egypt: Mustafa al-Babi al-Halabi wa Awladih.

Mandaville, Jon, E. 1979. "Usurious Piety: The Cash Waqf Controversy in the Ottoman Empire." *International Journal of Middle East Studies* 10 (3): 289–308.

Mango, Tamam. 2004. "Solidere: The Battle for Beirut's Central District." MA thesis, Massachusetts Institute of Technology.

Marcus, Abraham. 1989. *The Middle East on the Eve of Modernity: Aleppo in the Eighteenth Century*. New York: Columbia University Press.

Mardin, Şerif. 1962. *The Genesis of Young Ottoman Thought: A Study in the Modernization of Turkish Political Ideas*. Princeton, NJ: Princeton University Press.

Markesinis, Basil S. 1978. "Cause and Consideration: A Study in Parallel." *Cambridge Law Journal* 37 (1): 53–75.

Martin, John Jeffries. 2004. *Myths of Renaissance Individualism*. Basingstoke, UK: Palgrave Macmillan.

Marx, Karl. 1992. *Capital*. Vol. 1, *A Critique of Political Economy*. Translated by Ben Fowkes. New York: Penguin Classics.

Massouda, Abbas Yaphet. 1925. "Contribution à l'étude du 'wakf' en droit égyptien." PhD diss., Université de Paris.

Masud, Muhammad Khalid, Brinkley Messick, and David Stephan Powers, eds. 1996. *Islamic Legal Interpretation: Muftis and Their Fatwas*. Cambridge, MA: Harvard University Press.

Mattson, Ingrid. 2003. "Status-Based Definitions of Need in Early Islamic Zakat and Maintenance Laws." In *Poverty and Charity in Middle Eastern Contexts*, edited by Michael David Bonner, Mine Ener, and Amy Singer. Albany: State University of New York Press.

Mayeur-Jaouen, Catherine. 1994. *Al-Sayyid Aḥmad al-Badawī: Un grand saint de l'islam égyptien*. Le Caire: Institut Français d'Archéologie Orientale.

McChesney, Robert D. 1991. *Waqf in Central Asia: Four Hundred Years in the History of a Muslim Shrine, 1480–1889*. Princeton, NJ: Princeton University Press.

McGoey, Linsey. 2015. *No Such Thing as a Free Gift: The Gates Foundation and the Price of Philanthropy*. London: Verso.

Meier, Astrid. 2002. "*Waqf* Only in Name, Not in Essence: Early Tanẓīmāt Waqf Reforms in the Province of Damascus." In *The Empire in the City: Arab Provincial Capitals in the Late Ottoman Empire*, edited by Jens Hanssen, Thomas Philipp, and Stefan Weber, 201–18. Würzburg: Ergon in Kommission.

———. 2015. "Un *Istibdāl* révoqué: Raisonnement juridique et enjeux d'interprétation." In *Lire et écrire l'histoire ottomane*, edited by Vanessa Guéno and Stefan Knost, 87–106. Beyrouth: Presses de l'IFPO, Orient-Institut Beirut.

———. 2016. "The Materiality of Ottoman Water Administration in Eighteenth-Century Rural Damascus." In *Landscapes of the Islamic World: Archaeology, History, and Ethnography*, edited by Stephen McPhillips and Paul D. Wordsworth, 19–33. Philadelphia: University of Pennsylvania Press.

Méouchy, Nadine. 2006. "La Réforme des juridictions religieuses en Syrie et au Liban (1921–1939): Raisons de la puissance mandataire et raisons des communautés." In *Le choc colonial et l'islam: Les politiques religieuses des puissances coloniales en terres d'islam*, edited by Pierre-Jean Luizard, 359–82. Paris: Découverte.

Mercier, Ernest. 1899. *Le Code du hobous ou ouakf, selon la législation musulmane*. Constantine, Algérie: Imprimerie Nationale.

Mermier, Franck. 2015. *Récits de villes: D'Aden à Beyrouth: Essai*. Bibliothèque Arabe, Collection Hommes et Sociétés. Arles: Actes Sud.

Messick, Brinkley. 1993. *The Calligraphic State: Textual Domination and History in a Muslim Society*. Berkeley, CA: University of California Press.

———. 2001. "Indexing the Self: Intent and Expression in Islamic Legal Acts." *Islamic Law and Society* 8 (2): 151–78.

———. 2018. *Shariʿa Scripts: A Historical Anthropology*. New York: Columbia University Press.

Mikdashi, Maya. 2017. "Sextarianism: Notes on Studying the Lebanese State." In *Oxford Handbook of Contemporary Middle-Eastern and North African History*, edited by Amal N. Ghazal and Jens Hanssen. Oxford: Oxford University Press. https://doi.org/10.1093/oxfordhb/9780199672530.013.24.

Mitchell, Timothy. 2006. "Society, Economy, and the State-Effect." In *The Anthropology of the State: A Reader*, edited by Aradhana Sharma and Akhil Gupta, 169–86. Malden, MA: Blackwell. Essay first published in 1999.

Mittermaier, Amira. 2013. "Trading with God: Islam, Calculation, Excess." In *A Companion to the Anthropology of Religion*, edited by Janice Boddy and Michael Lambek, 274–93. Chichester, West Sussex, UK: Wiley-Blackwell.

———. 2019. *Giving to God: Islamic Charity in Revolutionary Times*. Oakland, CA: University of California Press.

Mohasseb Saliba, Sabine. 2008. *Les Monastères maronites doubles du Liban: Entre Rome et l'Empire Ottoman, XVIIe-XIXe siècles*. Paris: Geuthner; Kaslik, Liban: PUSEK.

Morris, Herbert. 1976. *On Guilt and Innocence: Essays in Legal Philosophy and Moral Psychology*. Berkeley: University of California Press.

Moukheiber, Ghassan. 2002. *Al-Jamʿiyyāt fī Lubnān: Dirāsa Qānūniyya*. Bayrut: Wazart al-Shuʿun al-Ijtimaʿiyya.

Moumtaz, Nada. 2015. "Refiguring Islam." In *A Companion to the Anthropology of the Middle East*, edited by Soraya Altorki, 125–50. Chichester, West Sussex, UK: Wiley Blackwell.

———. 2018a. "'Is the Family *Waqf* a Religious Institution?' Charity, Religion, and Economy in French Mandate Lebanon." *Islamic Law and Society* 25 (1–2): 37–77. https://doi.org/10.1163/15685195-02512P03.

———. 2018b. "Theme Issue: A Third Wave of *Waqf* Studies." *Islamic Law and Society* 25 (1–2): 1–10. https://doi.org/10.1163/15685195-02512P01.

———. 2018c. "From Forgiveness to Foreclosure: *Waqf*, Debt, and the Remaking of the Ḥanafī Legal Subject in Late Ottoman Mount Lebanon." *The Muslim World* 108 (4): 593–612.

al-Mudiriyya al-ʿAmma li'l-Awqaf al-Islamiyya fi al-Jumhuriyya al-Lubnaniyya. 1982. *Al-Mudīriyya al-ʿĀmma Li'l-Awqāf al-Islāmiyya Bayn al-Wāqiʿ wa al-Murtajā*. Beirut: Al-Mudiriyya al-ʿAmma li'l-Awqaf al-Islamiyya.

———. n.d. *Majmūʿat Qawānīn al-Awqāf*. Beirut (?): Al-Mudiriyya al-ʿAmma li'l-Awqaf al-Islamiyya.

Mudiriyyat al-Awqaf al-ʿAmma. 1938. *Mashrūʿ Qānūn al-Awqāf al-Islāmiyya li-Sanat 1938*. n.p.: Mudiriyyat al-Awqaf al-ʿAmma.

Müller, Christian. 2008. "A Legal Instrument in the Service of People and Institutions: Endowments in Mamluk Jerusalem as Mirrored in the Haram Documents." *Mamluk Studies Review* 12 (1): 173–91.

Mundy, Martha, and Richard Saumarez Smith. 2007. *Governing Property, Making the Modern State: Law Administration and Production in Ottoman Syria*. London: I. B. Tauris.

Murphy, Stacey. 2009. "'Compassionate' Strategies of Managing Homelessness: Post-Revanchist Geographies in San Francisco." *Antipode* 41 (2): 305–25.

Nadasdy, Paul. 2002. "'Property' and Aboriginal Land Claims in the Canadian Subarctic: Some Theoretical Considerations." *American Anthropologist* 104 (1): 247–61.

Nasif, Muhammad. 1928. "Ibṭāl al-Waqf al-Ahlī." *Al-Manar* 29 (2): 136–42.

Nucho, Joanne. 2016. *Everyday Sectarianism in Urban Lebanon: Infrastructures, Public Services, and Power*. Princeton, NJ: Princeton University Press.

al-Nusuli, Muhammad Anis. 2010. "Al-Fāsid: Bāʾiʿ al-Qubūr." *Essanad* (blog). 2010. https://www.maghress.com/essanad/1352.

Obeid, Michelle. 2011. "The 'Trials and Errors' of Politics: Municipal Elections at the Lebanese Border." *PoLAR: Political and Legal Anthropology Review* 34 (2): 251–67. https://doi.org/10.1111/j.1555-2934.2011.01165.x.

———. 2015. "'States of Aspiration': Anthropology and New Questions for the Middle East." In *A Companion to the Anthropology of the Middle East*, edited by Soraya Altorki, 434–52. Chichester, West Sussex, UK: Wiley Blackwell.

Oberauer, Norbert. 2013. "Early Doctrines on Waqf Revisited: The Evolution of Islamic Endowment Law in the 2nd Century AH." *Islamic Law and Society* 20 (1–2): 1–47.

Omar, Hanaa H. Kilany. 2001. "Apostasy in the Mamluk Period: The Politics of Accusations of Unbelief." PhD diss., University of Pennsylvania.

O'Neill, Kevin Lewis. 2013. "Left Behind: Security, Salvation, and the Subject of Prevention." *Cultural Anthropology* 28 (2): 204–26. https://doi.org/10.1111/cuan.12001.

Ongley, Frederick, and Horace Edward Miller, eds. 1892. *The Ottoman Land Code*. London: W. Clowes.

Opwis, Felicitas Maria. 2005. "*Maṣlaḥa* in Contemporary Islamic Legal Theory." *Islamic Law and Society* 12 (2): 182–223.

———. 2010. *Maṣlaḥa and the Purpose of the Law: Islamic Discourse on Legal Change from the 4th/10th to 8th/14th Century*. Leiden: Brill.

Ortaylı, İlber. 1983. *İmparatorluğum En Uzun Yüzyılı*. İstanbul: Hil Yayın.

Örücü, Esin. 1992. "The Impact of European Law on the Ottoman Empire and Turkey." In *European Expansion and Law: The Encounter of European and Indigenous Law in 19th- and 20th-Century Africa and Asia*, edited by Wolfgang J. Mommsen and Jaap de Moor, 39–58. New York: Berg.

Osanloo, Arzoo. 2006. "Islamico-Civil 'Rights Talk': Women, Subjectivity, and Law in Iranian Family Court." *American Ethnologist* 33 (2): 191–209.

———. 2019. "Subjecting the State to Seeing: Charity, Security, and the Dispossessed in Iran's Islamic Republic." In *Governing Gifts: Faith, Charity, and the Security State*, edited by Erica Caple James, 59–77. Albuquerque: University of New Mexico Press.

Owen, Edward Roger John. 1993. *The Middle East in the World Economy, 1800–1914*. London: I. B. Tauris.

Özbek, Nadir. 2005. "Philanthropic Activity, Ottoman Patriotism, and the Hamidian Regime, 1876–1909." *International Journal of Middle East Studies* 37 (1): 59–81. https://doi.org/10.1017/S0020743805050051.

Özcan, Tahsin. 2003. *Osmanlı Para Vakıfları: Kanunı Dönemi Üsküdar Örneği*. Türk Tarih Kurumu Yayınlarından. VII. Dizi, sa. 199. Ankara: Türk Tarih Kurumu Basımevi.

———. 2007. "Ömer Hilmi Efendi." In *İslam Ansiklopedisi*, 34: 70–71. Üsküdar: Türkiye Diyanet Vakfı.

———. 2008. "Legitimization Process of Cash Foundations: An Analysis of the Application of Islamic Waqf Law in Ottoman Society." *İstanbul Üniversitesi İlahiyat Fakültesi Dergisi*, no. 18: 235–48.

Özsu, Umut. 2012. "Ottoman Empire." In *The Oxford Handbook of the History of International Law*, edited by Bardo Fassbender and Anne Peters, 429–46. Oxford: Oxford University Press.

Öztürk, Nazif. 1995a. "Giriş." In *Elmalılı M. Hamdi Yazır Gözüyle Vakıflar: Ahkâmu'l-Evkaf*. Ankara: Türkiye Diyanet Vakfı.

———. 1995b. *Türk Yenileşme Tarihi Çerçevesinde Vakıf Müessesesi*. Ankara: Türkiye Diyanet Vakfı.

Pall, Zoltan. 2013. *Lebanese Salafis between the Gulf and Europe: Development, Fractionalization and Transnational Networks of Salafism in Lebanon*. Amsterdam: Amsterdam University Press.

———. 2018. *Salafism in Lebanon: Local and Transnational Movements*. Cambridge: University Press.

Pamuk, Şevket. 1987. *The Ottoman Empire and European Capitalism, 1820–1913: Trade, Investment, and Production*. Cambridge: Cambridge University Press.

Parry, Jonathan. 1986. "The Gift, the Indian Gift and the 'Indian Gift.'" *Man*, 453–73.

Peletz, Michael. 2001. "Ambivalence in Kinship since the 1940s." In *Relative Values: Reconfiguring Kinship Studies*, edited by Sarah Franklin and Susan McKinnon, 413–44. Durham, NC: Duke University Press.

Peters, R. 2012. "Waḳf: I. In Classical Islamic Law." *Encyclopaedia of Islam*, 2nd ed., edited by P. Bearman et al. Leiden: Brill. http://dx.doi.org/10.1163/1573-3912_islam_COM_1333.

Peters, Rudolph. 2002. "From Jurists' Law to Statute Law or What Happens When the Shariʿa Is Codified." *Mediterranean Politics* 7 (3): 82–95.

Peters, Rudolph, and P. J. Bearman, eds. 2014. *The Ashgate Research Companion to Islamic Law*. Farnham, Surrey, UK: Ashgate.

Petry, Carl F. 1983. "A Paradox of Patronage during the Later Mamluk Period." *Muslim World* 73 (3–4): 182–207. https://doi.org/10.1111/j.1478-1913.1983.tb03264.x.

———. 1998. "Fractionalized Estates in a Centralized Regime: The Holdings of al-Ashraf Qāytbāy and Qānṣūh al-Ghawrī according to Their Waqf Deeds." *Journal of the Economic and Social History of the Orient* 41 (1): 96–117. https://doi.org/10.1163/1568520982601421.

Philippe, Julie M. 2004. "French and American Approaches to Contract Formation and Enforceability: A Comparative Perspective." *Tulsa Journal of Comparative and International Law* 12: 357.

Piat, Théophile, and Iskandar Dahdah, trans. 1876. *Code de commerce Ottoman Expliqué*. Beirut: s.tinyurl.galegroup.com/tinyurl/57FMv3.

Pierret, Thomas. 2013. *Religion and State in Syria: The Sunni Ulama from Coup to Revolution*. Cambridge: Cambridge University Press.

Polanyi, Karl. 2001. *The Great Transformation: The Political and Economic Origins of Our Time*. Boston, MA: Beacon Press.

Pouyanne, Maurice. 1900. "Au Sujet d'un 'Essai sur les biens habous en Algérie et en Tunisie.'" *Questions diplomatiques et coloniales* 9: 94–99.

Powers, David S. 1989. "Orientalism, Colonialism, and Legal History: The Attack on Muslim Family Endowments in Algeria and India." *Comparative Studies in Society and History* 31 (3): 535–71.

———. 1996. "The Art of the Legal Opinion: Al-Wansharisi on *Tawlij*." In *Islamic Legal Interpretation: Muftis and Their Fatwas*, edited by Muhammad Khalid Masud, Brinkley Messick, and David S. Powers, 98–115. Cambridge, MA: Harvard University Press.

Powers, Paul R. 2006. *Intent in Islamic Law: Motive and Meaning in Medieval Sunnī* Fiqh. Leiden: Brill.

Qadri, Muhammad, 1942. *Code annoté du wakf*. Translated by Abdel Aziz Kahil Pacha, annotated by Umberto Pace and Victor Sisto. Paris: Librairie G. P. Maisonneuve.

Quadri, Junaid A. 2013. "Transformations of Tradition: Modernity in the Thought of Muḥammad Bakhīt al-Muṭīʿī." PhD diss., McGill University.

Quataert, Donald. 1997. "The Age of Reforms (1812–1914)." In *An Economic and Social History of the Ottoman Empire*, edited by Donald Quataert and Halil Inlacik, 759–943. New York: Cambridge University Press.

Rapoport, Yossef. 2012. "Royal Justice and Religious Law: Siyāsah and Shariʿah under the Mamluks." *Mamluk Studies Review* 16: 71–102.

Reinhard, Wolfgang. 2002. "Nepotism." In *The Papacy: An Encyclopedia*, edited by Philippe Levillain, translated by John W. O'Malley, 2: 1030–33. New York; London: Routledge.

Reinkowski, Maurus. 2005. "The State's Security and the Subjects' Prosperity: Notions of Order in Ottoman Bureaucratic Correspondence (19th Century)." In *Legitimizing the Order: The Ottoman Rhetoric of State Power*, edited by Hakan T. Karateke and Maurus Reinkowski, 195–212. Leiden: Brill.

Reiter, Yitzhak. 1995. "Family Waqf Entitlements in British Palestine (1917–1948)." *Islamic Law and Society* 2 (2): 174–93.

———. 1996. *Islamic Endowments in Jerusalem under British Mandate*. London: F. Cass.

———. 2007. "'All of Palestine Is Holy Muslim Waqf Land'—A Myth and Its Roots." In *Law, Custom, and Statute in the Muslim World: Studies in Honor of Aharon Layish*, edited by Aharon Layish and Ron Shaham. Leiden: Brill.

Repp, Richard Cooper. 1986. *The Müfti of Istanbul: A Study in the Development of the Ottoman Learned Hierarchy*. Atlantic Highlands, NJ: Ithaca Press.

Reynolds, Susan. 2010. *Before Eminent Domain: Toward a History of Expropriation of Land for the Common Good*. Chapel Hill: University of North Carolina Press.

Rida, Rashid. 1903. "Al-Waqf min al-Dīn." *Al-Manar* 6 (18): 729–36.

Ridwan, Murtadho, and Lisa Irwit Santi. 2018. "Revitalization of Sunan Muria's Waqf Assets: Maqasid Shariah al-Najjar Approach." *International Research Journal of Shariah, Muamalat and Islam* 1 (2): 54–63.

Rose, Nikolas, and Mariana Valverde. 1998. "Governed by Law?" *Social & Legal Studies* 7 (4): 541–51.

Rowe, Peter G., and Hashim Sarkis. 1998. *Projecting Beirut: Episodes in the Construction and Reconstruction of a Modern City*. Munich: Prestel.

Rubin, Avi. 2011. *Ottoman Nizamiye Courts: Law and Modernity*. New York: Palgrave Macmillan.

Ruedy, John. 1967. *Land Policy in Colonial Algeria: The Origins of the Rural Public Domain*. Berkeley: University of California Press.

Rustom, Joseph. 2011. "Conceiving Places of Worship in Postwar Beirut: The Cases of al-Omari and al-Amin Mosques." https://tinyurl.com/y25wkols.

———. 2012. "L'espace urbain de Bayrut al-Qadima et ses habitants vers 1860 à travers un registre du waqf sunnite." *Chronos* 25: 143–91.

Saad, Ahmed Zaki. 1928. "Le 'Wakf' de famille: Étude critique." Paris: Université de Paris.

Saba, Paul. 1976. "The Creation of the Lebanese Economy: Economic Growth in the Nineteenth and Twentieth Centuries." In *Essays on the Crisis in Lebanon*, by Edward Roger John Owen, 1–22. London: Ithaca Press.

Saidouni, Maaouia, and Nacereddine Saidouni. 2009. "Il 'Waqf' in Algeria e l'amministrazione francese: Il caso della Fondazione Degli 'Haramayn' (Algeri 1830–1873)." Translated by Benedetta Borello. *Quaderni Storici* 44 (132 (3)): 687–726.

Salami, ʿAbdallah bin Nasir al-. 2010. "Al-Mumāṭala: Maẓāhiruhā, wa Aḍrāruhā, wa Anwāʿuhā, wa Asbābuhā fī al-Fiqh al-Islāmī," 2010. http://fiqh.islammessage.com/NewsDetails.aspx?id=1306 and http://fiqh.islammessage.com/NewsDetails.aspx?id=1309.

Salti, Nisreen. 2015. "Income Inequality and the Composition of Public Debt." *Journal of Economic Studies* 42 (5): 821–37.

Salti, Nisreen, and Jad Chaaban. 2010. "On the Poverty and Equity Implications of a Rise in the Value Added Tax: A Microeconomic Simulation for Lebanon." *Middle East Development Journal* 2 (1): 121–38.

Salzmann, Ariel. 1999. "Citizens in Search of a State: The Limits of Political Participation in the Late Ottoman Empire." In *Extending Citizenship, Reconfiguring States*, edited by Michael Hanagan and Charles Tilly, 37–66. Lanham, MD: Rowman & Littlefield.

Sawalha, Aseel. 2010. *Reconstructing Beirut: Memory and Space in a Postwar Arab City*. Austin: University of Texas Press.

Sayyid, Ridwan. 1986. *Al-Umma wa al-Jamāʿa wa al-Sulṭa*. Bayrut: Dar Iqraʾ.

Schacht, Joseph. 1964. *An Introduction to Islamic Law*. Oxford: Clarendon Press.

Schatkowski, Linda. 1969. "The Islamic Maqased of Beirut: A Case Study of Modernization in Lebanon." MA thesis, American University of Beirut.

Scheper-Hughes, Nancy, and Loïc J. D. Wacquant, eds. 2002. *Commodifying Bodies*. Thousand Oaks, CA: Sage Publications.

Scherz, China. 2014. *Having People, Having Heart: Charity, Sustainable Development, and Problems of Dependence in Central Uganda*. Chicago: University of Chicago Press.

Schielke, Samuli. 2013. *The Perils of Joy: Contesting Mulid Festivals in Contemporary Egypt*. Syracuse, NY: Syracuse University Press.

Schmid, Heiko. 1997. "Der Wiederaufbau des Beiruter Stadtzentrums: Öffentliche Kritik und Akzeptanz in der Bevölkerung." PhD diss., Tübingen University.

———. 2002. "The Reconstruction of Downtown Beirut in the Context of Political Geography." *Arab World Geographer* 5 (4): 232–48.

Schroeder, Severin. 2017. "Grammar and Grammatical Investigations." In *A Companion to Wittgenstein*, edited by Hans-Johann Glock and John Hyman, 252–68. Chichester, West Sussex, UK: Wiley, Blackwell.

Scott, David. 1999. *Refashioning Futures: Criticism after Postcoloniality*. Princeton, NJ: Princeton University Press.

Scott, James C. 1998. *Seeing Like a State: How Certain Schemes to Improve the Human Condition Have Failed*. New Haven, CT: Yale University Press.

Sekaly, Achille. 1929. "Le Problème des wakfs en Egypte." *Revue des études islamiques* I–IV: 75–126, 277–337, 395–454, 601–59.

Shaham, Ron. 1991. "Christian and Jewish Waqf in Palestine during the Late Ottoman Period." *Bulletin of the School of Oriental and African Studies* 54 (3): 460–72.

Shakry, Omnia. 1998. "Schooled Mothers and Structured Play: Child Rearing in Turn-of-the-Century Egypt." In *Remaking Women: Feminism and Modernity in the Middle East*, edited by Lila Abu-Lughod, 126–70. Princeton, NJ: Princeton University Press.

Sharara, Waddah. 1975. *Fī Uṣūl Lubnān al-Ṭāʾifī: Khaṭṭ al-Yamīn al-Jamāhīrī*. Bayrut: Dar al-Taliʿa.

Sharma, Aradhana, and Akhil Gupta. 2006. "Introduction." In *The Anthropology of the State: A Reader*, edited by Aradhana Sharma and Akhil Gupta. Malden, MA: Blackwell.

Sharp, Deen S. 2018. "Corporate Urbanization: Between the Future and Survival in Lebanon." PhD diss., City University of New York.

Sharp, Lesley Alexandra. 2006. *Strange Harvest: Organ Transplants, Denatured Bodies, and the Transformed Self*. Berkeley: University of California Press.

Shaw, Stanford J. 2000. "Some Aspects of the Aims and Achievements of the Nineteenth-Century Ottoman Reformers." In *Studies in Ottoman and Turkish History: Life with the Ottomans*, 91–100. Istanbul: Isis Press. Essay first published in 1968.

Shaw, Stanford J., and Ezel Kural Shaw. 1976. *History of the Ottoman Empire and Modern Turkey*. 2 vols. Cambridge: Cambridge University Press.

Shibaru, ʿIsam Muhammad. 2000. *Jamʿiyyat al-Maqāṣid al-Khayriyya al-Islāmiyya fī Bayrūt, 1295–1421 H/1878–2000 M*. Bayrut: Dar Misbah al-Fikr li'l-Tibaʿa wa al-Nashr.

Shoard, Marion. 1997. *This Land Is Our Land: The Struggle for Britain's Countryside*. London: Gaia Books.

Shuval, Tal. 1996. "La pratique de la muʿâwada (échange de biens ḥabûs contre propriété privée) à Alger au XVIIIe siècle." *Revue des mondes musulmans et de la Méditerranée* 79 (1): 55–72. https://doi.org/10.3406/remmm.1996.1735.

al-Siddiq, Nazih. 2007. "Malas Yakhṭub Al-Muṣallīn wa Yaʾummuhum: Dār al-Fatwā wa Dāʾirat al-Awqāf Khāntā Masʾūliyyatahumā." *Al-Akhbar*, May 12, 2007. https://al-akhbar.com/Archive_Local_News/193265.

Silverstein, Brian. 2011. *Islam and Modernity in Turkey*. New York: Palgrave Macmillan.

Singer, Amy. 2002. *Constructing Ottoman Beneficence: An Imperial Soup Kitchen in Jerusalem*. Albany: State University of New York Press.

Singer, Joseph William. 2000. *Entitlement: The Paradoxes of Property*. New Haven, CT: Yale University Press.

Siraj, Muhammad, Ahmad. 2006. "Muqaddimat al-Taḥqīq." In *Qānūn al-ʿAdl wa al-Inṣāf fī al-Qaḍāʾ ʿalā Mushkilāt al-Awqāf*, 7–33. Al-Qahira: Dar al-Salam.

Skovgaard-Petersen, Jakob. 1997. *Defining Islam for the Egyptian State: Muftis and Fatwas of the Dār al-Iftā*. Leiden: Brill.

Slim, Souad Abou el-Rousse. 2007. *The Greek Orthodox Waqf in Lebanon during the Ottoman Period*. Würzburg: Ergon Verlag.

Smith, Joan, and Immanuel Maurice Wallerstein. 1992. *Creating and Transforming Households: The Constraints of the World-Economy*. Cambridge: Cambridge University Press; Paris: Éditions de la Maison des Sciences de l'Homme.

Smith, Wilfred Cantwell. 1964. *The Meaning and End of Religion*. New York: Mentor Books.

Starrett, Gregory. 1998. *Putting Islam to Work: Education, Politics, and Religious Transformation in Egypt*. Berkeley: University of California Press.

Strathern, Marilyn. 1988. *The Gender of the Gift: Problems with Women and Problems with Society in Melanesia*. Berkeley: University of California Press.

Tabit, Jad. 1996. *Al-Iʿmār wa al-Maṣlaḥa al-ʿĀmma: Fī al-Turāth wa al-Ḥadātha, Madīnat al-Ḥarb wa-Dhākirat al-Mustaqbal*. Bayrut: Dar al-Jadid.

Targoff, Ramie. 2001. *Common Prayer: The Language of Public Devotion in Early Modern England*. Chicago: University of Chicago Press.

Taylor, Charles. 1989. *Sources of the Self: The Making of the Modern Identity*. Cambridge, MA: Harvard University Press.

———. 1992. "Inwardness and the Culture of Modernity." In *Philosophical Interventions in the Unfinished Project of Enlightenment*, edited by Axel Honneth, Albrecht Wellmer, Thomas McCarthy, and Claus Offe, 88–110. Cambridge, MA: MIT Press.

———. 2007. *A Secular Age*. Cambridge: The Belknap Press of Harvard University Press.

Terras, Jean. 1899. "Essai sur les biens habous en Algérie et en Tunisie: Étude de législation coloniale." Lyon: Imprimerie et Lithographie du Salut Public.

Thompson, Elizabeth. 2000. *Colonial Citizens: Republican Rights, Paternal Privilege, and Gender in French Syria and Lebanon*. New York: Columbia University Press.

Ticktin, Miriam. 2006. "Where Ethics and Politics Meet." *American Ethnologist* 33 (1): 33–49.

Tillier, Mathieu. 2015. "The Mazalim in Historiography." In *The Oxford Handbook of Islamic Law*, edited by Anver M. Emon and Rumee Ahmed. Oxford: Oxford University Press. https://doi.org/10.1093/oxfordhb/9780199679010.013.10.

Touma, Toufic. 1972. *Paysans et institutions féodales chez les druses et les maronites du Liban du XVIIe siècle* à 1914. Vol. 2. Beirut, Lebanon: Publications de l'Université Libanaise.

Traboulsi, Fawwaz. 2007. *A History of Modern Lebanon*. London: Pluto.

Trilling, Lionel. 2009. *Sincerity and Authenticity*. Cambridge, MA: Harvard University Press.

Trouillot, Michel-Rolph. 2001. "The Anthropology of the State in the Age of Globalization: Close Encounters of the Deceptive Kind." *Current Anthropology* 42 (1): 125–38.

Tyan, E., and Gy Káldy-Nagy. 2012. "Ḳāḍī." In *Encyclopaedia of Islam*, 2nd ed., edited by P. J. Bearman et al. Leiden: Brill. http://dx.doi.org/10.1163/1573-3912_islam_COM_0410.

van Leeuwen, Richard. 1994. *Notables and Clergy in Mount Lebanon: The Khāzin Sheikhs and the Maronite Church, 1736–1840*. Leiden: Brill.

———. 1999. *Waqfs and Urban Structures: The Case of Ottoman Damascus*. Leiden: Brill.

Vause, Erika. 2014. "Disciplining the Market: Debt Imprisonment, Public Credit, and the Construction of Commercial Personhood in Revolutionary France." *Law and History Review* 32 (03): 647–82.

Vloeberghs, Ward. 2016. *Architecture, Power and Religion in Lebanon: Rafiq Hariri and the Politics of Sacred Space in Beirut*. Leiden: Brill.

Vogel, Frank E. 2000. *Islamic Law and Legal System: Studies of Saudi Arabia*. Leiden: Brill.

Waldron, Jeremy. 2002. *God, Locke, and Equality: Christian Foundations of John Locke's Political Thought*. Cambridge: Cambridge University Press.

Wali, Taha. 1993. *Bayrūt fī al-Tārīkh wa al-Ḥaḍāra wa al-ʿUmrān*. Bayrut: Dar al-ʿIlm li'l-Malayin.

Weiner, Annette B. 1985. "Inalienable Wealth." *American Ethnologist* 12 (2): 210–27.

Weintraub, Jeff. 1997. "The Theory and Politics of the Public/Private Distinction." In *Public and Private in Thought and Practice: Perspectives on a Grand Dichotomy*, edited by Jeff Weintraub and Krishan Kumar, 1–42. Chicago: University of Chicago Press.

Weiss, Max. 2010. *In the Shadow of Sectarianism: Law, Shiʿism, and the Making of Modern Lebanon*. Cambridge, MA: Harvard University Press.

Wensinck, A. J. 2012. "Niyya." In *Encyclopaedia of Islam*, 2nd ed., edited by P. Bearman et al. Leiden: Brill.

White, Benjamin Thomas. 2011. *The Emergence of Minorities in the Middle East: The Politics of Community in French Mandate Syria*. Edinburgh: Edinburgh University Press.

Williams, Raymond. 1976. *Keywords: A Vocabulary of Culture and Society*. New York: Oxford University Press.

Wittgenstein, Ludwig. 1974. *Philosophical Grammar: Part I, The Proposition, and Its Sense; Part II, On Logic and Mathematics*. Berkeley: University of California Press.

———. 2009. *Philosophical Investigations*, 4th ed., edited by P. M. S. Hacker and Joachim Schulte. Malden, MA: Wiley-Blackwell.

Wood, Leonard. 2016. *Islamic Legal Revival: Reception of European Law and Transformations in Islamic Legal Thought in Egypt, 1875–1952*. Oxford: Oxford University Press.

Yahaya, Nurfadzilah. 2020. *Fluid Jurisdictions: Colonial Law and Arabs in Southeast Asia*. Ithaca New York: Cornell University Press.

Yakan, Zuhdi. 1963. *Al-Tanẓīm al-Idārī: Tanẓīm al-Idāra al-Markaziyya wa al-Maḥalliya*. Bayrut: Dar al-Thaqafa.

———. 1964. *Qānūn al-Waqf al-Dhurrī wa Maṣādiruh al-Sharʿiyya fī Lubnān*. Bayrut: Dar al-Thaqafa.

Yanagihashi, Hiroyuki. 1998. "The Doctrinal Development of '*Maraḍ Al-Mawt*' in the Formative Period of Islamic Law." *Islamic Law and Society* 5 (3): 326–58.

Yayla, Hilmi Erdoğan. 2011. "Operating Regimes of the Government: Accounting and Accountability Changes in the Sultan Süleyman Waqf of the Ottoman Empire (The 1826 Experience)." *Accounting History* 16 (1): 5–34.

Yazbak, Mahmoud. 2010. "The Islamic Waqf in Yaffa and the Urban Space: From the Ottoman State to the State of Israel." *Makan, Adalah's Journal for Land, Planning and Justice* 2: 23–46.

Yediyıldız, Bahaeddin. 1985. *Institution du vaqf au XVIIIe siècle en Turquie: Étude socio-historique*. Ankara, TR: Société d'Histoire Turque.

Yıldırım, Rıza. 2011. "Dervishes, Waqfs, and Conquest: Notes on Early Ottoman Expansion in Thrace." In *Held in Trust: Waqf in the Islamic World*, 23–40. Cairo, Egypt: American University in Cairo Press.

Young, George. 1905. *Corps de droit ottoman: Recueil des codes, lois, règlements, ordonnances et actes les plus importants du droit intérieur, et d'études sur le droit coutumier de l'Empire ottoman*. Oxford: Clarendon Press.

Zahraa, Mahdi. 1995. "Legal Personality in Islamic Law." *Arab Law Quarterly* 10 (3): 193–206.

Zaman, Muhammad Qasim. 2012. *Modern Islamic Thought in a Radical Age: Religious Authority and Internal Criticism*. Cambridge: Cambridge University Press.

Zencirci, Gizem. 2015. "From Property to Civil Society: The Historical Transformation of Vakifs in Modern Turkey (1923–2013)." *International Journal of Middle East Studies* 47 (3): 533–54. https://doi.org/10.1017/S0020743815000537.

Zilfi, Madeline C. 1983. "Elite Circulation in the Ottoman Empire: Great Mollas of the Eighteenth Century." *Journal of the Economic and Social History of the Orient* 23 (3): 318–64.

INDEX

democracy, 155, 159, 192, 193n3, 206n35
destitution (*iʿdām*), 123n18, 127, 200n21. *See also* hardship; poor
development: and charity, 25, 39, 232; of Lebanon, 2n5, 7n17, 32; real estate, 56, 65; of waqf, 7n19, 62, 65, 70, 83, 89, 183n60, 211, 217, 220. *See also* neoliberalism; progress; property regime; real estate wealth
DGIW. *See* Directorate General of Islamic Waqfs
differentiation, 4, 101n70, 172–174, 228. *See also* separating religion and economy
dīn ("religion"), 93–95, 176, 178
Directorate General of Islamic Waqfs (DGIW): developing waqfs, 64–65, 110, 194, 212–222; and family waqf, 22, 55, 64, 186, 194, 215; and the shariʿa courts, 61, 100, 103–105, 110, 187; and the state, 16, 68–70, 100–106, 110, 215–218, 222, 225–226; suspicion and, 114, 150–151, 215, 219; and waqf jurisdiction, 32, 58, 60–61, 69–70, 100, 103–106, 110, 185–187, 194. *See also* expropriation; private waqf; waqf manual
Diryan, ʿAbd al-Latif, 109n91
discipline, 108n89; as form of power, 17, 43, 85, 231; of political economy, 12; of self-cultivation, 19, 140, 166
disenchantment, 5, 33
dismissal: of administrator, 41, 76–77, 81–82, 104; causes of, 76–77, 81–82, 104, 168n33; of General Supervisor, 98; of imam, 104n82; of judge, 116n5; of mufti, 168n33. *See also* appointment; competence; legal fiction
dispossession: of indigenous Americans, 179; of Palestinians, 59; of peasants, 129, 132–133, 145; of waqf rights holders, 55, 179, 194, 212–213. *See also* expropriation
disrepair. *See* ruined waqf
divine law. *See* shariʿa
divine ownership. *See* ownership
dominant legal opinion. *See* preponderance
Donzelot, Jacques, 17
Doughan, Yazan, 157n8
Doumani, Beshara, 1n3, 2n6, 2n7, 155n3, 159
downtown. *See* city center
Druze, 26, 113n1, 115n5, 131–134, 228n8
dunyā (worldly matters), 93–94. *See also dīn*
duress. *See* hardship

Ebüssuʿûd, Muhammad, 123n19, 137–139, 140n56, 202
economics, 4, 12, 178n53, 183
economy. *See* capitalism; debt regime; nation-state; political economy; property regime; separating religion and
Egypt: Beirut under rule of, 2n5, 87, 133; charity in, 8, 39n23, 232; Islamic law in, 24n48, 34n5, 35n9, 79n23, 183, 201; Mixed Courts of, 45, 49, 51n56; Ottoman, 43–45, 51n56, 55n69, 96; secularism in, 4n14, 149; state provision for poor in, 7n18, 36n12; waqfs in, 32, 35n9, 38, 48n43, 49, 51–52, 73n11, 79n23, 80n27, 108n87, 145n60, 175–180, 183, 201, 229, 232
elite, 13–14, 133, 194n5, 213–214, 217n52, 226. *See also* class
embezzlement, 82, 86, 153, 181. *See also* corruption; nepotism
eminent domain, 193n3, 207
endowment. *See under* waqf
England, 1, 19, 36, 56, 117n7
epistemology, 10, 24, 106, 169–170, 177, 184
epistle (*risāla*), 23, 24n47, 76n18, 176, 201. *See also* commentaries; legal manual
equality and inequality: of citizens before the state, 122n16, 155; economic, 223–224, 231–232; of human life, 163; of opportunity, 166, 170–171, 191; of religious communities, 227, 229; of waqfs before the state, 210, 224, 227
equity, 120, 126. *See also* equality and inequality
escaping debt through waqf: under the French Mandate, 145–147; in the Hanafi library, 119–120; in the Mamluk era, 60n75; under Ottoman reforms, 113–115, 131, 135–138, 140n56, 145, 151. *See also* ethic of abstinence; forgiveness; motive; suspicion
Esmeir, Samera, 15, 43n32
estate. *See* inheritance
eternal: rewards, 25, 185; waqf recipients, 36, 78n20, 136, 162, 187; waqfs, 3, 39–40, 47, 203, 221. *See also* hereafter; perpetuity; temporary waqf
ethic of abstinence, 147, 151–152. *See also* foreclosure; forgiveness; intent
ethic of care of the family, 21, 155–157, 160, 169, 173, 184, 186, 188, 192, 230; persistence of, 188–191
ethic of merit, 156, 170–174, 184, 192. *See also* competence; ethic of care of the family
ethics, 160, 169
ethnography. *See* notebook
Europe: cities of, 209; colonial settlers from, 50; economic regime of, 5n15, 17, 49, 121, 126, 132, 135, 143, 180n57, 188n67; education of, 44–45,

General Waqf Committee (French Mandate), 91, 98–99
Gennardi, Philippe, 52, 89–90, 96, 100, 141, 143–144, 146–147
Ghazzal, Zouhair, 21, 38n20
gift: and charity, 158, 163; to escape inheritance law (*tawlīj*) or debt, 118n9, 138, 178; to officials, 155; and tax exemptions, 225; and waqf after Ottoman reforms, 46, 48n41; and waqf in the Ottoman/Islamic library, 34–35, 39–40, 66, 138, 159n17, 161, 204; and waqf under the French Mandate, 53n60
gloss (legal supercommentary). *See Baḥr*; commentaries and glosses; *Ḥāshiya*; *Nahr*; *Tanqīḥ*
God: as actor in property relations, 1–2, 4–5, 18, 25, 32–36, 40–41, 46–49, 54, 56–57, 61–66, 159n17, 161, 192, 228; decree of, 150; fearing, 77, 120n13; giving for, 8n20, 9, 39n23, 232; and intent, 117, 140, 148, 151–152, 230, 233; as judge, 20; revealing law, 93, 177, 183, 196; rights of, 78n20, 151, 207; seeking the pleasure of (*see qurba*); sending inspiration, 59; and the state, 101, 216n51; worshipping (*see* worship). *See also* property regime; secularization; worship
government, 13, 17, 24, 44, 51, 70, 82, 83n30, 89, 92, 99, 102, 116n5, 122n16, 145, 157, 175, 179, 193n2, 194, 208–209, 223–225
governmentality, 13n31, 16, 43
governor, 60, 88, 99, 113–114, 115n5, 119–120, 131, 132n39, 135n47, 136, 140, 145
Graeber, David, 126, 131, 135
grammar (methodology): of benefit, 27, 195, 200, 210–211, 214, 218, 222; of concepts, 6–12, 16, 21, 24–25, 32, 55–56, 232; of family, 27, 156–157, 184, 191; of intent, 26, 114–115, 117, 136, 138, 140, 146–147, 149, 152, 230. *See also* architecture
grand mufti, 43, 60–61, 65, 68, 100, 103, 106, 109, 149, 151, 153–154, 180, 183, 191–192, 214, 216, 218–219
Greek Orthodox Christianity, 26, 216, 228n8
guardian (*waṣiyy*), 74, 76
guesswork (ẓann). *See* suspicion
guild, 122n16, 164, 166, 207
Gülhane Edict (1839), 83n30, 133. *See also* Tanzimat
Gupta, Akhil, 15

ḥabs. *See* confinement
hadith, 45, 169, 177–178; about faith, 140; about judges, 203n30; about *ṣadaqa*, 63, 158n11, 159–160, 161; about waqf, 35, 63, 177, 178n51; of Gabriel, 93
Hajj Tawfiq, 31–32
ḥajr. *See* interdiction
Hallaq, Wael, 9–10, 181–182
Hamdi Yazir, Elmalili Muhammad, 42
Hanafi school (Islamic law). *See* Abu Hanifa; Abu Yusuf; Ibn Nujaym; Ibn ʿAbidin; library; Muhammad al-Shaybani
Hanbali school (Islamic law), 23n44, 118n9, 130
handout, 39, 65. *See also* development; ṣadaqa
Haramayn waqf, 2n8, 38, 45, 75, 78n20, 186n62
Harb, Salim, 147–149
hardship (*iʿsār*), 115, 122–125, 138, 140
Hariri, Rafiq, 194, 213–214, 220
harm, 196–198, 200n20, 207, 210–211, 231; and benefit in shariʿa, 181–183, 196–198, 207; to creditors, 119, 138; to the economy by family waqf, 179–183, 191; forced sale as public, 123n17; through charity, 231; to the waqf, 200n20, 210–211. *See also* legal maxim; *maṣlaḥa*
Harvey, David, 3n11, 216–217
Ḥāshiya (Ibn ʿAbidin), 235–236; on benefit, 198; on debt/loans, 36, 125; on defining waqf, 36–37, 46, 60n76; on intent, 159, 162; on judges' jurisdiction, 75; on mosques as waqf, 36n10, 69n5, 104; on non-Muslim waqfs, 1n2; on officeholders, 165, 168n33; on recipients of charity, 157–158, 161–162, 173; on waqf exchange, 198, 201–204, 206. *See also Tanqīḥ*
al-Haskafi, ʿAlaʾ al-Din, 139, 235–236
Haydar, Ali, 42, 127, 130
heart, 19–20, 116–117, 122, 140–141, 150
heirs: bequests/gifts to one's, 118n9, 185, 188n67; collecting from the debtor's, 120, 127–129; and family waqf, 5, 56–57, 184, 186–187; of officeholder, 165, 170; seeking to revoke waqf, 41. *See also* debt regime; foreclosure; inheritance; legal fiction; transmission
here and now. *See* present
hereafter: God judging intent in the, 20, 117, 151–152; rewards in the, 1, 4, 41, 63, 65–66, 94, 158–159; shariʿa concern for the, 14, 43, 195–196, 208, 227. *See also* eternal; *qurba*; temporality
hierarchy: in the derivation of law, 125, 183; family as site of, 155n3; modern bureaucratic, 171; of modern Lebanese law, 69n4; Ottoman religious, 45n38, 113n2, 167; of Ottoman waqf administration, 84, 87; of property rights, 58. *See also* equality and inequality

trust (financial), 1, 36n11, 49n48, 102, 184n61, 225, 230n12
trustee, 41, 49n46, 95n60, 127; on board, 31, 58–60. *See also* waqf administration
trustworthiness, 77–78, 82, 84, 87, 169. *See also* uprightness
Tunisia, 49n50, 51, 91n50, 98n66, 229
Turkey, 9, 32, 49, 229
Turkish, 42, 44n35, 45, 206

ʿulamaʾ. *See* religious scholars
ʿUlamaʾ Waqf, 60–61
ulterior. *See* motive
ʿUmari mosque, 62–63, 75, 163–168, 186n62, 209, 235–236
umma (Muslim community), 72, 95–96, 227–228. *See also* community
uniformity. *See* standardization
United Kingdom, 36n11, 56, 184n61, 230n12
United States, 32n1, 36n11, 49n48, 64n82, 116, 157n7, 184n61, 188n67, 193n3, 225, 226n6, 230
upkeep (waqf), 2, 36, 69, 82, 100, 142, 163. *See also* maintenance; repairs
uprightness, 38, 77–78, 168, 170, 202–204. *See also* trustworthiness
uprising (2019), 223–224
urban, 15, 50n51, 63n80, 193, 205, 209, 219n55
usufruct (*manfaʿa*), 3n10, 34–36, 46, 60, 66, 147, 159n17, 160–161, 204; right of, 5, 54, 56, 114, 120, 128n31, 142, 147, 160, 179–180, 186, 212. *See also* defining waqf
usury (*ribā*), 3n10, 118, 123n19, 130–131, 134

validity: of cash waqf, 149, 181n58; of contracts, 118n9, 141, 145–147, 211; of debtor's waqf, 118–121, 137–139; of family waqf, 114–115, 140n56, 155n4, 156, 160–163, 172–177, 181–189; of imprisoning debtor, 123; inspecting waqf, 81n28, 136–137; and intent of waqf, 118–119, 136, 158n16, 160–161; and jurisdiction of waqf, 54–55, 57n72, 103, 113; of land to be waqfed, 48n43; of legal reasoning, 196n12; of loan, 120, 141; of non-Muslim waqfs, 162; of noncharitable waqf, 140, 160–163, 173; of temporary waqf, 47, 231; of testimony, 125; of unspecified waqf, 60n76; of waqf administrator appointment, 77n19, 165; of waqf conditions, 72, 130, 188; of waqf dedicated to the Muslims, 162, 227–228; of waqf exchange, 198–205, 222. *See also* cash waqf; charitable waqf; family waqf; interdiction; legitimacy; non-Muslims; Ottoman Land Code; permissibility; Real Estate Property Code; waqf exchange
Van Leeuwen, Richard, 1n2, 2n6, 76n18, 77n19, 139n53, 156n5
virtue, 8, 14, 19n38, 63, 77n19, 122n16, 140. *see also* uprightness
voluntariness, 66, 120, 158

wakīl (agent), 37, 74, 203
waqf abolitionism, 52, 133, 175–184. *See also* waqf conservationism; waqf revival
Waqf Administation Regulations (Ottoman), 83–87
waqf administration, 2, 14, 16–18, 20–23, 27, 109–110; Abbasid, 35, 79n23; after Ottoman reforms, 78–89, 126–140, 170–174, 206–210; between archive and library, 37; under the French Mandate, 51–58, 89–100, 141–147, 174–184, 210–212; and late Ottoman waqf manuals, 42–49; in the library, 71–78, 125, 156–169, 196–206; Mamluk, 41n27, 73n10, 79n23, 201–202, 210n41; between *mutawallī*s and supervisors, 79–82; in postcolonial Lebanon, 58–65, 68–71, 100–109, 147–151, 153–156, 184–191, 212–221; Umayyad, 79n23; and waqf deed, 38–41. See also dismissal; family waqf; *ḥüsn-i idâre*; judge; jurisdictional politics; maintenance; Mamluk era; *mutawallī*; qadi; repairs; stipulation; upkeep; validity; waqf beneficiary; waqf exchange; waqf expenditures; waqf subdivision; waqf supervisor
waqf assessment, 178–180
waqf beneficiary: claiming a waqf, 50, 57, 185; in court archive, 23; debts of, 37; extinction of, 3n10, 38, 78n20, 136, 146, 154–156, 161–162, 174, 184, 186–187, 200, 231; family as, 6, 18, 26, 55–58, 64, 140n56, 154–155, 156n5, 160–163, 166n30, 172–173, 179, 184–187, 230; as illegible, 57; and intent, 26, 119, 160–163; liability of, 65; the Muslims as, 95n60, 162, 197n12, 198, 227; oneself as, 160–161; particular people as, 76n17; the poor as, 1, 3n10, 26, 32, 34–35, 38–39, 140n56, 217; public, 191; religious institutions as, 2, 61, 75, 101, 154; stipulation of, 27, 38, 40, 160, 162, 171, 173, 187; and waqf administration, 54n64, 57, 69, 74–75, 77n19, 78, 81, 85–86, 89–90, 91n47, 103; and waqf dissolution, 108, 185, 191; and waqf exchange, 55, 197n15, 198, 201, 205, 212; and waqf manual, 44, 46; and waqf subdivision, 184–185; wealthy, 161–162, 173. *See also* family waqf; the poor; right

Founded in 1893,
UNIVERSITY OF CALIFORNIA PRESS
publishes bold, progressive books and journals on topics in the arts, humanities, social sciences, and natural sciences—with a focus on social justice issues—that inspire thought and action among readers worldwide.

The UC PRESS FOUNDATION
raises funds to uphold the press's vital role as an independent, nonprofit publisher, and receives philanthropic support from a wide range of individuals and institutions—and from committed readers like you. To learn more, visit ucpress.edu/supportus.